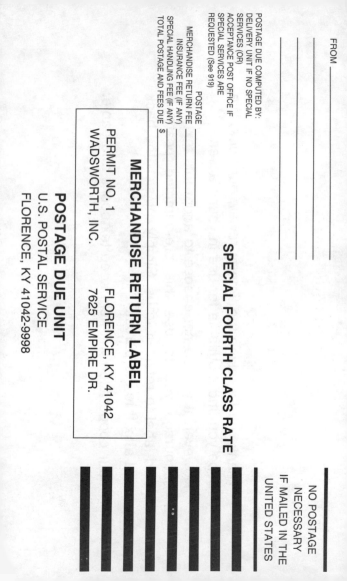

FROM _____

POSTAGE DUE COMPUTED BY:
DELIVERY UNIT IF NO SPECIAL
SERVICES (OR)
ACCEPTANCE POST OFFICE IF
SPECIAL SERVICES ARE
REQUESTED (See 919)

POSTAGE
MERCHANDISE RETURN FEE
INSURANCE FEE (IF ANY)
SPECIAL HANDLING FEE (IF ANY)
TOTAL POSTAGE AND FEES DUE $

SPECIAL FOURTH CLASS RATE

MERCHANDISE RETURN LABEL

PERMIT NO. 1   FLORENCE, KY 41042
WADSWORTH, INC.   7625 EMPIRE DR.

POSTAGE DUE UNIT
U.S. POSTAL SERVICE
FLORENCE, KY 41042-9998

NO POSTAGE
NECESSARY
IF MAILED IN THE
UNITED STATES

Thank you for taking the time to review our book. We hope you find it suitable for use in your classes.

However, if you do not choose to adopt this text, we encourage you to use this pre-gummed postage-paid label to return it to us. Simply moisten the back and affix it to the parcel.

Your cooperation will help keep textbooks affordable.

Integrated Language Arts
in the Elementary School

Integrated Language Arts
in the Elementary School

Susan Tchudi

University of Nevada, Reno

Wadsworth Publishing Company

Belmont, California

A Division of Wadsworth, Inc.

Executive Editor: Kristine Clerkin
Editorial Assistant: Kate Peltier
Production: Melanie Field, Bookman Productions
Interior and Cover Designer: Paula Goldstein, Bookman Productions
Print Buyer: Barbara Britton
Permissions Editor: Jeanne Bosschart
Copy Editor: Candace Demeduc
Photo Researcher: Chris Pullo
Illustrator: Martha Gilman Roach
Cover Photograph: Terry Wild
Signing Representative: Thor McMillan
Compositor: Thompson Type
Printer: Arcata Graphics/Fairfield

(Credits continue on p. 369)

 This book is printed on acid-free recycled paper.

I(T)P ™

International Thomson Publishing
The trademark ITP is used under license

Printed in the United States of America

1 2 3 4 5 6 7 8 9 10—97 96 95 94

Library of Congress Cataloging-in-Publication Data
Tchudi, Susan J. (Susan Jane), 1944–
    Integrated language arts in the elementary school / Susan Tchudi.
        p.   cm.
    Includes bibliographical references and index.
    ISBN 0-534-13092-5
    1. Language arts (Elementary)—United States.
    2. Interdisciplinary approach in education—United States.
    I. Title.
    LB1576.T78   1993
    372.6'0973—dc20
                                93-32878
                                     CIP

To our kids

Contents

■ 3 Language in Print: Reading   81

■ 4 Putting Language on Paper   128

■ 5   Bridges: Language Across the Curriculum   196

■ 6   Literature: Language and the Imagination   238

■ 7   On Being a Professional   279

■ 8   Orchestrating an Integrated Language Arts Classroom   306

 # Preface

Integrated Language Arts in the Elementary School reflects many of the most important recent developments in language arts teaching both in the United States and internationally. In keeping with current theory and research in children's language learning, the text emphasizes the view that the language arts should not be isolated into separate areas of study but should be integrated with an emphasis on whole, meaningful language experiences that absorb and engage students. Although reading, writing, oral language, language across the curriculum, and literature are described in separate chapters, each chapter develops the connections among all the language arts and indeed among all the disciplines studied in elementary school. In each chapter we provide many examples of language activities and units that demonstrate how language arts can be integrated. Moreover, because we believe it is necessary to understand children's language and learning in order to teach the language arts, we have included many examples of specific children learning language and using it.

In addition, we emphasize that there are many, many ways to integrate the curriculum, and the teachers who have contributed to this text (Linda Dinan, Janet Culver, Ann Urie, Mike Gazaway, and Diane Olds) describe the various ways in which they have experimented to create meaningful, holistic classrooms. Moreover, we provide specific help with classroom management, including how to set up reading and writing workshops, how to plan literature-based and interdisciplinary units, how to physically structure the classroom, and how to organize the day. We provide a good deal of specific, practical help for those just beginning to develop an integrated classroom.

For the teacher who no longer relies on the textbook or basal as the defining element of the curriculum, there is a need for new materials in the classroom. This text provides an exhaustive list of resources for the teacher who wishes to create a language-rich integrated classroom, including literature, other print and nonprint resources, community and government resources, and professional resources.

In writing *Integrated Language Arts in the Elementary School*, we hoped not only to provide information about the most recent theories and practices in language teaching and learning but also to encourage the notion of teachers as reflective practitioners, as professionals who look at their students' learning as a guide for instructional practices and who look to their colleagues for professional support. While this text presents a good deal of information on the background for integrated language arts—drawing on theories from whole language, interdisciplinary learning, literature-based programs, and reading-writing workshop approaches to the teaching of language arts—it also encourages teachers to test theories for themselves. We hope that preservice and practicing teachers who read this text will not simply accept our views of children's language but will themselves become "kid watchers," teacher-researchers who observe and on the basis of their observations build theories and create classrooms where joyful learning occurs.

Acknowledgments

We would like to thank the following manuscript reviewers for their helpful comments: Patricia J. Anderson, East Carolina University; Nancy Bacharach, Syracuse University; Ruth Beeker, University of Arizona; Howard E. Blake, Temple University; Susan Chevalier, Central Missouri State University; Linda DeGroff, University of Georgia; Viola Florez, Texas A & M University; Carol Mihalevich, Central Missouri State University; Robert Nistler, Drake University; Janet R. Reuter, the University of Akron; Carolyn Schluck, Florida State University; and Judith Washburn, California State University, Los Angeles. We would also like to thank Kate Peltier and Hal Humphrey at Wadsworth, and Candace Demeduc for her careful editing of the manuscript. A special thanks to Melanie Field at Bookman Productions for keeping the book on schedule and managing the nasty details.

Susan Tchudi

1

Children at Work:
The Nature of Language and Learning

M y five-year-old son Christopher climbed up the stairs of the big red double-decker bus ahead of his nine-year-old brother Michael and me and without hesitating proceeded toward the front seats, the ones right over the bus driver from which one could see everything: the storefronts and signs, the trees and gardens, the riders in the tops of other double-deckers, and the cars and people down below. All but one of the seats in front were occupied, so Christopher took the remaining one, leaving Michael and me to find seats behind him. After Chris settled in, he turned to check our location.

"Hi, Mom. I'm up here."

"Hi, Chris. I see you."

Chris turned to watch the city of London as the bus moved in fits and starts through the crowded street.

"You're American." The man next to Christopher spoke to him. He had an accent, but it wasn't English. Christopher was accustomed to encountering various shades of skin color in this multicultural environment in which he rode the bus every day. This man appeared to be eastern European.

"What?" answered Chris. He hadn't been expecting conversation.

"You're from America?" the man repeated.

Christopher turned to me with a question in his eyes. I nodded.

"Yes," Chris told the man. "We don't live anywhere in this world. It took us overnight to get here."

1

''Where are you from in America?''

Again Chris turned to me for the right answer. ''Michigan,'' I coached.

Christopher told his companion (though the man had already heard), ''Michigan. London is more busier than our place. We're just renting a house here.''

The man nodded.

Happy to have a companionable seatmate, Chris continued. ''We waked up at six thirty. What time did you wake up?''

''Nine o'clock.''

''Did we wake up before you?''

Chris's new friend explained that six thirty was two and a half hours before nine o'clock.

There was a lull in the conversation. ''Elefanto,'' offered Christopher. ''That's another language. My dad taught me that.'' For the fun of it, Chris's dad had been practicing Esperanto, an artificial language created for international use. This time it was the man's turn to be puzzled.

''Elefanto?'' The man sought clarification.

''I know one word of Esperanto.''

''Oh, that's Esperanto. If everyone spoke Esperanto then we could all understand each other.''

Chris nodded knowingly as he looked out the window. A now-familiar object on the London scene caught his eye, the red signal light outside of taxi companies. Inside the clear small dome was a shiny red disk that circled round and round to capture the attention of children, and presumably, those looking for transportation.

''Does that go around by wind or a motor?'' asked Chris.

''I don't know,'' answered his friend.

I have learned a good deal about what is known about the language of children—how it is learned and how it functions for them—by observing children, my own children (Christopher and Michael) and those I have encountered in my teaching and workshops for children. I start with this example of Christopher, because there is a great deal in it that illustrates how young children use language.

Children Learning Language Before School

The incident describing Christopher occurred the summer before he started kindergarten. Although he had not begun formal schooling, Christopher's language and thinking demonstrated an astonishing control over language for his own purposes and for a range of functions. Let's look more closely at how language functions in this situation for Chris. As in most language situations, the things that Christopher says often serve more than one function.

Christopher is using language *to establish a social relationship*. Though he was not looking to do that when he got on the bus, once he is drawn into conversation, he is more than happy to hold up his end. Christopher thinks about the needs of his audience right away. He is aware that the man does not know his background, so when he tells him he is from Michigan, he also tries to establish how unlike and remote it is from London, by telling him he had to travel all night to get there and that London is busier than his home. Another indication that Chris is thinking about his audience is his mention of *elefanto*. He introduces the word into the conversation seemingly out of nowhere. Back in Michigan Chris enjoyed participating in Esperanto lessons around the dining room table and knew that it was a different language. On the bus he observes that the man is from a cultural background different from his own and he knows that people from different cultures often speak different languages. Having made those observations, Chris attempts to accommodate his audience by trying out the only other language he knows.

Chris is also using language *to learn about his world and how it functions*. He's interested in what he observes (the red signal dome) and wants to know how it works. In the case of the dome's circling disk, he shows that he is able to think about alternative explanations for phenomena and has the language structures that set out the possibilities: Is it this or this? He's already thought of two possible causes for the circling disk, and he makes some guesses, hoping for confirmation from a more experienced person. Christopher uses language to make observations and to have those observations and perceptions confirmed.

Chris is also using language *to work on abstract concepts*. His efforts toward learning about time and space are different from his questions about the dome. Concepts of time and space are much more abstract than this physical object that interests him, and those concepts will take much longer to learn. At this point he is in the early stages of understanding time and is probably simply repeating what he heard about the time he got up. He has only very general ideas about time: morning, afternoon, and evening, and he connects some of these with numbers: twelve noon is lunchtime; midnight is very, very late. But his question about which is earlier, six thirty or nine o'clock, shows that he is still working on time relationships.

Chris is using language *to refine a frame of reference* that he often hears in his environment. He is in the process of developing his conception of time and the numerical terminology that accompanies the concept. To do that, he uses the appropriate words, even though he doesn't completely understand them. As he grows in experience, he will gather more and more data, which will allow him to understand the system and the words that describe it.

Likewise it takes children a long time to understand the concepts of city, state, country. They may know that they live in Los Angeles, or in California, or in America, but knowing just what the boundaries or structures are that define Los Angeles or California or America takes a long, long time. Even after children are able to say with confidence what city, state, and country they live in, we can't be sure what their concepts of those "units" are. We know that they begin to see the movement from smaller to larger units around the age of eight or nine, however; and at this point they all seem to take great joy in reciting some variation of the following: "I live in my house, on Harmont Drive, in the city of Phoenix, in the county of Maricopa, in the state of Arizona, in the United States, in North America, in the Northern Hemisphere, in the World, in the Solar System, in the Universe, in SPACE!" However, they work with those concepts from the time they are very young, asking again and again about where they live and is that a state or city and is that the same place that so-and-so lives. Children continually expand and refine their language and experience, using each to support the other in a complex interrelationship.

Clearly Christopher does not have the concepts of country, state, and city at this point, but he does have a sense of remoteness and establishes that in two ways. To communicate that it's not like London, he calls where he comes from "another world." He tries to be more specific about the place he lives by comparing size: "Our place is not so busy." And he tries to clarify just how far it is by explaining that it took overnight to get from his place to London. These are the beginnings of abstract geographical concepts.

It's important to note the difference in children's language and thinking between what they say and what they know. For example, Christopher tells the man that his family is "renting" a house in London. Because Christopher uses the word *rent* properly, one might assume that he knows what he's talking about. However, this is another case of his mimicking what he's heard a dozen times: "We're renting a house in London." At this point, however, his definition of rent is a gross one. He knows that the house is not our house, that it belongs to someone else, and that he and his family will be going back to our own house; but almost certainly he does not know the specific meaning of *rent*, as in paying to use the house. For him it has the more general definition of "temporary residence," which is close but imprecise.

Christopher is working on *other rules of language*. Although he already has the basic grammatical structures of his language under control, he is still in the process of refining his usage. Like many children his age, Christopher doesn't use appropriate irregular past-tense verbs. Instead of saying "We woke up," Christopher says "We waked up." And he says, "My dad teached me that," rather than "taught me." He also misuses the comparative: Instead of saying "London is busier than our place," he says "more busier." (Note, too, that he says "place" instead of town or city because he isn't sure what London or his "place" is called.) In both cases Christopher shows the great sophistication of thinking that accompanies language learning of young children. On the basis of participating in his language community, Christopher has made some generalizations about how the language functions. Christopher shows that he knows the rule for how to make a verb past tense, add -ed, and that he knows *both* ways to make a comparison, by using *more* or by adding -er.

At age five, Christopher is still working on *pronouncing some words*: He says callapitter for caterpillar and basketti for spaghetti and swamich for sandwich, but ridicule from his brother focuses his attention on his aberrant pronunciation and with concentration he can correct it. It's just a matter of time before his practiced pronunciations will become natural. In fact he would naturally conform, even without an older brother, just as his irregular verbs will come into conformity in his desire to say things the way the rest of his family and older friends do. Just the other day, for example, he ordered a "swamich" in a restaurant. The waiter, not hearing him, asked him to repeat. Fearing that his mispronunciation had caused the waiter's confusion, he carefully pronounced "sandwich." This, of course, is a big step from just a few months earlier, when he did not attend to the ways in which he pronounced words differently from other people. He is now at the point of recognition and will move to a conscious effort to change.

Christopher does other things with language. He *recalls and shares past experiences*, sometimes for pure pleasure, sometimes to keep the socializing going, sometimes to exorcise fears ("Remember that scarey part in . . ."). Christopher organizes with language ("First I'm going to . . . , then I'm going to . . ." or "I'll put this here and put that there . . ."). The range of ways that children begin to use language prior to beginning school is enormous (see Figure 1.1).

■ **IDEAS TO LEARN**   Spend time with a preschool child or visit a preschool classroom and listen to how children use language. Try to categorize the functions that language serves for very young children. Refer to Figure 1.1 ("Children's use of language and supporting strategies") to help you recognize the various ways children use language.

In piecing together the world, Christopher sees things in original ways and uses original language to express his perceptions, often creating the metaphors that we find so charming in children and that, again, reveal their powers of making sense of the world. For example, once on a walk, Chris and I saw a dog lying in the middle of the road, right near an intersection. I

1. Self-maintaining

Strategies

1. Referring to physical and psychological needs and wants
2. Protecting the self and self interests
3. Justifying behavior or claims
4. Criticizing others
5. Threatening others

2. Directing

Strategies

1. Monitoring own actions
2. Directing the actions of the self
3. Directing the actions of others
4. Collaborating in action with others

3. Reporting on present and past experiences

Strategies

1. Labelling the components of the scene
2. Referring to detail (e.g. size, color, and other attributes)
3. Referring to incidents
4. Referring to the sequence of events
5. Making comparisons
6. Recognizing related aspects
7. Making an analysis using several of the features above
8. Extracting or recognizing the central meaning
9. Reflecting on the meaning of experiences, including own feelings

4. Towards logical reasoning*

Strategies

1. Explaining a process
2. Recognizing causal and dependent relationships
3. Recognizing problems and their solutions
4. Justifying judgments and actions
5. Reflecting on events and drawing conclusions
6. Recognizing principles

5. Predicting*

Strategies

1. Anticipating and forecasting events
2. Anticipating the detail of events
3. Anticipating a sequence of events
4. Anticipating problems and possible solutions
5. Anticipating and recognizing alternative courses of action
6. Predicting the consequences of actions or events

6. Projecting*

Strategies

1. Projecting into the experiences of others
2. Projecting into the feelings of others
3. Projecting into the reactions of others
4. Projecting into situations never experienced

7. Imagining*

1. Developing an imaginary situation based on real life
2. Developing an imaginary situation based on fantasy
3. Developing an original story

---

*Strategies which serve *directing, reporting,* and *reasoning* may serve these uses also.

FIGURE 1.1 Children's use of language and supporting strategies (Tough, 1985, 80).

admonished the dog, warning him of the dangers he might face. Christopher had his own view of the situation. "Maybe that's a stop-and-go dog," he observed.

The Language Learning Environment

Although a chat with someone from another country on the top of a double-decker bus in London may be a somewhat unusual language situation, the kind of language behavior that Christopher engages in is not at all unusual for his age, nor are the processes by which he came to use language in these ways. How do children become adept users of language by the time they reach kindergarten? It's important to talk about child language acquisition, because the ways in which children learn language and their world through language can provide a model for teachers to help children continue to grow in their use of language. It is important for teachers to work with the current of children's growth rather than against it. The following observations of language learning can provide a basis for working with that current.

1. **Children learn language in meaningful situations.** From the time they are babies, most children live in environments that are geared toward helping the children make sense of their world. Parents and other care givers communicate with children about things in the immediate environment, about things of immediate importance. As a mother dresses her baby she talks about putting socks and shoes on baby's feet, about putting on a coat because it's cold outside. As a father gives his baby a bath, he talks about getting baby nice and clean and about being careful not to get soap in baby's eyes. As the baby-sitter serves lunch, she talks about baby eating all the peas and about being careful because the cereal might be too hot. On outings family members point out animals, plants, and cement trucks; chat about the sunny or rainy day; complain about how the car is running or about the traffic. Even when parents aren't talking directly to their children, a good deal of their talk is about what they are doing, what they have just done, or what they are going to do, much of which has been or will be demonstrated for the child.

In living day-to-day life, then, children are in a context in which language is connected to pertinent experiences, objects, and relationships. The language has a context and a referent. It is related to people's observations and actions. Words are not removed from reality but are fully integrated with it.

2. **Children learn language to participate in their "community," to interact with those around them.** Children are not simply passive

observers in this language environment but from infancy show a strong desire to participate. Communication or interaction with others is one of the driving forces in children's language learning. The early interactions of babies and their care givers demonstrate to babies the importance of language in their environment. For example, research conducted with infants and their mothers has shown that nursing babies and their mothers form patterns of communication. While the baby sucks, the mother remains quiet; when the baby stops, the mother talks to the baby. Researchers believe that this interaction establishes the turn taking that characterizes patterns of conversation ("Baby Talk," 1987).

In addition, early on babies begin making the same sounds that parents or other care givers use as the basis for the give-and-take of conversation. Psychologists have noted that parents treat their very young children as if they were full participants in the conversation. When a baby makes a sound, parents will often respond as if the sound had a specific intent; they will respond to it as meaningful. This encourages children in their desire to be understood and to understand, to participate fully in the social relations of the world around them. It is one way that babies begin piecing together how language means. We see further evidence of the desire for communication in babies' first words. We once assumed that the first words babies learn are nouns, words that refer to the "things" in a baby's environment; however, we now realize that babies' first words are socially tied: *hi, bye-bye, dada* and *mama*, and *thank you* ("Baby Talk").

Babies' early language shows that babies attempt to control their environment. Early words in their vocabulary include ones like *up* and *more* or nouns used as commands signifying that they want the object they name: *bear, ball, cookie, juice.* The fact that parents eagerly respond to babies' requests demonstrates for the babies that language is powerful indeed.

3. **Children learn language by using it and experiencing it rather than by being given rules about it to follow.** Observers have often been amazed at how quickly and thoroughly children are able to control the basic elements of their language. By the time they go to kindergarten, they can manipulate the syntax of the language (such things as word order and grammatical relationships). They know a good deal about the semantics of the language (the meanings of words and their relationships to one another). They also have significant control over the pragmatics of the language (the social uses of language) ("Baby Talk"). No one sat down and taught them the rules that govern language. The children didn't use a grammar book nor did anyone present them with lists of sounds so that they could learn how to put them together into the words we use in English (see Figure 1.2). Instead they learned by living in an environment in which the language was *used*.

How?

Bill Hull once said to me, "If we taught children to speak, they'd never learn." I thought at first he was joking. By now I realize that it was a very important truth. Suppose we decided that we had to "teach" children to speak. How would we go about it? First, some committee of experts would analyze speech and break it down into a number of separate "speech skills." We would probably say that, since speech is made up of sounds, a child must be taught to make all the sounds of his language before he can be taught to speak the language itself. Doubtless we would list these sounds, working our way down the list. Perhaps, in order not to "confuse" the child—"confuse" is an evil word to many educators—we would not let the child hear much ordinary speech, but would only expose him to the sounds we were trying to teach.

Along with our sound list, we would have a syllable list and a word list.

When the child had learned to make all the sounds on the sound list, we would begin to teach him to combine the sounds into syllables. When he could say all the syllables on the syllable list, we would begin to teach him the words on our word list. At the same time, we would teach him the rules of grammar, by means of which he could combine these newly-learned words into sentences. Everything would be planned with nothing left to chance; there would be plenty of drill, review, and tests, to make sure that he had not forgotten anything.

Suppose we tried to do this; what would happen? What would happen, quite simply, is that most children, before they got very far, would become baffled, discouraged, humiliated, and fearful, and would quit trying to do what we asked them. If, outside of our classes, they lived a normal infant's life, many of them would probably ignore our "teaching" and learn to speak on their own. If not, if our control of their lives was complete (the dream of too many educators), they would take refuge in deliberate failure and silence, as so many of them do when the subject is reading.

FIGURE 1.2 How children learn to speak (Holt, 1983, 118–119).

It was once thought that babies learn language by imitating what they hear around them. Closer observation of children's utterances, however, has shown that the language children produce is not identical to what they hear. Often, in fact, children produce utterances that they have never heard before. Moreover, some of their language is the result of an overgeneralization of the rules of grammar (for example, Christopher's use of *teached* for *taught*). In the early 1960s linguist Noam Chomsky (1957, 1972) hypothesized that humans are born with a specialized part of the brain for learning language, a language acquisition device. Though most linguists today recognize the biological roots of language, they believe that language acquisition is an interplay between children's cognitive abilities—that is, their ability to make generalizations that allow them to comprehend the world—and the language environment, the ways in which people talk to them and around them.

In early development, parents' routines in language and in matching language with experience allow children to make meaning from the situation. At first all language is heard by the baby as a stream of sound, but repetitions of words, words used in combinations with actions, baby's sounds turned into words by helpful care givers all give children clues to the relationship between sound and meaning.

Children begin their language production by babbling. (Actually their communication begins with their crying. Researchers have found that babies have different cries to represent different sorts of needs and feelings.) As parents talk to babies, babies begin to adjust their production to what they hear. Even before babies have words, they have intonation patterns that conform to those of adult syntax. It is often evident in a stream of baby talk whether the baby is producing an exclamation (*Kitty!* as in "How wonderful, a kitty!"), a statement (*Kitty,* as in "There's a kitty."), or a question (*Kitty?* as in "Is that a kitty?") In addition, in their early babbling children produce sounds that are used in their language (i.e., Chinese children will produce sounds used in Chinese, Mexican children will produce sounds used in Spanish, American children will produce sounds used in American English). Within months, babies use the sounds that are appropriate to the language that the people around them speak.

Children also learn the syntax of the language by establishing hypotheses and testing them. Children listen to the language around them and attempt to match what they hear. However, they do not simply imitate what they hear. On the basis of their vast experience with language, children make generalizations about how it operates. Some of the so-called errors that children make when they speak are based on their overgeneralization of rules. For example, when they first learn to speak, many children can match the irregular past tenses of their parents (*say, went, heard*). However, as they become more familiar with language (at age three or so), almost all children make the same generalization about language; that is, that we create the past tense of a verb by adding *-ed*, as we saw Christopher do. Children then begin to regularize their verbs, creating the past tense with *-ed*; their verbs become *seed, goed*, and *heared*. Although it may appear to be a step backward, this use of language demonstrates growth. Rather than seeing this as an error, then, we see it as a tremendous cognitive strength—the ability to take myriad instances and make a rule based on them. In time, given the same perceptiveness that led them to make the rule in the first place, children will note the exceptions to the rule and conform to the irregular past tense usage.

4. **Children learn language in an environment in which risk taking is encouraged and error is allowed.** The drive of parents and children to communicate compels them to work with each other to make themselves understood. Moreover, in attempts to understand children, parents and other good care givers are not only tolerant but are eager to praise and support children in their efforts to communicate. Each new attempt at a word, or even an intonation that sounds like a word, brings encouragement: smiles, cheers

of appreciation, and requests for repetition. Children, then, are reinforced and supported not on the basis of the correctness of their attempt but for the attempt itself and its appropriateness to the situation. Nearly all efforts to communicate, then, are seen as meaningful and productive and as having intent.

5. **Children learn language in the process of making sense of and getting control over their world.** The relationship of language to thought is an issue that has long been of interest to psychologists and linguists. Some have believed that first one must learn language, which then enables one to think. Recent work with children's language, however, points to the conclusion that language and thinking develop simultaneously and that each supports the development of the other. It's clear, for example, that children often use words and forms before they have pinned down the precise meanings; in fact it is their use of a word or a form that helps them begin to grasp meaning, that gives them something to hold onto while they are refining their sense of a situation or of words (for example, Christopher's use of the word *rent*). Language, then, is the means by which children come to know.

Often, too, children will learn a form before they understand the function of that form. For example, riddles and knock-knock jokes rely on the use of puns or figures of speech for their humor. When Chris's older brother Michael was four or so, his favorite riddle was: "What did one skeleton say to the other?" Answer: "I've got a bone to pick with you." Although Michael did know that skeletons were made of bones, he was unfamiliar with the saying "I've got a bone to pick with you." And yet he would tell the joke and laugh uproariously when he gave the answer. Five-year-old Christopher loves knock-knock jokes, but when he makes them up, even though he uses the form properly, "they don't make sense" (as his nine-year-old brother tells him).

Children spend much of their first five years exploring language and experience simultaneously and with the support and encouragement of those around them. Then they go to school.

Principles of Language Teaching

For many years children's facility for learning language was not exploited by teachers or reflected in the materials that children were given to learn language in school. In fact, a kind of conventional wisdom about how children could best learn to read and write dominated the schools for a long time: In order for children to learn language, teachers and writers of teaching materials needed to make things simple for children. And, it was assumed, the way to make things simple for children was to move from the small parts to the whole. Thus, for many years, children were given reading workbooks that moved from letters and sounds to syllables to words to sentences. They used basal readers with a controlled vocabulary; that is, only a few new words were introduced at a time. Children's early instruction in reading, then, began with workbook pages and simple (often boring) stories. As children got older, their books became more sophisticated, but exercises in syllabication and word analysis, with the addition of vocabulary exercises, continued.

In writing—if it were introduced at all—children began by copying. It was assumed that children could not write independently and would need to be taught about written language before they could write on their own. More often, however, the conventional wisdom dictated the use of weekly spelling lists and exercises in grammar that taught children parts of speech, subject-verb agreement, verb tenses, and so forth. It was assumed that if children were taught these aspects of the language they would be able to apply this information when they finally began to write.

For the most part, teachers, administrators, and creators of materials did not look at children's natural ability to acquire language as the basis for establishing instructional programs for children in school. Research in children's language learning, especially in the last twenty years, however, has called educators' attention to children's ability to master reading and writing in the same way that they have learned to speak. Ken Goodman has done significant work in children's language learning, particularly in learning to read, and has contributed to recent attempts to help language teachers bring their methods in line with what is known about children's learning. He claims:

> It had to come. Linguists and others are turning their attention from smaller bits and pieces to whole texts. They have begun to provide information on what makes a text a text and how people are able to produce comprehensible texts and make sense of them. Now we are beginning to realize that we've made mistakes in school when we tried to simplify language learning. Controlled vocabulary, phonic principles, or short, choppy sentences in primers and pre-primers produced non-texts. What we gave children didn't hang together, was unpredictable, and violated the expectations of even young readers who knew already how a real story works. Above it all hung the dark cloud of irrelevance and dullness. And we taught writing by drilling pupils on handwriting, spelling, and other mechanics, and so distracted them from what they already knew through oral language about producing whole functional texts.
>
> (K. Goodman, 1986b, 28)

Children learn to read and write in the same way that they learn to talk; that is, learning takes place when the tasks children encounter are meaningful, when the language environment is rich, and when children have some

What makes language very easy or very hard to learn?

It's easy when:	It's hard when:
It's real and natural.	It's artificial.
It's whole.	It's broken into bits and pieces.
It's sensible.	It's nonsense.
It's interesting.	It's dull and uninteresting.
It's relevant.	It's irrelevant to the learner.
It belongs to the learner.	It belongs to somebody else.
It's part of a real event.	It's out of context.
It has social utility.	It has no social value.
It has purpose for the learner.	It has no discernible purpose.
The learner chooses to use it.	It's imposed by someone else.
It's accessible to the learner.	It's inaccessible.
The learner has power to use it.	The learner is powerless.

These lists show that a whole language program is more pleasant and more fun for both pupils and teachers. Is it also more effective? Yes, it is. With the language they've already learned, children bring to school their natural tendency to want to make sense of the world. When schools break language into bits and pieces, sense becomes nonsense, and it's always hard for kids to make sense out of nonsense. Each abstract bit and piece that is learned is soon forgotten as kids go on to further fractured fragments. In the end, they begin to think of school as a place where nothing ever seems to make sense.

FIGURE 1.3 A whole language program (K. Goodman, 1986b, 8).

control over the discourse situation. Ken Goodman has outlined the circumstances in which learning language is easy and those in which it is difficult (see Figure 1.3). Once educators acknowledge the importance of language learning based on children's strengths, teachers can create an environment that supports children's natural inclination to grow in their use of language.

■ **IDEAS TO LEARN**   Explore some of your early memories of language. Were there funny words you used as a small child? Do members of your family tell stories about humorous misunderstandings or clever sayings you made when you were little? Do you or family members have any memories of your early interest in reading and writing?

Because the language expectations of school are often different from those at home, children who have been successful language learners before they go to school often become hesitant and doubtful about their own ability to learn once they enter school. Linda Dinan (1976) has written: "Some years ago when I was interviewing my first graders concerning their attitudes and knowledge about written language and school, one of my standard questions was, 'What would you do (about learning to read) if there were no teachers?' Most of the students either answered 'I don't know' or 'I'd ask my parents to help me,' but one determined little guy answered, 'I'd just come here and wait.' To me that was the quintessential statement about the relationship between many elementary school teachers and their students. We, as teachers, with assistance from parents, the media, and the public in general are responsible for a child's learning." There seems to be little recognition of the rich and detailed learning that children do within their family and community; thus, when they go to school, many children quickly become passive vessels for their teachers' instruction. Not only do the children's attitudes about learning change when they enter school, but the behaviors of the adult language "instructors" also change. When school begins, the natural and effective interplay that goes on outside school between adults and children is altered. Assuming the conscious roles of "teacher" and "learner," the characters in this drama become out of sync.

Linguist Judith Wells Lindfors (1980) refers to this as a "profound confusion" about the difference between teaching and learning. Often, Lindfors says, "teaching-learning connections are not apparent at all, with teachers' efforts to increase children's knowledge and skills, and children's efforts to make sense of their world, going on quite independently of one another" (600). Lindfors describes one such mismatch between "teaching" and "learning" involving her own son. While talking about school, her son reported that he "was not good in reading." Knowing that he could indeed read, she was stunned by his remark. After further discussion with him, she realized his confusion. "What he had done (learn to make sense of print) was effective; what the teacher was doing (sequencing and conducting activities toward a specific end) was, in this instance, counterproductive. But he believed wrongly, that his learning was the business of carrying out the teacher's sequence. He believed that he was doing HIS thing badly (learning) because he was not doing HER thing well (moving through her instructional activities)" (604).

This confusion is rampant: "I taught them but they didn't learn" is a common attitude. As Postman and Weingartner (1972) have said, teachers labor to create the perfect syllabus and the wrong students come through the door. An approach that suggests that teaching and learning are identical places the teacher's activity rather than the child's at the center of the curriculum. Lindfors concludes: "If the goal of teaching is, as some believe, to support children's learning . . . then we would do well to try to understand what children's learning is like, what the child is trying to do. At the very least, we must begin by distinguishing between the time-honored instructional activities of teachers, and the timeless sense-making processes of children" (Lindfors, 1980, 605).

Like Lindfors, educator Herbert Kohl sees teachers relying on textbook materials rather than looking at learners and learning. He admonishes teachers: "We should not depend upon packaged 'teacher-proof' materials to do our work, because frankly, if we continue to depend on those materials rather than on our knowledge and our ability to understand the learner, we will be replaced by people who can merely read answer books, control students and mark tests" (Kohl, 1982, 34). Kohl sees an important role for the teacher: "Experimentation is essential to good teaching, and teachers should be actively involved in inventing and testing new ways to teach old concepts. It's crucial that teachers ask themselves what they do that couldn't be done by any literate person" (34).

The danger of focusing on the program or the subject or the activity is present even with the most well-intentioned teachers and the most progressive programs. Ann Haas Dyson (1986), who researches children's language, describes a student teacher excited by the progressive classroom activities of her cooperating teacher. Dyson was skeptical of her enthusiastic response, because "she had no stories for me about the children—those seeming to do well and those struggling, those who were endearing and those who would be 'interesting challenges' in the coming months. Nor was she reflecting on her goals, on what she wanted to accomplish with these children as a 'teacher' and a 'learner.' The activities had caught this aspiring teacher's attention, not the children" (135).

Dyson suggests that teaching is not the "doing of activities but a dynamic interactive dance; teachers and children interact to create activities—to create curricula—as they work to reach their respective goals" (135–136). She warns that to avoid rigid approaches we as teachers need to deepen "our understanding of classrooms, language, learning, and learners, not only through keeping informed of the insights of others, but through critically observing the responses of students to our teaching efforts" (141–142).

Clearly in many classrooms the goals of the teacher and the teaching program often ignore children's skills, needs, and individual growth. Indeed children often choose very little of what they read and write; they study about language rather than engage in language processes; they fill in the blanks in workbooks that have them look at language from parts to the whole—all of which makes language almost meaningless and school work tedious. Many schools compound this situation by basing their reading programs on basal readers, which tend to use a simplified language that often makes for boring reading.

Things are changing, however. Especially in the past twenty years, research done in children's language acquisition and growth has begun to filter into classrooms, as more and more researchers and teacher-researchers have begun to appreciate children's tremendous language learning ability. In the coming chapters we will discuss specifics about the kinds of reading, writing, speaking, and listening activities that engage children's minds and imaginations and support their growth.

Creating a Classroom Environment to Support Children's Learning

So far we have looked at the individual child's language learning and at some recent theories about how schools can support and nurture children's growth in language and thinking. Now we will turn to the individual classroom and what you as a teacher can do to create an environment that promotes children's growth. The following suggestions are based on our current understanding of how children best learn.

1. **Create a rich and meaningful language environment.** Children learn to speak in an environment rich in language resources. We have already detailed how parents and care givers pull children from infancy into what language theorist James Britton (1970) calls a web of human relations. Children observe and participate in a language-drenched world. In addition to the obvious language-oriented aspects of child rearing—chanting rhymes ("This little piggy" and "Pat-a-cake"), reading books, and naming things—almost every aspect of a child's life (dressing, playing, shopping, eating, traveling) is connected to language. Children draw on this richness to construct their language world. Much of what they draw on is not simplified for them, but by constant contact they come to understand it.

The classroom needs to model the family in the sort of richness it provides. First of all, children should have opportunities in school to talk. In describing how children learn to write, Britton says that "writing and talking and doing must go on in close relationship, and talking and doing provide the essential foundation." Children need to talk about their firsthand experiences, he explains, in order to bring these to bear on secondhand experiences; that is, "other people's experience put into words." In addition, "the spoken language remains the 'recruiting area' for further linguistic resources. If you come to an unfamiliar area of experience about which you want to write . . . then the chances are you will talk before you write." According to Britton, "all that the children write, your response to what they write, their response to each other, all this takes place afloat upon a sea of talk" (Britton, 1970, 29).

In addition to opportunities to use language, children should have opportunities to hear the language of the literate community. Teachers should read aloud to children—at all ages and grades—every day. Hearing the language of print is precisely what allows children to learn how it functions, to develop a sense of story, to increase their understanding of words, and to develop a sense of the predictability of language that will help them as independent readers and writers. In addition, teachers can read to children who are already independent readers, from texts that may be slightly beyond them for reading on their own but that will help prepare them for the next step in their independent reading. Teachers should read literature of all sorts— poems, stories, articles from newspapers and magazines (perhaps related to the science or social studies pursuits of the classroom), and pieces written by children.

In addition to a rich oral language environment, children need a rich print environment from which to develop generalizations about how printed language functions. Most children come to school having a sense of reading and writing. They "read" the golden arch as "McDonalds" and the signs on service stations as "gas" and the labels on cans as "beans" or "corn" according to the picture of the contents. Some write with squiggles or random letters of idiosyncratic symbols to represent letters. Children, then, have skill in reading "environmental print," and they create print. Teachers can build on these skills by providing classroom environmental print. The print that is a part of the environment should be useful and interesting to the readers. Many teachers post such things as classroom procedures or rules, weekly or daily schedules, and sometimes colorful posters or pictures. To invite readers into the world of print, fill the classroom with useful and interesting language: newspaper and magazine articles, poems and stories, and texts written by the children (student-of-the week displays, stories, poems, informational articles).

The classroom should also have plenty of reading materials for children to browse through and read. Again magazines, newspapers, and books of stories, novels, poems, plays, jokes and riddles, and nonfiction (for instance, science and social studies trade books) should be readily available for children. Children should be encouraged to read not just during free time but as a central part of their day.

■ **IDEAS TO LEARN**   Develop an interest inventory of your own to learn more about children. How might the things you learn from children about their hobbies, skills, and interests be integrated into the classroom?

---

2. **Learn who the children are and what they can do.** Begin by finding out basic information about children through the use of inventories or (with young children) interviews (see Figure 1.4). Find out what they like to read, what they like to write, and what their special interests and hobbies are. You can uncover a wealth of child expertise and knowledge in class and

build upon it. Children may be rock or stamp or insect or butterfly collectors. They may help care for horses or birds or cats or tropical fish. They may play the piano or dance or enjoy painting and drawing. They may be hikers or bikers. They may have visited several states, been on a camping trip, or visited Hong Kong. All these experiences are the sources they will use as readers and writers to understand and describe their world. When teachers know the children's interests and experiences, they have a firm base for suggesting books to read, topics to write about, and projects to work on across the curriculum. Moreover, they can draw on these experiences to enrich the activities in the classroom by getting children to share their expertise—as rock or stamp collectors, as care takers of fish or iguanas, as bicyclists or ice skaters. And, as teachers encounter more and more children in their classrooms who do not share their cultural background, it is important that they learn what these children value and what interests them.

Interest Inventory

Name _____   Nickname _____

What are some of your favorites?

Books   Movies and TV shows

Heroes: real people and characters

Places: local and travels

Games/sports   Hobbies/pastimes

Talents/skills   Favorite school subjects

FIGURE 1.4 This interest inventory includes a few of many questions or categories you might want to ask children about. You might include more specific questions about reading interests or school subjects. Or you might want to know more about children's special hobbies, talents, and outside interests.

In addition to interest and reading inventories, teachers can learn about children's language abilities by observing what they do and how they do it. A recent movement in education calls for teachers to rely not only on research but on their own observations, because they work with children daily and have an opportunity to observe them closely. Teacher Patricia Candal (1988) describes how her awareness—her classroom research—helps her and her students to be successful. She describes four steps in her research: "I wonder. I read. I inquire. I document. . . . Wondering is to researching what rehearsal is to the writer's process: a time and a way to reflect upon what is working and what is not working, a chance to explore with questions what the problems are that need to be solved" (1). Candal learns more about an issue by reading and "finding out what others have said and done" about it (2). She also asks her students what they know and understand about what they are doing. Documenting involves "recording comments, impressions, behaviors, and reflections". She says this has "helped me learn to make more good decisions than bad ones in the classroom" (5).

Ike Coleman sees the issue of the teacher as researcher in more dramatic terms:

> If the people above teachers in the educational hierarchy are assumed to be the guardians of theory, then they're the ones who will hold the strings to classroom practice. We can't have it both ways; we can't remain in control of *what* we do in the classroom if we're not concerned about *why* we do it. In other words, until teachers join—and are allowed into—the discourse on theory and research, we'll be doomed, like the protagonist of "The Pit and the Pendulum," to an ever-decreasing space in which to do what we believe is best. The logical conclusion is frightening: the teacher's role would be simply to implement a series of steps dictated by those above, to teach a prescribed skill on a prescribed day in a prescribed manner.
>
> (Coleman, 1988, 82)

Teachers need to be aware of children's needs and abilities, then, because it is that awareness that allows them to be effective in supporting children's growth. That awareness is also the basis of a teacher's professionalism, which includes the power to make decisions and judgments about what happens and what should happen in school.

3. **Allow children to make choices and decisions.** One of the most distressing things about what happens in school is that children often do not leave school as readers and writers, even though literacy is one of school's central purposes. Certainly school alone is not the culprit. Perhaps children do not see parents read or write. Perhaps parents do not encourage their children to read and write (by setting aside time or providing books and

pencils and paper). Perhaps the easy and seductive world of television is in part responsible for children's lack of attention to the printed word.

It is easy to blame societal pressures for children's lack of interest in reading and writing. However, I believe that teachers have an obligation to provide children with opportunities to know the satisfaction of reading and writing. In addition, I strongly believe that the joys of reading, writing, and learning will engage children when the teacher has provided meaningful experiences. Many teachers often do not provide enough opportunities for reading and writing. Moreover, even when children are reading and writing, assignments are often teacher-generated: The teacher provides the *task*, the *requirements* for being successful at the task, and the *evaluation* of whether the child was successful.

As we have seen with very young language learners, children's needs and purposes are essential to their desire to use language and their process of learning language. When children enter school, teachers should encourage this desire to use language for one's own purposes. Ken Goodman (1986b) emphasizes: "Authenticity is essential. Kids need to feel that what they are doing through language they have chosen to do because it is useful, or interesting, or fun for them. They need to own the processes they use: to feel that the activities are their own, not just school work or stuff to please the teacher. What they do ought to matter to them personally" (31).

Providing opportunities for children to make decisions about what they read and what they write and how to evaluate the success and usefulness of their activities does not mean that the teacher is passive in the classroom. In fact just the opposite is true. In a classroom based on children's growth, the teacher must constantly assess the curriculum, the materials, and the classroom activities as well as the activities of individual children to make certain these are consistent with the needs and interests of the child. Teachers are much more involved with individual children rather than "teaching to a middle ground" (K. Goodman, 1986b, 29). Goodman values the role of teachers as they "seek to create appropriate social settings and interactions, and to influence the rate and direction of personal learning" (29). They "guide, support, monitor, encourage, and facilitate learning, but do not control it" (29).

Some teachers are afraid that students won't do anything unless they force, persuade, grade, or assign. But avoidance is not a natural response to work. Avoidance occurs when children have been asked to engage in meaningless tasks. In an article on management procedures in the classroom, David Berliner (1983) draws on the theories of executive management to describe human potential. He describes Theory Y, "a set of concepts about the inherent potential of all people" (30). He believes that these theories apply to students in the same way they do to workers. Theory Y states that:

- The expenditure of physical and mental effort in work is as natural as play or rest. The average human being does not inherently dislike work.

- External control and the threat of punishment are not the only means for bringing about effort toward organizational objectives. People will exercise self-direction in the service of objectives to which they are committed.

- Commitment to objectives results from the rewards associated with their achievement. The most significant of such rewards, such as the satisfaction of ego and self-actualization needs, can be direct products of effort directed toward organizational objectives.

- The average human being learns, under proper conditions, not only to accept but to seek responsibility.

- The capacity to exercise a relatively high degree of imagination, ingenuity, and creativity in the solution of organization problems is widely, not narrowly, distributed in the population.

- The intellectual potential of the average human being is only partially utilized.

(Berliner, 1983, 30)

All of us have seen children expend time, energy, and effort to get projects they are working on "just right"; they work with great care on things that they have chosen and invested themselves in. When children are given opportunities to take responsibility and to engage in meaningful activity, teachers will see Theory Y validated in their classrooms.

   4. **Encourage and support risk taking and see errors as indicators of growth.** (See Figure 1.5). As we have seen, risk taking is precisely what allows young children to learn language. They make guesses and they use the responses they get to those guesses to "evaluate" their effectiveness and determine what to do next. Their "errors" are what teach them, but no one spends a lot of time focusing on the errors or describing for children where they went awry. Rather all reasonably successful attempts are praised and encouraged. When our children were learning to talk, we rejoiced in every new attempt at a word—*key* for *kitty* was a wonderful accomplishment and *basketti* for *spaghetti* was close enough. Whoever was in the baby's presence when he said "key" would say "Yes, kitty" and pick up that end of the conversation by talking about how pretty the kitty was or how to be gentle to the kitty. And a request for "basketti" would always be rewarded with spaghetti, not a lecture on the *sp* sound. Eventually the children, wishing very much to be part of the grown-up community, said the words like everyone else.

   In school, children are often evaluated on the basis of their errors. If they have trouble spelling, they get back a test with a 65 percent on it.

The learning begins with immersion in an environment in which the skill is being used in purposeful ways. Readiness is timed by the internal 'clock' of the learner.

The environment is an emulative rather than an instructional one, providing lively examples of the skill in action, and inducing targeting activity which is persistently shaped by modelling and by reinforcement.

Reinforcement contingencies, both intrinsic and extrinsic, approach the ideal of immediate rewards for almost every approximation regardless of the distance of the initial response from the perfect 'correct' response.

Bad approximations—those moving away from the desired response—are not reinforced.

What aspect of the task will be practiced, at what pace, and for how long is determined largely by the learner. Practice occurs whether or not the adult is attending, and tends to continue until essential aspects of the task are under comfortable, automatic control.

The environment is secure and supportive, providing help on call and being absolutely free from any threat associated with the learning of the task.

Development tends to proceed continuously in an orderly sequence marked by considerable differences from individual to individual.

FIGURE 1.5 The foundations of literacy (Holdaway, 1979, 23).

Punctuation errors and spelling errors are often marked with red pencils on writing papers. Oral reading errors are immediately corrected. Children learn very quickly that their work will be viewed more favorably if it is error-free. Children's efforts at using language, then, are often directed toward avoiding error rather than experimenting by trying new words, more complex sentences, or forms that require difficult punctuation, like quotation marks or semicolons. Nor are they willing to guess at a word when reading. In fact, teachers who "grade down" or red-pencil a child's spelling are encouraging children to use simpler (and often more boring) words rather than the more difficult (and often more precise and expressive) words that they know but can't spell. But children enjoy the idiosyncrasies of printed language and will experiment with them in ways that augment their language growth when their efforts are understood and accepted rather than viewed as signs of inadequacy.

In fact, as children grow in their language, they are often working with a more complex and higher order of skills than those they've mastered, which can unbalance what they have already learned. We should be saying "Aren't you clever to have tried this?" rather than "Aren't you stupid because you haven't got it right yet."

5. **Describe, don't judge.** Although children do not benefit from criticism of their errors, they do benefit from adult feedback and response, from

someone who has perspective on their work and can look at it from another point of view or point out things that the child may not have noticed. Rather than marking wrong the spelling of a word, a teacher can describe how the child has constructed a word. When I taught writing workshop in first grade, many children were using very colorful and complicated words. Rather than telling them all their errors (in fact, they did that themselves by circling the words they felt they had misspelled), I would talk to them about those words. If a child had written *hrs*, for example, for *horse*, I would say "Look how close you were: you have the beginning sound and the end sounds. The vowels are harder. You just needed the o and the e at the end, which you couldn't hear."

In reading, the teacher will be more effective if he or she helps children describe their understanding of what they have read rather than to tell the child the meaning in the adult's terms. And if, in oral reading, children produce readings that don't make sense to us, we should ask them what they understood from what they just read. Then, we can provide feedback, reflecting back to the children what we heard them say or do without attaching a judgment.

6. **Adapt to variations in children's growth in literacy.** Often in schooling we've expected everyone at the same age and grade level to be doing the same thing, to be working on the same level. With the exception of the severely brain damaged and physically handicapped, all children have the linguistic and physiological skills to become readers and writers—and given the proper environment and materials, they will become readers and writers. In their extensive research into children's language Harste, Woodward, and Burke (1984) found that preschool children have a natural affinity for literacy tasks. This does not mean, though, "that all children start at the same place at the time of formal language instruction" (44).

When assessing a child's literacy achievements, it is extremely important not to rely solely on their products. Harste, Woodward, and Burke have concluded that even very young children make decisions "both in form and in kind, like those which we make as literate adults," and that the "young child is a written language user long before his writing looks representational" (16). Because a child's writing does not resemble that of adults, the work is sometimes underrated, but Harste, Woodward, and Burke caution that "in order to judge the quality of a literacy experience one must judge the quality of the mental trip taken, not the arrival point per se" (18). Finally they argue that "writing is not a monolithic skill. Language varies according to the circumstances of its use. Different settings mandate different products" (19).

In his first three years of elementary school, Michael produced very little writing and what he did produce was, to his teachers' eyes, messy and immature. At the same time, he was becoming an avid reader and adept user of oral language. Now a fourth grader, Michael has bloomed as a writer. He writes and writes and writes wild stories about his cats. One of the bases on which Michael has been assessed is his handwriting. He has difficulty with small motor skills and produces erratic handwriting. In addition, he does not or cannot color within the lines. It is easy for a teacher to be frustrated by a kid like Michael, because on the face of it he is not producing precise surface structures. Many fourth graders in his class are writing cursive and most of them have more precise handwriting. Yet many of the children adept at writing do not have the language or reading skills Michael possesses. In order to encourage Michael to continue to grow, his teacher must not overemphasize the surface structures that Michael produces and must not see children like him as linguistically or physically handicapped. When children have difficulty with surface structure, it's important to avoid feedback that will be discouraging and to try to assess the total literacy experience for these children, including the types of literacy activities in which they engage and the quality of their engagement.

7. **Expect children to succeed, to try, to care.** Teachers need to be very careful about placing too much stock in test scores, former teachers' assessments, parents' judgments, and grades or evaluation forms. These assessments may be accurate and true, or they may have been true, or they may not be true, but they needn't always be true. Research shows that teacher expectations have a substantial influence on how children perform and behave. Children will become the person that the people around them expect them to be. When they are labeled, they are treated as they are labeled and they become what they were labeled—the "brain," the troublemaker, the sweet one, the bad speller, the nonreader, the nonwriter. Every child has potential as a reader and writer, and teachers need to teach to that potential, not to past performance.

One myth that needs to be shattered is that children from lower socioeconomic backgrounds are less capable of work in language than children from middle-class backgrounds. Harste, Woodward, and Burke (1984) have found that "the child's sex, race, level of parental income, parental educational level, or where the child lives are poor predictors of what the child knows and can do in terms of literacy" (44). Teachers need to respect the language of the child's nurture. Regional and social dialects—variations in grammatical usage, the words people use, and the ways in which words are pronounced—often affect people's attitudes toward speakers of those dialects. Such attitudes about dialects often grow out of the attitudes toward the social class with which they are associated. As linguist Judith Lindfors (1980) states, "Less prestigious dialects are often not regarded as intact linguistic systems (which they are) but rather as error-ridden, garbled, inadequate at-

It seems incredible that these deficiency notions so totally dominated educational thinking as recently as the late 1960s, and more incredible still that they are prevalent even now. We know that every environment that offers people and things for children to interact with is a rich learning environment for young active learners, explorers, discoverers. BE [Black English]-dominant children have such a learning environment. We know that every culture socializes its children to behave in ways that are appropriate within that group. BE-dominant children have learned to behave in ways that are appropriate within their culture. We know that members of every community interact with children in a wide range of ways and for diverse purposes, and that the children figure out the language of those interactions that they engage in—they speak the language of their community. BE-speaking children have done precisely this. They come to school with the background and the abilities and the tools that are the stuff of valid and effective ongoing learning. What has been deficient all along has not been BE-dominant children's language, culture, or cognition, but rather our inadequate understanding of these areas.

FIGURE 1.6 How children learn the language of their culture (Lindfors, 1980, 370–371).

tempts of a group of people to speak a regional standard dialect (which they are not)'' (356).

Children whose language is at variance with the school or teacher norm are sometimes seen as language deficient. For example, Black English has been labeled by some as ''substandard'' and children from homes where Black English is spoken have been characterized in the past as being culturally or cognitively deprived. In the past twenty years, however, researchers have studied Black English and described its systematic nature and its communicative functions. Rather than seeing children who speak a dialect as deficient, we need to recognize the richness and contribution of the dialect to the lives of the children (see Figure 1.6). As Lindfors states, ''All of us, but most of all our school children whatever their background, can only benefit from . . . a widened interaction of language and life styles. Their cognitive and language growth can only be enhanced by an even broader range of experience and interaction'' (374).

Ken Goodman (1986) agrees. Recognizing the great diversity of dialects and languages that are spoken by school children, he states: ''Schools should welcome the dynamic, fluid nature of language. How marvelous the variety of language, dialects, and registers of pupils! How satisfying for teachers to support the full range of language development rather than confining it to arbitrary 'proper' or 'standard' language'' (15).

Like Lindfors, Goodman takes issue with the notion that ''bilingual children are disadvantaged in some academic way. They are at a disadvantage only if their linguistic strengths are underappreciated and schools are failing to build on their strengths'' (K. Goodman, 1986b, 17). Thomas Ricento (1988), a linguistics expert in English as a second language, agrees. He supports students' use of their own language: "Using the language that children bring with them to the classroom as a point of departure dramatically improves the development of English skills while reducing the negative effects of discrimination on students' self-image and self-confidence" (4). Harste, Woodward, and Burke's (1984) work with children underscores the need for accepting children's wide range of before-school literacy experiences as valuable: "Given our experience, we must conclude that one must approach all children as if they know quite a bit about reading and writing regardless of the circumstances of their birth. Working from that assumption, open-ended activities should be designed in order to allow children to demonstrate, use, and build upon the knowledge they have already acquired about literacy" (44).

8. **Put the needs of the children before the demands of the curriculum.** A curriculum that is transactional, that involves children in interactions they find of interest, value, and use cannot be, as Harste, Woodward, and Burke (1984) suggest, formulaic. "From our perspective, what we ought to do, curricularly, is to establish an environment in which the child can *experience* and *come to value* the psycholinguistic and sociolinguistic activities we associate with successful written language use and learning. This does not mean that convention—correct spelling, correct grammar—is not important, but rather that it is a fringe benefit of socio-psycholinguistic involvement in the authoring process" (xii).

Teachers are sometimes confused about when or whether they should intervene in children's language activity and about when or whether they should provide direct teaching in the classroom. Helen Slaughter (1988) believes that "often teachers trained in the conventional basal reader, skills approach to literacy instruction initially feel confused about their teaching role when changing to a whole language program" (31). In studying both whole language and conventional classrooms, Slaughter found distinctions between the two. But she also discovered a similarity: Direct teaching (in which learning is highly structured and the teacher plays a dominant role in the classroom) was present in the whole language classroom as well as in the traditional classroom. However, "what seemed important here was the teacher's conception or theory about how language learning occurs, and the degree to which the teacher was able to relate to the child's conception of literacy and build upon his or her strengths, rather than adhering to a prior script of text" (32).

9. **Question the value of setting universal standards.** The concerns about the decline in test scores, the decline in cultural literacy, and the decline of reading and writing abilities of children have led to a kind of panic on the

parts of politicians and educational administrators. We educators need to be very suspicious about the evidence being used to support claims about the decline in education and the decline in student performance. Moreover, we should question even more vigorously the value of establishing minimum objectives for language learning, or competency tests to judge linguistic skill, or required reading lists to enforce a standard in reading. Such recommendations are inconsistent with our understanding of the ways in which children's language grows.

As we have seen, many factors contribute to a child's growth in literacy. To expect that all children can or will do the same thing at the same time is absurd. To enforce such a policy is to ensure failure for many children. Although evaluation is important, it should be based on the behavior appropriate to the growth and activity of the individual learner and the teacher's responsiveness to that (see Figure 1.7).

Moreover, it is the role of informed teachers who know about children's language growth to educate the wider public. In the meantime we need to be clear in what we do in our own classrooms to establish the kinds of learning environments and classroom activities and behaviors that will support children's growth in literacy.

Guidelines for Creating an Integrated Language Arts Curriculum

Now that we have looked at how theory of children's learning influences what we do in the individual classroom, we'll turn to larger issues of the language arts curriculum. In the last several years curriculum reform has moved in the direction of the integrated curriculum. The whole language movement, the literature-based curriculum movement, and the language across the curriculum movement are all attempts to integrate language study in the schools. I have adopted the term *integrated language arts* to include all these approaches to language learning in both the theoretical bases and the practical applications suggested in this text.

To summarize,

1. **The integrated language arts curriculum/classroom integrates reading, writing, speaking, and listening.** The traditional language arts curriculum isolated these subject areas. Reading was taught separately from writing. Writing was often seen as copying or "taught" as workbook or grammar lessons. Speaking and listening were often virtually ignored. The integrated curriculum, on the other hand, emphasizes the relationships among these areas: Students write about, dramatize, or recreate what they read; write stories, poems, plays, and nonfiction pieces that they read or perform;

Informal Evaluation of Learning
In Whole Language and Conventional Classrooms

Whole language classrooms	Conventional classrooms
Global criteria	
Is the teacher in step with the student?	Is the child out of step with the curriculum?
Does the teacher accept and value approximations, risk taking, and efforts towards meaning?	Is the student successful in:
Is the child developing a sense of empowerment and an authentic view of what it means to be literate?	• Keeping up with age mates • Getting work done correctly • Following standard English conventions in oral reading, writing, and spelling
Is the child learning to read and write and communicate?	
Self monitoring: Does the child know when s/he is right or wrong?	Does the child follow externally imposed rules and directions?
Type of evaluation	
Focus on meaning and/or the learning process	Focus on correctness or convention
Focus on the communicative process, independence via peer support encouraged; generous learning time allowed for experimentation and using communicative processes	Focus on mastery of an isolated individual's performance, peer support overlooked or denied
Quality of thinking valued	Quantity of work products completed correctly valued
Intrinsic motivation, e.g., author's chair; communicating for purposes, including publishing	Extrinsic motivation; rewards for achievement, escaping sanctions
Progress measured as related to ability to orchestrate language processes holistically	Progress measured as related to task completion, often of subskills

FIGURE 1.7 Criteria for evaluating in whole language and in conventional classrooms (Slaughter, 1988, 33).

listen and respond to one another's ideas and performances; use peer groups to create, respond, collaborate. Children's writing becomes the literature of the classroom; professional writing becomes resource and is subject to critique and response.

2. **The integrated language arts curriculum/classroom integrates the learning of skills into actual language use.** Traditional language arts instruction relied heavily on the study of subskills—phonics, grammar, spelling, penmanship, and the like—using workbooks for children to fill in and tests to prove mastery. It was found however, that although children might

complete the workbooks and score well on tests, they still had difficulty reading and writing. Current theory has supported the movement to integrate the study of the skills of language into the actual use of language for authentic purposes. Skills are by no means ignored by advocates of an integrated language approach. Rather they are taught as children encounter problems and need instruction.

3. **The integrated language arts curriculum/classroom integrates the use of language development activities into every curriculum area.** Language is seen as the medium of learning, as partner to thought, as the means by which children come to know and to express their knowing. Moreover, the language across the curriculum movement has helped teachers see and develop relationships between subject areas. Teachers have begun not only to develop the logical connections between literature and social studies or math and science but to use these connections. The language across the curriculum movement has provided the impetus for a curricular approach that is whole and connected.

4. **The integrated language arts curriculum/classroom integrates students' interests and needs with the aims of the curriculum.** In fact the aims of the curriculum center on the interests and needs of the students. In order to promote authentic language growth, children need to be engaged in meaningful language activity. An integrated curriculum uses a wide range of individualized activities to match the different interests of the students. Moreover, because it doesn't require rigid adherence to teaching certain skills at certain times, it can accommodate students at varying stages in language and skill development.

The integrated language arts curriculum reflects an important current trend in educational improvement. In his study of the curriculum development process, Stephen Tchudi (1991a) studied Centers of Excellence, a number of school projects selected by the National Council of Teachers of English as exemplary. He discovered that "at the elementary level, focuses included whole-language and integrated language arts instruction, the use of computers in writing, 'real' book programs, interdisciplinary curriculum, and staff development in teaching literature" (22). Moreover, he discovered that most of the participants responding to his survey represented programs that were initiated by teachers. In fact the involvement of teachers in curriculum development is seen as key to a curriculum's success. The words of Sharon Knipp of the Ysleta Independent School District in El Paso, Texas, reflect this perspective: "I would like to encourage teachers who have a vision to trust themselves and that vision, as I feel the most successful innovative programs are developed by those who know students best—the teachers'' (in Stephen Tchudi, 1991a, 24).

You may be fortunate as a teacher to be involved in a school- or district-wide innovative curriculum project. Or you may have the pleasure of working in a school district with a well-thought-out, progressive, developing curriculum in place. However, even if your school district is not involved in innovative curricular activity, you can receive support for integrated teaching from supportive administrators and compatible teachers within your school.

Some Models for the Integrated Language Arts Curriculum

Throughout this text you will find many specific ideas for creating an integrated curriculum. Here, however, I will briefly describe some models for the integrated language arts curriculum.

The Writing Workshop

Many teachers found their way into an integrated language arts curriculum through the use of the writing workshop. The work of Donald Graves (1983), Lucy Calkins (1986), and Jan Turbill (1982, 1983) provides models for classrooms using students' writing as the starting point for.language activities. Teachers who use the writing workshop draw on a number of common practices. The writing workshop is held at the same time every day so that students are able both to become self-reliant in a predictable set of activities and to "rehearse" and mentally prepare for writing time. Students select their own topics and maintain a portfolio of their writing projects and skill development. Students share both in-process and finished products with one another, in pairs, in small groups, and as a class. Teachers help students develop their writing skills according to class and individual needs through the use of conferences and mini-lessons. Students read both professional literature as well as each other's work and draw on what they read for ideas and for information about how print works. Students' "publish," and their published work becomes part of the literature of the classroom. Chapter 4 discusses the writing process and the writing workshop in detail.

The Literature–Based Curriculum

The California Reading Initiative, a state-mandated program to improve students' reading acquisition, provided a tremendous impetus for change with its move from a curriculum based on children's learning of skills in isolation or through basal readers to a curriculum based on children's reading of literature. Proponents of a literature-based curriculum (Routman, 1988; Hancock and Hill, 1988) create thematic units based on literature; provide many opportunities for children to choose what they will read; provide students with a variety of ways to share their responses to what they read; use literature as a model for children's writing; and keep individualized records of children's reading progress through conferences, checklists, and children's self-evaluations.

Although children's reading may provide the basis for organization of the curriculum, writing, speaking, and listening are also integral to a literature-based curriculum. Regie Routman (1988) describes the powerful influence of literature on young writers: "The language of literature, with its imagery and phrasing, serves as a wonderful model and springboard. Beginning writers internalize the storyline and reuse it to suit their own purposes. They try out speech marks when they need conversation; they experiment with periods and exclamation marks to make the meaning clearer; and most begin to use capital letters and periods with some accuracy. They write chapter stories, include dedication and author pages, table of contents, and incorporate all manner of illustrations in various media" (94). Older children, too, develop a sensitivity toward language and become aware of increasingly complex syntax and language conventions. They also experiment with genres and forms as a result of their contact with a rich print environment that provides inspiration as well as models. Chapter 6 provides examples of literature-based teaching units.

The Reading/Writing Curriculum

The literature-based curriculum and the writing workshop differ from the reading/writing curriculum not so much in the teachers' methods or in their emphasis but in what they use as a starting point for organizing class activities and materials. Proponents of the reading/writing curriculum (Hansen, 1987, 1992; Atwell, 1987) emphasize the importance of giving students opportunities to make their own selections about what they read and what they write. Hansen (1987) emphasizes time and choice in teachers' efforts to place reading and writing at the center of their classrooms. Listening and speaking become important in a reading/writing classroom, because students' talking is a central class activity. They talk about their response to books and to one another's writing; they talk in pairs, in small groups, and in large class discussions; they talk with each other, with the teacher, and with other adults. In addition, as an ongoing description of their progress in language, students and teachers keep records of the students' language development (checklists, observation notes, self-assessments, etc.), of the books they read, and of the pieces they write.

The Interdisciplinary Curriculum

The interdisciplinary curriculum—also known as language across the curriculum (Stephen Tchudi, 1991a; Stephen Tchudi and Susan Tchudi, 1983; Stephen Tchudi and Margie Huerta, 1983)—emphasizes the role of reading and writing throughout the curriculum and seeks to establish relationships among all curriculum subjects. Although children's individualized reading and writing activities often allow them to make connections among various aspects of the curriculum, the interdisciplinary curriculum is structured so that students are encouraged to explore and discover these connections. Both the interdisciplinary curriculum and the literature-based curriculum use the *thematic unit* to organize class activities and materials. Sometimes the interdisciplinary units use literature as a jumping off point. For example, Lynn Butler's second and third graders began an extensive study of frogs and toads after reading Beatrix Potter's *Jeremy Fisher* and Arnold Lobel's *Frog and Toad Together* (Butler, 1992). The children's research included interviewing parents, reading trade books, creating wall charts, finding common characteristics of frogs and toads, verifying or refuting frog and toad mythology, and creating artistic representations. Interdisciplinary units can be based on a social studies topic, such as "Pioneers," and include literature, science, math, and art as a way of extending the dimensions of the topic and the children's understanding of it. A study of space or the solar system that begins with a science focus can lead to reading science fiction as well as studying the history of space exploration and using math to calculate the dimensions of space and time. You will find other examples of interdisciplinary units in Chapter 5.

Assessment: The Curriculum and the Students

Evaluating the Curriculum

Assessment is a major task in teaching. Thoughtful teachers constantly engage in the process of observing and evaluating the success of their students and of their own contributions to the design, structure, and activities of the classroom.

In order to evaluate the success of your program and your progress toward accomplishing your goals as a teacher, you need first to articulate your teaching philosophy and your goals as a teacher. This, of course, will probably be a lifelong process. The more you learn about children and their growth, the better you will be able to articulate your teaching philosophy and goals. Regie Routman's description of her beliefs and goals provides an understanding of the relationship between beliefs or assumptions about learning and the goals set as a result of those beliefs (see Figure 1.8).

My Beliefs

- All children can learn.
- Children learn to read by reading.
- Children need to read and write for their own purposes.
- Spelling develops through writing for real purposes.
- Children need many varied language experiences.
- Children develop self confidence through early school success.
- Children learn through trial and error.
- Teachers need ongoing support.
- Young children are capable of high-level comprehension.
- Independent work must be meaningful and relevant.
- Reading must be approached through strategies that focus primarily on meaning.
- Vocabulary is learned best in context.
- Parents have the right and need to be involved in their children's education.

My Goals

- Have high expectations for all children.
- Surround children with good books.
- Encourage daily, self-selected reading and writing.
- Accept invented spellings and teach spelling strategies.
- Provide opportunities for children to interact meaningfully with text and each other.
- Make learning to read and write easy, desirable, and pleasurable.
- Encourage and congratulate children for approximations and risk taking.
- Encourage in-service and provide teachers with opportunities for professional growth and interaction.
- Encourage, model, and give opportunities to practice brainstorming, predicting, and inferential questioning.
- Develop literature extension activities including the creative arts.
- Help children develop strategies that utilize semantics and syntax before phonics.
- Teach vocabulary during and after reading.
- Communicate regularly and clearly with parents and invite them to be part of the process.

FIGURE 1.8 An understanding of the relationship between beliefs and assumptions about learning (Routman, 1988, 27–28).

Once you have established goals for your classroom, you will be able to better assess your progress in accomplishing what you consider to be important. R. D. Walshe emphasizes the role of the teacher's self-evaluation in meeting her goals for the writing classroom:

> Evaluation has an overlooked side. While its obvious side is its attempt to estimate a child's progress, its overlooked side is what that estimate implies about the effectiveness of the teacher's program.
>
> Logically, then, the first step in evaluation ought to be taken before the class arrives, at the beginning of the year: the teacher needs to review the effectiveness of his or her last year's program.
>
> When such a self-evaluation has been made, the teacher will probably want to set down an outline of the improved program for the coming year.
>
> (R. D. Walshe in Turbill, 1983, 61–62)

Figure 1.9 is an example of priorities set for writing based on teacher's goals.

As a teacher you will likely be evaluated formally by administrators and informally by parents. Your ability to describe your goals for your students and your evidence for your progress in accomplishing those goals will help you to be more secure and focused in your teaching.

■ **IDEAS TO LEARN**   Begin developing your own philosophy for teaching language arts. You may wish to include a list of assumptions about the learning of language and some specific goals you would like to achieve. In addition to ideas you have read about here, you may wish to draw on other coursework and your own experience in describing your assumptions and goals.

Assessing Student Progress

Regie Routman (1988) emphasizes the relationship in evaluation between the goals of the teacher's curriculum and the performance of the students. "Evaluation involves two steps: first, collecting data, and secondly, making judgments about all aspects of teaching and learning for both students and teachers. I believe that evaluation should be consistent with the teacher's philosophy and the way the children have been taught. Consequently we evaluate the process, the product, and attitudes" (203).

Throughout this text we will make suggestions about ways in which you can evaluate children that are consistent with your goals as a teacher. Although there may be some institutional demands placed on you to use certain tests, forms, and report cards, it will be important for you to develop other modes of assessment that describe various aspects of children's growth. Informal, ongoing assessments—such as reading-response records, writing portfolios, children's lists of the books they have read and the books they have written, checklists of skills demonstrated in reading/writing projects, anecdotal reports, and observation notes—provide a much more detailed account of children's work that can be used to celebrate their successes and to provide information about areas of strength and areas that need attention. We will be discussing these in much more detail in subsequent chapters.

Reporting to Parents

One of the problems teachers have as they institute an integrated curriculum based on the needs and natural growth of children is that such a program is inconsistent with the categories in the grading system used by many school districts. Often, in fact, teachers are asked to give students letter grades—A, B, C, D, F—in reading (which may include discrete subskills such as word attack skills, syllabication, phonics) and language (which may include gram-

Writing Program: Priorities

1. *I will continually promote the importance of writing—*
   - will point to its importance in learning and adult life;
   - provide plenty of time to write;
   - show that it helps handwriting, spelling, language, reading;
   - read aloud daily to convey 'the sound of writing';
   - build up the spirit of a 'writing workshop';
   - myself write with the class at least once a week.

2. *I will secure an abundance and range of writing—*
   - will basically encourage free-choice, personal-experience topics, but also writing on classroom 'situations', e.g. improvisations;
   - allow a degree of choice in subject-area writing;
   - encourage, but not impose, writing about literature;
   - demonstrate ways to think-up, ask for, and research ideas.

3. *I will focus on experiencing writing as a 'process'—*
   - will continually explain 'process'—a steady clarifying of ideas;
   - foster everyday discussion of writing in 'process' terms, e.g. pre-writing, first draft, revision/editing, publishing;
   - notice whenever possible 'writing models' in literature, and use children's published work as models;
   - steadily attend to technical problems at the point of need, e.g. spelling, punctuation, grammar, structure.

4. *I will provide real readers for the children's writing—*
   - will respond myself to their writing at its 'process' stages;
   - do this chiefly through my 'conferences' with them;
   - also promote 'writing partners' and 'peer conferences';
   - publish child's choice (fully revised) of one in 4–5 pieces;
   - as well as classroom readers, sometimes find outside readers;
   - applaud and feature good writing whenever it appears;
   - keep asking, 'What will readers expect of your writing?'

FIGURE 1.9 An example of priorities set for writing based on teacher's goals (Turbill, 1983, 62).

mar, spelling, penmanship). Teachers who integrate reading, writing, speaking, and listening don't break up their subject matter in this way. They are often observing very different language activities, as well as the processes that students use to think and create in language. Most important, the idiosyncratic and individualistic nature of language development does not lend itself to making hard and fast judgments of students' language skills in the form of letter grades. In short, many teachers feel that the report card is not a useful or adequate means of describing children's progress in language.

In her report of a research project on evaluation of reading and writing, Jane Hansen (1992) describes how teachers in the project responded to their

Reading Record (for conferences)
Blackburn Elementary School
(adapted by Shirley Cochrane)

Name _____ Date _____
Title of Book _____

Familiar text?	Y	N
Chose appropriate reading level?	Y	N
Student influenced selection?	Y	N
Teacher influenced selection?	Y	N

Read Fluently?	Y	N
Read for meaning?	Y	N
Noticed miscues that interfered with meaning?	Y	N
Read word for word?	Y	N

Observation of Miscue Strategies

Used context clues?	Y	N
Used picture clues?	Y	N
Used beginning/ending sounds?	Y	N
Used other phonetic clues?	Y	N
Self-corrected?	Y	N

Observation of Self-correction Attitudes

Reads eagerly?	Y	N
Comfortable with reading?	Y	N
Guessed at meaning?	Y	N
Willing to take risks?	Y	N

Observation of Comprehension

Retold story?	Y	N	easily?	Y	N
Responded to text?	Y	N	easily?	Y	N
Repeats what others observe?	Y	N			
Language interference?	Y	N			

Response to Reading
Author: _____
Illustrations: Like? _____ Why? _____
Did you like the story?   Y   N   Why? _____
What was the story about? _____
Who were the main characters? _____
Why do you think the author wrote this story? _____

FIGURE 1.10 A reading record (Lamme and Hysmith, 1991, 636).

dissatisfaction with the district's report card: "They became unsettled about their standard report cards because the values their instruction now rested on did not appear on the card. The teachers received permission from their district to develop for their building the . . . reading-writing sheet to attach to the report card" (103). A committee of teachers met to discuss what they valued in reading and writing. "The list of values became the report card. The teachers now leave the reading, spelling, language arts, and penmanship sections of the regular card blank and use their new checklist instead" (103).

Of course it's possible that you will not be in a situation that will allow you to replace the report card with your own checklist. Nonetheless you may wish to supplement the report card with your own assessment of students' progress (see Figure 1.10). In your conferences with parents (and whenever you send home report cards or other reports), you can emphasize the language activities the children are working on and the individual students' progress and accomplishments in working on those activities.

Finally it is important to mention the role of children and parents in the evaluation process. In their portfolios, in their reading records, in their conferences with the teacher, children should be asked and can be expected to provide insights into their growth as readers and writers, speakers and listeners. Their own understanding of their accomplishments can and should become part of their record and part of what is communicated to parents. Moreover, parents can provide useful insights into their children's work in language by describing their children's home activities and outside interests.

2
Language Out Loud:
Listening and Speaking
by Linda Dinan

The listening and speaking that children experience prior to going to school is rich and diverse. Consider how Susan Tchudi describes the talk between herself and her preschoolers:

> I point out birds in the trees, the sounds of trains and sirens, the leaves after it rains, the silly cat sleeping with her paws hung over the arm of the chair, the worm holes in the cherries, the dead squirrel in the middle of the road; I explain to a not-very-self-controlled-baby Christopher why he can't bite Michael (it hurts) and to Michael why he can't hit Christopher back (it hurts) and why Emily is crying over the accidental death of a school friend (another kind of hurt). I answer questions about why I peel carrots, why cars have different kinds of hubcaps, and what makes lightning, why we brush our teeth, why we can't eat too many sweets, and why Andrew has to go home if he keeps pounding on the other kids. I explain why there's a picture of Miss Piggy on the Cheerios box and what the words say on street signs and what the skull and crossbones means on a box in the garage. We sing silly songs and Daddy's barbershop songs and make up our own words. Anyone who has cared for a preschooler can continue the catalog of intriguing minutiae that attract the thoughts, feelings, and perceptions of one getting control over the environment. James Britton's observation that all of life is afloat on a sea of talk is true in spades with preschoolers.

> (Susan Tchudi, 1985, 464)

Even though this ''sea of talk'' still exists when these children arrive at the school-house door, in many classrooms the tide has turned. The ''listening and speaking'' by which these children have become formidable language users suddenly moves out of their control.

Linguist Courtney Cazden (1988) notes a particular difference in the control of the right to speak. ''To describe the difference in the bluntest terms, teachers have the right to speak at any time and to any person; they can fill any silence or interrupt any speaker; they can speak to a student anywhere in the room and in any volume or tone of voice. And no one has any right to object'' (54). Judith Lindfors offers a similar observation of what occurs when children attempt to communicate in the classroom: ''It is interesting that traditionally many teachers who have all along sincerely professed an intense concern for children's oral language development, punish children more for talking in school than for any other single 'offense.' More children miss recess, stay after school, have their seat moved to an isolated area of the class-room, write paragraphs about what constitutes good (quiet?) behavior for their 'offenses' relating to talking than for any other 'misbehavior' includ-ing a host of various deliberate and calculated unkindnesses.'' (Lindfors, 1988, 337).

When compared to the rich texture of the language learning environ-ment at home, the school's environment can indeed be threadbare. When teachers align themselves with the traditional philosophy that the quieter a classroom is, the better a classroom is, they are acting in direct opposition to what has worked for children prior to their arrival at school.

More than twenty years ago British writer James Britton cautioned teachers that

> in school we cannot afford to ignore all that has gone on before. So often in the past we have tried to make a fresh start, at the risk of cutting off the roots which alone can sustain the growth we look for. It is not only that the class-room must more and more merge into the world outside it, but that the proc-esses of school learning must merge into the processes of learning that begin at birth and are life-long. We can no longer regard school learning as simply an interim phase, a period of instruction and apprenticeship that marks the change from immaturity to maturity, from play in the nursery to work in the world. School learning must both build upon the learning of infancy and foster something that will continue and evolve throughout life.
>
> (Britton, 1970a, 129)

The merging process that Britton describes does exist in many class-rooms. The supportive language community that these children know outside of school can be recreated by knowledgeable classroom teachers. Such teach-ers know children, language development, and language theory and are aware of the special demands of the classroom community. Successful language arts teachers operate with a thorough, albeit at times an almost intuitive, understanding of the complexities involved in language learning. In order to foster a flourishing language community, teachers must be aware of and sensitive to the issues described in the following pages.

The Importance of Listening and Speaking in All Learning

Listening and speaking opportunities are critical to learning. In a review of language research Christopher Thaiss identified three important considerations that should influence decisions about the quality and quantity of oral language in the classroom:

1. Children will understand, and thus remember, only what they have the opportunity to talk about (and, perhaps, to write about, sing about, make plays about, etc.) (6).

2. Children can learn to read and listen beyond mere recognition only if they regularly practice expressing their own meanings in speech and writing to themselves and others (8).

3. Children learn only if knowledge is defined in action as a dialogue, or conversation, between teacher and student, student and student, student and text, and student and the world (11).

(Thaiss, 1986)

Listening and Speaking as a Part of All Classroom Interactions

To establish a flourishing language community in elementary classrooms, teachers must be keenly aware of their interactions with students. From the morning greeting, through classwork, recess, lunch, and dismissal, students learn about language, especially about listening and speaking. Although oral language permeates the day, teachers frequently keep students from meaningful language situations rather than exploiting the opportunities. Almost considered "part of the furniture," the language of the classroom often suffers from benign neglect or worse. Neither the teachers nor the students are consciously aware of oral communication as something to be developed, other than perhaps a concern for correctness. Consequently little is done to improve an area that is the lifeblood of the entire operation. Every interaction with students, either in individual conferences, in small groups, or with the entire class, is an opportunity to model and refine listening and speaking skills.

An important first step in developing a successful speaking and listening program in a classroom is for teachers to closely examine their own listening and speaking behaviors. In many classrooms the teacher talks too much and, perhaps because of that, the students listen too little. A frequent complaint from teachers is "These kids just don't listen!" In many classrooms the children could be making the same comment about their teachers. With so much language in the environment, both adults and children become accustomed to not listening and to not being listened to. As teachers, therefore, we need to be especially sensitive to the model of listening and speaking that we present to our students. By making eye contact and giving a speaker full attention, a teacher shows students what careful listening looks like. In a busy interactive classroom it is tempting to try to listen to several children at once, but that type of modeling is counterproductive.

Attention to what children mean as well as to what they say is also important. A teacher's thoughtful response, such as "I think I understand how you came up with that answer," will encourage children to stay in a discussion rather than retreat because they produced a "wrong" answer. Moffett and Wagner (1976) note: "Your basic job as the teacher is to create a good climate for talk and listening to talk—relaxed and concentrated. The tone must be warm and friendly but not saccharine. You do not have to revere children's words; but everything you do should show you truly value what your students say. You need to see to it that the class members do the same. The art of conversing is a profound cognitive activity, not an application of etiquette like practicing table manners. Mere polite attention is not what you are aiming for; relevant, perceptive, insightful response to one another is" (74–75).

Determining what to attend to from the cacaphony of sounds in which we live is sometimes difficult even for adults. Listen to the world. Do people respond to each other while they are watching TV? Can they ignore the blasting stereo while talking on the phone? In our multimedia world we are all very skilled at ignoring each other and much of our environment. We expect to have information repeated more than once and to hear things more than once. Examples of untidy interactions are easy to find. Watch parents with their children at shopping malls, restaurants, or museums. When are people listening? When are people tuning out? And how many times has tuning out been a wise decision? Probably as many times as it has been wise to attend. Untidy interactions are regularly played out in elementary classrooms as well.

■ **IDEAS TO LEARN**   Experiment with the nature of listening (and not listening). Find some public place (a cafe, a lobby, a mall, a playground, a library, an airport or train waiting area, etc.) in which you can sit and listen. Record everything you hear for thirty minutes. What sounds do you hear? What sounds are dominant? Hear anything unusual or surprising? How does this illustrate the ways in which we select what we listen to and what we ignore?

Teachers can rectify some of this breakdown in communication by watching their own behavior when giving directions or asking for attention. Verbal cues such as "I need you to listen carefully now" or "It's time to listen" help children focus on the message that follows. Some teachers find that asking young children to assume a listening position—eyes on teacher, hands folded on desk, speaking suspended—gets their attention. For young children visual clues can also be crucial to a successful transfer of information. Role-playing the expected behaviors can also improve comprehension. Finally it's important to make certain that students understand why they should listen. Children learn very quickly if we're willing to repeat directions. If we *are* willing, our students *will* ask for such repetitions.

In addition to not listening at all, other breakdowns can occur. "There is a long, torturous trail between speaking and listening in the communication act. The listener 'creates' the language of the speaker. Thus, while the message is ideally the same for the speaker and the listener, contrasts are usually present" (Lundsteen, 1979, 13). At times, Lundsteen says, listeners "become preoccupied with the message they want to formulate and then send back," and they fail to attend to the whole message (13). Young children are especially susceptible to this type of listening interference. One word may trigger a powerful memory that supersedes any current concerns. For instance, for a particular child a discussion of amusement parks may trigger a frightening memory of frantically searching for "misplaced" parents during a recent visit.

■ **IDEAS TO LEARN**   Observe a situation in which a number of people are present—at home, at school, in the library, in the dorm, and the like. Describe the listening behavior you observe. Can you tell when people are listening? How? What are people most attentive to? What do they ignore? How do they demonstrate their lack of attention?

Further complicating oral communication is the mismatch in the capacities of every human being's physical apparatus for listening and speaking.

The human brain processes verbal information much more rapidly than most individuals can speak. Therefore during any ''listening'' experience, part of the brain is available to be used for other purposes. Teachers can explore this phenomenon with their students. Why is it that sometimes it looks like you're listening but you're not, while at other times it looks like you're not listening but you are? Discuss successful listening behaviors and strategies. You might model listening behaviors such as looking at and even leaning toward the speaker.

As teachers we should encourage conscious awareness of the complexity of listening. In order to sensitize children to the process of listening we might discuss variations of the following questions:

- Is there a difference in how we listen to a story and how we listen to directions?
- What happens to our body and mind when we are listening intensely?
- When is careful listening necessary and when isn't it?
- How does our listening and responding adapt to group size?
- What clues other than language can support our understanding of the spoken message?

After attention to the listening process, you can ask students to keep a list of the various listening situations they encounter during a school day (Winn, 1988, 145). Gathered over a series of days, the lists can be shared and categorized. The types of listening, pleasurable and purposeful, can be labeled and described. Winn also suggests that teachers share their own strategies for different listening situations. Is there a difference in the way we listen to directions on how to get to the new fast-food restaurant and the way we listen to the evening news report?

Referring back throughout the school year to the information developed from these activities will help students refine their perceptions of listening and their responsibilities in oral communication. Students and teachers who have increased their sensitivity to the listening decisions that people make throughout the day seem to be able to hear each other better.

> The weaver carefully threads the first set of threads—the warp—onto the loom. The warp gives the fabric its strength. Similarly, a writing/reading program begins with listening, and listening holds the program together. . . . Traditionally, we have pictured the students as listeners and the teacher as the person to whom the children listened, but now we see ourselves as the number one listener. This role reversal hits us unexpectedly and catches us unprepared.
>
> We spend a lot of time developing our listening skills. We find this basic skill a prerequisite if learning is to happen among our students and between them

and us. The children must know that we hear what they say in order to believe in themselves, a hallmark of an independent learner.

(Hansen, 1987, 69)

Classroom Environments that Encourage Listening and Speaking

An often-repeated bit of teacher advice goes something like this: "I never smile at them until the second week of school." While this may create a quiet classroom, it can also create a classroom that is uncomfortable for children. "During the first few weeks of school, teachers turn children into pupils by teaching them to be quiet, not to initiate conversations, and to respond briefly when the teacher speaks to them. Our management concerns don't permit children to use talk as a way to learn—a way to figure things out." (Hansen, 1987, 80). In order to create an effective environment for the development of oral language, such a philosophy must be modified.

In creating environments that are good for kids and aligned with current language theory, teachers should consider the issue of "noise" or classroom talk in general. Is it reasonable to ask children to spend six or seven hours a day in almost total silence? Certainly the silence does not fit with linguists' views on how children acquire language. Judith Lindfors challenges teachers to consider whether their classrooms reflect the talking constraints present in our society. Consider the following concerns about "talk":

1. *Talking when working.* . . . In the real world much of our work involves talk (338).

2. *Talking when one should be listening.* . . . We often make listening a negative thing, refraining from talking. But listening, real listening, is far too important to be treated this way. Real listening requires mental activity, the processing of new information into one's existing cognitive structure, the encounter with the new idea that triggers a new question one never had before. This active process is listening (338–339).

TEACHING IDEA

Have children keep a weekend listening diary. Have them describe what people in their family listen to: each other? stories? the radio? TV? When do people listen most carefully? When do they seem to tune out? You may want to develop a chart or a check-off sheet to help children focus on the variety of listening situations they may encounter.

3. *Talking too loud.* . . . . It is important to learn the difference between simple noise and the sound of meaningful verbal interaction (339).

4. *Talking in the wrong place.* . . . [In] many classrooms . . . there is no right place for talking (339).

5. *Talking about the wrong thing.* . . . [P]erhaps we need to reexamine the subject itself: Is it one that is of genuine interest to the children in the first place? (340)

6. *Talking to the wrong person.* . . . Children elicit conversation for purposes that are real to them, and carry on these conversations with the appropriate people (340).

7. *Talking without raising one's hand* (340).

8. *Talking too much.* . . . Be sure that we provide plenty of opportunities for acceptable talk within our classrooms (341).

(Lindfors, 1988)

Obviously there are times when talking is not appropriate in the classroom. But having to be quiet all day long contributes little to the language development of elementary students. Together students and their teachers should describe the talk that is appropriate for a variety of classroom purposes.

Throughout the school day teachers should consider two other critical aspects of their verbal interactions with children—the pace of the interactions and the control of those interactions. First the issue of pace, or "wait time." After twenty years of classroom research, Mary Budd Rowe, a science educator, has determined that the time between a teacher's question and a student's answer affects the quality of both the teacher's and the student's performance. She states that "when teachers ask questions of students, they typically wait 1 second or less for the student to start a reply; after the student stops speaking they begin their reaction or proffer the next question in less than 1 second" (1986, 43). When the response time is increased to three seconds or more, profound changes occur in the quality of students' responses and in fact in the entire tenor of the classroom. Rowe's research, as well as that of many others, documents the following consequences of increased wait times:

1. The length of student responses increases between 300% and 700%, in some cases more depending on the study.

2. More inferences are supported by evidence and logical argument.

3. The incidence of speculative thinking increases.

4. The number of questions asked by students increases, and the number of experiments they propose increases.

5. Student-student exchanges increase; teacher-centered "show and tell" behavior decreases.

6. Failures to respond decrease.

7. Disciplinary moves decrease.

8. The variety of students participating voluntarily in discussion increases. Also the number of unsolicited, but appropriate, contributions by students increases.

9. Student confidence, as reflected in fewer inflected responses ("Is that what you want?"), increases.

10. Achievement improves on written measures where the items are cognitively complex. (44–45)

The effects on teachers' behaviors are equally dramatic.

1. *Teachers' responses exhibit greater flexibility.* . . .

2. *The number and kind of questions asked by teachers changes.* There are fewer questions, but more of them entail asking for clarification or inviting elaboration or contrary positions.

3. *Expectations for the performance of certain students seems to improve.* (45)

Although these behaviors were observed in questioning situations, similar response patterns can be observed in other teacher-student interactions. Obviously one way to encourage students to participate in classroom discussions is to give them time, both before they respond and after they have responded.

When a teacher responds to a student's response, there are a number of possible verbal reactions to consider in addition to the issue of wait time. A not-uncommon teacher response is to merely mimic what has been said. Not surprisingly "a high mimicry rate cuts off extended wait times and reduces the quantity and quality of student responses" (Rowe, 1986, 48). But teachers can enhance the quality of classroom discussions when they respond to student input in other appropriate ways. Instead of asking another question, teachers have these alternatives:

1. Make a declarative statement (for example, give an opinion).

2. Make a reflective restatement (give the sense of what a student has said).

3. Describe the student's state of mind ("I'm sorry, I'm not quite getting your point.").

4. Invite the student to elaborate on a statement ("I'd like to hear more of your views on that.").

5. Encourage the student to ask a question.

6. Encourage students to ask questions of each other (until the student resumes or another enters into the discussion).

7. Maintain a deliberate, appreciative silence.

(J. Dillon, 1984, 55)

Moreover, teachers also need to consider the power of their messages. Not only must they be aware of the *negative* things that they may say to students, they must also be aware of the *positive*. In his book *Between Teacher and Child* (1972), Haim G. Ginott describes what he considers to be the cardinal principle of communication between teachers and students: *"Talk to the situation, not to the personality. . . .* Translated into classroom procedures, this principle would change a teacher's basic approach to children—his expression of anger and the tenor of his commands, his method of criticism and style of praise, his system of evaluating and categories of grading, his ways of comforting and means of reassuring, his routine of testing and manner of speaking" (71). In successful communication situations teachers do not evaluate the individual but describe the product or the current conditions. For example, by acknowledging a child's emotional state with "You're upset" or describing a stellar piece of writing with "This story is exciting!" we allow children to say to themselves, "My teacher recognizes how I feel" or "I'm a successful writer." Empowering children to positively describe themselves and their accomplishments is critical to the development of their confidence and self-image.

But sometimes a teacher's enthusiasm over a child's work or behavior denies the child the opportunity to think independently. Lowell Madden (1988) contends that we teachers "at times treat our students as if they were dogs" when we use the language of praise—"Great job!" "Super work!" (142). We serve our students better when we allow them to determine their

TEACHING IDEA

Develop a file of "This is worth listening to" materials. Ask children to contribute. You can include short poems, jokes and riddles, weird facts, interesting current events items from magazines and newspapers, and the like. Share them and have children share them at various times in the day—perhaps when you want the whole class to regroup after engaging in small group and individualized activities. (Another good time is when you are lining up for lunch or to travel somewhere else in the building and you want children calm before they enter the hallway.) Make sure these listening activities are *worth* listening to.

own worth by limiting ourselves to descriptions of their "growth or contributions." Ginott (1972) says that "praise consists of two parts: What we say to
the child and what he in turn says to himself. Our words should state what
we like and appreciate about his efforts, help, work, and accomplishments.
The child then draws conclusions about himself. When our statements describe the events and feelings realistically and appreciatively, the child's conclusions about himself are positive and productive" (104).

Other writers have recounted debilitating results from the way certain
questions are worded. "Over and over I hear teachers asking questions, hundreds of them, and the vast majority of those questions begins with 'tell me.'
Those queries are presented as follows: 'Who can tell me what the noun is in
this sentence?' 'Can you tell me if this is a long vowel or a short vowel?' 'Tell
me which syllable is accented.' I want to be transmigrated immediately into
one of those young bodies and shout to the teacher. 'No I will not tell you. I
will tell my classmates, I will tell myself, but I will not tell you. I am not here
for your benefit; I am here for *my* education.'" (Lucking, 1985, 173).

Lucking continues: "If teachers are to capitalize on the intrinsic excitement of language at work in the classroom, they will have to surrender some
of their authority in the manner in which they involve children in talk and in
the manner in which they respond to that talk" (174). In creating a comfortable classroom for children, teachers must reflect on all of their interactions
with students.

Pamela Bailis and Madeline Hunter (1985) suggest that teachers examine their choice of words with students to determine whether they are "think
stoppers" or "think starters." "If you say 'Put your papers in your desk,' for
example, the student just has to follow a simple direction. But, if you say, 'The
bell's rung; think about what you need to do before you leave,' he must decide
for himself what to do and then direct himself to do it" (43).

In many schools by the time the children reach the upper elementary
grades, they are extremely reticent about asking questions or expressing any
type of confusion. Barbara Comber (1988) describes what she and Marija
Baggio, a teacher, observed about a class of fourth and fifth graders: "We
realized the need to give children explicit permission to be confused and ask
questions to explore or seek help. We also realized the need to provide time
when asking questions or seeking help *was* the curriculum agenda. The children needed to trust that such requests from them were not considered signs
of failure and would not be negatively received" (150).

After devoting time to modeling useful questioning strategies and predicting problems prior to starting a task, the children began to use questions
to get information from each other and from the teachers. Not only did this
information help the students, but the teachers also realized that "by listening
to their questions over a number of episodes, we could see patterns in chil-

dren's approaches which directed our helping. The first step was for the children to trust that they could ask for help" (152).

In the classroom specific physical setups often promote successful speaking and listening. "Proximity promotes interaction" claims Jane Hansen when describing reading/writing classrooms (1987, 77). The size of the group and the setting can often contribute to children's level of comfort. "Moving chairs can seem a nuisance in classrooms, especially with young children who have to learn how to carry them in safe ways. But in addition to the particular value of a circle for discussions, it may be generally helpful, especially for young children, to have different physical arrangements for events where different discourse norms prevail. Just as learning a second language is facilitated by the separation of languages by setting, learning to shift ways of speaking should be helped by visual signals as well" (Cazden, 1988, 59).

However, maintaining the *same* physical arrangement for sharing the work of both professional and student authors has the power of emphasizing the importance of the children's work. When a first grader is asked to clamber into the "Author's Chair" (the chair from which child authors read) to share his or her latest piece of writing, it becomes an important event for all the children in the class, verifying the importance of their own work.

By becoming conscious of our own language use and attitudes, of how children learn language, and of the uses of language, we will become more sensitive and effective teachers of language.

Children and Language Play

Preschoolers love messing around with language. They try out new words, they laugh uproariously at nonsense sounds, they explore and appreciate all facets of oral language—the sound as well as the meaning.

As these children advance from their playpens to the playgrounds of the world, they continue to explore the sounds and purposes of language with jump rope chants, ridiculous riddles, catchy songs, insulting epithets, scathing parodies, commercial jingles, off-color jokes, and perhaps occasionally an obscene word. Along with the pure joy of this play, "children almost everywhere use such jokes, rhymes, and wise remarks to explore taboos relating to bodily functions, sexual differences, and sex" (Nilsen, 1983, 195).

When children enter a classroom, their natural interest in language gives teachers the opportunity to further increase their students' delight in language. Appealing oral language in the form of chants, riddles, jump rope rhymes, tongue twisters, nursery rhymes, and songs allow children to play with language in the classroom. But to get the most out of this language play,

---

■ **IDEAS TO LEARN**   Take a journey into the rich world of childhood. Begin a collection of chants, riddles, tongue twisters, jump rope rhymes, nursery rhymes, and songs to share with your classmates or coworkers. Write reminiscences and memoirs based on your experiences with these pieces. List ten ways in which you can integrate children's oral language world into your own classroom.

---

students need to believe that their contributions are genuinely accepted. Geller warns that "programs for word play need to be developed as a partnership—children together with teachers providing the interest and the opportunities. In the beginning, teachers need to observe and listen, to stimulate play by making it an accepted part of daily exchange between adults and children. Subsequently, as I've discovered, children can be counted upon to take the lead in finding ways to play" (1982, 125).

Vocabulary

"Now there's a word to tip your hat to." That quote, attributed to Emily Dickinson in William Luce's play *The Belle of Amherst*, reflects an attitude toward language that most preschoolers adhere to. They love to add new words to their speaking vocabularies, and their parents delight in the almost daily increase. Sometimes preschoolers use their new words inappropriately; other times they can be almost poetic in their precision. After hearing us frequently use the word *appropriate* to describe any number of things, our seven-year-old daughter Lindsay revealed her ambiguous feelings about the new beige living room carpet with this comment, "Is this new carpet *appropriate*, Mom? It looks kind of dry like a desert."

By the time children enter school, they can easily become "word detectives" or "word catchers." Characters from books like Leo Lionni's *Frederick* can lead the way. The book's hero, Frederick, spends his time collecting words and images to store for the winter months when things are dull. Establishing a place in the classroom (mobiles, bulletin boards, charts, etc.) to display words works well with children in the early elementary grades (see Figure 2.1). Older students can make their own personal word collections (including definitions). The words can be chosen by the teacher, by the students, or even taken from a commercially produced word-a-day calendar. Soon students will become word collectors on their own; they'll spontaneously identify "Words for Frederick" or "Words to Tip Your Hat To." They'll get excited whenever they find any of the chosen words in their readings.

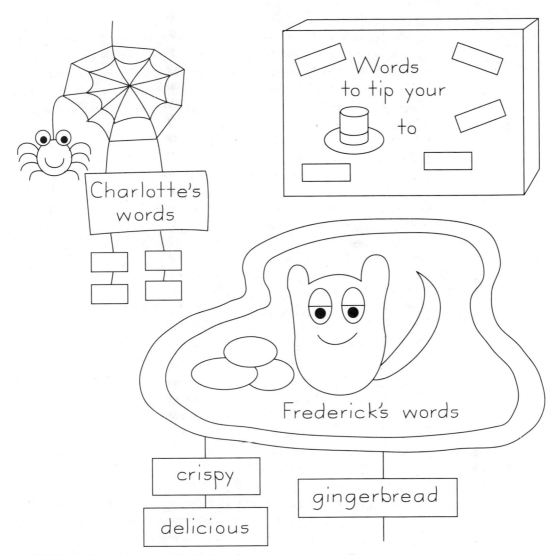

FIGURE 2.1 Displaying words in the classroom.

Patterned Songs

Your students will enjoy familiar childhood songs such as "Bingo," "The Bear Went Over the Mountain," and "Do Your Ears Hang Low," which can form the basis for messing around with language patterns. You can change the words to these songs to fit seasonal, regional, or curricular interests. For example, "The Bear Went Over the Mountain" could become "The Pioneers Went Over the Mountains" or "The Bat Went Over the Haunted House."

These could even be assigned as homework. Familiar nursery rhymes can also be messed with to produce satisfying language fun. "Little Jack Horner" may become "Little Jack Ghost who sat on a post, eating his vampire toast."

Music in general can provide rich resources for language play. Many camp songs and songs from early childhood offer singers the chance to play with language and imagery. The song "Down by the Bay" is one such example:

> Down by the bay
> where the watermelons grow
> back to my home
> I dare not go. For if I do
> my mother will say,
> "Did you ever see a (*fly*) with a (*polka-dotted tie*)?"
> Down by the bay
> (Repeat)

This can be repeated endlessly and happily, with each new verse providing an opportunity for a new ridiculous image of "llamas in pajamas" or "raccoons using spoons."

Riddles and Jokes

For young children, experimenting with riddles is pure fun. Preschoolers work doggedly to determine what makes a riddle successful or a joke funny. "Q: Why did the chicken cross the road? A: Because he wanted to. Is that one for the books?" five-year-old Lindsay regularly asked when trying out what she thought might be a joke. The elementary years are filled with active exploration of humor. Some of the most popular books in the classroom are riddle anthologies. They are, however, also opportunities for oral interaction and *no one* can pick up a riddle book and not feel a need to say to someone, "Hey, listen to this." Riddles provide opportunities for language play, reading, writing, listening, speaking, and laughter. In order to be a successful riddler, children must understand language and its inconsistencies, because so many riddles depend on a play on words. (Q: What happened when the baseball catcher missed the ball? A: He didn't get a chance to dance with Cinderella.) "To bring the art of riddling into the classroom requires little more than finding time to have regular riddling sessions" (Geller, 1981, 674).

Poems

Short, easily memorized poems are another rich source of language fun. Some children find memorizing them as easy as learning a new song; others prefer to collect them in writing in a poetry folder. Regardless of how children collect them, poems provide an opportunity to enjoy refined images and language. As with some children's songs, the structure of certain poems allows word substitution. A delightful image such as this:

> Grapes hang purple
> in their bunches
> Waiting for September lunches.
> Gather them no minutes wasting,
> Purple is delicious tasting.
>
> Leland B. Jacobs,
> *The Random House Book*
> *of Poetry for Children*, 1983

can be messed with to sound like this: "Apples hang red upon the trees, Looking like plump autumn leaves. Gather them no minutes wasting, red is crispy tasting."

Chants

Chants appear on TV screens as advertisements or at sports events as encouragement for our favorite teams. They present teachers with another opportunity to play with language. In an anthology of chants, Sonja Dunn claims that we all can be chant writers. She and her son combined talents to produce the following:

> **Crackers and Crumbs**
> crackers and crumbs
> crackers and crumbs
> these are my fingers
> these are my thumbs
> these are my eyes
> these are my ears
> they'll all grow big
> in the next ten years

Simple actions make this chant very involving whether done with one child or with many. Fingers, thumbs, eyes, and ears can be shown at the appropriate line. A great leap into the air demonstrates the growing in the last two lines. In a group situation, several children can be given a line to chant and act out together.

As in most chants, finger-snapping, foot-stamping, and clapping can be added to establish the beat. Several people can be a chorus, chanting "crackers and crumbs" in the background while others do the complete chant.

(Dunn, 1987, 31)

Figurative Language

Idioms provide upper elementary students with an endless opportunity to have fun with language. Requests to "pick up the room" or "keep an eye on your sister" will be greeted with groans and attempts to literally perform the requested task. "It appears that once the ground had been prepared, so to speak, for alerting youngsters to search for idioms with which to play, most began to 'hear' these words and phrases with increasing frequency in everyday exchanges" (Geller, 1984, 159). A class book with illustrations of idioms can be added to throughout the year. Literature such as Gwinn's *The King Who Rained* add to the fun.

Messing about with language in the elementary classroom bridges the gap that sometimes occurs between the language of home and the language of school. Children will bring the chants, the jokes, the riddles, the poems, and the words with them as they travel their worlds. The pleasure and the power of language will be theirs. Furthermore they will become increasingly aware of other ways in which to play and grow linguistically.

Language for a Variety of Functions and Contexts

"Children's experiences with language determine their view of language— what it is, what it can do for them, and what they can do with it" (Jaggar, 1981, 152). Preschoolers and their parents intuitively know that people learn language by being encouraged to use it for a variety of purposes in increasingly sophisticated contexts. How can classroom teachers create equally stimulating situations in their classrooms? The matrix developed by R. R. Allen in 1977 for the Wisconsin Alternative Curriculum Design illustrates some pos-

TEACHING IDEA

Ask some adults of various ages to reminisce about their experiences with memorization in elementary school. Some of these will be horror stories; some will be happy memories. Invite some folks into your classroom to share some of the pieces they still remember.

Consider giving the children in your classroom the option of memorizing and sharing poems (including chants, nursery rhymes, and jump rope rhymes) for one of their classroom projects. Share short, memorized poems yourself. We predict that children will choose and enjoy this speaking/listening time.

Dimension One: Functions of Communication

	Informing	Expressing Feeling	Imagining	Ritualizing	Controlling
Mass Communication					
Public Communication					
Small Group Communication					
Dyadic Communication					
Intrapersonal Communication					

Dimension Two: Communication Contexts

Each cell involves both message initiation and message reception skills.

FIGURE 2.2 The Wisconsin Alternative Curriculum Design matrix (Allen & Kellner, 1984, 220).

sible intersections of the functions and contexts of communication (see Figure 2.2). It can provide a framework for innumerable authentic communication activities.

Functions of Communication

Informing—People communicate for the purpose of informing in a wide variety of contexts: authors write informative essays; teachers lecture and distribute handouts to inform; and students write informative reports, give demonstration speeches, and participate in discussions about information. As receivers, people read the morning paper, search out information in the library, and watch the evening news on television, and read their favorite "self-help" book before retiring for the night.

Expressing feelings—Affective communication is a necessary and powerful ingredient of life. People initiate and receive various messages expressing positive and negative feelings about themselves and others. They express positive feelings of love, appreciation, and admiration, and negative feelings of disappointment, anger, and frustration. A variety of forms are used for affective messages: poems, greeting cards, love notes, hate mail, pats on the back, a glance, a glare, a raised eyebrow, a prayer. As empathetic readers and listeners, people try to see the world from the perspective of the person communicating so that they may celebrate or commiserate as appropriate.

Imagining—The imaginations of students may be engaged through a wide range of creative communication activities. Students may be given opportunities to dramatize, fantasize, tell stories, invent limericks, brainstorm, theorize, role-play, and pantomime. Through appreciative listening, viewing, and reading, students may enjoy the results of creative efforts of others whether that creativity is revealed through literature, film, television, stage, or face-to-face encounter.

Ritualizing—Many communication exchanges are largely ritualistic in nature. On any given day, people engage in such ordinary speech acts as greeting, leave-taking, introducing, teasing, commenting on the weather, and demonstrating social amenities. They perform rituals appropriate to home, school, church, bus, elevator, and office settings. Rituals are used in conversations, interviews, small-group discussions, parliamentary debates, ceremonial speeches, letters, diaries, printed invitations, thank-you notes, and announcements. As listeners and readers, people note and often respond to violations of social expectations and ceremonial requirements. From "Hey, it's my turn," to "Point of order," they demand that ritualistic requirements be honored.

Controlling—People seek to influence the thoughts and actions of others by using such diverse strategies as threats, commands, arguments, psychological appeals, and entreaties. Controlling messages take such diverse forms as television commercials, printed advertisements, legal briefs, editorials, election posters, and schoolyard squabbles. When on the receiving end of a controlling message, one is well-advised to be a critical listener, viewer, or reader.

(Allen and Kellner, 1984, 217–219)

Communication Contexts

Intrapersonal communication—Intrapersonal communication simply means talking to oneself. It takes such forms as rationalizing, goal-setting, speculating, praising, blaming, and debriefing. Intrapersonal messages may be thought, verbalized, written in diaries, or scrawled on "to do" lists.

Dyadic communication—Two-person communication is both pervasive and important. On a given day, one crosses paths with a relatively large number of people with whom one engages in dyadic exchange. Certain of these exchanges are with people who are of the greatest significance in one's life—parents, offspring, friends, life companions. The ability to establish and maintain such dyadic relationships is important to a happy and fulfilling life.

Small group communication—Two conditions are necessary for an assembly of people to be considered a small group: they must be in face-to-face contact, and they must be psychologically aware of each other. A group of strangers on a city bus are not a small group; they become one when the bus stalls in a flooded underpass and they begin discussing their predicament. Among the most significant small groups in life are families, peer groups, teams, clubs, and classroom groups.

Public communication—Public communication tends to involve larger groups of people in situations in which initiator and receiver roles are relatively fixed. Public messages are given in such diverse settings as auditoriums, banquet rooms, courtrooms, street rallies, and rock concerts.

Mass communication—The communicator and the audience in this form of communication are physically separated, necessitating the use of technology in bringing the message to the audience. Messages are often initiated by groups and are often intended for large, heterogeneous audiences. Common mass communication forms are radio and television programs, films, audio tape recordings, newspapers, and magazines.

(Allen and Kellner, 1984, 219–220)

For the most part it would be difficult to design a classroom language experience that was exclusive to one of the contexts described above. For example, when students prepare a dramatic production for their classmates, a number of speaking and listening contexts and purposes present themselves: Students have to determine role assignments; imagine how the characters talk and walk; locate objects for props and costumes; perhaps advertise to the public, and so on. In any long-term group project in any subject area, the purposes fluctuate as does the size of the group.

Your goal as a teacher should be to provide opportunities for students to refine their speaking and listening skills in a variety of contexts and curriculum areas. The following ideas may inspire your own thinking.

Dyadic Communication

Reviewing with partners   In any area of the curriculum where students will be questioned about material they have read, viewed, or discussed earlier, students can review the topic with a partner. For example, before a general class discussion about a recent field trip to a pond, student partners could describe for each other the habitat and the organisms they observed there.

Explaining a process to partners   When performing a process or applying a skill, students may benefit from "talking through" the process for another student. In this situation a student might verbalize the in*tra*personal communication, or self-talk, that commonly occurs when working through a difficult problem. For example, while doing an arithmetic problem, say, multiplying 23 by 45, a student could observe to a partner: "First, I multiply 3 times 5, which is 15. I put the 5 under the line and carry the 1 up over the 2." Both listener and speaker learn from each other's insights into the procedure.

Answering with partners   This procedure may be used with the partner review. As the teacher asks the group a question, individuals *must* tell their partners their answer before they can tell the group. The partners may make refinements or corrections to the information before it is shared.

Reading written work to a friend for a first response   This dyadic relationship happens almost inevitably in classrooms where children are writing. Most children feel an almost physical need to share their written words with someone else. "How's this sound?" and "Listen to this!" are natural exclamations in a comfortable classroom. In the classroom we describe in Chapter 4, one of the early stages of the writing process is the formal directive to "Read your writing to a friend." A special place to sit, perhaps an old beanbag chair, facilitates this interaction.

Time-fillers   During a normal elementary school day there are minutes that need to be filled while you organize the lunch tickets or wait for the music teacher to arrive. Those minutes can be used for a multitude of language activities, including the development of fluent and imaginative thinking. Here are some possibilities suggested by Petreshene (1988):

1. Present an effect and ask students in pairs to provide possible causes. Sample: The cookie jar is empty.

2. Make a prediction, such as "There must have been an accident near here." Ask students to list possible observations that would support such a statement.

3. Present an answer such as "in a minute" or "under the bed" and ask partners to determine possible questions.

Cross-age learning buddies   In most schools children have little opportunity to develop relationships with children from other grade levels. It would be unusual for a kindergartner to have a relationship at school with a fourth grader. Teachers, however, can be matchmakers for this type of dyadic interaction. For example, fourth graders would delight in meeting with a kindergarten buddy once a week. The two teachers could arrange a mutually convenient time and try to pair children with mutual interests. Activities could be formal or not. For instance, the older students could prepare picture books to read to the younger students each week. The readers might use a bookmark to indicate a spot in the book where the younger children could be asked to predict what they think will happen next. At other times the older children could act as scribes or readers; they might help the kindergartners write thank-you notes to classroom visitors or read the messages and signatures on their Valentine cards.

My colleague, kindergarten teacher Margaret Stokes, asked her class's fourth grade learning buddies to assist the kindergartners with research projects. The older students accompanied the younger ones to the library to find picture books on their specific topics; they read them the pertinent picture captions and paragraphs. In addition, with the help of the teachers, the students were able to interview someone in the fourth grade group who was an "expert" on the topic under study. For example, if a kindergartner wanted to learn more about cats, he or she would find an older child who was a cat "expert" and ask that person questions. Finally, with the help of their parents, the kindergartners presented their information in displays complete with pictures, models, and captions.

Small Group Communication

Cooperative learning   Recently educators have become interested in refining the skills of students and teachers working on projects in small groups. Thanks in part to the research, theory, and implementation of ideas described by Roger Johnson and David Johnson at the University of Minnesota, cooperative learning groups are becoming commonplace.

> The importance of cooperative learning experiences goes beyond improving instruction, increasing student achievement, and making life easier and more productive for teachers, although these are worthwhile activities. Cooperation is as basic to humans as the air we breathe. The ability of all students to cooperate with other people is the keystone to building and maintaining stable families, career success, neighborhood and community membership, important values and beliefs, friendships and contributions to society. *Knowledge and skills are of no use if the student cannot apply them in cooperative interaction with other people.* It does no good to train an engineer, secretary, accountant, teacher, or mechanic, if the person does not have the cooperative skills needed to apply the knowledge and technical skills in cooperative relationships on the job, in the family and community, and with friends.
>
> (Johnson and Johnson, 1986, 8–9)

In examining the structures and strategies that are part of the cooperative learning experience, the opportunities for refining oral communications skills are obvious. Roger Johnson describes five basic elements of cooperative learning:

> The first is what we call "positive interdependence." The students really have to believe they're in it together, sink or swim. They have to care about each other's learning.
>
> Second is a lot of verbal, face-to-face interaction. Students have to explain, argue, elaborate, and tie in the material they learn today with what they had last week.
>
> The third element is individual accountability. It must be clear that every member of the group has to learn, that there's no hitchhiking. No one can sit on the outside and let others do the work; everyone has to be in there pulling his or her own weight.
>
> The fourth element is social skills. Students need to be taught appropriate leadership, communication, trust building, and conflict resolution skills so they can operate effectively. To say it slightly differently, if students have not developed social skills, a lot of the benefits of cooperative learning are lost.
>
> The fifth element is what we call "group processing." Periodically the groups have to assess how well they are working together and how they could do even better.
>
> (R. Johnson in Brandt, 1987, 17–18)

Handling conflicts   The school setting (classroom, playground, lunchroom, bus lines) gives children ample opportunity to come into conflict with each other in a number of ways. Frequently the conflicts involve language, and most certainly language is needed to resolve them. Teachers can be heard saying, "How many times do I have to tell you not to play with Billy?" Meanwhile Billy is screaming at Jake, "He's the one who started it!" If that brings back memories, it's because you've heard these words time and time again—they are probably being repeated on some playground as you read this. But language can improve a situation as well as inflame it.

Some elementary schools have implemented a plan to resolve minor playground conflicts with language, oral and written. Applications are taken from fourth, fifth, and sixth grade students for the role of "conflict manager." The conflict managers are trained to help other children resolve minor conflicts with a set procedure of oral and written exercises. The combatants are first asked to sit down with the conflict managers and observe one minute of silence. (An example of the power of silence that Mary Budd Rowe [1986] has researched.) After the silence each student is given the opportunity, without interruption, to tell his or her view of the situation. The conflict manager writes a description on an official form; then the conflict manager and the combatants decide on a strategy for handling this type of conflict in the future.

FIGURE 2.3 Interviewing community workers.

They record the strategy on the same form. This program has given students the opportunity to use language in a manner that will be a "life skill."

Other small group activities   Less formalized small group activities across the curriculum give children opportunities to expand their oral language skills. Experimenting with math manipulatives or games provides language experiences. Observing and classifying leaves, rocks, and other material objects or conducting an experiment in science does the same. Social studies projects involving simulation or community exploration are also small group language experiences (see Figure 2.3). Finally the language arts themselves provide opportunities for small group discussions.

When students are involved in small group interactions, the teacher can become "a roving on-the-spot consultant" (Lindfors, 1988, 211), observing, questioning, encouraging, and finally appreciating that learning is possible when the teacher steps away from the front of the room.

Public Communication

Along with death most people rank speaking in front of a group as one of life's most terrifying experiences. In order to help children develop confidence in themselves as public communicators, experience in speaking to groups should be part of a comprehensive language arts curriculum.

Although still found in most early elementary classrooms, show-and-tell has a mixed reputation as a speaking activity. In some classrooms it may be the only opportunity outside of the moments before school begins for students to share anything of a personal nature (Cazden, 1988, 8). All teachers might examine their own classrooms to determine whether that is the case for their children.

If teachers do decide that sharing should be part of their daily or weekly schedule, they can limit the sharing to information that might be of general interest. Topics appropriate for sharing with the whole class might be limited to happenings in the community (local to international), items that complement the curriculum, something the children have made, or a treasure from the natural world that the others might be interested in. Some educators suggest limiting topics to items that have good stories behind them, that students made or grew, or that move or work in a funny or interesting fashion (Moffett and Wagner, 1976, 74).

Teachers can adjust the size of the sharing groups to permit more participation. At sharing time you can divide the class into five groups, each with one or two individuals with information or objects to share. Before trying this, ask the children to describe or perhaps to role-play appropriate listening and speaking behaviors.

Everyday small-step performances   As part of the daily morning schedule, you can plan enjoyable performance activities. You can ask students to provide a joke a day, a riddle a day, or a poem a day to keep their antennae tuned to entertaining tidbits to share with the class. With twenty-five students, each student will have the opportunity every twenty-five days to tell a joke or riddle or read or recite a special poem. This assignment will entice them to explore poetry and joke books, thus making this an integrated activity.

The "Guessing Can," which is described in the Math Their Way program materials, also provides a daily opportunity for thinking, writing, and speaking. Every night one child takes home the special can (for instance, a cookie tin). At home the child places an inanimate object inside the can and writes three clues that will help the class determine the object. The next day the Guessing Can child stands in front of the group, gives the clues, and calls on respondents.

Comic strips like "Peanuts" can be used as a source of literate dialogues that can easily be turned into a "vaudeville-type skit" (Suid, 1984, 58). Again this is a performance activity that asks students to read, speak, persuade, and enjoy bits of pithy language.

TEACHING IDEA

Create a listening center in your classroom. Include music (classical, traditional, and folk songs, songs for children); children's books with accompanying tapes; tapes that children create of dramatizations; readers theater (more about this later); and dramatic readings of their own stories and children's literature. Children will mostly listen for pleasure. At other times you will want them to write their responses to the things they listen to.

All these activities not only engage children in integrated language arts experiences, but because they are performed continuously throughout the year, students must keep searching for jokes, poems, and objects to delight their peers. By limiting the performances to one a day from each of the areas, your language-loving students will relish each and every morning in your classroom.

Performances with props   Children benefit from giving public presentations. Since using props helps kids feel more comfortable "on stage," activities like magic tricks, science experiments, and how-to demonstrations are good choices. There are many books available describing simple science experiments or magic tricks. Performed for classmates, these activities allow children to integrate language skills through reading, writing, speaking, and listening in a self-selected activity.

Dramatic opportunities   Drama has a special place in children's lives. Outside the classroom well into their elementary school years, children relish lengthy episodes of dramatic play. They can entertain themselves for hours playing dress-up, pretending to be kings, queens, paupers, moms, dads, dancers, or rock stars. Not only do they put on clothing to "dress up" their images of these characters but they "put on" language as well. They know there is a difference between the way the baby and the mom speak as well as between the queen's directives and the pauper's pleas. Almost as soon as they can talk, preschoolers initiate dramatic play. "You be the mom and I'll be the baby" matures into "Let's say that I'm a prince and you take care of my horses, but we don't have enough food for them."

With dolls and adventure figures children extend and elaborate their views of the world. Dramatic play is powerful and irresistible and absolutely appropriate for learning all the language arts as well as problem-solving with peers.

Dramatic Play Themes and Props

House Play

1. Kitchen furniture: a stove, sink, refrigerator, table and chairs, shelves.
2. Tablecloth or place mats.
3. Small chest of drawers and doll bed.
4. Artificial flowers.
5. Several dolls and stuffed animals.
6. Dolls' clothes, blankets, and bottles.
7. Old adult clothes: hats, gloves, jackets, neckties, scarves, jewelry.
8. Plastic replicas of fruits and vegetables.
9. An assortment of dishes, silverware, pots and pans, and cooking utensils.
10. Empty containers from food, cleaning products, and toiletry items.
11. Dustpan and small broom.
12. Play telephones.
13. Brown paper bags or plastic net bags to use for "shopping" or "picnicking" trips.
14. Container of play-dough.
15. A "cookbook" consisting of a collection of recipe charts used in classroom cooking projects.
16. A "telephone book" consisting of children's names, street addresses, and telephone numbers.
17. Paper, pencils, and envelopes.
18. Wall plaques with appropriate sayings such as "Home Sweet Home."

Fire Station Play

1. Climbing box or building blocks to use in creating a fire station.
2. Firefighter hats.
3. Old shirts to use as firefighters' jackets.
4. Small lengths of garden hose to use as water hoses.
5. A bell to use as a fire alarm.
6. Old flashlights.
7. Play telephones.
8. A sign that says FIRE STATION.
9. Very simple labelled maps of the classroom for use in locating "fires."
10. Picture posters with appropriate fire safety messages.
11. A large "log" book made with blank sheets of paper.
12. Pencils.

FIGURE 2.4 Suggestions for using language arts through drama (Schickedanz, 1978, 715).

Children play at castles on the playground. For hours, they fight battles and search for treasure. But in the classroom, in units of study on castles, where teachers do not have a method to tap into a child's ability to play, a student will usually only read information from a text, memorize vocabulary, take tests, and write the essay on castle life. Something is lost to this student. That teacher who can make the castle live through drama in the classroom has tapped the rich resource of the student's imagination to totally involve the entire human being in the learning process. It is the child involved in the second teaching method that really learns, remembers, and comes to understand the material. Drama is the learning medium. Drama makes castles in the sky a reality in the classroom.

(Erickson, 1988, 9)

Doctor's Office Play

1. Old, white shirts and blouses for use as doctor and nurse dress-up clothes.
2. Medical props such as stethoscopes, popsicle sticks or straws (thermometer), strips of white cloth (bandages), plastic syringes, cotton balls, and old flashlights.
3. Play telephones.
4. Dolls and dolls' clothes.
5. DOCTOR IS IN and DOCTOR IS OUT signs.
6. An "appointment" book for the receptionist.
7. Pencils.
8. Model of clock face with hands that move.
9. An alphabet letter or picture "eye chart."
10. Exposed x-ray films obtained from a doctor.
11. Poster showing the human skeleton, or body parts.

Grocery Store Play

1. A shelving unit.
2. Cardboard boxes that can serve as cases for "dairy products" or "produce." (Place smaller box inside larger one to make a raised surface.)
3. A large variety of empty containers from foods and other household products.
4. Plastic fruits and vegetables.
5. Play money.
6. A cash register (toy or old, real one).
7. Large food sale poster obtained from local grocers.
8. Brown paper bags of various sizes.
9. Newspaper pages containing food ads.
10. OPEN and CLOSED signs.
11. Old shirts for store employee costumes.
12. A kitchen scale to weigh produce.
13. A large selection of food and household products coupons clipped from magazines and the newspaper.
14. A small pad or small pieces of paper, and pencils.
15. Magnetic board and letters to use in making signs for special sales.

FIGURE 2.4 *continued*

Unfortunately classrooms seldom ring with the same genuine sound of children at work in dramatic situations. In fact, as Betty J. Wagner claims, "informal classroom drama—activities that are largely improvisational (as opposed to performances of scripted plays), including creative dramatics, educational drama, or role playing—is one of the most widely heralded and yet least practiced models of integrating the language arts with one another and with the content areas" (1983, 155).

Early elementary classrooms are often the only places where dramatic play is a daily event. Judith Schickedanz (1978) suggests ways to ensure that all the language arts are employed in a drama center (see Figure 2.4). Using props—especially writing utensils and paper—children will naturally develop the written materials they need to support their play. In addition to providing the necessary materials and creating environments where children are encouraged to explore those materials, "teachers should suggest uses for the material, model literacy behaviors, and change materials periodically to keep the interest high" (Morrow and Rand, 1991, 401).

Dramatic activities are often the first to be eliminated and the last to get scheduled into busy elementary school days—but for children these activities can often be the most memorable, engaging, and satisfying in the school year. Dramatic activity is too often limited to special events such as holiday plays, with tremendous pressure for teachers and students to perform at an almost professional level. But by placing less emphasis on the performance and more on the process, drama can be a frequent and comfortable school experience. In fact "a performance may eventually grow out of a drama but this is not the initial goal of the exercise" (Johnson and Louis, 1987, 144).

With a more relaxed perspective on dramatic activities, teachers can attend to the valuable listening and speaking that occurs in the process. The interaction is real and focused. Mem Fox claims children use language during drama experiences for:

- bossing each other around
- asking questions
- making suggestions
- trying to be friendly
- giving opinions
- pretending to be other people in role-play
- demanding things
- informing other people
- organizing themselves through problem-solving
- reflecting on what happens (Fox, 1984, 2)

Many introductory dramatic activities ask children to take mini-steps toward total involvement. Brian Way suggests presenting a "still photograph" as a method for easing teachers and students into drama. After putting children into groups of three, he gives them a few minutes to organize themselves into "a still photograph that we could put into a book, just a quiet, still photograph" (in Dillon, 1981, 359). These photographs should fit whatever concepts are being discussed in the classroom. "It could be three astronauts coming out of a rocket, the president of the United States taking his oath of office, three soldiers returning from the war, three miners from the days when mining conditions were horrible staggering out of the mine, or whatever it is they are studying that day. They can make their own photo and perhaps bring it to life for a few seconds" (359).

Students can imagine they are a character in a familiar story. "Questions to stimulate imagination might include: 'What does your character look like? Make a picture of your character in your head. How does your character move? Awkwardly? Gracefully? Quickly or slowly? How does your character talk? Dress?'" (Cook, 1993, 42). You can also make comparisons between characters like Father Bear and Baby Bear.

Students can dramatize stories they themselves have written. Children assume roles and "act out" the story as it is being read. Deciding whether all the elements of the story should be part of the piece becomes obvious when characters have nothing to do but stand during the reading.

As students become comfortable with this type of mini-activity, you can introduce more advanced "pieces of life." These can be taken from any curriculum area or from any written material the students have shared as well as from any reading text. "Any form of dramatization is a comprehensive exercise par excellence. The demands placed on a reader taking cold printed text and turning it into a convincing simulation of reality, replete with the cadences of living language, movement, gesture, costume, setting and timing, go far beyond anything demanded by comprehension questions" (Johnson and Louis, 1987, 143).

You can also use puppets for dramatization. You can create puppets out of socks, paper bags, gloves, sticks, paper plates, paper cups, your own hands, and more (see Figure 2.5).

Creative "light shows" make exciting performances. You can use an overhead projector or the light from a filmstrip projector to present dramatic shadow productions (see Figure 2.6).

If these dramatic situations develop to the point of being performance worthy, it's usually easy to find an appreciative and unintimidating audience. For example, kindergartners would enjoy the first graders' performance of several folktales.

In addition to the obvious oral language experiences present in drama, Mem Fox (1984) identifies two other benefits. First "it gives all children the chance to be successful" (4). Second a "group feeling . . . develops in a class through closer understanding and knowledge of each other. Instead of relating only to the teacher, the children relate to each other and become more tolerant, more settled, and more mature" (4).

Readers theater   In the elementary classroom, readers theater is an attractive alternative to a major theatrical production. Pieces of literature are arranged so that a narrator and the necessary characters can *read* the story to an audience. Because readers theater doesn't require much in the way of props, sets, and costumes, and because the script does not need to be memorized, it is an almost perfect device for integrating all the language arts processes

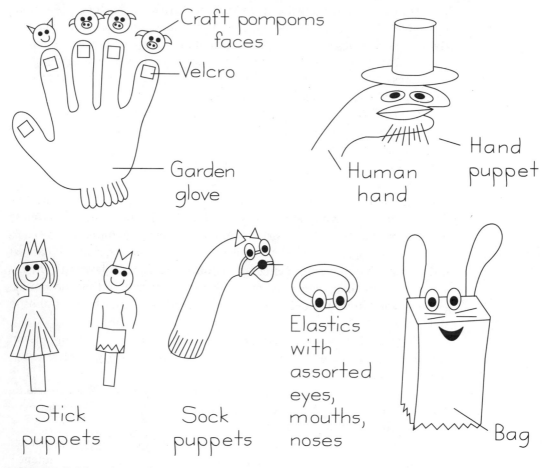

FIGURE 2.5 Ideas for making puppets.

(reading, writing, speaking, listening) in a satisfying experience for both students and teachers.

Because there is little action and few props, the reader's voice must convey the excitement, drama, mystery, or melodrama of the writing. In their book *Putting on a Play*, the Judys (Tchudis) describe how young readers can create drama with just their voices. Here are the five methods they describe:

- Use different *rates* of speaking. We usually associate speaking slowly with being relaxed and calm. People who speak very slowly are sometimes thought of as lazy or dumb. You can also express tiredness through slow speech. Increase your rate of speaking to express anxiety or nervousness. Fast speech also can be used to show fear or excitement. We also associate fast speech with people who are trying to pull a fast one, so liars and crooks are sometimes portrayed as speaking very fast.

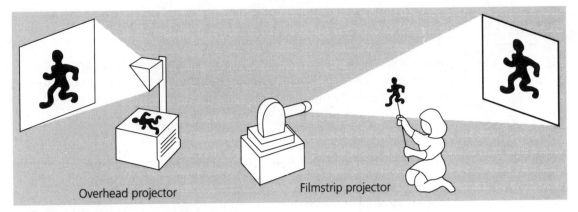

FIGURE 2.6 Creating light shows.

There is a general tendency when you are nervous to speak quickly. This is one thing you will want to concentrate on controlling. Consciously make yourself read slowly, even overemphasizing the slowness for a time to keep yourself from racing through your reading.

- Use different *rhythms* in your speaking. Rhythm refers to the pattern of the accents, the pitch, the rate, and the volume of your speech. For example, some people speak in a monotone. Their voices don't get any higher or lower in pitch. Some people speak very haltingly. They speak quickly and then they stop; then a few more words come out and then silence. We often can guess what section of the country people come from in part because of the rhythm of their speech. Use a halting rhythm when you are trying to express insecurity on the part of a character; use a steady, even rhythm to express confidence; use a slow singsong rhythm to express boredom.

- Change your *pitch* in speaking. Pitch refers to highness or lowness of your voice. In general, women's pitches are higher than men's. We often associate very low pitches with tough, rugged cowboys and policemen, and very high pitches with sweet young things. When people are excited they tend to speak not only faster, but higher. People who are angry are sometimes described as ''shrill'' because their voice gets higher. Use a lower pitch to tell a secret or to express dismay, disappointment, or sadness.

- Change your *volume* in speaking. Some characters have loud, booming voices; others speak quietly because they are reserved or shy or frightened. Show anger and give commands by speaking louder; show close relationships with quiet talk.

- Use *pauses*. Sometimes silence can communicate as much as talk. Avoid the tendency to rush through your play with each line quickly following the previous one. Use pauses to let characters think. Show shock or surprise through a pause. Emphasize an important development in the plot with a pause. Give the audience time to feel an emotional exchange through some

---

TEACHING IDEA

Begin a collection of photographs and art reproductions that capture dramatic action. (It's best if the pictures contain three to five people.) Children may work with these pictures in several ways.

- They may create a "still life," assuming the poses of the people in the picture.

- They may dramatize the event that is taking place in the picture.

- They may improvise the events that led up to or occurred after the moment captured in the picture.

You may want to apply this idea in a social studies/science unit using pictures that relate to the topic under study.

---

silent time. Emphasize important words by pausing just a moment after delivering them.

(Judy and Judy, 1982, 53–54)

Staging a readers theater production is different in several ways from putting on a play. In the same book the Tchudis give students six helpful tips on the staging of the script.

- **Arranging the players.** The most important thing in arranging the actors is that you feel and look like a unit. You should not be too far apart, except for the narrator who stands or sits alone to the side. The players may stand or sit, or you may have a combination, with some actors standing and some sitting. Avoid lining up in a straight row. You should stay stationary throughout the performance, though you may move your heads and torsos. Although in readers theater the players communicate directly with the audience, you need not always face the audience; you can look at one another as it fits the dialogue of the play.

- **Scenery.** Scenery is not required for a readers theater production. You may wish to have a simple backdrop or curtain to create a mood. Remember that dark colors express a quiet, serious, perhaps even a depressing feeling; light colors express warmth, lightness, and happiness. You may also use simple cardboard cutouts to suggest a place—trees, the skyline of a city, etc.

- **Lighting.** Again, lighting can be used to establish a mood, and it should be very simple. A crook-neck lamp or two can be used to light up the players— white light bulbs for daytime or happy scenes, green or blue for nighttime or somber scenes. If you use cardboard cutouts, you can place a simple desk light behind them to create a silhouette.

- **Costumes, Makeup, and Props.** Keep them simple. No costumes are necessary (and they create problems if any players are doing more than one part), but it is attractive if everyone dresses in similar fashion, say everybody in T-shirts and jeans. Simple props might be used to differentiate among the characters: a professor wearing a pair of glasses, for example, and a baseball player wearing a cap. You might want to use a little makeup to highlight your features, but it should not be used as a means of establishing a character. You can also scatter a few props about the stage to set a mood—baseball bats and gloves for a baseball story; stuffed toys and dolls and a banner or two to represent a girl's room—but do not try to handle or use these props during the production, since your hands will be filled with the script.

- **Music.** You may also use music to set the mood of your performance. Have an appropriate record playing as your audience enters and even very quietly as the narrator begins to speak and set the scene. Music can be used as an interlude between scenes, too. Sound effects can be employed sparingly throughout the reading to highlight the reading.

- **The Performance.** Begin the play by having the narrator introduce it, perhaps saying a bit about why the group selected it and what it is about. The narrator should then introduce the players and the characters they are representing. It will be helpful to the audience in following the play to know in advance who the characters are.

(Judy and Judy, 1982, 56–57)

Besides giving students the opportunity to perform before an audience, readers theater has other value in students' lives. In adapting a piece of literature for performance, students must make important decisions about what it means and how they can communicate that meaning. Since there is no physical action in readers theater, students must employ their writing skills to prepare introductions, orient listeners, and create transitions. In addition, they will learn to edit out unnecessary language. Finally students involved in readers theater become experienced in speaking and listening in small and large groups, as they negotiate interpretations of the literature, work out interpretations of characters, and solve any number of problems involving emphasis and presentation.

The first step in a readers theater presentation is to choose what to read. This piece of writing can be by a student or by a professional writer. "Children's books are a rich source for scripts, often with little adaptation. All types of books—folk tales, myths, fantasy, poetry, biography, or informational—are appropriate. Plays can be used if the story stands without action. One scene or episode, or an entire short book, can be used. For instance, Cleary's *Ramona the Brave* (1975) combines humor, strong action, interesting relationships, and strongly drawn characters with just enough individuality for children to capture. Children of all ages enjoy the story and benefit from the snappy, intelligent language" (Busching, 1981, 335).

Storytelling   In recent years there has been a resurgence of interest in storytelling. There are professional storytellers in most communities, and storytelling conferences are held worldwide. Even in our electronic, commercially packaged world, a storyteller can still captivate. Perhaps it is the intimacy and courage of someone coming before an audience without props, scripts, or actions that makes storytelling so compelling.

Happily everyone already has experience at storytelling (explaining how the vase got broken or why you have a scar on your hand), and with some encouragement those skills can be refined even further.

Spellbinding an audience without props is a wonderful goal, but for novice storytellers, both students and teachers, support materials can be comforting. In her book *The Story Vine*, Anne Pellowski gives a number of suggestions for using simple props. These include string stories (see Figure 2.7), picture drawing stories, sand stories, stories with dolls or figurines, stories using musical instruments, and finger-play stories.

Your students will be excited and motivated by a visit from a professional storyteller. After pushing aside the desks and gathering my fourth graders in a circle around her, Sheila Dailey, a Michigan storyteller, shared a folktale called "The Extraordinary Cat" (see Figure 2.8 on page 76).

Dailey practiced what she preached about the art of storytelling—pausing before beginning and adding sounds and using phrasing to sweep the children into the story. The children sensed that "a special gift was being given" when the story was being told (Dailey, 1985, 2). When the story was over, the class worked on telling their own versions. First they paired up and one of the partners started telling the tale. Throughout the retelling, the partners were directed to "switch," which meant that the other person took up the retelling. "This activity teaches listening skills and sequencing and memory skills, as well as being an effective way for children to learn to be storytellers without having the whole burden for the story" (Dailey, 1985, 5).

Dailey also taught the children to use drawings of the events and/or important characters from the story to help trigger the story sequence in the teller's mind. The pictures in Figure 2.9 on page 78 helped order the telling of "The Extraordinary Cat."

Developing some of the critical techniques used by successful storytellers enhances general skills in oral expression. Kathryn Farnsworth (1981) uses the two following large group activities to develop storytelling techniques:

1. *Phrasing,* or "where to take a breath." Each child has a copy of the story to write on as the group makes decisions about appropriate phrasing and words worthy of stress: "There was once/ a *shoemaker*/ who worked hard, and was very *honest*/ but still/ he could not earn enough/ to live upon" (165).

2. *Coloration*, or saying the same word in different ways. From a list of words (greedy, peace, old woman), children choose one and say it in different ways.

Storyteller Jay O'Callahan (1980) suggests polishing a story by practicing it in front of three types of mirrors: a real mirror, a human reviewer, and an audio recording. He also suggests rehearsing the telling in silence by using only gestures as the story runs through your mind. Listening to professional storytellers on audio tapes will help develop a sense of pacing.

Ritualization

"Hello, this is the Cunningham residence, Cleo speaking."
"Mom, this is my friend, Zack. Zack, this is my mom."
"Good morning. How are you today?"
"Excuse me, but I think you dropped this mitten."
Ritualized statements like these are part of everyone's life. Children learn many of them by observing older language users in their communities. Here as in other language learning situations, your students can benefit from becoming aware of and exploring language rituals. Ask the children where they have heard these expressions and which ones they are comfortable using and which they are not.

Language rituals provide opportunities for role-playing, for playing out both the "proper" and "improper" procedures for handling such events in our lives. Aside from the everyday rituals of meeting and greeting and the like, students can be introduced to formal ritualized situations at school—in student senates or councils or in individual classrooms conducting "official" business meetings using established parliamentary procedures. Have your students identify the ritual, observe it in action, and then role-play it for critical review, before employing it in an authentic situation.

Mass Communication

For the most part children are the receivers, or perhaps the victims, of the tremendous power of mass communicators. Children receive information from the radio, television, and sometimes the newspaper. As consumers they need to develop critical thinking skills to counter these assaults. Advertisers, politicians, and other persuaders in children's lives commonly use the following propaganda devices:

1. *The Glittering Generality*. Every item or incident may fit into *some* generality. Propagandists try to select for their purposes a generality so attractive that

The Mosquito

This string figure has been called "The Fly" by (among others) the Patomana Indians of Guyana, the Melanesians of New Caledonia, and some of the people in Ghana. In Uganda it was known as "The Locust".

I have followed the directions given by Lyle Alexander Dickey in his book *String Figures from Hawaii* but have added the part about weaving. That illusion can easily be created by exaggerating and repeating the in and out movements and by keeping the hands in constant motion, even though the string remains in the same places.

The story is most effective with young children between the ages of three and eight. They will duck and try to avoid the "mosquito" and then, at the end, ask in wonder: "Where did it go?"

Recommended string length before knotting: 40 inches (100 cm)
Recommended strand length when braiding yarn: 50 inches (125 cm)

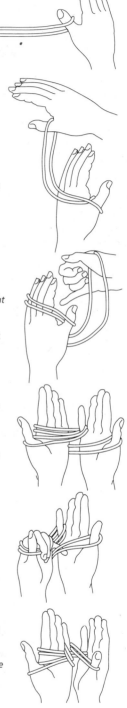

| A woman sat weaving one day, when suddenly she heard a buzzing noise nearby. | *Loop string around the two thumbs.* |

| She looked up and saw nothing, so she continued her weaving, | *Lift both strings around back of left hand.* |

| in | *Hook little finger of right hand under the two strands between left thumb and index finger.* |

| and out, | *Pull right little finger (with string) back as far as it will go. Keep strings taut, moving them as far down on the fingers and thumbs as they will go.* |

| in and out. | |

| The buzzing noise now got louder and the woman looked around again, but seeing nothing, continued her weaving. | *Bring left little finger toward right palm and from the top, curl it under the two strands running from right thumb across the palm.* |

| In and out, | *Move the left little finger, with string, back into position so the hands are side by side, palms facing you. There should be almost no space between the hands.* |

FIGURE 2.7 The mosquito string story (Pellowski, 1984, 5–8).

With the right thumb and index finger, pick up the two strands of string running from the left palm to the back of the left hand.

up and around.

Bring the two strings over all four fingers of the left hand and let go of them.

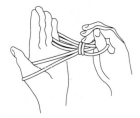

Suddenly the buzzing grew very loud. The woman looked at her weaving and saw—

a giant mosquito!

Quickly wiggle both hands back and forth, tightening the knot in the middle so that the figure ends up looking like a big mosquito. If necessary, use your right index finger to ease the knot to the center.

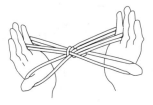

The mosquito began to buzz around her head. It buzzed into her ears and under her chin. It buzzed past her eyes and the tip of her nose. It buzzed in her hair and down her cheek. It was driving her crazy!

Move the "mosquito" close to the ears, chins, eyes, noses, hair, cheeks, etc., of the individual children in the front rows of the audience.

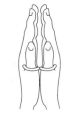

"I am going to catch that mosquito," said the woman. She waited until the mosquito flew right in front of her. Then she clapped her hands over it—

Move two hands with "mosquito" all around through the air and end up right in front of your face.

Clap hands together.

and the mosquito

As hands begin to move apart, point little fingers slightly downward, releasing strings from little fingers as quickly and inconspicuously as possible. The "mosquito" will be gone.

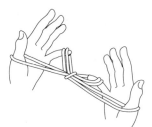

was gone!

FIGURE 2.7 *continued*

The Extraordinary Cat

Once there was a King who was given the gift of a cat. But this cat was the biggest and the fattest cat you ever saw. It was so fat that servants had to haul it in on a wagon. It ate so much the King could hardly keep food in the royal kitchen. But the King needed to name the cat. He thought to himself, "I want to name my cat the biggest and the best thing I can think of. Something worthy of its size." And he thought for a long moment. Then he said, "I shall name my cat Sky because sky is the greatest thing of all. Here Sky, nice Sky." He tickled the cat under the chin.

"Meow, purr," said Sky.

Things went along pretty well. Until the Queen happened to be walking by the throne room. She stopped, looked in and she said, "Husband, what a cat, what an extraordinary cat. What do you call that cat?"

"Oh, I call my cat Sky because sky is the greatest thing of all," said the King, please to be asked.

"Oh, husband, any old fool knows that clouds can cover a sky, therefore cloud is greater than sky. You should call your cat Cloud." The Queen walked away in a huff.

"Oh," said the King, "very well. Here Cloud. Nice Cloud."

Cloud only said, "Meow."

Things went along fairly well until the King was getting his annual checkup. The Court Physician came in. He had four black bags, two stethoscopes, and ten tongue depressors. He marched up to the King and said, "Good day your Majesty. Stick out your tongue. Cough. Breathe deeply."

The King obeyed. Then suddenly the Court Physician stopped his exam, looked at the fat cat and said, "Excuse me your Majesty. But do you know that there is an enormous cat right next to you?"

"Oh, yes," said the King, pleased to have the physician notice.

"What do you call that cat?"

"Ah, I call my cat Cloud because a cloud can cover the sky and the sky is the greatest thing of all."

"Your Majesty," the physician checked the King's ears, "isn't it also true that wind can blow away a cloud and therefore, shouldn't you call that cat Wind?"

FIGURE 2.8 Using a storyteller in the classroom can stimulate children's creativity (Dailey, 1985).

listeners will not challenge the speaker's real point. If the candidate for public office happens to be a mother, for example, the speaker may say, ''Our civilization could not survive without mothers.'' The generalization is true, of course, and listeners may—if they are not careful—accept the candidate without asking such questions as: ''Is she a mother? Is she a good mother? Does being a mother have anything to do with being a good candidate?''

2. *The Testimonial.* To persuade listeners to have strongly favorable feelings about some item, person, or event, the persuader links it with another that does have prestige and respect. To convince people to like a product, an advertiser associates it with a popular, well-liked athlete or film star: ''Bozo Cereal

"Oh," said the King, looking suddenly tired. "Oh, very well. Hello Wind."

Wind wouldn't come at all. In fact, it only growled "Yeoww."

Things went less and less well. Then the Court Wise Man came sweeping in with a monical on one eye and a long, red robe draped across his shoulders. He took one look at the cat and said, looking down his long nose. "Whaaat an extraordinary cat. Whaaat do you call that cat?"

"Oh," said the King looking a little confused, "I call my cat Wind because wind can blow away the clouds, the clouds can cover the sky and the sky is the greatest thing of all."

"That's so true your Majesty, but isn't it also true that a wall can withstand wind and therefore, isn't waaaall a better name for your caat?"

"Wall?" said the King scratching his head. "Oh, very well. Here Wall. Nice Wall."

The cat bit the King! Things were growing worse all the time. The Court Jester came in then. He had bells on his fingers and bells on his toes. He looked at the cat, twirled on one toe, and said, "Oh, greetings your Majesty. What an extraordinary cat. What do you call that cat?"

"Oh," said the King looking very upset. "I call my cat Wall because a wall can withstand wind, wind can blow away the clouds, the clouds can cover the sky and the sky is the greatest thing of all."

"Oh, that's true your Majesty," the Jester danced around the King. "But isn't it also true that

a mouse can burrow into a wall and make its nest there? Shouldn't you call your cat Mouse?"

"Mouse?" The King's eyes crossed. "Ohhh, very well. Nice Mouse. Good Mouse."

Well the cat could hardly be found. He wasn't even eating his food. From then on things were terrible, just terrible, until the King's youngest daughter came in. She looked at the cat and said, "Oh, father, what an extraordinary cat. What do you call that cat?"

"I call my cat Mouse because a mouse can burrow into a wall, a wall can withstand wind, wind can blow away the clouds, the clouds can cover the sky and the sky is the greatest thing of all," said the King breaking into a sweat.

"Oh, father. Well now it may be true that," the Princess very quickly counted off on her fingers, "a mouse can burrow into a wall, a wall can withstand wind, wind can blow away the clouds, the clouds can cover the sky and the sky is the greatest thing of all, but anybody knows that a cat can catch a mouse. Shouldn't you call your cat . . . Cat?"

And that is exactly what the King did.

FIGURE 2.8 *continued*

must be good because Joe Footballstar eats it every morning." Students generally have had much experience with this particular propaganda device.

3. *Name Calling.* Here the advertiser, propagandist, or persuader tries to pin a bad label on something listeners are to dislike so that it will automatically be rejected or condemned. In a discussion of health insurance, for example, an opponent may label the sponsor of a bill a socialist. Whether the sponsor is or is not a socialist does not matter to the name-caller; the purpose is to have any unpleasant associations of the name rub off on the victim.

4. *Transfer.* In this device, similar to the Testimonial, the persuader attempts to transfer the authority and prestige of some person or object to another person

FIGURE 2.9 Drawings reflecting the story sequence of ''The Extraordinary Cat.''

or object that will then be accepted. Good examples are found regularly in advertising: Miss Starlet-of-the-Year is seen using Super Soap, and viewers are supposed to believe that they too may have healthy, youthful skin like the starlet's if they use the same soap. Likewise, politicians like to be seen with famous athletes or entertainers in hopes that the luster of the stars will rub off on them.

5. *Plain Folks.* Assuming that most listeners favor common, ordinary people (rather than elitist, stuffed shirts), many politicians like to assume the appearance of common folk. One candidate who really went to Harvard and wore $400 suits, campaigned in clothes from J. C. Penney's and spoke dialect. "Look at me, folks," the candidate wanted to say, "I'm just a regular country boy like you; I wouldn't sell you a bill of goods!"

6. *Card Stacking.* In presenting an argument where the issues are complex, the unscrupulous persuader often chooses only those items that favor the positive side of an issue. Listeners get only the facts that support one point of view, and any unfavorable facts are suppressed.

(Devine, 1982, 39–40)

Television relentlessly and often unscrupulously bombards children with commercial messages. Children need help to critically evaluate those messages. Use a VCR to record examples of these advertisements. At the same time ask children to provide examples of the toys, cereals, or other products seen in the advertisements. Viewing the commercials with critical ears and eyes, looking for examples of propaganda strategies, will help students become critical and perhaps wise consumers (Tutolo, 1981; Allen, Wright, and Laminack, 1988; Kehl, 1983). You can use these viewing, listening, and speaking experiences with any age level to develop literacy skills that are immediately applicable to life outside of school.

Summary

As teachers of young, developing children we need to examine our own listening and speaking and what we believe about language learning.

> We do not, cannot, give children our ready-made concepts or our language to express them. Each child must build her understanding and expression out of personal experience. We serve her well if we provide worthwhile experiences, and the endless opportunity to express what she feels and what she understands as she engages in them. We serve her well, too, if we leave pathology notions of child language behind us. Ours is not to hunt for deficiencies (diagnose) to eradicate ("treat"), but rather to understand the growth in progress and exploit opportunities for enhancing it. We know that the child's language has grown steadily and continuously in form, in content, in social flexibility, in function up to the moment she arrives at the school door. What reason would we have for supposing that that continuous growth would stop or slow down now, at the very time she comes to an environment, our classroom, which offers more people to interact with every day than she has ever had at home, and a wide variety of daily experiences to communicate in and about? The possibilities for contributing richly to the child's steady language growth are there, but

only if we see our classrooms as communities for communicative interaction, rather than as locations where children mindlessly follow our dictates. We would do well to understand the child's continuous language growth process and, believing in it, align ourselves with it.

(Lindfors, 1988, 204)

In summary, teachers must learn to be alert to what their students are trying to do with language, raise the "linguistic consciousness" of their students as well as themselves, provide meaningful opportunities for children to experiment and expand language skills, and *celebrate* successes, big and small.

3
Language in Print:
Reading

Some Views on the Beginning Reader

What do you remember about learning to read? Did you learn to read at school or at home? Was the first book you read on your own a school reader or a book that your family shared with you again and again? Do you remember reading your book to anyone who would listen? Do you remember the feelings you had about books, and the anticipation you had at learning to read?

Many people remember their anticipation about learning to read and the importance that learning to read had in their lives, but few remember the actual process. In fact there is a good deal of confusion, contradiction, and controversy about how people learn to read, some of which we would like to explore in this chapter.

Right now Terry, age five, is in the process of learning to read. Although he is not in kindergarten yet, he has already taken the first steps in learning to read. Actually you could say that children begin their preparations for learning to read when they are learning to speak, but we will take as our starting point the actual process of learning to recognize and comprehend print.

Terry knows several things about reading. First of all he knows that printed language has meaning. He knows that the words written on signs, on labels, in books, and on pieces of paper mean something. He knows this because people have read books, signs, and notes to him.

Second he knows that what surrounds the language—buildings, pictures, the structure of the material (sign, scratch paper, magazine, box or can)—has something to do with the meaning of the language. Thus when he sees a golden arch, he knows that the sign says McDonald's; when he sees a can with a picture of peas on the outside, he knows that somewhere on the can it says peas; he knows that a story book with a picture of a dog is likely to have something about a dog in it.

Terry knows that letters make up words and that there is some relationship between what one writes down and what one pronounces. He knows this because he has listened to his brother figure out how to spell words when he writes and has watched other family members write down words for him that they pronounce as they write. These observations also show him that words read from left to right and that pages in books and magazines start on the left and proceed to the right. Moreover, Terry knows a little bit about how the structure of words relates them to one another. He knows that *Terry* and *terrific* start the same way. He knows that *cat, rat, bat*, and *hat* rhyme. From here it is not a big leap for him to see that they look alike.

Finally Terry knows a lot of "sight" words, words that he sees in his daily life—*stop, exit, Mom, Dad, Kinder Care, McDonald's, free, Terry*—on which he will draw to make generalizations and analogies about new words he encounters. At this point in his development he also believes that it is all right to guess when you are reading. Recently one such guess involved a candy wrapper. After noting a series of question marks on the paper, he asked, "Why does this say *hmmmm?*" Although he doesn't know the exact meaning of a question mark, he knows it implies wondering, so he made a good guess.

Terry understands all these things about reading not because his family "taught" him but because he is in an environment in which print is important and people read. But it is important to note that it is not just children from "bookish" homes who make these generalizations (see Figure 3.1). In fact the usual variables associated with the development of children's literacy—sex, race, setting (urban, suburban, etc.), and age—are currently being questioned. In their work with preschool children, Harste, Woodward, and Burke (1984) have discovered that it is the *number* of encounters with literary or the *quality* of the encounters that are more significant than those other factors. They discovered, too, that preschool children have "an almost natural affinity for books and for paper and pencil activities if the environment makes these things available."

Language researcher Yetta Goodman has also studied the interactions of preschool children with print. She has concluded that children ages two, three, and four "construct a variety of principles about language relevant to

The experts have begun to examine in detail what happens when children learn to read on their own, and why they can be successful without a teacher. One of the best documented cases, not usually included in books for parents, concerns a boy from a poor home in a southern state of the USA who became an expert reader by learning the words of the TV advertising slogans by heart and reciting them as they appeared on the screen. Another study tells of a number of Glasgow children who arrived in school able to read and confident of tackling anything, as a result of their parents' help and an early understanding of what reading is all about. It is not the bookish home, nor necessarily the middle-class family (except insofar as they are usually aware of what is at stake), not high intelligence, good eye movements, acute ears, right-handedness, nor even extensive vocabulary that makes the successful beginner. The supporting adult, who shows him what a book is and how print works, who helps him to discover reading and expects him to be successful, makes all the difference. Together, adult and child learn about reading.

FIGURE 3.1 What happens when children learn to read on their own (Meek, 1982, 31).

their developing literacy'' (1983, 73). These principles ''develop idiosyncratically, depending on each child's environment, and they overlap and become integrated. Over time, children must sort out which principles are the most significant in any particular written language event or situation'' (75). According to Goodman, children learn functional principles in which they ''discover when and how written language is used and for what purposes'' (75). In addition, children discover linguistic principles; that is, they figure out how written language is organized. They learn the alphabetic nature of English; they learn the directionality of writing; they learn about spacing and punctuation. Finally children ''learn to relate written language to meaning and where necessary to oral language'' (80). They discover that written language has meaning and they come to recognize elements of language that are related to a specific text. For example, six-year-old Lindsay demonstrated how much children assimilate about the world of print on the basis of experience. As a first grader reading ''chapter books,'' Lindsay was given her first comic book. Although she had had plenty of experience with reading the funny papers, she hadn't experienced the story format of comics. After reading a few of the comic-book stories, she confessed that she didn't ''get the joke.'' Her experiences with the comic form had led her to expect a gag rather than a narrative story. Lindsay and Terry, then, like most children, have begun to develop principles of language without any formal training.

John Holt, who wrote *How Children Learn* over twenty years ago, described Lisa, a kindergartner, at work on reading:

> One day she and I were sitting in the living room both reading. From the children's section of the public library she had just taken out four books, the maximum. Picking the one that looked most interesting, she had settled herself in

a big chair and had begun to work on it. I could hear her murmuring, though most of the time I could not hear what she was saying. From the tone of her voice, and her silences, I got a feeling that while there were many words in the book that she knew and could recognize at sight, there were others that she had to stop and figure out, perhaps using her rough knowledge of phonics, perhaps guessing from the context, perhaps both. Some words, she was willing to skip; she didn't feel that she had to get every one. But every now and then she would come to a word that she could neither figure out, nor guess, nor skip. On this day she found such a word. Slowly she climbed out of her chair and, holding the book, came toward me. I looked at her as she came. She had a set, stern expression on her face. Pointing to a word in her book, she asked, "What does it say?" Her look seemed to say very distinctly, "Now please don't ask me a lot of silly questions, like: 'what do you think it says?' or 'have you tried sounding it out?' or anything like that. If I could do those things, I wouldn't be up here asking. Just tell me what the word says; that will be enough." I told her. She nodded, went back to her chair, and continued reading.

(Holt, 1983 [rev. ed.], 80–81)

Holt's experiences with children's learning supports the view that learning to read is a naturalistic process in which children solve their problems based on their needs.

These studies of young children and my own observations of children's language confirm the view of many language educators today that children learn to read in much the same way they learn to speak. They observe and participate in the world around them in a way that allows them to make meaning of their environment; on the basis of their observations and need to understand, they make generalizations about how something works; they then test their generalizations by using them and seeing if they work. In short, as we said in Chapter 1, they move from the whole to the part—from the meaningful language-rich situation to an understanding of its parts.

■ **IDEAS TO LEARN**   Write your own learning-to-read autobiography. Try to remember the first words you were able to read. What were your favorite books? Who read to you and when? How did your family and home contribute to your reading development? What sorts of reading did you do in school? Do you remember any books that were read out loud to you? Where did you like to read?

Children's early experiences with books introduce them to "the literacy community" and give them information about how people function within that community. Don Holdaway describes the ways in which young children form connections with books. He emphasizes that the purpose of parents reading to their children is not to teach them anything but "to give pleasure."

And the experiences of being read to for a child are "among the happiest and most secure in his experience. The stories themselves are enriching and deeply satisfying—there is something emancipating in the experience which transcends normal time and space." In addition, the relationship with the parent in this situation is unique: "The parent is giving complete attention; there are none of the normal distractions most of the time. . . . Thus the child develops strongly positive associations with the flow of story language and with the physical characteristics of the books" (Holdaway, 1979, 39–40).

Children who are read to regularly and whose parents interact with them as they read begin to develop ideas about how to read a book. In fact they develop their responses to books as well as their basic reading behavior while their parents read to them. When parents talk to children while reading, the interaction between parent, child, and text is rich, as the parent responds to both the words and pictures and encourages the child to respond to them as well. The things parent and child say about the book as well as what is presented by the book itself (the language and the illustrations) create the meaning of the text. *Responding* to literature, then, becomes a basic activity of *reading* literature (Susan Tchudi, 1985).

In his descriptions of children learning to read, Holdaway describes the ways in which young children who have had shared experiences with books approach them independently (see Figure 3.2). Children who have interacted with text make it their own, recreating it in their own language, often with great energy and excitement—and with obvious pleasure in the process.

Early Instruction in Reading

Often in school the complex processes that children have developed to make sense of print are not recognized or built on. In fact methods for teaching reading focusing on subskills such as word structure and graphophonics (the relationship of sounds to letters) conflict with children's natural learning processes. There is little doubt that children make use of sound-letter correspondences when learning to read, but when they are overemphasized and arbitrarily taught, reading is made more difficult. In fact many of the exercises purporting to teach reading in school are ones that get in the way of children's own efforts to make sense of print (see Figure 3.3). Constance Weaver summarizes some of the shortcomings of emphasizing phonics to teach children to read:

> (1) Since vowels are relatively unimportant in identifying words, it seems unnecessary to teach numerous vowel rules, as many phonics programs do; (2) spelling/sound correspondences are often very complex and not easily reducible to rules that can or should be taught; (3) only a few of the frequently

Leslie has just turned four and will obviously be a high progress reader when she begins school. She is enjoying Sendak's *Where the Wild Things Are*—which has been read to her four times. Note the way in which she determines the precise relationship between the story and reality as she 'reads' the title:

> " 'Where the Wild Things Are'—see! (sighs) I'm scared of these things but they're only in books—not in real countries. Only in books."

We now sample her reconstruction of the text beginning about a quarter of the way through the book.

Text	Re-enactment
and an ocean tumbled by with a private boat for Max and he sailed off through night and day	Max stepped into his private boat and sailed off one day and one night
and in and out of weeks and almost over a year to where the wild things are.	then when he came to where the wi——OO look at that thing—he's blowing smoke out of his nose
And when he came to the place where the wild things are they roared their terrible roars and gnashed their terrible teeth and rolled their terrible eyes and showed their terrible claws	and where the wild things are they lashed their terrible claws—*oh no*! they lashed their terrible teeth—Hrmm!—(Interviewer: "What did they gnash?") They *lashed* their terrible claws!—showed their terrible claws and showed their terrible yellow eyes (but we've got blue eyes)
till Max said "BE STILL!" and tamed them with a magic trick of staring into all their yellow eyes without blinking once and they were frightened and called him the most wild thing of all	till Max said, "BE STILL!" that's what he said. One of these ones have toes (turns the page to find the toed monster) Toes! (Laughs) until Max said "BE STILL!" into all the yellow eyes without blinking once. And all the wild things said, "You wild thing!" (Note the elegant transformation into direct speech.)
and made him king of all the wild things. "And now," cried Max, "let the wild rumpus start!"	And then Max said, "Let the wild rumpus start!"
No text. (Picture of wild dance)	That's got no words, has it? He'd better pull his tail out of the way.

FIGURE 3.2 The foundations of literacy: A beginning reader at work (Holdaway, 1979, 46).

taught rules are both consistent and comprehensive—that is, applicable to a considerable number of words; and (4) most of these rules do not need to be explicitly taught to whole classes of children, since most children can and will internalize spelling/sound patterns just by reading and writing a lot, and/or with minimal guidance. In the long run, however, the most crucial problem with phonics instruction may be this: that a heavy instructional emphasis on phonics encourages readers to use just one language cue system, the grapho/phonemic. And sole reliance on grapho/phonemics makes the task of reading inordinately difficult, if not impossible.

(Weaver, 1988, 101)

Weaver, too, believes that we need to support children in the variety of ways they use to make sense of text. To teach them to rely only on the graphophonic system handicaps them. ''If beginning reading instruction emphasizes just phonics, only those children who intuitively use context to make sense of a text will be using all the resources that a successful reader needs to draw upon. Those who do just what they are taught will be in serious trouble'' (101). Thus it is the child who tries hardest to do what the teacher is teaching who often has the most trouble learning to read.

Often in teaching children to read, the goal is to get them to reproduce flawlessly what is on the page. But real reading is not simply decoding written language. Real reading (as opposed to word calling) is making meaning from print. Moreover, a child's oral production is not always a reliable indicator of whether the child is making sense of what he or she is reading. Research done with miscue analysis demonstrates that one can correctly reproduce what is on the page without having a clear sense of the meaning therein (Goodman, Watson, and Burke, 1987). Conversely a child may struggle to read aloud what is on the page, pronouncing what seem to be nonwords, but when done be able to tell you accurately what the text meant. Moreover, by observing children's miscues (unexpected responses that deviate from the text), teachers can discover why children produce something different from what's on the page. Listening to children read and having them describe what they have read helps teachers understand the meaning that children have made.

Twelve Rules for Reading Teachers

1. Aim for early mastery of the rules of reading.
2. Ensure that phonic skills are learned and used.
3. Teach letters or words one at a time, making sure each new letter or word is learned before moving on.
4. Make word-perfect reading the prime objective.
5. Discourage guessing; be sure children read carefully.
6. Encourage the avoidance of errors.
7. Provide immediate feedback.
8. Detect and correct inappropriate eye movements.
9. Identify and give special attention to problem readers as soon as possible.
10. Make sure children understand the importance of reading and the seriousness of falling behind.
11. Take the opportunity during reading instruction to improve spelling and written expression, and also insist on the best possible spoken English.
12. If the method you are using is unsatisfactory, try another. Always be alert for new materials and techniques.

FIGURE 3.3 Twelve rules for making reading difficult (F. Smith, 1973, 185).

TEACHING IDEA

You may be in a teaching situation that emphasizes phonics and word attack skills as early reading strategies. What are some activities and strategies you can use with your students to help them use their other language strengths? Develop a list of ideas to extend beyond the reading workbook.

Activities for the Beginning Reader

As we have seen, children come to school knowing a good deal about how written language functions. Simply by being consumers, by being TV watchers, by participating in a society that confronts them daily with printed language, they know something about the system of language and the relationship between written and oral language. Those with more experience know something about how stories are structured and the relationship between the kind of printed material and the content it contains. How, then, can you as a child's early reading teacher build on this knowledge to help children become independent readers?

The most important element in helping children learn how to read is *meaning*. To learn, children must have activity that is meaningful. First, then, all reading activities should make sense to the learner. Children are much more likely to find meaning in whole pieces of literature, not nonsense (word parts, sentence parts, or story parts) or overly simplified stories with simplified language. Moreover, children's experiences with literature should involve them intellectually and emotionally. And children should be encouraged to describe their reactions, their meanings, their understandings. As Louise Rosenblatt (1983) has pointed out, reading is a transaction between the reader and the text; children bring to bear all their knowledge and experience to create meaning from literature.

Children, then, should enjoy and care about what they read, rather than being made to perform a series of drills, after which, it is supposed, they will be able to read something of interest to them. Children should be actively engaged with the text, creating and developing meaning. You can use the activities that follow throughout the curriculum, as part of a reading/writing workshop or interdisciplinary unit. The activities encourage you to interact with your students, providing them with experiences that extend their relationship with print and allowing them to interact with the literature they encounter.

■ **IDEAS TO LEARN**   As an experiment listen to a few children read aloud, then talk to them about what they read. What is the relationship between their oral reproduction of the text and their understanding of it?

Reading Aloud to Beginning Readers Every Day

To build on children's knowledge of what is available in print, choose a wide variety of reading materials. You may use picture books with large pictures so that the children can see as well as hear. At times you can choose stories with no pictures so that young children have an opportunity to focus on listening to a story. Select stories that involve children's imaginations, thoughts, and feelings. In addition, provide variety in the styles and language structures of the stories that you read, to expose your students to language that they may not have previously encountered. Remember that children do not have to understand every word that is read to them. As with babies learning language, hearing new words in familiar contexts helps children begin to create new meanings. It is the experience of being in a rich, complex language situation that allows children to grow and assimilate new structures, words, understandings. Read all genres of literature to children—poems, stories, short novels ("chapter books"), and a wide range of nonfiction. Early in the year create a checklist of your students' interests, hobbies, and special talents, and choose stories and nonfiction pieces based on the list. Share reading that you especially love, because your pleasure and enthusiasm for literature will inspire and involve your students.

Discussing Literature with Beginning Readers

Talking about literature can help develop in children the notion that their reading should make sense, that they should be predicting what will happen next based on their own knowledge and experience, and that they should be

TEACHING IDEA

Begin to develop a list of read-aloud pieces to share with your students. You may focus on a particular grade (keep in mind that fifth graders enjoy picture books too). Choose from a variety of genres—poetry, fiction, nonfiction—and styles that will appeal to children's imaginations, feelings, and thinking.

raising questions that will be answered by the text. In short, involving children in discussions reinforces the notion that reading is an active process. So before you begin to read, tell your students the title of the poem or story or nonfiction piece and ask them whether they know it or its author. Ask them what they know about the subject. Ask them what they think the story is going to be about. At times you will want to stop during the reading and ask them what they think is going to happen next. At other times you will not want to interrupt the emotion, the rhythm, or the drama of the story. You will need to gauge this on the basis of your sense of the story and your sense of the children's involvement and understanding. At the end of the story ask your students what they liked about it, who their favorite characters were, which parts, if any, confused them, and so on. Discussions like this encourage children to make meaning and to form predictions and responses to what they read.

Creating "Lap" Experiences

For many children the biggest impetus in learning to read is sitting on someone's lap so they can see and hear the story at the same time. The emotional climate created by this experience is so important that you should try to reproduce it in the classroom whenever possible. Don Holdaway (1979) calls this attempt to reproduce home reading experiences the Shared Book Experience. Although it's not always easy to do this when you have twenty to thirty students, the benefits are so great that you should make the effort.

Allow readers to read to nonreaders. You may have children in your classroom who already read; ask for volunteers who enjoy reading out loud and are pretty good at it to read to their classmates. Or get volunteers from the upper grades to come in at scheduled times to read to your K–2 students. In our household we are convinced that our third grader's reading was really boosted by his sharing a bed with his five-year-old brother and reading him to sleep. In your classroom a small couch, a beanbag that holds two (or more!), or carpet squares will allow children to sit side-by-side so that the "listener" can "read" with the reader.

Invite parents or grandparents to read to small groups of children (three or four). Provide a cozy setting and a variety of read-aloud stories. Set up a schedule for these volunteer readers.

Use audio tapes in conjunction with books. Although they lack the intimacy of being read to by a person, taped poems and stories give children the opportunity to look at the words while listening to them. If your school has a tape player with several headsets, several children at a time can listen. After reading give children the chance to talk about the stories. Your students may also want to draw pictures or write about what they have read and listened to.

Use big books. Recently a number of publishers have been putting out "big books." These are oversized books of popular children's stories that can be placed in the front of the room and read from almost anywhere in the room. Teachers and children can then read the book together or the children can join in on refrains, which they come to memorize after having read the story several times with the teacher. Teachers can also point to specific words and talk about them or cover words and ask the children to guess what word comes next. Because commercial big books are quite expensive, Dorothy Watson and Paul Crowley (1988) suggest that you make your own big books or "even better, invite children to make them. In making *Big Books*, the children print the exact text of the story on either the top or bottom of a large page of light cardboard . . . , talk about the pictures, and make decisions about who is going to illustrate each page" (253). The completed pictures are glued onto the cardboard and are then ready to be shared by the whole class or in small groups.

Oral Sharing

Have children talk about their own experiences, about objects they bring to class, about favorite stories. Whenever children can build their own language, they develop the strengths they need to understand print (see Chapter 2 for oral language activities).

Getting Beginning Readers to Write and Share Stories

Chapter 4 discusses in detail how to get children to write and how to establish a writing workshop in your classroom. When very young children write, they test and experiment with their generalizations about how language functions. In addition, as authors they participate in the cycle of writing and the chance to express themselves to others. When you help children revise and edit their language, you give them the sense of creating meaning in the same way that authors do. Moreover, when children work in a writing workshop, they learn

TEACHING IDEA

Develop a list of books on tape that you would like to have for your classroom. Remember that a good deal of young adult literature is available on tape that upper elementary children would enjoy but may not be able to read independently. If you are interested in primary age children, develop a list of big books. Determine how you can integrate the big books or taped books into your classroom activities.

to raise questions about one another's meaning and technique. Jane Hansen (1983) describes three kinds of workshops in which children's responses to one another carry over to their reading of professional writers: "All three of these response sessions—when the children ask their friends questions about pieces in progress, when they ask a friend questions about that author's published books, and when they ask questions about each other's published books—are all response sessions where readers learn to question print. These response sessions can only happen in a classroom where readers are writers" (973–974).

Using the Language Experience Method

Although it is vital that very young children write down their own stories themselves, I also like the idea of taking dictation from children. This approach, described by Roach Van Allen in *Language Experiences in Communication*, emphasizes the relationship between oral and written language; it demonstrates for children that what they say can be written down and can be read. The children's own language provides the reading material, enabling them to "read" it. Because the process of writing something down is so demanding for young children—involving both the struggle of getting the little hand to make those crazy shapes and of trying to remember how to make the words look like they do in "real" language—children will often write much less than they know or think about. For that reason it's a good idea to let children tell their stories to an adult or older child who acts as scribe, writing down exactly what the children dictate. Children can also use a tape recorder and then write out their story later. Teachers can even use the language experience approach as a whole class activity, allowing children to dictate stories based on shared experiences, such as a field trip or a study of some particular theme or process (growing plants, caring for animals, observing the seasons, etc.). Children's language experience stories may be made into individual books, class books, or posted on bulletin boards for others to read. Most important, because the language experience stories use the children's own language, the children are much more likely to be able to read them. Some reading programs use the child's own language as the primary basis for teaching children to read.

Filling the Classroom with Print

Kindergarten and first grade teachers have traditionally labeled objects in the classroom, and that's a fine starting place—but don't stop there. Provide children with lists of language that they have helped you generate. Typically classrooms contain lists of classroom rules and guidelines and lists of classroom tasks (collecting milk money, feeding the gerbil, passing the paper, etc.).

Instead of making up these lists yourself, get the children to generate the ideas and do the writing. At the beginning of the year create a chart that shows each individual class member's special talents, areas of interest, and expertise (you may want to change this chart to follow children's interests); set aside a bulletin board for the "children of the week" to display photos of themselves, draw pictures, and write (or dictate) information about themselves to share with the rest of the class; devote a wall or bulletin board or clothesline to children's writing; bring in magazine and news articles that relate to subjects the children are studying (place them on the bulletin board for the children to read after you've read them to the class); bring in interesting posters (educational publishers provide many for free), bumper stickers, and pamphlets on subjects of interest to your students; encourage the children to bring in the same sorts of things; have children create posters and pamphlets relating to subjects they are studying in class; have children put labels and captions on the artwork that they display. With your students' help, you can fill the classroom with interesting things to look at and to read.

Playing Language Games

In *A Book of Puzzlements*, Herbert Kohl states that "play and invention are central ways of acquiring power over speech, of learning to command one's language and use it in the service of one's thoughts" (x). Kohl's book demonstrates the range of possible language games and includes play that involves letters and words, parts of speech, phrase and sentence variations, sense and nonsense in meaning, figures of speech, proverbs and fables, songs and poems, and codes and ciphers. Children's language games include telling riddles and jokes (both their own and those learned in books and from others), solving brain teasers or mysteries, making and using rhymes, singing and chanting rhymes or verses, making and breaking codes, creating puns, solving crossword or acrostics puzzles, and playing with sentence structure or word meanings. Older children can even create their own games. Kohl says this heightened involvement with language can help children "learn that speech can be used in many ways—it can trick, persuade, question, ridicule, insult, praise, delight, inform, etc.—and therefore it has great power" (x).

Using Drama

The use of drama allows children to develop their imaginations, to use their bodies and their language to express meaning, and to physically engage in their reading. Have children act out familiar stories. Read a new story and ask children to move or talk in a way that they think the various characters would. Create readers theater scripts from stories the children have read. Chapter 2 describes dramatic activities more fully.

TEACHING IDEA

A game that I learned as a child and have passed on to my own children and my students is "teakettle." First you think of a homonym, *bare/bear*. Then you create two sentences that use those words, which you replace with the word *teakettle*: "Make sure you are 'teakettle' before you get into the bathtub." "When you go camping, put your food away so a 'teakettle' won't get it." Recite the sentences to the class and ask your students to guess the homonym. Begin a collection of your own games—ones that you played as a child, that you've learned from friends, or that you've found in books. How might you make games a part of your classroom activities?

Rereading Favorite Stories and Poems

Choose stories that allow your students to participate in the storytelling, by repeating refrains or finishing phrases or sentences. Reproduce the refrains in large print so that children can read and recite at the same time. Use predictable books and encourage children to guess what will happen next, so that they become involved in telling the story. Again the experience of participating in language situations builds children's sense of structure and their repertoire of language possibilities.

In addition, children can participate in the reading/writing process by adding to the text they are reading. Have children write new verses to songs or poems or create their own version of a familiar story.

Using Art

Have your students draw pictures of settings or characters from stories you are sharing with them. Encourage them to create nonrepresentational art in response to the mood or feeling of a poem. Let them create collages that represent the meanings or images that they take from the things they read. Have them create sculptures from wire, styrofoam, clay, and "junk" that signify the meanings or moods of literature; let them create mobiles of important objects from the piece. The whole class can create a landscape or a village from an important book that the class has read.

Involving Parents

Marilyn Wilson and Celeste Resh have developed a pamphlet for parents to help their children with reading (see Figure 3.4). The International Reading Association (IRA) also has a series of pamphlets for parents. The pamphlet

Good Books Make Reading Fun for Your Child by Glenna D. Sloan describes how important to the learning of reading it is that children see reading as worthwhile and interesting. The pamphlet encourages parents to share rhymes with very young children ("Pat-a-cake" and other nursery rhymes); to read colorfully illustrated picture books (*Bruno Munari's ABC, Brian Wildsmith's Mother Goose, Richard Scarry's Best Word Book Ever,* Leslie Brooke's *Johnny Crow's Garden,* Marcia Brown's *The Three Billy Goats Gruff,* and Barbara and Ed Emberley's *Drummer Hoff*); to provide their children with a variety of books: "folktales, funny tales, exciting tales, tales of the wondrous and stories that tell of everyday things"; to introduce the classics (E. B. White's *Charlotte's Web,* George Seldon's *A Cricket in Times Square,* Mary Norton's *The Borrowers,* Robert Louis Stevenson's *Treasure Island,* Lewis Carroll's *Alice's Adventures in Wonderland,* and Rudyard Kipling's *Jungle Book*); and "to keep up with what is new and best in children's books" by reading such publications as *The Horn Book Magazine.* The pamphlet encourages parents to share the joy of reading with their children: "Young children want to read what makes them laugh or cry, shiver and gasp. They must have stories and poems that reflect what they themselves have felt. They need the thrill of imagining, of being for a time in some character's shoes for a spine-tingling adventure. They deserve to experience the delight and amazement that comes with hearing language that puns and plays. For children, reading must be equated with enjoying, imagining, wondering, reacting feelingly. If it is not we should not be surprised if they refuse to read."

Other titles in IRA's pamphlet series include *You Can Encourage Your Child to Read, You Can Help Your Child In Reading By Using the Newspaper,* and *You Can Use Television to Stimulate Your Child's Reading Habits.* These pamphlets provide guidance to both teachers and children on how to focus on the needs of the child.

It is vital that reading skills be taught in context. Teachers must make the connection between children's oral reading and the language children encounter on the page. In doing this, however, teachers must avoid round-robin reading, which emphasizes performance over constructing meaning. Oral reading might take the form of group reading, using big books or familiar songs, stories, or poems in which children can join in reading refrains or choruses. Children may read out loud to small groups of other children or to a reading buddy. They may also read to parents or classroom aides who can help them as they read. When my son was in second grade in an Australian school, parent volunteers listened to children read one-on-one and assisted not only beginning readers but also the more advanced readers in third grade.

In his research in the New Zealand schools Claude Goldenberg discovered that teachers taught all reading skills in the context of meaningful situations with real books, no basals or worksheets. Teachers provided instruction and support to help young children read fluently.

FIGURE 3.4 Reading in the home pamphlet developed by Marilyn Wilson and Celeste Resh (Michigan State University).

If a child did not know a word or read it incorrectly, the teacher assisted. She might call the child's attention to context or to sound-symbol cues, although the former was used much more frequently. Children were encouraged to predict or estimate a word they did not recognize, using either visual, semantic, or syntactic cues.

"What would make sense there?" might be appropriate in some instances. In others, the teacher might ask, "What does that look like? Make your mouth ready to say it." If the teacher had chosen the selection well for the group, however, and had done a good job before the actual reading commenced, the number of instances where children were completely stuck would be minimal.

In correcting oral reading errors, the most frequent type of feedback we heard teachers give was, "Does that make sense? But does it look like _____?" In this way, the teacher reinforced the use of context, while simultaneously

READ ALOUD TO CHILDREN AND LET THEM READ TO EACH OTHER OR TO YOU:

Signs	Children's books
Letters	Comic strips
Recipes	Catalogues
Maps	Cereal boxes

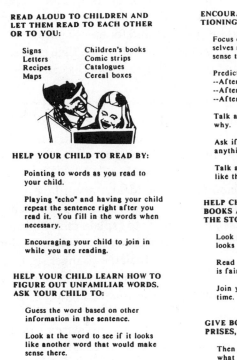

HELP YOUR CHILD TO READ BY:

Pointing to words as you read to your child.

Playing "echo" and having your child repeat the sentence right after you read it. You fill in the words when necessary.

Encouraging your child to join in while you are reading.

HELP YOUR CHILD LEARN HOW TO FIGURE OUT UNFAMILIAR WORDS. ASK YOUR CHILD TO:

Guess the word based on other information in the sentence.

Look at the word to see if it looks like another word that would make sense there.

Skip the word and come back to it later if the reading doesn't continue to make sense.

If none of these ideas work, then ask someone.

ENCOURAGE THINKING AND QUESTIONING BY ASKING READERS TO:

Focus on meaning by asking themselves as they read, "Does this make sense to me?"

Predict what will happen next:
--After looking at the title.
--After looking at the pictures.
--After reading a few pages.

Talk about what has happened and why.

Ask if the story reminds them of anything or anyone they know.

Talk about why they do or do not like the story.

HELP CHILDREN CHOOSE THEIR OWN BOOKS AT THE LIBRARY OR AT THE STORE. LET THEM:

Look at a few pages to see if it looks interesting.

Read a few lines to you to see if it is fairly easy to read.

Join you in a quiet, regular reading time.

GIVE BOOKS AS PRESENTS, SURPRISES, AND REWARDS:

Then ask children to tell you about what they've read so they will know you think it's important.

GIVE CHILDREN'S MAGAZINE SUBSCRIPTIONS FOR HOLIDAYS, BIRTHDAYS, AND OTHER OCCASIONS:

Cricket	*Electric Company*
Ranger Rick	*Jack and Jill*

USE TELEVISION TO ENCOURAGE READING BY:

Helping your child become an active rather than a passive viewer (see suggestions for encouraging thinking and questioning).

Reading the print shown on commercials, news, and game shows.

Reading the t.v. schedule together.

Reading the books on which children's specials are based:

--*Peanuts*	--*Peter Pan*
--*Dr. Seuss*	--*The Wizard of Oz*
--*The Berenstain Bears*	

SHARE PARTS OF THE NEWSPAPER WITH YOUR CHILD:

Comics	Advice columns
Sports	Advertisements

Kids' games and puzzles
Funny feature stories
Current and local events
Pictures and captions

Discuss articles and ask your child what he or she thinks about them.

FIGURE 3.4 *continued*

prompting students to attend to letter (that is, visual) cues to verify their reading.

Teachers generally did not interrupt to correct an error. Unless the child were completely stuck, the teacher would wait until the end of the page or passage, then go back.

(Goldenberg, 1991, 556–557)

The Developing Reader

As children progress in school, the reading demands placed on them become greater and greater. Much of their school learning relies on textbooks; in addition, they are often asked to read newspapers, magazines, and other print resources. As students face these new demands, teachers should support them in several ways. First, teachers must continue to provide plenty of opportunities for their students to read for pleasure and for emotional and personal enrichment. Equally important, teachers must provide their students with strategies of critical thinking and reading that the students can bring to bear on more sophisticated texts.

Recent findings of the National Assessment of Educational Progress (1983) looked at the ability of over one hundred thousand nine-, thirteen-, and seventeen-year-olds throughout the United States to interpret literature and defend their interpretations. The results showed that students were able to answer multiple choice questions at the "literal or inferential" level but were "unable to examine, explain, or elaborate on the ideas." According to the NAEP, "most students were satisfied with their initial responses to what they had read and were puzzled when asked to defend or to explain their interpretations. Even the 'better' responses showed little evidence of problem-solving strategies, and seventeen-year-olds were no better than the younger students at explaining or defending their ideas through reference to personal experience or to the text" (National Assessment of Educational Progress, 1983, 1031).

We have evidence not only from the NAEP but from our own experience that students are not making judgments about what they read, that they are not intellectually involved. How can teachers help students develop active thinking as they read? Watson and Crowley (1988) suggest that helping students to become conscious of the reading process and discussing strategies for reading will increase students' success in reading. Drawing on the work of Kenneth Goodman, Watson and Crowley describe strategies that involve the "reader's sampling from print, predicting on the basis of on-the-page and off-the-page information, confirming when the effort makes sense and sounds right, correcting when the effort results in nonsense or is garbled, and finally integrating new information with old." Students must be made to recognize that what they already know and think can actually help them understand what they read. Watson and Crowley conclude that "bringing reading to a level of awareness so that a child can reflect on the process is a powerful teaching-learning experience. Fortunately, it is not difficult to do this because children are interested in language and how it works; that is, they are interested unless their curiosity is killed by skilling and drilling" (257).

Students who rely on their own knowledge and experience to make judgments about the text will become critical readers. Too great an emphasis on activities that focus on mere recall or specific facts mislead students about the nature of reading. In fact many educators see students' reading problems as the result of schools' heavy reliance on workbooks and ditto sheets that ask children to fill in the blanks, provide short factual information, answer multiple choice questions, rather than to interact with the text, to bring their own experiences to bear on it, to ask questions of it, to evaluate it in light of their own knowledge. Problems with texts will be discussed further, but first we would like to explore the kinds of experiences with reading that will help developing readers to read actively and critically.

Activities for the Developing Reader

As with beginning readers, the heart of the reading experience is the creation of meaning that occurs when readers interact with the text; that is, when readers create meaning on the basis of their own knowledge and experience rather than simply passively stacking up facts (which can't be assimilated or processed in the absence of an active mind and structure). Reading material for older children needs to be not only appropriate for their intellectual and emotional development but also engaging, interesting, and personally involving.

Since the processes and purposes of reading are similar for older readers to those for beginning readers, many of the activities I suggest are also similar. I'll describe how older readers might use them.

Reading Aloud to Developing Readers Every Day

Once children become independent readers, teachers are often tempted to abandon oral reading. However, the benefits of reading to intermediate children are tremendous and worth the time they take in the busy class schedule. Oral reading of good literature creates a bond among learners, providing shared experiences that they can talk about; children can extend their understanding of a piece of literature by sharing their thoughts and by listening to the different interpretations and responses of their classmates. In addition, oral reading introduces children to literature that they may not be able to read on their own but that they can understand and appreciate. Literature from different times and places often uses unfamiliar language or complex syntax; these new words and metaphors demonstrate the richness of language and encourage children in their language development.

Allowing Students to Read for Enjoyment

Reading for pleasure should be a part of every child's day, not reserved as a reward for the child who finishes up work early. By providing time in class for children to read, you accomplish two important goals: (1) You demonstrate to children that reading is valuable, so important that you set aside class time to do it and so important that you as the teacher do it also (rather than grading math quizzes). (2) You provide time for children to read who may not have time, attention, or value given to reading at home. Remember that some children's lives are so filled with outside activities or with TV watching that they won't read or get hooked on reading unless you set aside class time for that to happen. Allow children to read anything that they want but insist that everyone have a book. Provide books for those who have forgotten to bring one. Make sure that the books you have on hand are real grabbers, ones that help hook kids rather than serve as boring punishments for kids who "forgot to bring their books *again!*"

Discussing Literature with Developing Readers

Have your students read a poem or story and then talk about it with them: their favorite parts, their favorite characters, their favorite words, anything that confused them, anything they didn't like. Louise Rosenblatt (1938) describes the importance to young people of discussing literature: It helps them discover how responses differ and how experience influences the way one interprets what one reads. When children discuss their differences, they are able to reflect on their own meanings and encouraged to go back to the text to see what led them to their conclusions. This is an important step in the process of creating students who are critical readers and thinkers.

Valuing Independent Reading

In almost every elementary school in the country, children go to the library once a week to check out a book for their independent reading. Often, however, teachers simply ignore these or, worse, make them the basis for the dreaded book report. Instead of doing either, demonstrate to the children the value of their reading. First of all institute reading time. Then allow time for students to talk and write about their independent reading: Set aside a few minutes before or after reading for kids to chat about their books; hold book talks several times a week so that children can give the class a brief description of the books they've read and make a recommendation; provide alternatives to the book report. Instead of a traditional report, have your students

- Make a book cover that includes art, a description of the contents, a recommendation for readers, and a brief biography of the author.
- Make a poster that advertises the book.
- Create a rhyme, jingle, or song to reflect their response to the book.
- Make a pamphlet that describes the book.

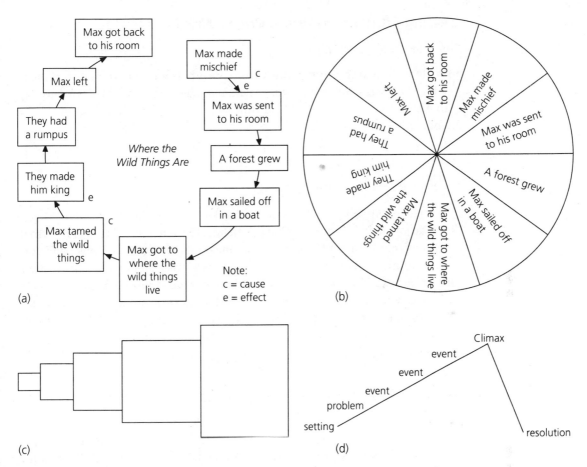

FIGURE 3.5 Students can use maps to interpret and describe the action of a story (Galda, 1987, 56–57, 91).

- Dramatize a section of the book or give a readers theater performance of it.
- Create a radio, magazine, or television ad for the book.
- Draw a picture or make a sculpture or mobile that reflects the book's content.
- Use maps to interpret and describe the action of the story (see Figure 3.5 for examples of various kinds of maps).

Although you are eager to have children develop responses to what they read, don't make your students write or create a project for every book they read. Occasionally allow them to simply read and enjoy.

Getting Students to Write, Write, Write

Give children opportunities to

- Write their own stories that draw from the whole world of their experiences with life, books, and language. It's amazing how reading inspires students to experiment with writing and how writing arouses children's curiosity about how writers write.

- Experiment with form: jokes, riddles, poetry, scripts, mysteries, fables, myths, science fiction, domestic humor, scary stories, and so on.

- Respond to what they are reading.

Nancie Atwell (1987), a middle school teacher, has her students keep dialogue journals, which they share with her. The journals consist of informal dialogues in which students can raise questions, describe feelings, and formulate opinions about their reading. She responds as a person who is interested in her students' thoughts rather than as a judge who tells them what is right and wrong, valid and invalid. Under these nonjudgmental circumstances students feel free to explore and to risk having opinions. Both elementary and junior high/middle school teachers have found success with the reading/writing/sharing workshop that Atwell describes.

Getting Students to Explore Authors

Read books and create displays and activities that center around some of your students' favorite authors. Young children might enjoy learning more about such authors as A. A. Milne, Beatrix Potter, Janet and Allen Ahlberg, John Burningham, Maurice Sendak, and Brian Wildsmith. Older children would enjoy learning more about Shel Silverstein, Jack Prelutsky, Katherine Paterson, Roald Dahl, E. B. White, Madeline L'Engle, Beverly Cleary, and Betsy Byars. Displays can include pictures of the author, the author's description of how and why he or she writes, lists of other books the author has written, biographical sketches, and reviews of the author's books. If the writer is also an illustrator, students can display some of the pictures. In some cases students may be able to find manuscript drafts that show how the book changed as the writer revised it.

Part of the focus on the author should include reading a number of his or her books and comparing them in terms of subject; upper elementary and middle school children can compare the type or style of writing the author employs. Having many of an author's books on hand allows students who really appreciate him or her to read more.

By learning about an author and reading that author's books, children can make a number of discoveries. First of all they learn that books are written by real people and that books reflect the interests, the values, and the experiences of their writers. If children are able to see writers' drafts, they will have a greater appreciation for the process by which books are written, a recognition that will help them in their own authoring process. They will have opportunities, too, to see that each author has a particular approach to experience and to writing that makes his or her work unique.

■ **IDEAS TO LEARN**   Learn more about your favorite authors. In addition to reading as many of their books as you can, try to find out more about their lives and their development and interests as writers. Learn how they work as writers. If an author is alive, you may consider writing a letter to get answers to specific questions. Perhaps this person would even be willing to share some rough drafts! Create a display and share it with your students as they themselves prepare to learn more about their favorite authors.

Getting Developing Readers to Share with Beginning Readers

Volunteer your fourth, fifth, and sixth graders as readers for kindergartners and first and second graders. If you teach junior high or middle school, have your students create books for younger children, which they can share during a field trip to the elementary school. You can have these students research (by survey and interviews with parents, the librarian, and younger children) what kinds of stories younger children really like; have your students search their own memories for their favorites. Then give your students a chance to practice reading with meaning and feeling. They may also like to record literature for younger children, to be used in classrooms or in the media center (where children who are just learning how to read can be helped by hearing and seeing a book at the same time).

Using Drama

Help children physically and imaginatively participate in what they read. Use improvisation, dramatization of scenes, staging of plays, and writing and staging scripts for readers theater. All these activities get children to participate in literature by using their bodies and voices, which intensifies their involvement. (See Chapter 2 for more ideas on dramatic activities.)

Involving Parents

Think about creating your own pamphlet (similar to the IRA pamphlets we mentioned earlier) recommending books and language activities for the home that coordinate with activities in class. Parents also appreciate receiving letters with suggestions for other ways they can support classroom activities. Moreover, by communicating with parents you are educating them about children's language development, about books, and about developments in education.

Reading Materials

For many years basal readers and workbooks have been the primary texts for teaching reading. But teachers are becoming increasingly aware of the limitations of these materials. Workbooks are supposed to teach children skills to help them read by moving from the part to the whole. Workbooks have been used, then, to teach all the little parts that *seem* to make up reading. One workbook exercise, for example, asks children to analyze sound-letter correspondence.

A recent text series published by Scott Foresman, *The House of Reading*, takes children through four steps that purport to develop "early decoding independence through a systematic pattern of phonics instruction," as an advertisement from the publisher attests. First, children are given a picture with an accompanying row of pictures. The teacher pronounces the word for the single picture and then the words for the other pictures. The teacher asks the children to circle all the objects in the accompanying pictures whose names begin with the same sound as the object in the first picture; this is supposed to teach "auditory discrimination." Second, "children see the letter and associate it with the sound" by again matching a picture with rows of objects "whose names begin with the letter . . . and sound." Third, children "write the consonant to kinesthetically reinforce the letter-sound relationship." Again they listen for the sound and write the letter under the pictures whose names begin with the same letter and sound. Finally the teacher gives the children a different word that starts with the same letter and asks them to write that word several times in a blank provided in "sentences."

The publisher of this material asserts that this "systematic instruction lets students immediately apply phonics skills to new unit vocabulary." The same company also provides "optional vowel instruction [that] can begin as early as Kindergarten and Readiness; regular vowel instruction begins with Preprimer 2 and also follows a consistent pattern of instruction."

Some educational materials are taught in the form of "games" that break language down into its smallest parts. One company provides thirty games that provide information about how language is structured. Unlike the games we have recommended, these require analysis of subskills. The publisher (Holland) states in its catalogue: "The syllable rules (closed, open, magic e, double vowel blockers and singers, R-control, consonant le, and special) are taught by mnemonic stories. The students sort words according to syllables, read words, spell words, name the syllable, and use the words in sentences. Students learn to watch for consonant and vowel patterns to determine the vowel sounds. There are ten vowel decks of A, E, I, O, U, single consonant and consonant blend words. Each deck contains two decks of four syllables, a total of twenty decks. The games help teachers understand individual learning styles and adjust to meet student needs."

The theory behind this approach is that children learn by having principles of words presented to them, learning those principles, and then applying them. In Chapter 1 and in this chapter we have tried to demonstrate how that concept of learning does not reflect the way children actually learn language. Although children need some understanding of sound-letter relationships and word patterns to get started in reading, this sort of heavy emphasis distracts them from their primary task of reading. Although many schools still use materials like these, most teachers see their own role in reading as much expanded from the drill emphasis found in workbooks.

The basal reader is used in many schools, often in conjunction with a workbook. Traditionally this early reader has most often contained stories written by in-house writers (rather than trade literature writers) using a controlled vocabulary. The assumption is that if children are presented just a few words at a time, they can learn those and then go on to add more words as the stories in the book become more complex (that is, as the stories add new words). Along with the workbook the basal reader provides lessons in "language skills" for children to master on the assumption that skill mastery will make them competent readers (see Figure 3.6).

Throughout this chapter I have demonstrated the weaknesses in this model of teaching reading, and raised concerns about the paucity of the language provided for children. Many teachers nonetheless find that a workbook or textbook gives them some sense of direction. In a recent poll conducted by the journal *Learning*, more than 85 percent of the 339 respondents said that they used basal readers, but 56 percent of the respondents said that they were "not required to strictly follow a basal reading program, and 64 percent are encouraged by their districts to go beyond the basal and adapt it to their personal needs." Many more teachers, then, are using basals than are required to do so. The reason, they say, is that basals "provide a sequential skill structure that allows teachers to cover the basics in an organized, logical manner" (62). Teachers do not feel confident that children are learning to read unless they "cover" the basic skills. Teachers want to take the guesswork out of teaching and teach "the great variety of beginning reading skills in an organized, spiral manner." (62) Many teachers feel that structure and sequence must be provided in order for children to learn what teachers teach.

So What's Wrong with Basals?

1. They put undue emphasis on isolated aspects of language: letters, letter-sound relationships, words, sentence fragments, or sentences. Often, particularly in workbooks, there is no cohesive meaningful text and no situational context.

2. That leads learners to put inverted value on the bits and pieces of language, on isolated words and skills, and not enough on making sense of real, comprehensible stories and expository passages.

3. Basals discourage risk taking by requiring right answers on trivial details.

4. They introduce arbitrary sequences of skills which involve readers in abstract exercises instead of reading to comprehend.

5. They isolate reading from its use and from other language processes.

6. They often create artificial language passages or text fragments by controlling vocabulary or by building around specific phonic relationships or word-attack skills. They also often create artificial texts by applying readability formulas to real texts.

7. They minimize time spent on reading while monopolizing school time for skill exercises.

8. Even the use of real children's literature is marred by gearing it to skill development, rewriting it, or using excerpts instead of whole books.

9. Basals cost so much that they do not leave funds for school and classroom libraries and other more authentic reading material.

Particularly in the United States, the basal reader often becomes the entire reading curriculum. If some pupils don't make progress in the regular basal it is often augmented by extra "practice," either in additional components of the same program or in another, even more highly structured set of materials. That leaves no time for writing, social studies, science, math, oral language, and the arts. Ironically, it often leaves no time for reading!

FIGURE 3.6 Basal readers: A call for action (K. Goodman, 1986a, 361–362).

Some teachers in the survey, however, recognize that essential to children's learning to read is their involvement and interest in their reading. Their goals are to help children love reading, to help children think creatively rather than seek the correct answer, to challenge children in their thinking rather than using stories that have been "dumbed down," to get children to read rather than simply working with isolated skills. Despite the fact that teachers in general are critical of skill work, 60 percent of the teachers in the survey said "they use their workbook all or most of the time." Only 10 percent of the respondents said that they don't use their basals at all (63). Some teachers, however, are adamant about the effects of basals on their students (see Figure 3.7).

With the growing knowledge about how children learn and the recognition of the limitations of basals, then, the movement these days is clearly

No basal at all

Only 10 percent of our respondents say they don't use basals at all, but they were perhaps the most eager to state their views:

- "Basals are so programmed they take away my professionalism in knowing what my kids need. I refuse to lower students' self-esteem by putting them in reading groups, and most basals are structured that way."

- "I want children to learn to read fine, crafted writing, to be inspired by it, to learn writing from it. Basals don't do this. Instead, they isolate skills, control vocabulary, and don't allow the sustained involvement that's so necessary to comprehension."

- "We are a very poor community with low socioeconomic status. Our children always did poorly in school—until we dropped the basal and allowed students to read real books. We use no workbooks, and our children now think of themselves as readers and writers, capable of learning. This change was not entirely due to dropping basals, but it was the first step. In my experience, teachers only use basals because they don't know of any alternatives. When we demonstrate what we're doing, they become eager to switch to trade books."

Taking charge

Despite the criticisms, the fact remains that most of our respondents use basals in one way or another. Many of them commented on the role teachers must take in improving their own destiny. For example:

- "I truly believe that basals, used as they are in our schools, are the ruination of the love for reading that must be fostered. But it's not the basals that need improving—it's the way teachers use them. Basals have become too many teachers' security blankets."

- "New teachers feel they need to do everything in the teachers' manual. These guides should be written so that teachers feel free to pick and choose what they want to use and know how important it is to spend class time letting children pick books to read."

- "Workbooks are intended to provide additional practice, not to teach. Too many teachers feel every page must be done no matter what. That's not true. Children who do well on the workbook pages usually already know the material. Children who don't, need to have it introduced orally first."

- "Teachers must realize that they can use their basal as a basic source, but it is also important that they enhance the program themselves."

A number of teachers sent a clear message to publishers that they'd like to be respected as professionals who may use basals but won't be ruled by them:

- "It's time we take advantage of our freedom to make choices. We should let publishers know the specific strengths and weaknesses of their programs."

- "The teachers' manual should be written to help teachers realize that they are the professionals and are the ones who should decide which pieces to use. Support like that would help us with paranoid administrators."

FIGURE 3.7 Who uses basals? (Turner, 1988, 64).

away from controlled-vocabulary basals and workbooks that break language down into separate skills. Some textbook publishers have taken up the whole language banner; they have begun to publish materials for teachers who are trying to build on what children already know and the ways in which they learn. Many publishers have also responded to the notion that reading can best be taught by providing children with real literature rather than controlled-vocabulary stories.

Some critics are unhappy with the new basals provided by the publishers, even though these include real literature. There are three reasons to be somewhat suspicious of these reading books:

1. Some reading books have "tampered" with the literature that they include in their series. They have abridged the story or made the language simpler.

2. Even when the literature is intact, the reading book is different from a "real" book. The "reader" is something you do as a school activity, not something you do for your own enjoyment. If we want children to see reading as something they do outside the classroom, if we want them to be lifelong readers of literature, then we should offer them real books.

3. Reading books often distort the reasons for reading, by providing ready-made reasons for reading a story other than students reading for their own meaning and their own purposes. A friend of mine is concerned that many teachers don't really know how to involve children in positive experiences with literature. He fears that teachers who make students answer factual questions on study guides, take tests over trivia, or write formulaic book reports may produce the first generation of children to hate *Charlotte's Web*.

Nonetheless many teachers find themselves in situations in which the basal is part of the materials supplied to their classrooms. Because publishers seem to be responding to the criticism of basal readers, they have updated many of the reading series to include a wide variety of literature by outstanding classic and contemporary writers, providing children with a good overview of literature. If in fact these basals include unchanged and unabridged literature, a teacher might want to use one. Used in conjunction with an individualized reading program, a basal reader allows teachers to provide whole class experiences with literature, which all the students can discuss in class. Because most pieces in basals are short, a number of brief sharing opportunities can expand children's sense of how to talk about literature and demonstrate the varieties of responses that different people can have to the same work.

■ **IDEAS TO LEARN**   Review a number of reading series with the following in mind. What seems to be the theory of how children learn to read? What apparatus is included with the series? (Introductions to the literature? Questions or exercises at the end of the pieces or the sections?) What sorts of language activities are children asked to engage in? What sorts of reading/ thinking skills are emphasized? Choose one of the series and describe how you might use it in your classroom.

The need, finally, is for a reading program that is based on children's reasons for reading. The thoughtful teacher will review all the materials available and develop ways to make reading significant to the students and to fully integrate it into the life of the classroom. Reading, then, is not an isolated subject taught during a particular period each day but occurs all day long. The goal of reading in the classroom is not to teach reading but to use reading in all the ways that people in the real world do: for pleasure; for understanding other times, people, and places; to reflect on one's own experience; to learn new things; and to extend one's knowledge as interest and expertise dictate.

Using Literature in the Integrated Language Classroom

Charles Reasoner (1975) has puzzled over teachers' notions that they have to *motivate* children to read "as if reading were a bitter pill to be swallowed" (10). Reasoner believes that all it takes for children and books to get together is a classroom where children have access to appropriate books. Children don't need outside stimuli to encourage their reading. "Children WANT to read. Children DO read. And children WILL READ without coercion or extrinsic rewards when the reading fare is *right*: the right material, for the right child, at the right time" (10). The important goal, then, is to make it possible for children to *have* the right reading material at the right time. Reasoner debunks the myths about individualized reading that often interfere with teachers' attempts to create an individualized program. It is not necessary, he says, to have a reading conference each day or spend a good deal of time chatting with children about their comprehension; nor are required textbooks and/or a required curriculum an insurmountable hurdle; nor is it impossible to evaluate and grade children in an individualized program. Reasoner provides a number of guidelines for an individualized program.

- Children need time to make selections; allow them to browse, choose a book, sample it, return it, choose another. Give them choices about when they read and the option to continue reading when they just can't put a book down.
- Let children choose where they read—at school, at home, on the playground, in a chair, on the floor, in small groups, alone. Give them opportunities to share with others while they are reading and after they are done.
- Give children options for *how* they share their reading comprehension with you. You can use conferences with children to diagnose their reading needs and provide help specific to the individual.

- Avoid public displays of what children have read. Charts and bulletin boards often lead children to read competitively, for quantity; they read quick and easy books or fake what they've read in order to build up their chart. Rather, have children use a simple form to keep track of everything they've read, in and out of school, which they share with you. From these records you can compile your own log of your students' reading.

- Set minimum expectations for individual students. You might set a minimum number of books to be read (though children choosing and reading for their own purposes will probably not need such minimums); have your students select two or three books to share with you so that you can gauge your students' comprehension.

- Evaluate your students by keeping all records and logs of their reading and responses on file. Instead of comparing children with one another, evaluate each student on the basis of his or her own reading and response logs and individual growth.

Nancie Atwell has written about her efforts to create a literate environment for her students. As a teacher Atwell had long been running a writing workshop in her class, in which she and her junior high students took time "to think, write, confer, write, read, write, change our minds, and write some more" (1985, 150). But she realized that there was a contradiction between what she did in her writing workshop and what she did in her reading course, a kind of "watered-down lit. crit. approach"—pass out the anthologies, introduce the vocabulary, lecture about genre or theme, assign the story or parts of the story, give a quiz on comprehension and vocabulary, conduct a whole-class post mortem, and sometimes assign an essay" (151). Atwell decided to extend the invitations of the writing workshop—time and responsibility—to her teaching of reading. Students would choose what they would read (usually fiction, autobiography, biography, or poetry) and the rate at which they read. In addition, she wanted to give them the opportunity to do what she and most of us do as readers—talk and think about what we read. To accommodate the large number of students, she established dialogue journals with these instructions: "This folder is a place for you and me to talk about books, reading, authors and writing. You're to write letters to me, and I'll write letters back to you. . . . In your letters, talk with me about what you've read. Tell me what you thought and felt and why. Tell me what you liked and didn't like and why. Tell me what these books meant to you and said to you. Ask me questions or for help. And write back to me about my ideas, feelings and questions" (152).

Atwell's hunch and hope—that written response and sharing would be more reflective and sustained than oral conferences and that students would make connections between what they wrote and what they read—turned out to be justified. Students who had not before been connected with books be-

The most dramatic change I have made as a teacher occurred in the last three years, in the area of reading.

In the past, my emphasis in reading was on reading skills. My fifth graders were divided into three groups based on a timed reading test I gave at the beginning of the year. I relied on workbooks which included endless pages on finding the main idea, selecting supporting details, determining the correct meaning of vocabulary words printed in boldfaced type; choosing an appropriate title from a list of four, and numbering sentences in the order in which they occurred in a given paragraph. My fifth graders filled in the blanks, guessed at multiple choice answers, and tried to make sense out of the sequencing exercises. I felt secure that at least I was teaching reading skills, the same skills that would show up on the reading achievement test at the end of the year.

But, were these children learning to read? Were they even learning isolated skills? I didn't know. What I did know for sure was that they hated reading workbooks, and I hated correcting them.

In those days I also gave my class a reading period for 20 to 30 minutes a day. Students had to have a book to read for the reading period. I often suggested or assigned books that I thought would be appropriate for their reading level—not their interest—their reading level based on the test at the beginning of the year. During the reading period I would see five or six students a day. They would come to my desk individually, and I would hear them read their books aloud, checking to make sure they could pronounce every word and teaching them to sound them out if they couldn't. If they didn't know the meaning of isolated words or couldn't pronounce some of the words, I suggested they return the book and get an easier one.

That was my reading program, and I worked hard at it. I wanted my students to become good readers which meant to me, at that time, that I wanted them to have high scores on the end-of-the-year reading test. Yet, despite my hard work, I heard from their parents, "Michael doesn't like to read," or "She doesn't read at all at home." And I observed my students during the reading period as I corrected their workbooks. They turned the pages of their books, but they looked out the window, sighed, whispered to each other, passed notes, and watched the clock. They did not like reading. In fact, the reading period was a chore for them.

Today my reading program is dramatically different and so are the results. Today my students read between 25 and 144 books a year. Children listen to each other and seek recommendations for their next book selections. They wonder about authors and look for feelings, for believable characters, for interesting words, and they are delighted with effective dialogue. And my students and I always talk books before school, during school, at lunch and after school, something we never did in my "workbook" days.

Test scores are gratifying, too. With this program that departs from the teaching of isolated skills, test results remained constant or showed gains of from two to six years in reading comprehension.

FIGURE 3.8 How one teacher changed her reading program (Five, 1988, 103–104).

came engaged with reading and writing, becoming what she calls "insiders." By allowing students to choose and respond to literature in individual ways, Atwell created a literate environment: "By literate environment I mean a place where people read, write, and talk about reading and writing; where everybody can be student and teacher; where everybody can come inside" (148).

Teacher Cora Lee Five (1988) describes how she changed her reading program from one based on the traditional workbook to one based on students' needs and interests, a program that gave the students "time, ownership and response" (105) (see Figure 3.8). Five replaced workbook pages with mini-lessons to help students while reading and writing to think about such things as "character development, setting, titles, flashbacks, and other techniques writers and readers need to know." (105) Five used mini-lessons to introduce different genres, often basing these lessons on the books she was reading aloud to the class. Other types of mini-lessons included:

- How to select a book. Students share information about how they choose a book, such as recommendations from friends, the title, information on the inside flaps or cover.

- What to do about a book that isn't "working." Students discuss how long they read before they abandon a book and what different people mean when they say a book is boring.

- What the value and meaning of copyright, publisher, and date are.

- Activities such as creating a time line for the life of a character, graphing the plot of a story, and so on.

As with Atwell the heart of Five's reading program is that students select their own books, read them, and respond both orally and in writing to what they have read. In addition, students may express their interpretations of literature through art, drama, and mapping. In this process Five felt that her students attempted "to search for greater depth in their reading if their responses [were] accepted and not treated as comprehension problems" (108).

Younger children should also have opportunities to choose literature, to respond on the basis of their own tastes and experiences, and to explore relationships in writing. In reaction to the limitations she perceived in basal readers for her first graders, Marcia Burchby established a reading program that used literature. In addition, Burchby emphasized the role of reading across the curriculum, with children at the center. "As children follow their interests, I attempt to integrate all aspects of language arts (as well as other subject matter) into the activities they are pursuing. Children are at the center: they share in the decision-making and bring their personal experiences, creativity, and interests to shape the curriculum. In all these ways, children are empowered, democratically empowered, to read. They use reading as a way to make sense of the world and to act within it" (1988, 118).

Acting on this theory, Burchby chose a theme, such as fairy tales, and organized a multitude of resources and plans, speakers, field trips, and projects. Her classroom resources include:

- Trade books, children's magazines, class-made and individually made books, reference books, tapes with books, poetry, joke and song books, photo albums with captions, shape books, and experience stories made by the children.

- Predictable reading materials for beginning readers—from a McDonald's logo and Cheerios box to songs, nursery rhymes, and children's literature.

Reading activities include:

- Read-aloud time by the teacher and/or ''other accomplished readers, sustained silent reading, small group reading, paired reading, browsing through magazines'' (119).
- For beginning readers, ''paired reading in which two children read together with big books which have enlarged print so that a number of children can see at once, with tape recorded and with shared book experiences in which an accomplished reader points to the word from the top as a beginning reader points from the bottom'' (119).

Children in Burchby's class also wrote freely on meaningful topics and without fear of mistakes. The writing process was modeled for them, and they gradually used it in their own writing, rewriting fairy tales to rework or extend the story or change the ending. Children also discussed the validity of what they read in literature and what they wrote, putting forth their own views on the ethical questions they encountered, such as whether it was right for Jack to steal from the giant. In addition, they created their own fairy tale games, newspapers, and museum.

Burchby also suggests ways to use literature to provide background for social studies or science lessons. ''A study of houses and structures coincides with the Fairy Tale theme in our room. Children construct houses of various materials (straw, sticks, bricks, clay, thatch, mud, fabric, and blocks) and examine the durability of those materials. We discuss the availability of housing materials in environments and cultures around the world and survey housing styles and materials in our own community. We create a gingerbread house, which is later talked and written about and happily eaten'' (122).

Teachers like Atwell, Five, and Burchby are alive and thriving throughout the country. They have discovered, not only through the exploration and development of language and learning theory but also through the revitalization of their classrooms, the joy and power of language and reading, when student and teacher together take control and make choices.

Struggling Readers

Learning to read is not a successful enterprise for all children. In your teaching you will encounter children who can't, won't, or don't read. Although you may have standardized test scores for your students that indicate at what ''grade level'' they are purported to read, you will probably know very little about what is actually going on with individual readers. Part of your responsibility, then, will be to discover whether children can't, won't, or don't read and how to help them become readers.

As I suggested earlier, some children have difficulties with reading because they try to follow the rules or procedures of well-meaning teachers. Children who try to rely solely on sound-letter correspondence to the exclusion of the other cueing systems—the meaning of the words, the grammar of the language, and the context in which they find the discourse—are doomed to failure. Exclusive use of graphophonic cues restricts children to a fragmented, letter-by-letter approach to creating sound (decoding print into speech) to get meaning. Frank Smith (1979) has shown that phonics rules are not consistent enough and short memory not sufficient to create meaning simply from sounding out. Word analysis and word attack approaches may create word callers who have difficulty understanding what they read because they are focusing on accurately reproducing words. Children will not learn to read fluently if they rely solely on sound-letter correspondences rather than also using their own knowledge of language and their own understanding of the world to sample the text and to predict, confirm, and create their meaning as they read.

Susan Church and Judith M. Newman (1985) provide a case study of Danny, who—they conclude—is an example of a student whose reading problem is "instructionally induced." They describe Danny as being "from an intact middle-class family, emotionally and socially well adjusted, of average intelligence" (170). Despite the fact that Danny "received special help from a learning-disabilities teacher, a reading teacher, many classroom teachers, as well as a university reading clinic," his reading level at the beginning of the ninth grade was a 2.6 on a standardized reading test (170).

In reviewing his school history, Church and Newman report that Danny was successful at the skills deemed necessary for learning to read. In grades primary, one, and two Danny scored in the 80s, 90s, and 100s in the vocabulary and word analysis sections of the end-of-the-unit skills test. But his teachers were concerned that he was not applying graphophonic information or other word attack skills in his reading. His second grade teacher retaught the final unit to improve his comprehension, which earned him a score of 100%. Church and Newman note:

> It is interesting to consider what Danny's test scores show us. The instruction Danny had been receiving and the evaluation of his progress were both based on an accuracy model; that is, his teachers emphasized word analysis (phonics) and word identification (skills) in their teaching. The end-of-unit test results confirm Danny was learning those subskills but what about his comprehension scores? According to a linear accuracy model if Danny can analyze words and identify them he should be comprehending. This he clearly was not doing. His teachers, mystified by his poor comprehension performance, were unable to see that his test scores were violating their reading instruction model. Rather

than questioning their model, however, they concluded Danny needed more practice with word analysis and word identification.

(Church and Newman, 1985, 171–172)

This pattern continued through Danny's elementary school years. In third grade Danny's vocabulary and word analysis scores were still high (90 and 92 percent) but his comprehension was lower (67 percent), and he was somewhat behind his age group. He was referred to the resource teacher for remedial help and changed to another basal series to provide different content while teaching the same skills. During third and fourth grade Danny's resource teacher worked with what she thought were "auditory and visual perceptual problems."

Because his reading comprehension did not improve (though his visual-perceptual performance did), he was referred to the reading teacher in fifth grade. Her diagnosis: "Suggest that perceptual deficits have affected reading growth. Recommend total remedial reading program including reteaching of basic skills beginning with blends and digraphs, and Dolch sight words." At the end of the year the reading teacher reported that Danny had mastered the Dolch words and that his phonic skills had improved, but that his reading was still "slow and laborious above the second grade level" (173). In sixth grade Danny was placed in yet another basal series. The reading consultant tested him at reading at the 2.8 grade level orally and the 4.5 level silently, meaning he was able to gain more meaning from reading when not required to reproduce orally what he read. Nonetheless the consultant recommended that "he be taught digraph 'th,' long/short vowels, then other vowels" (173). Referred to a university clinic in eighth grade, Danny spent a bit more attention on meaning, but there was still emphasis on decoding and word recognition. By ninth grade, "despite the great deal of instruction in phonics and word analysis, Danny now scored poorly on letter/word identification and word attack. His comprehension was similarly low" (174).

Church and Newman conclude that despite everyone's best efforts Danny failed to become a fluent reader. His teachers were concerned and tried numerous strategies to help Danny. "Their instruction wasn't haphazard: they provided individualized instruction; they did what they could so that learning to read wouldn't be frustrating for him; they tried to prepare him for reading by drilling the vocabulary he would encounter; they taught him word attack skills; they used controlled-vocabulary reading material. Both he and his teachers worked hard. Yet Danny seemed worse off in spite of all their efforts" (174). In fact Danny learned exactly what he was taught. The problem was that those processes are not the ones that create readers.

Danny's reading disability, then, did not come from a deficiency in him but in the inappropriate teaching that led him to try to read in ways that did not work. What other sorts of students struggle with reading, and what causes their struggle?

In their book on teaching learning disabled and remedial students to read and write, Lynn Rhodes and Curt Dudley-Marling point out the difficulties involved in labeling children and the confusion in the area of remedial and learning disabled identification. Students who don't succeed in reading and writing at the same rate as their peers may be labeled in any number of ways, as "learning disabled, dyslexic, underachievers, remedial readers, and the like." Rhodes and Dudley-Marling wondered, as teachers, "why some students were placed in remedial classes while others were placed in learning disabilities classes; their reading and writing performance seemed quite similar to us and, in fact, often resembled the performance of normally achieving younger students" (Rhodes and Dudley-Marling, 1988, 1).

Rhodes and Dudley-Marling try to shed some light on just what learning disabilities are and how those labels attempt to define the deficiencies that children have. To do that, they provide an official description of who may not be labeled as learning disabled, drawing on the official federal definition of learning disabilities from the *Federal Register* (1977): "The term does not include children who have learning problems which are primarily the result of visual, hearing, or motor handicaps, of mental retardation, of emotional disturbance, or of environmental, cultural, or economic disadvantage" (in Rhodes and Dudley-Marling, 1988, 3). Children in these categories may have learning disabilities, but they are considered learning disabled only if their problems cannot be "adequately explained by other handicaps or environmental influences" (3).

A recent definition proposed by the National Joint Committee on Learning Disabilities [reported in Rhodes and Dudley-Marley (4)], which has received the endorsement of many organizations concerned with the language development of children, defines the term *learning disability* as a generic one referring to a heterogeneous group of "disorders manifested by significant difficulties in the acquisition and use of listening, speaking, reading, writing, reasoning or mathematical abilities. These disorders are intrinsic to the individual and presumed to be central nervous system dysfunctions."

According to Rhodes and Dudley-Marling, one problem in identifying learning disabled children is the difficulty of separating intrinsic and extrinsic factors. "Many parents and professionals are frustrated by the apparent vagueness of most accepted definitions of learning disabilities. LD definitions have not been particularly useful for determining eligibility for LD services nor do they help teachers and parents decide what to do for a child instructionally" (4).

For the most part, learning disabilities are "identified in terms of a discrepancy between measures of ability, usually an IQ test, and measures of academic achievement." However, discrepancy measures often fail to "discriminate LD students from other underachievers, especially students who are placed in remedial classes. Researchers have shown that school psychologists and special education teachers aren't able to discriminate reliably between students in the lowest quartile of academic achievement and children identified as learning disabled. . . . Other studies indicate considerable overlap in the characteristics of LD students and underachievers . . . and even between LD and normally achieving students" (4–5).

Rhodes and Dudley-Marling conclude that "the available evidence indicates that the characteristics of learning disabled children and remedial learners are quite similar. Additionally, LD and remedial learners are likely to be served in similar programs, often using similar teaching methods" (10).

The work of Rhodes and Dudley-Marling and the research of Church and Newman both point to the problems of placing children who are struggling with reading into programs based on a skills-oriented, deficit model. Rhodes and Dudley-Marling see the deficit model as having "a devastating effect on the lives of many LD and remedial students," because it puts them through endless drills and meaningless practice, it constantly reminds students of their inadequacies, and it encourages passivity in students rather than helping them become responsible and active in their own learning (10). For children who are having difficulty with language, all these researchers recommend holistic approaches that "take a developmental view of children's reading and writing problems, focus on children's strengths and not children's weaknesses or deficits" (Rhodes and Dudley-Marling, 1988, 10). They support programs that "encourage children to actively integrate what they are learning into what they have already learned" (10).

Teachers of language are also concerned about how they can support students who are linguistically and culturally different. They are becoming aware that students from "different" backgrounds come to school with not only different language patterns but with different experiences and different strategies for learning. In their book *Children of Promise: Literate Activity in Linguistically and Culturally Diverse Classrooms*, Shirley Brice Heath and Leslie Mangiola explain that "all sociological groups have some unique ways of transmitting to their children background knowledge about the world and of asking their children to display what they know" (14). However, rather than seeing these children as being "at risk" or "different," teachers should see them as "offering classrooms 'expansions' of background knowledge and ways of using language" (17).

All students should discover in school "a range of ways of seeing, knowing, thinking, and being that . . . will be equally challenging to all students and teachers to imagine other possibilities, to take risks with learning, and transcend the boundaries of the immediacy of personal knowledge" (17).

Heath and Mangiola's instructional goals for teaching students who are culturally and linguistically different are based on a basic premise: "Across individual, as well as across cultures, the learner possesses a range of bodies of expertise, and it is on this expertise that learning from books and responding to texts and tests will build" (36).

Heath and Mangiola have a number of suggestions for ways that teachers can address differences in culture and language:

- Involve students in the assessment of their own language and learning. Here and elsewhere I suggest student self-assessment as a significant contribution to students' self-understanding. According to Heath and Mangiola, when students collect and analyze instances of their use of their own language and style of communication, they come to see themselves as "experts over their own communication abilities" (47). They become aware of the effectiveness of their communication by consciously being aware of and giving attention to it.

- View language as an object of study as well as an instrument. Teachers in the Heath-Mangiola study helped students see language as "central to accomplishing the tasks at hand" (34). Using audio tapes and field notes, students recorded their own language habits and those of their family, their community, and their classroom. The discussion and analysis of these data helped students begin "to see how language works as an instrument of social interaction" (34).

- Use cross-age tutoring with students who share a language and/or culture. Teachers in an interactive, cross-age tutoring project in California allowed Spanish-speaking tutors and tutees to "read and interact in the language they felt most comfortable using" (22). However, teachers found that over time students who started out reading and discussing books in Spanish eventually began to use English. An added bonus was that the tutors themselves gained confidence and participated more in class. In addition, it was found that "cross-age tutoring provides numerous authentic occasions for extensive and highly motivated student writing"(25). It also allowed teachers to become facilitators and provided "more time for individual consultation" with students (25).

- Make schooling equally "strange" for all students. Although Heath and Mangiola support ways to develop the skills for academic success for all students, their intention "is not to urge teachers to teach in special ways to students whose everyday cultural and linguistic habits differ from those of the classroom. Instead, we want to urge teachers to make schooling equally strange for all students and thus to expand the ways of thinking, knowing, and expressing knowledge of all students through incorporating many cultural tendencies'' (37).

Stephen Krashen (1982), an expert in second language acquisition, emphasizes language learning in which students *use* language, not just study it. He advocates a movement away from grammatical description that reflects a concern for *product* and that includes procedures for drilling to promote ''real communication in the classroom, helping students *understand* spoken and written input and participate in conversations.'' Using the three approaches for understanding how people learn language—second language acquisition theory, applied linguistics research, and ideas and intuitions of teachers and students—Krashen concludes that ''language acquisition does not require extensive use of conscious grammatical rules, and does not require tedious drill.'' Krashen recommends patience because real language acquisition takes time ''and speaking skills emerge significantly later than listening skills, even when conditions are perfect. The best methods are therefore those that supply 'comprehensible input' in low anxiety situations, containing messages that students really want to hear.'' Krashen counsels against a forced early production, recommending approaches that ''allow students to produce when they are 'ready,' recognizing that improvement comes from supplying communicative and comprehensible input, and not from forcing and correcting production'' (Krashen, 1982, 6–7).

Curtis W. Hayes and Robert Bahruth (1985) agree. As teachers in a small rural community near San Antonio, Texas, they worked with twenty-two migrant children from Mexican-American families who spent only part of the school year in the community. The children, ages ten to sixteen, spoke Spanish ''in the home, on the job, and on the playground. Most know little English. Their only exposure to English came from television, the radio, and from school. Their reading abilities were also limited: most were reading three or more years below grade level. Some were nonreaders'' (97). Hayes and Bahruth wanted to help these children develop their reading and writing skills simultaneously, to help them have success in school, and to lessen the risk of their dropping out in ninth grade.

Hayes and Bahruth's language immersion program tapped into the common experience of the students: ''This experience is at the heart of student interest and was more meaningful to our children than the material in texts'' (98). They began by engaging the students in projects, often art, that ''encouraged cooperation and involved just the slightest amount of reading and writing,'' activities that had no wrong answers and thus no threat of failure (98). They also read to the children daily and had students illustrate and retell their favorite stories. Students were encouraged to write in journals on topics of their own choice, which the teachers did not correct but simply responded to. "The dialogue journal also provided a reading lesson each day, a conversation between two readers who are also writers, each writing for the other and each reading what the other has written" (100). Concentrating primarily on fluency, Hayes and Bahruth did not see errors as a cause for alarm: "Children learning English as a second language will make errors, but as they become more proficient, as their production increases, as they read and write more, the number of errors will decrease" (102).

Dialogue journals provided a bridge for the kind of reading and writing children would be expected to do in school. Students began to collect ideas for objects and natural phenomena that they wanted to investigate, and language itself became a topic of investigation. Using a handbook of idioms, students explored the meanings of expressions that didn't make sense to them. Students "acted out each expression and wrote the meaning in their own words. Next, they illustrated the literal meaning and wrote the actual idiomatic meaning underneath the illustration" (103).

Hayes and Bahruth noted tremendous growth in their students over the year. Evaluations in April demonstrated growth from one to four grade levels, with most students advancing by three. Hayes and Bahruth conclude: "Our children now know they can learn; they have learned how to learn, and they are proud of their achievements" (107).

Textbooks for ESL students are also a problem. Like some of the language arts texts we have already described, ESL texts often trivialize language learning. Krashen worries that the "use of exercises, questions that test students on content and drill them on vocabulary used" may "ruin the pleasure of reading" and "encourage reading more for form and less for content." In addition, he states, "current readers simply do not provide enough." Students should have a wide range of topics about which they may choose to read. Finally texts contain materials for readers in which "each line, each paragraph, must count and introduce some new structure or vocabulary item" (Krashen, 1982, 183–184).

Krashen advocates that students be able to read material that they would choose to read in their first language for pleasure. "In doing pleasure reading, readers have the option of skipping whole sections they find either too difficult or less interesting. . . . They even have the option of putting the book or story down and selecting another after reading a few pages. They can skip words they do not understand, if they think they are following the main point, and they have the option, of course, of looking up every word, if that is their style" (164). Krashen believes that pleasure reading gives students what they need for the acquisition of language: It is comprehensible, it is interesting and relevant, it is not grammatically sequenced but based on real language, there is a good deal of it available, it does not create demands for performance (so students do not get defensive), and it provides tools for being able to engage in conversation, if the text includes dialogue (165).

Assessment in Reading

Establishing clear goals for your students' progress in reading is of course central to your ability to assess your students. The following are some criteria you might apply:

- The child likes to read.
- The child reads for pleasure.
- The child reads to answer questions and satisfy curiosity.
- The child reads outside of school.
- The child tells others about what he or she has read.
- The child responds to and forms ideas and opinions about what he or she has read.
- The child has strategies for creating meaning from reading that is difficult or new.
- The child reads a variety of materials (fiction, nonfiction, magazines, books).
- The child uses the library.

Remember that these are only *general* guidelines—you should apply them flexibly. For example, sometimes children get on reading jags and focus all their attention on one kind of reading—mysteries, joke books, nature books. They don't want to bother with other reading. That a child can be so absorbed in reading is probably a sign of strength rather than weakness. Moreover, a child who hasn't had significant access to a library can't be negatively judged for not knowing how to use one, and the teacher will look for other signs of involvement in reading.

Chapter 1 touches on some of the evaluation techniques for reading, which I will describe in more detail here. In her literature-based literacy program, Regie Routman (1988) values informal, ongoing procedures for assessing children's progress and cautions teachers against placing too much stock in standardized tests. "While standardized testing has its place in evaluation, we need to be sure that we do not overfocus on mechanical accuracy and detail. At best, standardized testing gives an individual's performance on a given day in a group situation and in comparison to other children. . . . It is important to use other means of evaluation which focus on meaningful communication in the language processes—listening, speaking, reading, and writing—and the individual's day to day progress. Such focus relies on careful teacher observation and teacher judgment and implies trust in teachers as professionals'' (204). Routman suggests a number of methods for evaluating individual progress that ''give the teacher specific information on individual instructional needs and growth'' (204). They include the following:

- Keep records of students' repetitions, substitutions, insertions, omissions, self-corrections, and so on as they read a teacher-provided text of one hundred to two hundred words; you can get a sense of your student's understanding of and engagement with what they are reading.

- Tape record students' oral reading throughout the year; this allows you, your students, and their parents to track reading progress.

- Ask students to respond orally—in general discussions and those specific to literature—to demonstrate what they know and understand.

- Keep records of what your students read, its level of difficulty, their ability to interpret and respond to it, and their appreciation of it.

- Hold conferences with your students to assess their ability to articulate their own growth; together analyze the students' progress and help them solve any problems they encounter.

Jan Turbill (1983) also suggests that teachers keep ongoing evaluation records. She includes the following, which are not time-consuming:

- ''In the head'' assessment may not be a record of a child's achievement but it is very significant to teachers' understanding of their students on the basis of conferences and observations throughout the school year. Some teachers, says Turbill, claim that they have all they need to know about their students in their heads. However, it is important to be able to document children's progress with parents and administrators.

- Anecdotal records can help you assess your students. Much of what you learn about students will be a result of your daily observations of them. Often your insights will happen in the midst of a busy activity and often they are fleeting glimpses. It is valuable to get these down in some sort of concrete form so that you can substantiate your impressions and see progress. I recommend using a three-ring binder in which you devote a page or two (or three or four as the year goes on) to each child in your class. The entries may be very short and you may make an entry for each child only once or twice a week. Note various behaviors that form a basis for your assessments of children's reading: ''Pat is reading another book that is a bit easy for him.'' ''Sarah is over-relying on phonics in reading; needs to use context cues.'' ''Dana is reading this book with more fluency; not so much word calling." Date the entries and look through your book weekly to note progression (and regression) and to make sure that you're making entries for all children. (Some kids seem to escape our notice more easily than others.) These records are particularly useful in substantiating your impressions about a child's work when you conference with parents.

Self-Assessment

Many teachers emphasize the value of self-assessment both as a way to get children to share the responsibility of record keeping and to make them aware of their own progress. From the beginning of the school year, have children keep a record of their own reading—both what they read and their responses to it. Among various other self-assessment records are:

- A list of all-time favorite books from preschool and previous ages.
- A list of favorite genres: mystery, science fiction, poetry, nature study, animal books, and so on.
- A list of the books the student reads with dates of completion (including a record of books started but not completed).
- A list of the books the student has written about or responded to.
- A record of successes and difficulties in reading. For example, have students keep records of a style or an aspect of a book (first person narration, dialogue, use of metaphors) that they've integrated into their own writing; of a complex book that they have been able to read to the end; of books that are too hard.
- A list of goals for future reading. These might include reading in a new genre; rereading a book enjoyed in the past; reading a certain number of books a week, and so on.

You might want to keep these records in file folders or expandable booklets. For example, students could use the front covers of file folders to list all the books they have read, the inside front covers to list all the books they have written about or responded to, the inside back covers to list reading successes and challenges, and the back covers to list goals for reading. Inside they could keep written responses to reading, letters exchanged with class members and the teacher, and so on.

The Reading Portfolio

The reading portfolio is a collection of students' work with commentary and interpretation by both students and teachers that gives teachers, parents, and administrators a detailed view of students' work that authentically charts their growth, their strong points, and the areas in which they are working. You will see references to the portfolio through this text, because as an assessment tool it is consistent with an integrated view of learning.

Elaine Parker emphasizes that the portfolio substitutes "for proficiency tests and more nearly resembles the process." She sees its value both as a diagnostic and a teaching tool. Among its teaching advantages is that it "postpones evaluation so that students are less frustrated in early stages of the class when they are less likely to succeed"; "allows the instructor to concentrate on process rather than product"; "develops a critical sense within the student toward his writing"; "allows instructors to tailor classes to the students' needs"; "allows readers to address specific problems or offer encouragement in response"; "provides multidimensional/multifaceted assessment"; "diagnoses specific problems or progress in students' writing skills" (unpublished broadside).

All the assessment tools mentioned here can be a part of the reading portfolio—the students' self-assessment records, teachers' checklists or observations of students' reading, informal miscue analyses. Lamme and Hysmith (1992) report on an assessment project at an elementary school in Florida that involved extensive use of portfolios to demonstrate the reading and writing progress of early elementary students (from prekindergartners to second graders). All teachers used the portfolio system but "specific strategies for doing so were left up to individual teachers. Three different types of information were gathered by most teachers" (630). These were "Collection and Analysis of Student Work (Artifacts)," which included "writing folders, reading response journals, dialogue journals, day books, projects, and writing notebooks" (630); "Student Reflection and Self-evaluation," which involved students choosing their best work and explaining why (632); and "Observations, Checklists and Scales," which included "observational data, checklist data, and interview or conference data" (634). For the most part, teachers involved in the assessment project found that the portfolios enabled them to learn much more about their students than before and focus on positive aspects of their growth. Moreover, they found that the observations, insights, and record keeping became easier as they learned what to look for. It was noted, however, that portfolio assessment—which involves conferences, observation, analysis of the students' work and their self-assessments—is labor-intensive. The payoff is that teachers have a much more precise picture of their students and of learning that can guide their practices in the classroom.

Controversies and Conflicts

It is probably clear to you from reading this chapter that there are conflicts and differences of opinion about the best way to teach children to read. Tradition runs deep in schools and practices are slow to change, even as new research and knowledge becomes available about how children learn. The attempt in this chapter and throughout the book is to provide you with current understanding in children's literacy development (and the resources to extend and deepen your understanding), but you will need to form your own hypotheses and do your own classroom experiments to discover how to create a language program that is based on your students' interests and needs and their natural ability to learn. As a teacher you may work in a school district whose objectives for reading are separate from objectives for writing and where none exist for speaking and listening; the curriculum may be a list of skills that children are to be taught at each grade level; or the curriculum may be a textbook that consists of a hodgepodge of phonics drills, word attack activities, grammar exercises, bits and pieces of reading and/or "literature," and questions that ask children to draw conclusions. Children may take standardized tests to see at what grade level they read or what their language ability is.

Moreover, your administrators and colleagues may be committed to a particular curriculum and/or a particular textbook. They may believe that test scores represent some absolute reality rather than simply providing a sense of who is testwise or who has lots of experience with a certain kind of task.

Often when new teachers begin teaching they are pooh-poohed for their idealism. But as Stephen Judy (Tchudi) says in the *ABCs of Literacy*, having an ideal is what allows you to create a master plan. You need to know what *ought to be* in order to *approximate* it. Even though your theory may not have been tested by years of classroom encounters, it can provide the starting point for experiments and explorations.

■ **IDEAS TO LEARN**   Articulate your theory of how people learn to read and how reading is connected to listening, speaking, and writing. To develop your theory, you may wish to recall your own background, interview others about their experiences and observe readers reading and talking about their reading. You may choose to read more from the works cited in this chapter (other works of interest include Cullinan, 1987; Gates, 1983; K. Goodman, Shannon, Freeman, and Murphy, 1987; and Lehr, 1983). Take every opportunity to learn from your students about how they manage and master the process of reading.

If you are a new teacher and have not had the opportunity to build up a lot of materials, or to develop a highly complex reading theory, or to try various approaches, you will probably need to begin to experiment slowly. Most likely you will be given a set of materials, perhaps (but probably not) a copy of the curriculum guide, and more likely, advice from experienced teachers. Some of this advice will be useful and some not. You will have to judge on the basis of your own knowledge, intellect, and experience. You may be tempted to rely on the materials or the practices of those around you to define your teaching. But do begin to experiment in your teaching and to learn from your students about how best to reach them. You can use the following ideas in conjunction with published teaching materials as a starting place for developing your own program.

- Set aside some time every day for students to read what they choose to read.
- Set aside time to talk about what you are reading and what your students are reading outside of school.
- Have students write every day and spend time sharing their writing. Allow them to read, publish, and display what they've written.
- After reading a story in the basal (if you must use it), have students talk about their thoughts and feelings (or write about them) rather than answering the questions at the end of the chapter.
- Allow students to pick and choose pieces to read from the basal rather than reading them all together in the same order.
- Check with your administrator to see if you are required to use the basal. If not, begin gathering and using materials to supplement (and perhaps eventually) replace it.
- Instead of teaching a section on phonics, have students write individual stories or do class experience stories using the "rules" being taught. For example, if students are learning about the *sh-* sound, have them write a story about "the sheep who shared a shopping cart" or other stories using phonics rules. Have them share with the class.
- Chat about your responses to books, telling what you liked best and the ways in which the author achieved his or her effects. Encourage children to do the same.
- Instead of doing a workbook task on homonyms have children play homonym games. (Remember the "Teakettle" game mentioned earlier. Example: The "teakettle" was running so fast, I almost fell off; I'm really "teakettle" from yelling so much at the game. Answer: horse and hoarse.) There are many many language games that raise children's consciousness about how language functions.

- Find ways to enrich your classroom library with diverse and interesting reading resources. Visit garage sales and used books sales (often organized by libraries or service organizations), ask whether parents have books and magazines they would like to donate to the classroom, have kids run candy sales to raise money to buy books, draw on the services of the librarian or media specialist (who is often willing to bring in a cart filled with books on a particular topic or present a talk about books that have appealed to your students' age group), and of course bring in books from the public library.

These suggestions are meant to help you begin to enrich your classroom and engage your students. If you are new to teaching, you might feel you have to rely on basals and workbooks for various reasons: they may be required; everyone else may use them; they provide a sense of security and accountability (you can say to parents and administrators that you taught specific skills); they provide ready-made assignments so you don't have to create a program on your own. However, as you develop an understanding of how children learn language by watching children at work, and as you gauge their involvement and satisfaction in their tasks, you and your students will soon be charting your own course.

4

Putting Language on Paper

by Linda Dinan

Early Writing Development

My husband almost always carries a ballpoint pen in the breast pocket of his shirt. When our daughter Lindsay was six months old, she would remove the pen from his pocket and use it for teething. By the time she was a year old, however, she *knew* what to do with the pen. Just as she headed for the front door after grabbing my keys or ran for the broom when something was spilled, she understood the function of *this* tool—and demanded paper for it. She knew what a pen was for—making your mark on the world. Children entering school possess similar confidence that they know how to write. ''They want to write the first day they attend school. This is no accident. Before they went to school they marked up walls, pavements, newspapers with crayons, chalk, pens, or pencils . . . anything that made a mark. The child's marks say 'I am' '' (Graves, 1983, 3).

What Preschoolers Understand About Writing

Careful observation of preschool children provides insight as to what children understand about written language and what they need to do it. For example, researchers Harste, Woodward, and Burke note that young writers

128

begin very early to make distinctions about the writing process, even including which tools are appropriate to correctly produce a written message.

> If a three-year-old is given a pen and asked to write without first engaging in drawing, about 25 percent of all three-year-olds will draw rather than doing what is asked, which is to write. If the contract is clarified by asking what the three-year-old expects, almost all children will make the distinction wanted. We say "almost all" because Joan Chubb, a research assistant on our project, found that if a three-year-old is given a pen, as opposed to a crayon, and asked to write, the confusion is reduced. Children at three know that usually pens are used for writing and crayons for drawing. In fact, when Joan asked one of her three-year-olds to write with a crayon, her young sophisticate said, quite matter-of-factly, "No. I need a pen."
>
> (Harste, Woodward, and Burke, 1984, 34)

By the time children enter elementary school, they have already begun to refine numerous hypotheses about written language. Among these is an effort to control what their writing should *look* like. After a period of random scribbling, most children's writing begins to develop a recognizable pattern. If encouraged and given the opportunity to observe adult writers, most preschoolers will write in a linear scribble that is faintly reminiscent of the writing that they've observed in their world. For example, in Figure 4.1 showing a sample of a three-year-old's writing, it's obvious that the child understands the left-to-right linear orientation that is characteristic of writing in English.

Preschoolers also refine their understanding of how writing is employed for communication. Initially, young writers expect the adult readers in their lives to provide the meaning for what is written on paper, from storybooks and newspaper comics to cards and notes from grandparents. When small children want their own "writing" to be read, they get the adults in their lives to do so.

Three-year-old Caroline, for example, clearly understands how written communication works, as the following incident demonstrates. Bringing her scribbles to an adult, she asked, "What does this say?" The adult "reader" playfully began to "read" the story of The Three Bears from Caroline's scribbles. Stopping abruptly after the hot porridge is on the table, the reader handed the piece back to Caroline, who grabbed her pencil and diligently began to add to the story, demonstrating that she knew the writer has responsibilities to put marks on paper. After returning the expanded version to her reader, she listened with great interest as the adult read through several more events, again stopping abruptly before the story was finished. Caroline immediately grabbed her story and added more. This continued until Caroline was satisfied that the whole story was told.

Preschoolers like Caroline recognize that written language contains messages, but the youngsters are still confused about who is responsible for

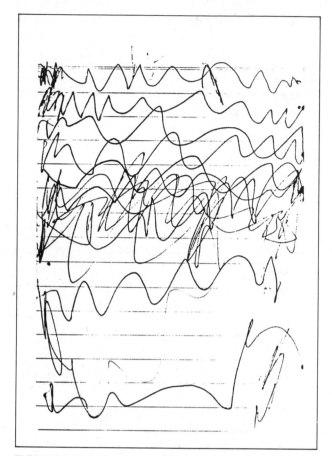

FIGURE 4.1 A three-year-old's writing.

creating the meaning of the messages. They often assume that the reader has the power to make sense of *any* scribble made by a fellow human. But as they experience print more frequently, they begin to refine their understanding of how the writer must make meaning for the reader.

Fledgling Writers and the Alphabet

As children become familiar with the alphabet and can identify specific letters, they begin to understand how these symbols are used for communication. Initially children overgeneralize their understanding of how the alphabet makes meaning. At three-and-a-half, my daughter Lindsay knew that her name and my name begin with the letter L, so when our family stopped at a Lum's restaurant, she exclaimed, "Our name is on the sign, Mom!" Although she recognized that letters contributed to messages, she was yet unaware that the twenty-six letters of the alphabet are used over and over in an endless combination of meaningful communications.

Often coinciding with their entrance in school, children begin to recognize and label specific *signs* (alphabetic letters) used in written messages. Four- to six-year-olds will "write" using any letters that they know, especially those found in their own names.

Many of the sound-symbol relationships of the alphabet readily support these initial attempts. Repeating the desired sound until they hear the name of a letter such as "/K/-/K/-K" works for many letters (i.e., B, D, F, G, J). It's clear that young writers are using this spelling system when a sound such as /w/ is written with a Y, because of the obvious similarities in the letter name Y and the phoneme /w/. The invented spellings of fledgling writers often demonstrate these obvious letter-phoneme connections. Children make other connections between sounds and letters because many sounds that are different from one another are created by similar alignment of the tongue and mouth. For example, beginning writers will often encode /TR/ with a J. The similarities in mouth and tongue placement for these phonemes make this substitution an obvious one. Although not "taught," these developmental patterns are remarkably universal in young children's writing (Read, 1975; C. Chomsky, 1971; Bissex, 1980).

Because of the close and logical sound-symbol connections seen in early writing, experienced readers like teachers and parents have little difficulty constructing its meaning. The surprise and delight in the faces of young writers when they hear someone "read" their intended message accurately confirms the significance of this step in writing development. As with speaking skills, adults who are accepting and encouraging play an important role in young children's acquisition of writing skills. As responders we listen or look for the meaning within the message and celebrate the child's approximations, which will gradually develop more and more accuracy.

Fledgling Writers and Space Constraints

Fledgling writers occasionally start their writing on the right side of the paper. With no room available to write left to right, to fit the letters, they simply reverse their direction and begin to write from right to left rather than left to right. This often alarms their caregivers, but unless it is accompanied by other unusual behavior related to writing, the adults should consider it a sensible solution to a space problem.

Children usually begin to try to place space between words in kindergarten and first grade. Marie M. Clay (1975) notes that "this difficulty is often more than just a problem of motor co-ordination. It is a complex mixture of knowing the word segments in the language statement, of knowing the function of the space in the written code, and having the skill and coordination to produce the appropriate spatial record" (55). When children attempt to reread what they have written, they quickly become aware of the need for some type of division between words. Teachers often suggest using a "finger space" between words, but some children choose to use dots or dashes to indicate where one word ends and another begins.

For many six- and seven-year-olds these space markers are retained in their writing for several months; for others the dots or dashes disappear within days in favor of white space. Still others develop very sophisticated spelling and punctuation skills before they regularly use space to indicate word boundaries.

Teachers will also notice a difference in what children can successfully manage in controlled writing situations and what they do when they write on their own. Clay (1975) reports that "while the idea of space is becoming established, copied stories are likely to include space and creative stories are likely to omit it. *It is as if the attention can be given either to the visual and spatial aspects of the product or to the language aspects but not to both*" (54). Similar patterns of behavior occur in other areas of writing as children increase their fluency. They can demonstrate knowledge of punctuation, capitalization, spacing, or paragraphing in something copied from the board or a book but show little or no evidence of any of those skills in their independent writing. This gap between abstract and operational knowledge occurs in other areas of learning when new information is introduced—but it is especially evident in the development of writing abilities.

Support for Fledgling Writers

In writing classrooms it is crucial that teachers support their students' efforts to write. Given the fact that sometimes writing can even overwhelm adults, teachers must remember that the challenge for children—who may be uncomfortable holding a pen or pencil, unsure of letter formations, and undecided about their message—can be especially daunting. Despite these challenges, kindergarten and first grade writers whose teachers support and recognize the children's approximations—who focus on what students *can* do rather than what they can't—become fluent, confident writers in a very short period.

Developmental Patterns in Early Writing

When children first put words on paper, the pictures that accompany the writing contain most of the meaning. The written words are almost incidental, and teachers will often need to encourage fledgling writers to add a letter or label to these early creations. Teachers can say, "Can you write something about this picture?" or "What have you decided to write about this picture?"

When children do start writing, most select a consonant or two that they can distinguish in the words they want to write. For example, "I am raking the lawn" may appear as a glorious fall picture of a child and his or her rake and the letter K. Later in children's development, they'll use one consonant for each word; later still they'll use consonants for each syllable. As children begin to understand *wordness*, they begin to use initial and final consonants and blends. Finally, just before they learn to spell, young writers include medial consonants and short vowels.

You can easily document the stages of a child's early writing development by collecting samples of writing done by the child over time. Another informative procedure is to periodically ask children to write down the words to a poem or nursery rhyme they know by heart. The advantage here is that you already know what the children's message is. Figure 4.2 shows a young writer's development by displaying his efforts to write "Humpty Dumpty" at different points during his first grade year. Progressive samples like these help you document, for parents and children, how a child's control of space and symbols has matured. Since the message stays the same in each attempt, even first graders can see how their writing has changed. This type of assessment obviously does not reflect the possible content and meaning that a child could produce, so you can't use it to provide a complete picture of a child's writing progress.

Risk Taking

If first graders are allowed to "think-spell" or "sound it out," most of them can communicate in writing. Most first graders who ask for you to spell a word will be satisfied if you say something like, "I will say it slowly for you, and then you write down what you hear." Some children, of course, are more hesitant than others. Their previous experiences with writing and their unique personality traits will determine their willingness to take risks.

Children who want everything to be "perfect" will need extra support as they set off on their own. Judith Schickedanz (1990) has noted that some early readers are uncomfortable using approximations of correct spellings, and they won't be happy until they get the spelling right. She maintains that "inventive spellers are not taking risks; they think they are spelling words *right*. The reluctant child knows more, and digs in his heels" (105). Schickedanz's son lost confidence in his own spelling ability early in his first grade career, and he depended on a mini-dictionary for a few weeks until he rebuilt his independence.

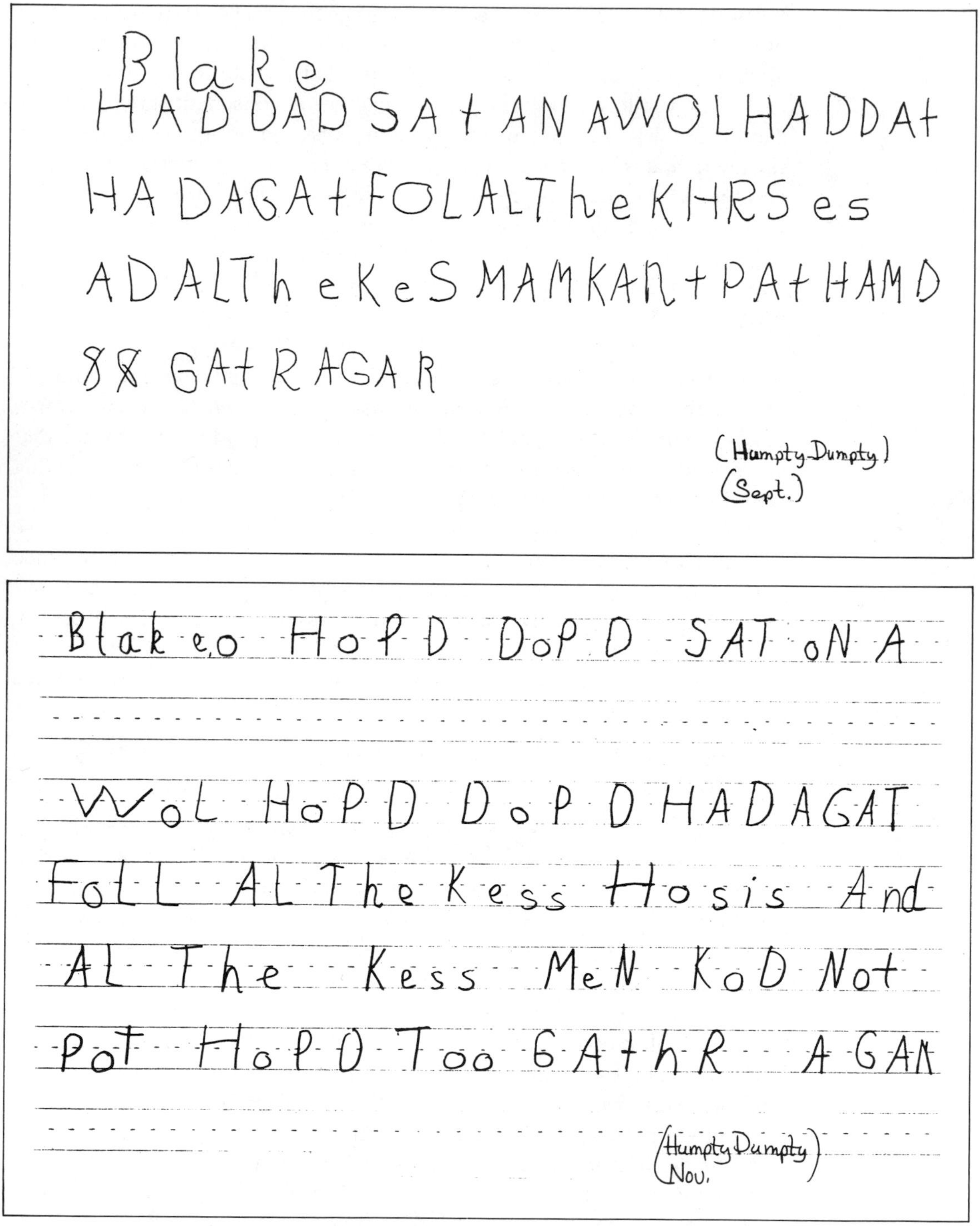

Blake
HAD DAD SAt AN AWOLHADDAt
HA DAGAt FOLALThe KHRS es
ADALThe KeS MAMKARt PAt HAMD
8𝓧 GAtRAGAR

(Humpty-Dumpty)
(Sept.)

Blake o HoPD DoPD SAT oN A

WoL HoPD DoPD HADAGAT
FoLL ALThe Kess Hosis And
AL The Kess MeN KoD Not
Pot HoPD Too 6AthR AGAN

(Humpty Dumpty)
Nov.

FIGURE 4.2 The "Humpty Dumpty" rhyme written by a first grader at different points in the school year.

Blake

Hump   de   dump   de

sat   on   a   woll.   Humpde

dumpde had   a   grat   foll.

Oll   the   kegs   horsis   and.

Oll   the   kegs   men.

Kod not put   humpde   to

gethr   a   gen.   (Humpty Dumpty) Feb.

FIGURE 4.2 *continued*

For most beginning writers who are given dictionaries, however, the message is, "I don't believe you can do this on your own." Consequently children spend too much of their writing time waiting for someone to give them the correct spelling of a word. Save dictionaries for the editing process, when they can be a real help, rather than encouraging them in the earlier stages of writing, when they can be a hindrance. Although we teachers must be sensitive to the needs of each individual young writer, we should always remember that our goal is to support children's independence in writing and their ownership of the writing process as soon as possible.

Teachers often find it difficult to support risk taking in writing because "every false start, every misguided hypothesis, every mispronunciation or misspelling, every incoherent thought . . . is available for analysis for both the language user and any would-be language teacher in the immediate environs" (Harste, Woodward, Burke, 1984, 134). Teachers and parents must respond to children's written approximations the same way they respond to children's first words, with praise and encouragement. It is decidedly unhelpful to demand error-free writing, which would be tantamount to forbidding a baby to speak until he or she mastered all the elements of correct speech. Nevertheless, when it comes to teaching children to write, many teachers and parents find fault rather than something to celebrate. We must remember, instead, to acknowledge children's meaningful approximations, just as we do for fledgling speakers. We must not discourage young writers by denying their efforts and their risk taking. ''Show us a safe writer and we'll show you someone who doesn't write much, often, or well (English teachers are prime but sensitive examples). By not rooting curriculum in the functional strategies which successful writers use, we convince children to abandon their more functional approach and lament the results, compliment them on writing achievements which do not merit comment, and fail to appreciate that what they have learned to orchestrate are our demands and not the process'' (Harste, Woodward, Burke, 141).

Changes in the Emphasis on Writing in Elementary School

Thanks in part to close observation and documentation of the behaviors and attitudes of young writers in actual classrooms, writing rather than penmanship has become part of the daily elementary program during the last fifteen years with an energy and prominence it previously did not possess. The evidence is widespread: elementary language arts textbooks are finally beginning to devote a large percentage of their pages to writing; undergraduate and graduate writing courses have appeared in college catalogues; conferences and workshops on writing are filled to capacity; and the number of national writing centers has increased steadily. Although the new emphasis on writing is a breakthrough to some, it is interesting to note that this ''new'' way of looking at writing instruction has been discussed for years by numerous experts. In a retrospective issue of the elementary journal of the National Council of Teachers of English (1983), Julie Jensen collected articles from the past seventy years that offer us insight and inspiration that are appropriate today.

> *1925*
> They have vivisected a living, vital, throbbing beautiful English and the parts have become dead—spelling, writing, composition—each separate, lifeless, unused. We poke them up and turn them over with a little drill and contemplate them sadly—they are so dead—and we keep each in his cell—the dimensions vary—ten, fifteen, possibly twenty minutes. . . . I observe a little child who is the victim of this senseless division of subjects. He talks and writes about a cat—not his own cat, because a classifier split child interests into ''subject matter and method'' and after the division of the two the child and his own cat can't get together in the classroom, but cats in general—cats—just cats. I do not

need to tell you the process but as a result of it he yields up his prosaic tale—he is getting to be a classifier.

"There are very many cats. Some cats are black."

Very good—capitals correct, periods in. Very commendable—but the composition is as dead as the cats, and the teacher was the proof-reader who put in most of the periods. She does not have time to breathe life into either the cats or the composition because she must swiftly turn to the Standardized Spelling list. . .

I observe another classroom. A little girl has a new kitty. What does it mean to have a new kitty!—wonderful experience! She wants to talk about it—to tell how soft and cunning it is. Others have kittens too and each wants you to see just how his kitten looks and each will try to help you see it—some on the board. One little girl writes—you help her spell the words she needs and show her how to make the hard letters—"My little kitten is as dark as a cloud in summer when it rains."

She knows that you can see her kitten better because she wrote it. And she writes it to take home to Mother, and in doing this she writes "dark" several times to "get it nice." And she learns to write and to spell it and it is entirely possible for her to do it with her head up and feet flat. She has something to say—and what child does not!—and says it naturally, happily, carefully. Every day she has something to say if permitted to say it. She will cover the standard list—we will risk a checking.

Ethel Salisbury
Los Angeles City Schools (15–16)

1933
We train children to write in the lower grades, these three-sentence stories we thrust upon them as models. "I have a cat. He is black. I like my cat." This is sheer inanity—and children are not naturally inane, whatever else they may be. Nor is it the children who are at fault; it is ourselves. We seem to argue that because children have small hands, they must write small stories. Give the children a chance to tell their stories in their own fashion, real, or imaginary, and then get set for a long-winded, far-ranging chronicle of epic proportions, grandiose, hugeous, magniloquent.

Walter Barnes
President, NCTE (8)

1953
It ought to be unnecessary to say that writing is learned by writing; unfortunately there is need. Again and again teachers or schools are accused of failing to teach students to write decent English, and again and again investigations show that students have been taught about punctuation, the functions of a paragraph, parts of speech, selection of "vivid" words, spelling—that the students have done everything but the writing of many complete papers. . . .

. . . Only by writing themselves can the young people in our classes learn the seriousness of putting words down on paper where all may see. What they write needs to be written for their classmates. These classmates need to listen, to question, to challenge.

Lou LaBrant
New York University (72–73)

1978

The most serious problem facing the language arts curriculum today is an imbalance between means and ends—an imbalance between too much attention to drill on the component skills of language and literacy and too little attention to their significant use. . . .

. . . Only linguists have language as their subject matter. For the rest of us—especially children—language is learned not because we want to talk or read or write about language, but because we want to talk and read and write about the world.

Courtney B. Cazden
Harvard University (121–122)

The recent enthusiasm for including more writing in the classroom has not come from an expert's new theory or from a publisher's new package but instead from careful observations of what children can do. A unique part of this reenergized thrust comes from the writing done by classroom teachers themselves as they have found their voices along with their students and have begun to share their own stories of how writing has become part of their classrooms. Perhaps the addition of these authentic and passionate voices will bring a permanent change to the instruction of language arts in our schools.

Critical Components in Learning to Write

Despite the voices recorded in the retrospective journal just mentioned, many elementary teachers have had limited personal experience with the writing process in their own education. Consequently they may operate with a limited view of writing "as an act of retrieving a fixed body of information and putting it into correct form to meet the requirements of the teacher and the institution" (Ritchie, 1989, 159). This vision is *not* supported by recent research on writing and is a view that will *not* support a successful writing classroom. Understanding writing and the needs of writers demands a new approach that includes all the elements of successful language learning.

New Zealand educator Brian Cambourne (1988) lists the following as critical components of successful literacy learning:

- **Immersion**—Children must see that reading, writing, listening, and speaking are important in their world.

- **Demonstration**—Children must have literacy modeled for them and must be motivated to do the same.

- **Expectation**—Children must interact with proficient language users who *expect* that the children will learn literacy skills.

- **Responsibility**—Children "need to make their own decisions about when, how and what 'bits' to learn in any learning task" (33).

- **Use**—Children learn how to listen, speak, read, and write by listening, speaking, reading, and writing—not by practicing parts of these wholes.

- **Approximations**—Children must feel that they will not be penalized for attempting to use whatever knowledge they possess, even though it's limited or incomplete.

- **Response**—In order to refine their learning, children must have authentic and timely responses to their approximations.

The writing workshop that I describe later in this chapter includes all of the components for successful literacy learning.

As a result of being invited into the world of literacy as described above, young writers view themselves in a new light—as learners who are independent, active, and eager rather than dependent, inactive, and passive.

> The classroom, as seen here, can open for students a process of "becoming" which ultimately prepares them for more than the narrow vocation of academic life. It encourages them to be more than pliant members of a community, more than bureaucrats who can use the required conventions with ease, or people who can "recite by heart" what teachers and others want to hear. It allows students to gain a sense of the personal, social, and political relationships from which all our words arise and of the new idioms that are likely to be born as we appropriate those words to our own purposes. It educates people who can participate in a constant evolution of personal and communal meaning and who will not be easily silenced.
>
> (Ritchie, 1989, 173)

The Writing Process

Understanding the complexities of writing is critical to implementing a successful writing program at any level. Writing teachers must simultaneously pay attention to the chronological dimension of the process (prewriting, drafting, revising, editing) and its messy, looping-back-on-itself nature. Many

Other writers have chosen other labels to describe the processes involved in composing. The chart below compares three such models.

Murray (1987)	State of Michigan (1983)	Flower & Hayes (1981)
Collecting Focusing Ordering	Prewriting	Planning
Developing	Drafting	Translating
Clarifying	Revising/editing	Reviewing

FIGURE 4.3 Models of the writing process.

writers and language theorists have devised models of the writing process that focus not only on the *product* but also on the *process*.

Among the most common divisions of the process are *prewriting, writing, revising, editing* (or *proofreading*), and *publishing*. This model reflects our understanding that writing projects take place over a period of time, usually beginning with an assignment of some kind and ending with a finished product, usually in response to a deadline. Writing teachers must call attention to the stages of writing by using techniques such as establishing a series of deadlines for each stage, requiring that students "finish" a minimum number of pieces, asking students to be responsible for accomplishing a certain amount of work in a certain amount of time, or requiring them to keep records of their progress in a writing project.

One danger of presenting writing stages linearly is that it implies that each stage occurs one after the other. But in most writing, the steps intermingle until the writer produces a satisfactory piece. A writer may begin a draft, stop, go back to prewriting, stop, revise or edit, stop, then draft some more. Writing is *recursive*, constantly cycling through the different stages.

Other writers have chosen other labels to describe the writing process. See Figure 4.3 for a comparison of three models. Each of the models in the figure describes a three-stage process—prewriting, writing, and postwriting. Flower and Hayes (1981) introduce the term *monitoring* into their model, which occurs across all three stages and incorporates the notion of recursiveness. Even the very youngest writers are seen to stop, reread, insert a missing word or punctuation mark, pause, reflect, and then continue to write.

Writing is an idiosyncratic activity. All writers adjust the process to fit their needs as writers and to fit the needs of the writing situation. For some writers, prewriting is completely internal; other writers labor over "clusters"; some make outlines before they write, others after the piece is done. Teachers sensitive to these preferences do not demand that every writer follow the same procedure. Instead they give their students a wide repertoire of strategies from which to choose.

As writers mature, their approaches to the various stages of the writing process change as well. The chart in Figure 4.4 describes some of the developmental changes that may appear as writers develop. As with all other human development, changes do not occur at the same age for all writers, nor does having sophisticated revising skills mean that a student's editing skills will be equally developed.

The Writing Workshop

"A successful unit of instruction can be seen as a dance between two types of classes: presentation classes, where the teacher charts the direction of learning, and workshop classes, where students have more control over their learning" (Marzano, 1992, 159). To teach writing effectively teachers must combine both *presentation* and *workshop* in their classrooms. Most of you are familiar with presentation, which you can use to model the writing process. For instance, you and your students can use the overhead projector or large chart paper to create community stories or reports. You can model how to select a topic, how to revise, and how to edit.

However, many of you may not be familiar with the workshop, so we'll provide a detailed description. (In addition to its use in writing instruction, the workshop model can be applied in other curriculum areas, such as math, science, and art.) Workshop classes usually include a mini-lesson, an activity period, and a sharing period (see Figure 4.5).

Mini-Lessons

Five- to ten-minute *mini lessons* should meet the needs of the students and teacher in a particular writing community. The mini-lessons cover all aspects of writing, using literature or writing done by students in the classroom. During the first few weeks of a writing workshop, your mini-lessons should probably focus on management issues, such as what to do with materials and how to ask peers or the teacher for assistance.

Other opportunities for mini-lessons come from observing students in the classroom, both their needs and their triumphs. Some of the best

Pre-writing

Beginning (K-2)	Developing (3-5)	Maturing (6-8)	Mature (9-12)
often draws first	beginning awareness of audience	consider purpose & audience	have clearer vision of purpose & audience
not concerned about audience	benefit from small group work	formally explore topics	more self-directed in selecting appropriate pre-writing activities
enjoy sharing	like to try out ideas before committing to paper	study works of other authors	more time on pre-writing
little pre-planning		more time for pre-writing	
need reading and vicarious experiences			

Drafting

produce single draft	internalized some of the mechanics of writing	consider topics more fully	manipulate sentence structure and vocabulary to affect tone
fatigue interrupts flow of ideas	select language more consciously	more able to organize ideas	begin to develop own style
conclusions abrupt	sense need for revision while drafting	more clearly delineate form, audience, and purpose	able to write for a variety of purposes & audiences
assume audience understanding	easily discouraged		
confident if correctness is not overemphasized			

Revising

view revision as unnecessary	begin to recognize needs of readers	revise for many reasons	feel responsibility to their audience as well as to themselves and the ideas they are trying to express
see revising as recopying or as adding on	begin to consider what is said & how it is said	accept suggestions	
need help in re-seeing their ideas	revise with encouragement	extensive revisions can cover tone, style, & organization	seek help from peers & teachers
	revisions tend to be piecemeal		

Proofreading/Editing

overlook mechanical errors	become aware of correct standards	see significance of correctness in form	anxious to present their work in its best form
need help in accepting their efforts	need help in searching their writing for selected types of errors	need help in accepting responsibility for errors	use a variety of resources to help them determine correct forms
		use resources to help them determine appropriate form	

FIGURE 4.4 The developmental nature of the writing process (Michigan Board of Education, 1985).

Publishing

motivated by published stories	take special efforts in revision & proofreading in order to publish their work for class or community	need opportunities to bring writing to polished form	try to correct all errors
find it difficult to read own work when invented spelling is transferred to standard orthography	need help, encouragement, & recognition	begin to identify their own audiences	seek wider audiences for their work need help in locating and selecting publishing opportunities

FIGURE 4.4 *continued*

A Workshop Class

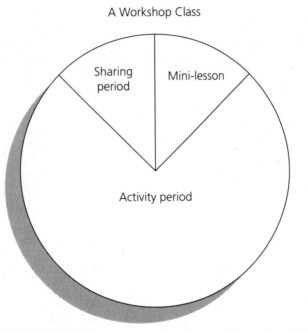

FIGURE 4.5 The components of a workshop class (Marzano, 1992, 163).

mini-lessons are those conducted by the students themselves, as they demonstrate how they wrote a captivating lead, substituted a powerful verb, included vivid details, or successfully punctuated a complex piece of language. You might ask a second grader to talk about how he figured out how to spell a difficult word or a sixth grader about how she used an appositive correctly.

There is nothing sacred about having mini-lessons at the beginning of the workshop. Some teachers combine a mini-lesson with sharing time or stop in the middle of the activity period for an emergency mini-lesson when it is obvious that numerous students are struggling with the same problem.

Another option is to hold mini-lessons during reading-related activities rather than the writing workshop. While reading a favorite author, you can point out word choices, story structure, and other language-related issues. In an integrated curriculum, reading and writing are woven together. When the class is discussing a reading selection, they are also discussing writing. These relationships should be part of all language arts instruction.

The mini-lesson overview in Figure 4.6 is based on a similar form devised by fifth/sixth grade teacher Jan Craven.

Mini-Lesson Record Sheet

The following is an overview of possible mini-lessons. Teachers must determine by observation what information might be helpful to students at a particular point in time. The Source columns record which piece of literature or which student's work was used as part of the lesson.

Writing Workshop Procedures	Source Date	Source Date	Source Date
Care of materials			
Weekly and daily schedules			
Student record keeping (date stamp, name)			
"What to do if . . ." procedures			
Steps in the writing process			
Daily use of the writing folder			
The permanent file			
Goal setting			
The writer's attitude toward own and others' work			
Pre-writing			
Finding a topic			
Purposes for writing (functional writing)			
Where authors get ideas			
Literature invitations			
Writing contests			

FIGURE 4.6 Sample of a mini-lesson record sheet (based on Craven, 1991).

Themed classroom collections			
Brainstorming and listing			
Clustering and webbing			
Writing/Drafting			
Sloppy copy (or *Rough draft*)			
Re-reading often			
Spelling "spectacular" words			
"Show, not tell"			
Illustrations			
Genre information (models and facts)			
Point of view			
Figurative language			
Revising			
What makes writing "good"?			
• Ideas and content			
• Organization			
• Voice			
• Word choice			
• Sentence structure			
Revision mechanics			
• Caret marks			
• "Spider legs"			
• Cut-and-paste			
Switching genres			
Predicting audience questions			
Adding stronger verbs			
Transitions in time and space			
Paragraphing			

FIGURE 4.6 *continued*

Conferencing			
Model listening and telling back			
"I noticed . . ." statements			
"I wonder . . ." statements			
Deciding on the next step			
Editing			
Ending sentences ?, !, .			
Capital letters			
Commas			
Dialogue			
Apostrophes			
Colons, semicolons			
Hyphens, dashes, ellipses			
Using colored pencils for editing			
Checking spelling			
Usage			
Publishing			
Options for the cover			
Dedication			
"About the Author"			
Copyright			
Table of Contents			
Sharing			
Author's Chair			
Audience responsibilities			
Dramatizations			

FIGURE 4.6 *continued*

The Activity Period

After the first day of writing workshop, when everyone launches a writing project at the same time, your students will rarely ever *all* be at the same stage again, but instead scattered among the various stages of the writing process—prewriting, drafting, revising, conferencing, editing, and publishing—on any given day. For obvious reasons, students need to know the steps of the writing process. You might post these on a wall chart or include them as guidelines in each individual's writing folder.

It's a good idea to begin the activity period by finding out where your students are in the process, what Nancie Atwell (1987) calls the "Status of the Class." A "status check" might go like this:

> "Ann?"
> "Editing final draft of my cat story."
> "Erin?"
> "Writing first draft of a poem."
> "Nathan?"
> "Abandoning my piece on my trip, so I'll be finding a new topic."
> "I'll be by to check with you soon. Jacob?"
> "Continuing my draft of nonfiction piece on snakes."

If this is Wednesday, the teacher's Status of the Class recording sheet might look like the one in Figure 4.7.

As students report their personal status to the teacher, they are making a verbal contract, which often helps them focus on just what they need to work on that day. They also get to hear the topics that their peers have selected, which often inspires them. In addition, the teacher finds out who needs attention immediately.

Some teachers like to follow the status reports with five to ten minutes of USSW, or Uninterrupted Sustained Silent Writing, which they themselves

Students		Mon.	Tues.	Wed.	Thurs.	Fri.
1. Ann		D'Cat	Revise	Ed.		
2. Erin		Pub.	Pub.	poemD'		
3. Nathan		D'Trip	D'Trip	Ab		
4. Jacob		Pub.	D'Snakes	D'Snakes		

FIGURE 4.7 A status-of-the-class recording sheet.

may do as well. If you do decide to write, be sure to report your status to the class too. This can be a powerful modeling tool. You might show your students a rough draft of the letter that you will send home to parents on Friday or a description of your pet parakeet's latest antics as a mini-lesson during sharing time.

Finally comes the activity period, providing the teacher with the most intense, active, challenging, and exciting part of a workshop class—*cruising the room*—making a multitude of decisions about who needs face-to-face attention immediately, who just needs a pat on the shoulder, who needs help finding a personal topic, and then—how to meet those individual needs in two- to five-minute conferences.

The teacher's responsibilities during activity period include instruction and motivation and nonstop assessment. You might carry a clipboard with an open-ended recording sheet (see Figure 4.8) so you can keep track of the children you talk with and record your observations of each student's attitude and control of the process. "In this sense, the teacher becomes like a classical anthropologist. Like an anthropologist, she alternates between participant observer, detached observer, and collector of artifacts. At times she observes the 'member of the tribe' from a distance, recording her observations for later analysis. At other times she asks questions of various informants about what they know and think and about the ways they produce their artifacts, all the time recording their responses. Her records become her store of knowledge" (Cambourne, 1988, 122).

Although this recording sheet may seem almost too simple to be useful, it is a powerful tool for "kid watching." (The sheets can alert you, as well, to those students to whom you haven't paid attention lately.) Some teachers find it useful to cut the sheets apart so that as they complete them they can put them in a looseleaf notebook, where each child has a page. (You can also use gummed labels, which are easy to transfer from one sheet to another.) In this way you can build up an annotated record of a child's progress based on your observations. This, combined with the collection of the child's actual writings gives a more complete picture of writing development. (The Kid Watching sheets can also be used in math or science workshop, or even at recess.)

Teachers new to the writing workshop often worry about what to say to students in order to make a difference. There is no one *right* way to respond to a child, but the model described in Figure 4.9 offers simple but effective guidelines. Always remember that the two to five minutes of individual attention and genuine interest that you give to each student during writing workshop sends a powerful message: "My teacher is interested in me and my work."

Workshop classrooms demand that teachers become reflective practitioners, that they watch their students, listen to their interactions, and continuously refine what works for them as teachers and for their students. Since

Kid Watching

1.	2.	3.	4.	5.	6.
7.	8.	9.	10.	11.	12.
13.	14.	15.	16.	17.	18.
19.	20.	21.	22.	23.	24.

FIGURE 4.8 A Kid Watching recording sheet.

The Pattern of Teacher/Pupil Interactions During Activity Time

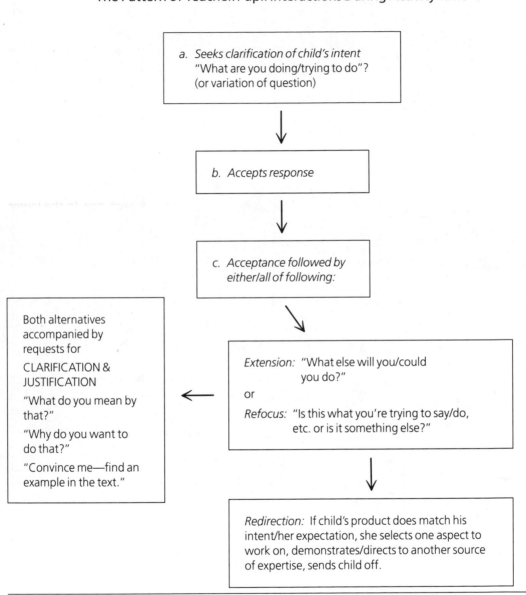

FIGURE 4.9 Guidelines for conducting the activity period in the writing workshop (Cambourne, 1988, 121).

many of us were never trained to manage writing workshops, learning how to do so and sharing our experiences with other teachers provide a wonderful opportunity for us to collaborate with each other as we continue to learn about literacy development.

Sharing

Follow the writing workshop activity period with the sharing period. The transition is often difficult for children. Groans and "Do we have to?" are frequent responses to the teacher's request for sharing time, which is when students read what they've written to the class. Jeanne Lintenmuth, a Mt. Pleasant first grade teacher, plays a tape or record of a special piece of music to make the transition painless. Rather than groaning or complaining, her students start to sing along. They know how long the song is so they know how much time they have to finish a sentence or two before handing in their writing folders.

The number of students who share each day should be kept manageable so that the sharing period is not too long. In the upper grades, students' pieces are longer, so only a few students can read their work each day. In the lower grades, however, children write a new piece every day, and most of them want to share every day. To control the frenzy in those classrooms, establish a sharing day for each child. This way Amanda knows that on Tuesday she must be prepared to read her favorite piece from the week's work.

The sharing child sits in the Author's Chair, which can be as simple or as elaborate as you like. Once in the chair, the child takes control of the gathering, waiting for silence before beginning to read, reading the selection, and then calling on classmates to respond. Spend time early in the year to establish this routine. Once everyone knows the rules, it's magic time.

For the most part, children are very interested in hearing their peers' work, and their listening and speaking abilities are at their best. The author may ask for comments or questions. If you encourage students to preface their statements with "I noticed that . . ." or "I wonder . . .", they will naturally look to the work itself in order to complete the thought. Encourage them to avoid simple comments such as "I liked your picture," which elicit little from the other students. Because your students run the sharing session, you are free to record your observations, both of the sharer and the classmates who respond.

After students have shared their pieces of writing, display these on a bulletin board or on the shelves of the classroom library—providing more evidence that this is a community of writers.

To be successful, students as well as teachers must know the structure of the writing workshop. In the words of eighth grade teacher Linda Rief (1992): "Organization has to be right up front. I want to be 'so dammed organized' I can concentrate on the students: Who are they? What do they know? How have they come to know that? How can I help them become better readers, writers, and learners?" (33).

Teachers must decide what is the best way to divide the stages of the writing process for their grade level (see Figure 4.10). For instance, most first

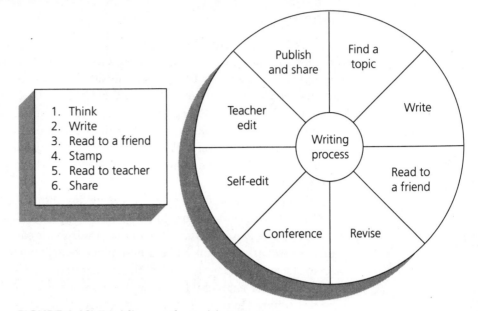

1. Think
2. Write
3. Read to a friend
4. Stamp
5. Read to teacher
6. Share

FIGURE 4.10 Dividing up the writing process.

graders enjoy reading their work aloud to the teacher before filing it in the finished box. Moreover, since young writers will not be able to read their pieces if too much time passes, their reading aloud is important in making their meaning evident. With older students this contact would not be necessary. Once you've decided how to handle the writing stages, establish a writing center, which should include places for the children to keep their work. A box or basket labeled "Ready for Editing," "Ready for Publishing," and "Ready to be Shared" might be part of the writing center, depending on how you've set up the process for your writing community.

The Writing Center

The writing center in the classroom should have paper in a variety of sizes, colors, and types (provide unlined paper for the youngest writers). There should be a variety of writing implements, including colored pencils and markers. (Early writers, who almost always draw before they write, seem most comfortable using markers. Since markers can easily be used for both drawing and writing, the youngsters don't need to switch from crayons to pencils.) The center should also include rubber stamps that say *Date* and *Draft* (and an ink pad, of course). Draft stamps come in a variety of styles, from very simple for more sophisticated writers to very cute for beginners. The

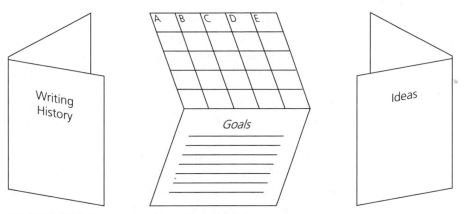

FIGURE 4.11 A sample of a writing folder.

draft stamps confirm for students as well as their parents that this particular piece of writing is still at an early stage in its development, so errors should be expected.

The center's references should include dictionaries, thesauri, and handbooks as well as several files, including address files for famous people; genre files containing examples of the genre and a list of its characteristics (Rief, 1992), and files for "genres of power" (Lemke, 1989, 307), such as letters to the editor or letters of complaint.

The materials in the writing center convey a message to students about what the teacher believes about the writing process. Tape and scissors along with models of cut-and-paste revisions testify to the idea that writing can be messed with. Special editing pens emphasize that editing is a specific and separate step in the writing process. Materials for the final, published piece— special paper for the text and the front and back covers—motivate students to complete a piece of writing and say to them, "Your writing deserves preferential treatment."

Each student should have a writing folder, which can be a simple pocket portfolio or a manila folder with special recording forms attached (see Figure 4.11). The four sides of the folder might contain the following information:

Personal writing goals   One of the goals of a writing program is to help writers become better able to assess their own work. Asking students to identify areas of their writing that need attention will help them define and reach their goals. These might include "I want to add more colorful words to my writing" or "I want to write longer pieces." As the writers identify what they want to work on, they develop their own understanding of what constitutes good writing.

Writing history   Keeping a tally of completed writing provides evidence for a student that "I am indeed a writer." Since most writers encounter dry spells, when engaging in writing is difficult, this list of past accomplishments can be comforting as well.

Writing ideas   Everyone has talents, interests, and experiences that can provide fertile ground for writing ideas. Students add to the list all year long.

Personal dictionary   A six-by-four grid of the alphabet helps students create personal dictionaries for words they frequently misspell. First graders can use the grid to record the words they've learned to spell, in celebration of their growing competence.

■ **IDEAS TO LEARN**   Begin your own writing folder. On the outside cover list your goals for yourself as a writer. Inside begin a list of topics you can write about. Experiment with the various topics and take one piece to publication. Use one of the ideas suggested later in the chapter to publish your piece.

Establish a permanent file for each student's work. Again this provides evidence that "Yes, I am a writer" and allows the student, the teacher, and the parents to observe growth over time. Share this folder with parents at conferences; regularly send home copies of individual writing pieces, so parents can see how their children's writing is progressing. At the end of the year have students select a piece from their files that they consider their *best work* to put into a cumulative portfolio that will travel with them throughout their school career, documenting their writing growth. For a complete discussion of the writing portfolio, see "The Writing Portfolio" section later in this chapter.

Without question the final ingredient necessary for a successful writing workshop is the teacher who understands the developmental nature of the writing process; who is sensitive to the needs of the students; who respects their language and their efforts; and who fills the classroom with exciting literature, language play, and opportunities for students to get their hands on numerous, enriching materials in literature, science, math, and art. This teacher understands that young writers must discover topics they care about, have time to write about those topics, and have an audience to help celebrate their accomplishments. Throughout the year the teacher must model a love of language, strategies for getting words on the page, techniques for improving writing, and the satisfactions and frustrations of his or her own writing.

■ **IDEAS TO LEARN**   Describe your own writing process. Do you need a special place to write? Do you like to use particular writing implements? (Felt-tipped pen? legal pad? word processor? note cards? number two pencil?) How do you get started? What sorts of prewriting techniques do you use? How many drafts do you write? Do the number of drafts differ with the different kinds of writing that you do? Who reads your drafts? What sorts of things are you likely to change when you revise? How do you catch errors when you edit?

Prewriting

In a process that is unique to each individual anyway, prewriting may be the most idiosyncratic stage. Each writer will develop his or her *own best way* of capturing information to put on paper. These best ways, in fact, may be different for the same individual depending on the type of writing to be done. The key to becoming a writer is to think like a writer at all times, to see the writing topics that are part of our lives. Pam Owens, a Mt. Pleasant, Michigan, mother of a first grader who was an eager participant in a classroom of writers, reported overhearing this comment from an interchange between her sons as they involved themselves in some backseat silliness while driving home from school: "Hey, thanks. You just gave me an idea for my next book."

Peter Clark (1987) observes that "writers see the world as a storehouse of writing ideas. . . . Such is the reporter's fate: She cannot drive home or get a haircut or go to church or go to the bathroom without discovering something to write about, or encountering some things she wants to know more about" (12).

The first step in the writing process is to identify a topic. In earlier models of writing instruction, teachers assigned the topic, the format, and in some cases even the first line. When writers select their own topics and have identified familiar audiences, their writing improves; they become active rather than passive learners. Some children may need help in finding topics on which to write. Teachers can provide this by suggesting the strategies that follow.

Expertise   Writers write about what they know. Have your students make up individual lists of areas of expertise, to which they can refer when they need a topic.

Within each of their areas of expertise, children may find several stories or poems. If a student feels he or she has depleted an area with just one piece of writing, you can help the child explore the area further by brainstorming or by conducting a mini-interview to help determine subtopics within the major area. If a child loves and knows horses but feels he or she must cross off that topic with one fictional piece, point out other possibilities, such as a how-to book on the care of horses, a reference guide to the types of horses, a book of poems on the feel, smell, sight, and thrill of horses, or a letter to a summer horse camp requesting information.

Journals, logs, or daybooks   Writer Donald Murray (1990) keeps track of potential writing topics by compiling what he calls a daybook. Within this book he keeps "questions, fragments of writing, leads, titles, notes, outlines, diagrams, observations, quotes, newspaper clippings, titles of books to read, pictures, schedules, letters from other people, or lists" (21).

Lucy Calkins (1991) is enthusiastic about the use of notebooks or journals in the elementary classroom. "We can't give children rich lives, but we can give them the lens to appreciate the richness that is already there in their lives. Notebooks validate a child's existence. Notebooks say, 'Your thoughts, your noticings, your fleet of orange slices matter'" (35). Notebooks provide a place to gather pieces of life and an opportunity to reflect on those pieces. They also keep us in touch with ourselves.

It is important to recognize that these collections of ideas should reflect the interests, ideas, and passions of the writer. This description of an old diary by a young girl describes what happens when life is left out of your notebook: "Grandmother has just gone through ten years of Great Aunt Jessie's diaries and found absolutely nothing worth saving in them. They just said things like, 'went to Dougans for dinner today,' 'cold and snowy,' 'great-grandma died today,' and never showed any of her feelings or even had more than a sentence or anything that happened so they just threw them out. I would bore myself silly if I kept something like that. What's the use of even writing it?" (Jackson, 1974, 94).

Sometimes the best stories come from life's most mundane experiences. Even the "most boring" day in a person's life can provide material for an interesting story.

Personal experience   "Guess what happened to me last night!" is a refrain familiar to most teachers. These enthusiastically recalled happenings are often rich writing topics. Keep mental files on each of your students and be ready to retrieve them when students are searching for something to write about. Make your response "Hey, that would make a great story for writing workshop" so familiar to students that they automatically say, "I *know* I should write about this."

Parents can help their children find personal, involving topics as well. As a homework assignment ask students to interview their parents for ideas for classroom writing projects.

1-15-90

Dear McDonalds,

I like your food but I don't come to your restaurant any more. I don't come any more because you use styrofoam. You probably haven't noticed that styrofoam can't be recycled so all you can do is throw it away and it takes an incredibly long time to turn into dirt. Most other fast food places don't use it. If you switch to cardbord I will come back but until then I'm going to Burger King and Wendy's.

Sincerely,
Lindsay Dinan

Name: Lindsay J. Dinan
Address: 914 Southmoor Rd
        Mt. Pleasant MI
        48858
Phone: 773-4714
Age: 9
School: Vowles
Teacher: Mrs. McFarlane

FIGURE 4.12 Students' concerns are rich sources of writing topics.

Students' concerns are another rich source of topics. The following comments—"This toy busted and I only had it one day!" "I wish we didn't have to line up by the big kids after lunch recess." "Why do the first graders always have to sit on the floor at assemblies?" "Why does my dog throw the new cereal from his bowl?"—can provide *real* reasons to write and often elicit positive responses. A letter to a toy company or to the school principal may even result in real change (see Figure 4.12).

Children can express their feelings when they write to each other. Even first graders find that some things are better said in writing than aloud (Figure 4.13).

Curiosities   "I'm going to get a gerbil for my birthday." "My grandpa gave me these rocks and I wonder what kind they are." As we will describe in Chapter 5, natural curiosities can lead naturally to writing projects.

Literature invitations   The stories written by professional writers invite readers and listeners to explore memories and emotions from their own lives. Judith Viorst's book about the death of a family cat, *The Tenth Good Thing About Barney*, never fails to elicit heartfelt stories from children about their

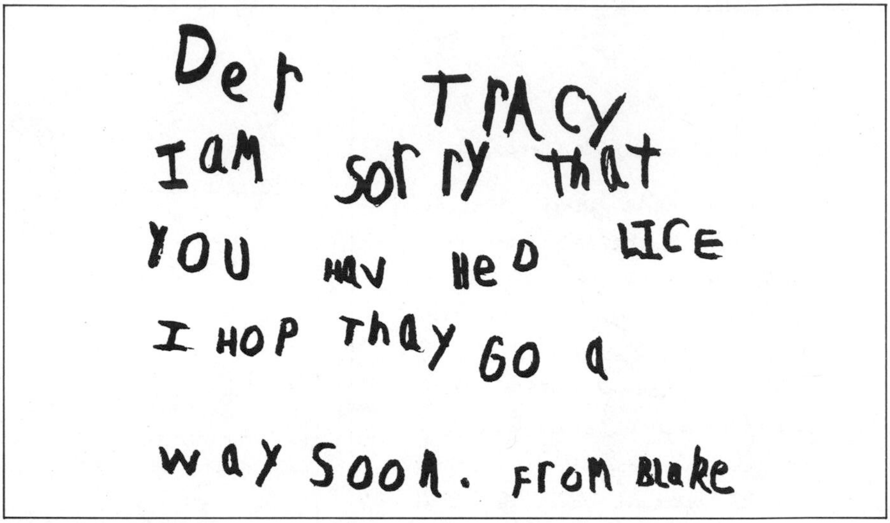
Der TrACy
I aM sorry that
YOU HAV HeD LICE
I HOP Thay GO a
way Soon. From Blake

FIGURE 4.13 Children learn that some things are better expressed in writing.

pets. Mem Fox invites readers to look for the little memories that make up our lives in *Wilfrid Gordon McDonald Partridge*.

Other professional works have literary patterns that are inspiring. For example, along with other alphabet books Chris Van Allsburg's *The Z was Zapped* provides a structure for organizing information on a topic. Exercise caution, however, when asking students to use literary patterns in their own writing. Do not give students the impression that they must depend on professional writers for their structures and ideas. "Literary patterning allows little opportunity for students to reflect on new ideas, to integrate and apply these ideas in new ways, or to make them their own. Students who write literary patterns then equate learning to write with the ability to manipulate sentences rather than the ability to communicate ideas" (Wason-Ellam, 1988, 293).

After a topic is selected, the next step is gathering ideas from which the writing will be generated. Some writers benefit from just putting pencil to paper and beginning, but most benefit from time spent exploring the topic. The following section describes several productive prewriting activities for generating ideas about a topic.

Clustering (or webbing) One of the most useful prewriting strategies, clustering is elegant in its simplicity and in its ability to fully develop topics. Students place their topic in an oval in the center of a blank sheet of paper. From this center they spin off ideas relating to the topic, as shown in Figure 4.14.

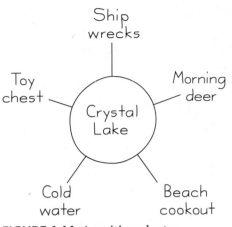

FIGURE 4.14 A writing cluster.

If students know how they are going to organize a piece of writing, they can make a more structured cluster. For example, a narrative developing over a series of events can be placed around a sequence cluster.

Maps   Maps are an inviting way to launch a story. Several children's classics (*Wind in the Willows, Rabbit Hill,* and *Winnie the Pooh*) contain maps that detail the setting of the story and help orient readers. Creating a map as a prewriting experience can do the same for writers.

Six questions   The traditional reporter questions of Who? What? Where? When? Why? and How? are useful for generating information for certain types of writing, such as news stories or simple narratives.

Outlining   Most adult writers have stories of how they created the outlines for their term papers *after* they wrote the papers. For some children in the upper elementary grades, outlines may be useful *before* they write.

Key questions   If students want to write nonfiction, they can create an organizing framework from the key questions they plan to answer as writers. For example, if they want to explore the care of horses, they might place the following questions at the top of four blank pieces of paper, one question per page:

What do horses need to eat?

What shelter do horses need?

What grooming do horses require?

How do you keep a horse happy?

Then they gather information on these questions—through interviews, books, or videos—and add it to the appropriate piece of paper. When they've answered the questions to their satisfaction, they can develop their answers into a complete piece of writing.

■ **IDEAS TO LEARN**   Choose one of the topics you have listed in your writing folder. Try two or three of the prewriting activities here to generate ideas for drafting your topic. Which activity generated the most material? Was the value of the prewriting topic related to the topic you chose?

Drafting

Staring at a blank sheet of paper can be intimidating to a writer. It helps to write "Rough Draft" in heavy squiggly lines across the top (stamping the sheet with a draft stamp has the same effect).

First lines are important to readers and writers. Some writers claim that the first sentence is the crucial one because all else must fall in place behind it. E. B. White tried numerous drafts before he settled on the provocative "Where's pa going with that ax?" Young writers can try White's strategy and write several different leads.

Get writers who just can't seem to find the right beginning sentence to fold the paper in half and begin on the bottom section. Later they can settle on an appropriate lead.

You may have to take dictation for some reluctant writers, as least for the first paragraph of their piece. Young writers who have experienced only failure and injury may need to dictate their first few stories in their entirety. (They could also record their stories on tape for later transcription.) You must try to convince these students that they have stories to tell, that they are writers. For some students the risk is too high to even try at all, so they would rather not. It's your job to convince them that they have a voice and marvelous stories to tell.

■ **IDEAS TO LEARN**   Try writing five or six different leads for a topic. What is the effect of having so many different possible beginnings for your piece?

When writers are writing they often talk—to themselves, to others nearby, to themselves again. Sometimes your students may talk to avoid the paper, but a few minutes of Uninterrupted Sustained Silent Writing can help them. However, fledgling writers are often almost physically unable to sit quietly and write as they sound out words and labor to put symbols on papers.

Kindergarten through second grade teachers should expect many writing-related conversations during writing time.

Some young writers may need a mini-lesson on the necessity of rereading from the beginning what they've written. They often become so involved in the transcription of their ideas to paper that they lose the flow of the story.

The appearance of the rough draft should also be a topic of a mini-lesson. First, if writers are using lined paper, they should write on every other line so that they can easily include additions and make corrections later. Inexperienced writers may need help coping with words they cannot spell. Being able to circle the attempt and just keep going gives some writers confidence and peace of mind to forge ahead and fuss with spelling later.

Conferencing

When students feel they've written enough to need the response of an audience, they read to a classmate. In some classrooms special areas are designated "Read to a Friend" areas. This first reading is an informal opportunity for writers to find problems in their pieces before taking the work to a wider audience. Sometimes the teacher might want to listen in on these one-to-one conferences. As children read their work orally, they become aware of any gross problems in structure, syntax, and even semantics. If you observe these interchanges, you will often see the writer adding information on the spot or saying, "I'll have to fix that."

After responding to the needs of the piece that became evident during the conference with a friend, writers might ask for a more formal, small group conference. In some classrooms these conferences, which always involve the teacher, are done on the move as the teacher circulates in the classroom. With writers from third grade on, small group conferences may more efficiently meet their needs. At the conferences the writers speak first, detailing what they have written about and then indicating where they think they need help. After hearing the story, the group comments on the work and questions the writer.

When you first set up a writing workshop in your class, you must demonstrate the kinds of responses that are appropriate and helpful to writers during conferences. Sometimes it might be helpful to the writer if the teacher notes down some of the group's suggestions. (Sticky notes make non-offensive reminders of peers' questions.) The writers always maintain final say over what will and will not be added, deleted, or rearranged. These groups are usually very supportive, since everyone knows that they too will eventually have their writing reviewed.

Typical problems in children's writing are distracting characters who appear and then disappear without a word; abrupt, unrelated endings; confusing story sequences; and flat, voiceless writing. Sometimes it helps the group to focus on the genre of the writing. For instance, if a child has written a mystery, the group can identify the mystery, the clues, and any foreshadowing that may be present.

Often teachers don't have time to conference with all the students who they want to see. Velerie Johnstone's (1990) idea of having a "write back" option solves this problem. In addition to in-class responses to writing from peers and teachers, students can ask their teacher to provide a written response to their writing. Students might want this in the early stages of a piece, for a specific problem, or late in a draft, or for the final edit. When students turn in the finished piece, they include all the drafts and the teacher's write-backs, so the teacher can see how the responses were incorporated.

Revising

If writers decide to include the ideas generated in the conference, they begin to work on revising. Adding revisions to a paper is not easy and does not come easily to children. Most young writers don't understand that a piece of writing can still be "unfinished" even after words are on the paper. (In fact first graders seem for the most part opposed by their very nature to doing any writing over.) You will need to teach your students how to add to or delete from an existing text. Provide numerous mini- and maxi-lessons on revision in your writing workshop.

Students can place some of the additions they make to their writing in the lines that they skipped throughout the paper, or at the end of the paper—but often the information won't fit the available space. One way to handle this is to tape bits of writing on long strips of paper to the side of the paper at the appropriate spot. Nancie Atwell (1987) refers to these as "spider legs" for obvious reasons. Papers can also be cut apart and restapled in a new order or with space to incorporate the new text. You should model these procedures under fairly close supervision the first few times your students attempt to revise.

A less messy strategy is to use starred additions on a second sheet of paper. The first addition has one star, the second two, and so on. Color-coded highlighters also work well. For instance, all the parts that should be in the paragraph describing how the animal gets its food might be highlighted in green. The description of the animal's habitat might be highlighted in pink and then recopied in appropriate segments.

Editing

Although first graders can handle some rudimentary editing (such as "Do I have a period somewhere in this piece?"), formal editing usually begins some-

■ **IDEAS TO LEARN**   After you have drafted your piece of writing, share it with a friend. You can begin your writing conference in several ways. Tell your partner where you are having problems with the piece and ask for suggestions about how to solve them. Or ask whether a certain technique, explanation, or description makes sense or works. Or listen to your partner's reaction to the paper before you tell him or her anything about it. Your partner may tell you two or three things he or she liked best and then ask two or three questions about the piece. After you have shared your paper with a friend, use his or her advice and your own ideas to revise the piece. You may want to add, delete, or move things in order to make your piece clearer, more exciting, or more interesting.

time in second grade. When writers feel their work is ready for final polishing, they begin what we call "self-editing." Some teachers provide personalized self-editing lists on the outside of the child's writing folder or special editing checklists designed by the group. But editing one's own writing is difficult, even for experienced writers. Don't expect young children to find *all* their mistakes.

Editing in "living color"—that is, using colored pencils for different aspects of editing—helps children focus on the various conventions in writing. For instance, students can mark end punctuation in red and capitals in green. They might use an orange pencil to circle all the *ands* and *and thens* that appear in their writing. That way they can easily tell, even from across the room, that they've got to find some other transitions because they've overused those two. They can use a purple pencil to underline all the verbs. Then they can go back and replace some of these with more colorful verbs.

Together the class can create a chart of transition words—*immediately, suddenly, later, before, after, while, in (so many) weeks (days, years, minutes), between, meanwhile*, and the like—to remind writers of ways to move a story through time. Student editors can track down other overused words (*said, happy, sad*) and substitute them with more exciting words from other lists they've created.

Some teachers have used editing teams successfully (Harste, Short, and Burke, 1988). Set up an editors' table in the classroom and have *all* students take turns working in teams.

Publishing

Presenting one's writing to the public is the final stage in the writing process; it's a satisfying and motivating experience. Although occasionally students can properly celebrate their finished work by simply reading it to the class, often they deserve to see it in a more permanent form, like a book. After copying their work in their best handwriting, students can choose from a variety of bookmaking methods to present their piece with a touch of class.

If students prefer, they can copy their finished piece of writing on the computer to produce a spiffy-looking printout. But because most young writers have limited keyboarding skills, they would probably do better to copy long pieces by hand or to have an adult type them into the computer. Poetry is by far the easiest and most effective genre for computer work.

Making Books

Simple wallpaper   Most home decorating stores are delighted to get rid of their out-of-date wallpaper sample books, which provide a multitude of textures and designs. Children love to browse through the selections until they find one that is just right. After they select a cover, they staple it and the writing together to make the book. (You can precut the wallpaper in several different sizes to expedite the bookmaking process). Apply titles to the front covers with permanent magic marker or labels. Colored plastic tape on the binding improves the book's appearance even more.

Complicated wallpaper   Although these take more work, the results are usually worth the effort. In addition to the wallpaper, you need blank cardboard (cereal boxes or dry-cleaning shirt cardboards work well). To save your sanity, deal with only one or two sizes of these elaborate covers. Students can produce the front and back covers separately or at the same time. When they make them separately, they tape the front and back together after covering them. When they want to do both covers at the same time, they tape the front and back together first and then glue the wallpaper to the cardboard. Either way, students then insert the pages (which they've already stapled or stitched together) by gluing the first and last pages to the inside of the wallpaper covers.

File folders   Students can cut up old file folders to any size they want. (You might even consider getting brand-new folders when a special at an office supply store makes them cheap enough.) The young writers can easily decorate and title these covers.

Construction paper   Although this paper fades and tears easily, it can still make attractive covers. Students can improve durability by adding library tape to the edges, or folding pieces to make a double-layered cover.

Marbleized paper   Students can turn ordinary white paper into extraordinary paper with two or three bottles of model airplane enamel paint. To make the paper, fill a large shallow pan with water. In a well-ventilated area use toothpicks or pencils to scatter drops of paint on the surface of the water. Gently swirl the paint into patterns. (Too much stirring will destroy the marbleized effect.) Carefully lay a piece of paper on the surface of the water. Pat it gently until you can see the paint adhering to the paper. Carefully lift the paper out and allow it to dry. Pick off unwanted paint from the water's surface with a paper towel before starting the next design. Since you use very little paint, this is a fairly inexpensive way to create dramatic paper. Students can use the marbleized paper over cardboard for covers or as endpapers. (Students can make stationery this way too. Substitute black India ink for the paint. On the envelopes be sure to leave space for the address [Wiseman, 1975].)

Assembling Books

Motivate students by providing interesting formats for assembling books. Below are two unique methods.

Accordion books   Use a long narrow sheet of paper (twelve-by-eighteen-inch paper cut to six-by-eighteen works well.) Fold the paper in half and then again in fourths (or eighths if you want narrow pages). You can tape two sections together to make the book longer. To make tiny accordion books, use adding machine tape. Attach ribbons to both sides of the back cover so the book can be tied shut.

Fold-a-book   The origami book-folding design shown in Figure 4.15 is one that all teachers and students should have in their repertoire. Once mastered, the procedure can be used with any size paper to produce quick, sturdy books.

Posters and Murals

In addition to multipaged books, students can display their writing, especially poetry, on posters and in murals. They can use paints, watercolors, collage, markers, chalk, crayons, and special papers from foil to tissue to celebrate a piece of writing.

■ **IDEAS TO LEARN**   Use one of the publishing techniques described in this section to publish your final piece of writing. Share it with other students and friends.

Commercial Publications

Many commercial publications publish children's writing. (See Chapter 7 for a list of periodicals.) Some children are highly motivated by the possibility of

Fold-a-Book

Use any size paper. Large sheets of newsprint work well.

1. Fold paper in half lengthwise.

←fold

Fold in half again.

Fold in half again.

2. Open to step 1 lengthwise fold. Cut narrow strip A to C on fold of two middle sections.

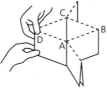

3. Open the slit.

4. Refold side D with pinches to make a fold. Crease the outside.

5. Pull points D and B out while pushing A and C to the middle to make a plus sign.

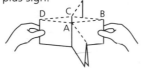

6. Bring points D and B toward you.

7. Bring remaining page toward you to make a book.

8. Crease the book edge.

9. To make a book with more pages, paste two books together.

PASTE

Acknowledgment: This sharing of fold-a-books is a way of thanking the many teachers who have used them to help children enjoy reading and writing. We do not know the original origami reference; the folding format has been, and continues to be, passed on from teacher to teacher.

FIGURE 4.15 Instructions for creating a book by folding (Bohning and Cuccia, 1990, 526).

being published in a national magazine. In addition, there seem to be an endless number of writing contests that children can enter. One success story will provide energy for countless others. Use part of the writing center to display the flyers announcing contests or the magazines that publish student work.

Exploring Less Traditional Forms of Writing

The writing process strategies just described are usually associated with conventional writing assignments—stories, reports, research projects, and the like. An effective, stimulating writing classroom, however, engages students in nontraditional forms of writing as well. Such writing activities help young learners see that writing serves a variety of audiences and purposes, which is critical to their development as writers. They also get to experience the *playfulness* of language that more traditional writing projects often deemphasize. Below are some nontraditional writing forms that you might want to use in your classroom.

Riddles and Jokes

Typically children become interested in jokes and riddles in kindergarten and first grade. They spend a lot of time trying to determine what indeed is amusing to other people. Five- and six-year-olds love to experiment with humor. By second or third grade they know what makes people laugh and enjoy telling and hearing jokes.

In classrooms this natural interest in humor is obvious—new joke and riddle books quickly become dog-eared. Children *cannot* read joke books during silent reading time, because they simply cannot be silent.

Mike Thaler (1988), author of numerous children's books, describes a riddle-making activity that is great fun. His procedure involves first selecting a topic and then brainstorming a list of related words (e.g. pigs: *snout, ham, oink, mud,* etc.). Then you and your students can employ several tactics. One is to omit the initial letter(s) from the related words, then look in the dictionary for words that begin like the altered words. For example, *snout* without the *sn* becomes *out*. After looking in the dictionary, students discover that they can play around with words such as *outlaw, outskirts,* and *outgrown* to create riddles, as shown in Figure 4.16.

Another strategy Thaler suggests is to take proper nouns, particularly the names of people and places, break the names down into syllables, and look for places to add a pig-related word. For example, Albert Einstein might

FIGURE 4.16 Creating riddles in the classroom.

become Albert Swinestein or Alboar Swinestein in answer to "What pig created the theory of relativity?"

Pamphlets

Pamphlets are tidy combinations of graphics and script that get positive responses from all kinds of audiences, and are therefore exciting to create. The first step should be a close examination of the form as it is found in our world. Both teachers and students will be surprised at the variety of types of pamphlets available in stores, theater lobbies, doctors' offices, travel bureaus, public libraries, and almost everywhere else you go. In fact the types of folds found in pamphlets can be a research project on its own. At any level pamphlets are an attractive alternative to research papers or end-of-unit exams. Their audience appeal is obvious. "No one ever wrote a pamphlet to be read by only one person" (Skean, 1982, 86).

Pamphlets are a good way to integrate reading and writing into content areas. They can be a perfect culminating activity to most science, social stud-

FIGURE 4.16 *continued*

ies, or health units. Titles might range from *The First Settlers* and *Disease and You* to *Simple Machines* or *Barn Safety*.

Students can make pamphlets to promote books in the classroom, as part of a reading project. Such a pamphlet might contain the following elements on one book or on a series of books by one author:

Page one: title, author, illustrator, copyright, awards

Page two: pictures and/or descriptions of the characters

Page three: pictures and/or descriptions of the setting

Page four: description of the story problem

Page five: tantalizing quotes from the book

Page six: testimonial(s) from readers describing the book's merits

Creating a pamphlet on a curriculum topic can help students understand it more fully. For instance, if your students prepared a pamphlet for future classes that described the writing process, they would have to examine the concepts and procedures closely. They would then be able to present them in a manner that an audience their age could understand (see Figure 4.17).

1

2

3

For one kid
One stuffed
bunny and 20
Jelly beans

For 2 kids it's
2 stuffed
bunnies and
40 jelly beans

For 3 kids it's
3 stuffed
bunnies and
60 jelly beans.

FIGURE 4.17 A student-created pamphlet can be a perfect culminating activity for most science, social studies, or health units. This pamphlet is created with six panels—two sheets back-to-back and folded in thirds. The cover is at the far right.

TEACHING IDEAS

Creating pamphlets is a good collaborative activity for the classroom. At the end of a unit—on animal habitats or the pioneers or a featured author—have students work in twos or threes to create pamphlets on some aspect of the subject they just studied. A unit on pioneers, for example, might yield ten or fifteen pamphlets on pioneer crafts, recipes, or medical cures. See whether you can set up a pamphlet stand in the library to give your students' work wider circulation.

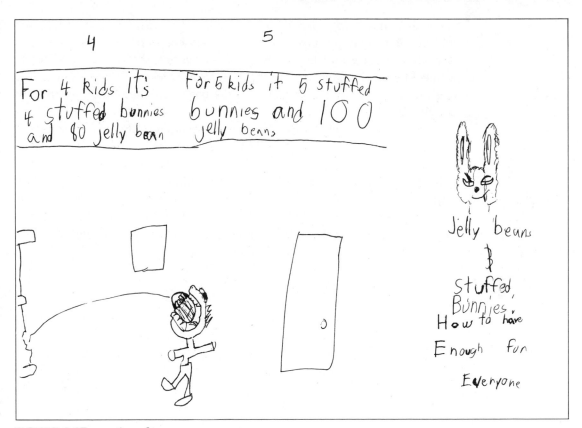

FIGURE 4.17 *continued*

Newspapers

Classroom and schoolwide newspapers provide a wide variety of genres to write in. First have groups of students identify as many different types of genres as possible. Classroom newspapers could include news features, special reports, interviews, sports reports, weather, ads, book and TV or movie reviews, comics, editorials, polls and surveys, poetry, and crossword puzzles.

A two-page, double-sided newspaper is a good format for a classroom paper. Before assigning topics, have students divide the space in the paper into sections and then have them cut blank paper to that size. For example, put the poll on a vertical half-sheet and divide the front page into three equal horizontal sections. When the writers get their assignments, they also receive the piece of paper on which their article must fit. Working collaboratively, pairs of students discuss their topic and make decisions about what will appear. If they are going to be taking a survey, they must determine the question and set up a format for collecting the data from their classmates. As they write their articles, they support each other by taking turns writing, spelling for each other, or revising. They then present the article to the Senior Editor (who will be the teacher, in most early elementary classrooms) for final editing. After the Senior Editor makes the final corrections, the writers rewrite the article in publishable form onto their cut-to-size pieces of paper. As the articles are finished, students reassemble the pages and tape them together for copying (see Figure 4.18).

A schoolwide newspaper demands more organization and time as well as external support. The hassle is balanced by the skills the writers learn as they gather news from a larger community, edit other people's work, sell ads, collate, staple, and sell papers—and by the applause and appreciation of that large community. Clearly, this is a rich, integrated language arts experience, but one probably best handled by upper-level students. Classroom newspapers, on the other hand, can be put together in one or two days and offer rich writing and reading experiences to all levels.

Plays

Some children enjoy the challenge of writing a play and are thrilled by the unique "publishing" possibility of someone actually performing it. Occasionally you'll see these young playwrights assigning the roles of the main characters after writing only a few lines. In fact the number of characters in the play may depend on the number of friends available to assume roles.

In order to write a play, students must be familiar with the format specific to plays. To understand this, they must read actual plays to see how dialogue is transcribed and how stage directions are used.

Although the characters and conflict in a play are usually developed through dialogue and action, young playwrights often use a narrator to carry large parts of the story.

 TEACHING IDEAS

Students can also create a newspaper in conjunction with reading a piece of literature. With *Charlotte's Web*, for example, children could create a newspaper that might come out at the county fairgrounds. Another newspaper might be created for and by the animals that inhabit the worlds of Beatrix Potter or A. A. Milne. Have children create feature and news articles, puzzles, advice columns, comics, advertising, and the like that would be of interest in this world.

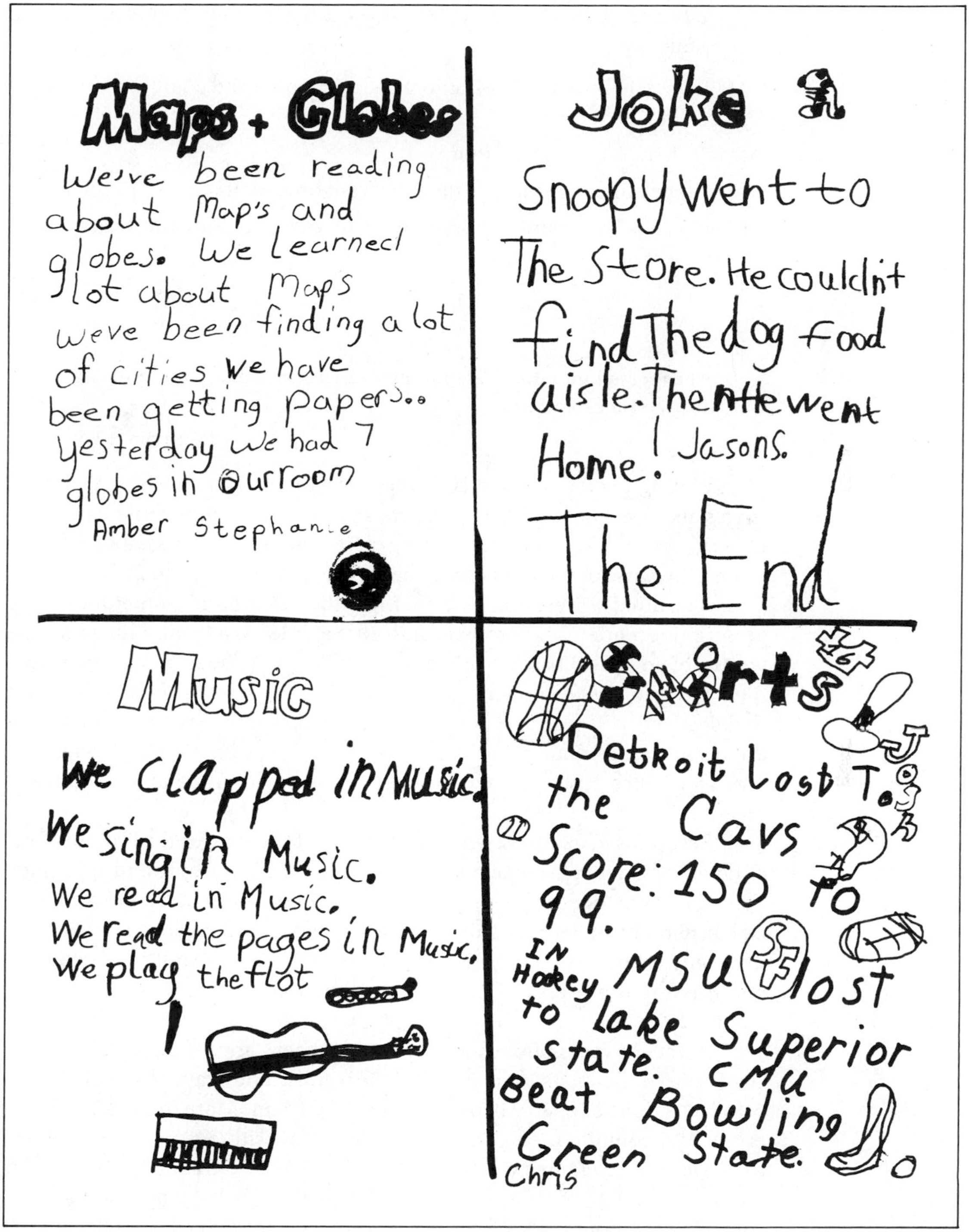

Maps + Globes

We've been reading about Map's and globes. We learned lot about Maps We've been finding a lot of cities we have been getting papers.. Yesterday we had 7 globes in our room
Amber Stephanie

Joke

Snoopy went to The Store. He couldn't find The dog food aisle. Then He went Home! Jasons.

The End

Music

We clapped in Music. We sing in Music. We read in Music. We read the pages in Music. We play the flot

Sports

Detroit Lost To the Cavs Score: 150 to 99. IN Hockey MSU lost to lake Superior state. CMU Beat Bowling Green State.
Chris

FIGURE 4.18 A classroom newspaper.

Judy and Judy (Tchudi) (1982) suggest the following guidelines for a successful play:

- Make sure there is plenty of action: people coming and going, events taking place.
- Don't change scenes too often.
- Introduce minor conflicts or subplots from time to time.
- Make sure the ending of the play is in keeping with the traits of the characters.

Poetry

> When something is too beautiful or too terrible or even too funny for words: then it is time for poetry.
>
> (Merriam, 1992, 18)

Writing poetry in the elementary classroom offers both special challenges and special rewards to teachers and students. On the one hand, prewriting, drafting, revising, and editing may seem more manageable to young writers, because of the limited number of words in poems and in many cases a specific, almost prescriptive format. On the other hand, sometimes those prescriptive tendencies dominate until all that is left is a blank-filling exercise worthy of any basal-based workbook. New York City poet-in-residence Matthew Cariello (1990) cautions teachers that using poetry primarily as a formulaic activity "leads to a poetry of constriction rather than expansion, of exclusion, rather than inclusion, of writing and reading to the demands of forms and rules, rather than to the energies of experience and the depth and breadth of the mind" (833).

Becoming acquainted with poetry is one of the most critical components of helping students become poets (see Chapter 2 on listening and speaking). You can honor poetry books and poets in the classroom by creating special displays or bulletin boards. You may even want to create a special chair used only while reading poetry. X. J. Kennedy (1981) describes the chair in one classroom as resplendent "with sequins and ablaze with fresh gold paint" (273).

In recent years publishers have issued more appealing anthology and single-poet collections than ever. Teachers must find ways to develop their own collections of poetry books for their classroom. More important, teachers should compile their own collections of favorite poems, which reflect their view of *good* poetry. Search your school and community libraries for attractive collections. In some areas, a teacher's only hope of establishing a collection is to purchase his or her own copies of poetry books (local children's bookstores may give discounts to educators). Perhaps if every teacher purchased one book of poetry for the classroom each year, even more delightful books would become available.

Poets and anthologists with whom teachers should be familiar include:

Arnold Adoff	Byrd Baylor	Harry Behn
Gwendolyn Brooks	John Ciardi*	Elizabeth Coatsworth
Beatrice S. deRegniers	Eleanor Farjeon	Aileen Fisher*
Paul Fleischman	Eloise Greenfield	Nikki Giovanni
Mary Ann Hoberman	Lee Bennett Hopkins	X. J. Kennedy
Karla Kuskins*	Nancy Larrick	Richard Lewis
Myra Cohn Livingston*	David McCord*	Lilian Moore*
Ogden Nash	Mary O'Neill	Jack Prelutsky
Shel Silverstein	Judith Viorst	Valerie Worth*

*Winners of the National Council of Teachers of English Poetry Award

Peggy Harrison and Sheryl Reed, fifth and sixth grade teachers, acted on their belief that poetry should be the center of the classroom community. They asked their students to immerse themselves in reading and writing poetry. The following describes their philosophy.

> We feel that involvement with poetry increases children's sensitivity and awareness, helps them become more observant, causes them to look deeply within themselves, and to reach far beyond themselves to universal truths, provides them a vehicle to get in touch with the feelings of others as well as their own feelings, brings to the surface that spark of truth within each of them, gives them the opportunity to be in communication with the aesthetic side of life, and initiates a habit which can bring joy to them for the rest of their lives.

> Reading, hearing, and especially writing poetry helps children become better overall writers and readers. Their prose becomes more poetic, more truthful,

TEACHING IDEAS

Begin a file of favorite poems. Copy your favorite poems on five-by-seven cards, poems you like for yourself and ones you would like to share with your students. You may want to categorize your poems by topic—poems about animals, autumn, food, the sea, sports, and so on. Try to develop a broad, eclectic collection. Ask your students to find poems that they would like to add to the file. You might want to mount your poetry collection on large art tablets, which you can decorate and then share with the class as a big book.

> *Wishing With Whistpers*
> *If someone saw a shooting star*
> *and decided to wish upon it, they*
> *wouldn't say it very loud. for*
> *some one would hear it. They would*
> *whistper it so very soft, not fly, nor*
> *bee would hear it. Who knows what*
> *you would wish for, for you say it very*
> *low. Only you would hear it only*
> *you will know.*

FIGURE 4.19 Students' first poems often don't look like poetry.

more fluent, and more to the point. They learn to say what they mean in a few words—to be concise. We develop a sense of the uncommon and endeavor to make the common come alive.

(In McClure, 1990, 64)

Along with sharing poetry daily, Harrison and Reed required their fifth and sixth graders to write in poetry journals every day, either writing a new poem or adding to or revising earlier ones.

As part of the program, students discussed the poems they read and soon were able to "make connections between poets and between poems with similar themes or styles, thus communicating the idea that poetry is a body of literature with common ties to content and technique" (64). As they discovered how poets make their pieces unique, the students tried the same techniques in their own writing. They began using elements like repetition, figurative language, and nonsense words to make their own pieces "sound more poetic," as they termed it. To guarantee that their students continued their contact with poetry, Harrison and Reed periodically asked students to find a poem that illustrated a theme, topic, or subject area to be added to a group or individual collection.

As was noted earlier, teachers should be cautious with prescriptive models for poetry. In his anthology *One at a Time*, poet David McCord (1977) offers delightful examples of poems written in a specific form *about* that specific form. For example, there are haikus on how to write haikus and ballads about ballads, doubly challenging language play. But more important than form to a poem is its quality, which teacher Gregory Denman (1991) emphasizes with "Mr. D.'s Three C's" for his students in charts, in reminders pasted into their writing folders, and in chants:

1. Create images.
2. Convey feelings.
3. Communicate with association.

The use of space in writing a poem takes time and experience. The first poems students write on their own, especially those not based on a prescriptive format, will probably not look like poetry (see Figure 4.19). Revising a poem to its most effective presentation takes some effort. Because poems usually don't have a lot of words, students can use computers to revise their work. On a computer, experiments with line breaks and arrangements are easy and fun. The poem from Figure 4.19 might look like this:

WISHING WITH WHISPERS

If someone saw a shooting star
and decided to wish upon it,
they wouldn't say it very loud
for someone might hear it.
They would whisper it
so very softly
not even a
fly nor bee
would hear it!
Who knows what
you might wish for,
for you say it
very low,
only you
would hear it,
only you
would know.

Lindsay Dinan, 10

Many of the elements that make poetry attractive to us are the same elements that make any piece of writing appealing: powerful images, strong metaphors, and important ideas. Therefore time spent on refining poetry skills is time spent on writing. In Matthew Cariello's (1990) words, "Being a poet is a way of being alive: children are poets" (838).

Letters

Emily Dickinson wrote "letters to the world" through her poetry. Your students, however, can write letters to real people in the real world: Questions to the First Lady or appreciation sent to the star of the newest TV show often get answered. Authors often respond to notes from children (most authors can be reached through their publishing companies). Students can correspond with pen pals in classrooms across town, across the country, or around the world.

Writing to Learn

As students become comfortable with the writing process, they can use writing to help them think. Given permission to express themselves without worrying about punctuation and spelling, elementary students can write to discover what they know about a topic.

> To use writing as a tool of learning means using writing much like a crescent wrench of the mind, as a device which organizes, manipulates, channels, and gives extra leverage to thinking. This tool-like kind of writing works best when it's personalized: when students use language that is informal, colloquial, loose, and personal—as close as possible to everyday speech; when experimentation and risk-taking are invited; when the demands for proofreading and the risks of grading are eliminated; and when the results of writing-to-learn activities are frequently *used* in class, as contributions to an ongoing exploration of content.
>
> (Daniels and Zemelman, 1991, 1)

At the beginning of a unit of study, have students write about the topic to find out what they know and to help them focus. This is a useful exercise before and after viewing a film or video.

Fifth grade teacher Christine Sobray Evans (1984) conducted a limited but intriguing classroom research project in her math classroom. She asked her students to do three types of writing during units on multiplication and geometry: explanations on how to do something, definitions of math terms, and troubleshooting, in which students specifically explained their errors on homework and quizzes. Posttests in both units showed impressive gains, particularly in geometry, where her group outscored the control group by 10 percent. See Chapter 5 for many more ideas for using writing in all subject areas.

Writing Conventions

For years teachers filled many of the classroom minutes labeled "Language Arts Instruction" with exercises in grammar and usage. Although most of these teachers were simply following the teachers' guides distributed by their school districts, the effectiveness of their efforts were minimal. The only guaranteed result was the dislike for "English" that was generated in students. Although the exercises were expected to improve students' speaking and writing, there was rarely time left during the school day to see whether this was the case.

In a meta-analysis of research on writing, George Hillocks (1987) identified those classroom activities that had a positive impact on students' writing performance. Of all the activities reviewed, only one had a negative impact on writing instruction: grammar drill. Such evidence, however, does not necessarily deter language arts teachers from their obsessions with errors in writing. In fact in many classrooms, "whether we mean it to be so, our students recognize what they already have learned so well: this is what the teacher looks for, this is what writing is all about: The Avoidance of Error. Our students tell us so, in many ways" (Halsted, 1975, 245).

For many years this quest to squelch "error" at its earliest appearance has reached into elementary classrooms right down to the primary grades. Spelling and punctuation errors were *not* acceptable in the work of first graders. Teachers felt compelled to correct every error on every paper, while parents carefully checked to make sure none was missed. It is no surprise that young children were not allowed to write anything that wasn't copied or spelled out for them. As we bring our knowledge of how oral language is learned into the arena of written language, however, we are beginning to understand that the pattern of development evident in a piece of language such as "Me, water" will also appear in the punctuation and spelling of fledgling writers.

Viewing writing as a performing art, akin to such activities as playing the piano or playing tennis, helps us understand this complex process. No one questions that it takes years to develop and refine abilities in such activities. And so we all understand that—when it comes to learning tennis or the piano, at least—lack of polish (error, that is) is an expected and probably even necessary part of the growth process children go through when developing their skills. It helps to see writing errors in the same way—more common in new performers than in experienced ones, more likely to occur in harder "pieces" than in easier ones, less of a concern in practice sessions than in "recitals," something young performers need to consider—but not so much that they begin to move mechanically or, worse, stop hearing the music altogether.

Holding on to this vision of writing demands that teachers address the instruction of writing conventions differently than before. If we break language down into small, meaningless parts and demand isolated drill on those parts, little is transferred into the actual writing process—it would be like practicing one note on the piano.

Painless Instruction

A painless method for dealing with conventions and developing a common vocabulary is to have the whole class focus on one or two sentences a day. *The*

Write Source 2000's Teacher's Guide (1990) calls these mini-exposures to grammar MUG (*M*echanics, *U*sage, *G*rammar) Shots. To do MUG Shots, place a sentence in need of editing on the chalkboard or overhead; for example, "at the minnesota zoo chris lacie and tyler discovered many interesting animals" (use your students' names and classroom topics in the sentences). Have groups of students collaborate for a few minutes, then ask them to take turns editing and explaining why they made the changes: "The A in *at* should be capitalized because it's the first word in the sentence." (This activity works well after lunch or recess to refocus attention.)

By discussing language conventions, students learn quickly. As they edit together and hear their peers' reasons for making changes, they develop a common vocabulary and a common body of knowledge for future reference. They also come to understand that conventions sometimes play an important role in written language. For instance, first graders may notice that several of their big books use ellipses. When their teacher explains that these let readers know something exciting is coming on the next page, the first graders begin to use ellipses in *their* writing. Obviously ellipses would not normally be taught at the first grade level—but when they and other conventions are observed in a meaningful context, children can understand their function and begin to apply them.

Children come to school already expert at the grammar of the English language. Although they cannot discuss language at an abstract level, they can apply very abstract information in order to construct grammatical utterances. "The study of grammar requires an act of self-consciousness that literally asks young people to step outside themselves to describe how they juggle. In time such a step has immense value and is a giant step for self-knowledge. Attempted at the wrong time, the step results in confusion and frustration, a backward step educationally and personally" (Sanborn, 1986, 77). Therefore it's critical that teachers watch for those *right* times.

Spelling

Spelling holds an exalted position in American society. In fact, if you are a successful speller, you may even get to visit the President of the United States via the National Spelling Bee. Spelling errors in public documents and on signs are regularly reported and complained about in the media (a recent misspelling on the diplomas of the graduates of the Naval Academy as graduates of the "Navel Academy" got a lot of press nationwide). Schools reflect society's attitude toward spelling. Few parents would fail to recognize (and remember) the Friday morning panic associated with the wail: "I forgot to study my spelling words!" This hyperattention to spelling places two challenges before language arts teachers: first to understand the nature and function of spelling and second to share that understanding with the public.

Many people view spelling as a simple act of memorization. But anyone who observes children's writing would certainly notice that the words that students spelled correctly on Friday's test often appear incorrectly in their own writing. There is more going on here than simple memorization.

Because they don't understand how children develop written language, some parents and teachers fear that errors seen in early writing efforts will become permanent. The same people have no qualms about the errors they hear in children's speech—in fact most recognize that errors are a part of the normal development of oral language. This same acceptance is evident in other areas of early development as well.

> Like early attempts to walk, talk, and draw, initial attempts to spell do not produce habits to overcome. No one worries when a child's first drawing of a person is a head propped up on two stick legs. As the errors become more sophisticated—two stick arms protruding from the head where the ears should be—no one fears this schema will become a habit though it may be repeated a hundred times. Although deficient by many measures, the drawings are not interpreted as signs of visual, cognitive, or fine motor problems. They are greeted as a display of intelligence and emerging proficiency.
>
> (Sowers, 1986, 47)

It's up to teachers to let parents know what their children's early writing will look like. When parents understand how writing develops, they can provide more effective support for their children—and the language arts program will be more successful.

J. Richard Gentry (1982) has identified the following five stages of spelling development in children's writing: precommunicative spelling, semiphonetic spelling, phonetic spelling, transitional spelling, and correct spelling. At the **precommunicative stage,** young writers use letters as well as numbers or other nonalphabetic symbols. Their writing may or may not move from left to right, and they may mix uppercase and lowercase letters randomly (but they show a strong preference for uppercase).

During the **semiphonetic stage,** young writers begin to see a relationship between letters and the sounds of the language. At this point they frequently use abbreviated spelling, so one letter may represent an entire word. For example, they often use the letter R to represent the word *are*. Gentry says that teachers can support these writers with instruction that "may focus on alphabet knowledge, directionality of print and its spatial orientation, children's concept of words, matching oral language to print, and representing sounds with letters" (199).

As young writers begin to employ an almost one-to-one correspondence between sounds and symbols, their spelling behaviors belong to what Gentry identifies as the **phonetic stage.** "During this stage, writers often begin to negotiate word segmentation and spatial organization as well. Phonetic

Oral Language Stages	Written Language Stages	Level of Understanding
Babbling & cooing	Scribbling	Exploration of medium
Language intonation	Linear/repetitive drawing	Refining the form
Native language forms	Letterlike forms	Cultural relevance
Creative grammar	Invented spelling	Overgeneralization of rules
Adult speech	Standard spelling	Formal structure

FIGURE 4.20 A comparison of the early stages of speaking and writing (Fields, 1989, 899).

spellers are ready for introduction to the conventions of English orthography: word families, spelling patterns, phonics, and word structure" (199).

At the **transitional stage,** spellers display even more sophistication about the rules of written English. They recognize that vowels appear in every syllable; they abandon letter name strategies (vowels are included with the R to spell *are*); and they begin to regularly use silent vowels, common English letter sequences, and inflected endings (ed, ing, s). Finally these spellers are ready for regular spelling instruction, and teachers can expect the learned words to appear in the writing.

Gentry places writers at the **correct stage** when as second graders children have mastered "a certain corpus of words that has been designated as 'second grade level.' 'Correct spelling' is usually viewed from the instructional scheme rather than the developmental scheme because developmental research beyond the age of eight or nine is limited to a few studies" (197).

These stages in spelling closely parallel the stages that children pass through as they learn to speak. Since the errors children make on their way to becoming proficient users of oral language are very familiar to most adults, the table in Figure 4.20 developed by Marjorie Fields (1989) provides a succinct, informative comparison of early speaking and writing.

Helping Students Become Better Spellers

1. **Allow students time to apply spelling knowledge in authentic writing experiences.** Spelling is not a subject in itself: it is a subskill of writing. Children are not good spellers unless they spell correctly at their developmental level in their own writing. Some of the time currently devoted to extensive spelling activities should more appropriately be spent on writing.

2. **Help students develop an eye for what "looks" right.** As children develop to the level of transitional and correct spelling, they will begin to develop an eye for what "looks right." After first developing the ability to

find those words in their own writing that "look wrong," students need to learn how to make educated guesses about how a word is spelled. Most adult spellers use this strategy in their own writing when they write a problematic word over in a variety of possible forms before selecting the one that "looks right." Teachers should model this strategy and then ask students to practice it.

3. **Help students learn to spell words that appear frequently in writing.** Not all words are worth their weight in gold in the storehouse in our brain. Although it may be fun to be able to spell *Mississippi*, it is not one of the words that anyone writes often. There are one hundred words that make up more than 25 percent of what we write; being able to spell those words would guarantee that 25 percent of a student's writing is spelled correctly. There are one thousand words that make up almost 89 percent of everything we write (Sitton, 1989). Focus your spelling program on these words rather than seldom-used words like *encyclopedia* or *Mississippi*.

4. **Help students learn rules that promote good spelling rather than hinder it.** Disagreements over which spelling rules should be taught have occupied researchers for years. The rules below, from *Spel . . . is a Four Letter Word* seem a sensible choice, given what we know about the English language and its exceptions.

- the rules for using periods in abbreviations
- the rules for using apostrophes to show possession
- the rules for capitalizing proper names and adjectives
- the rules for adding suffixes (changing *y* to *i*, dropping the final silent *e*, doubling the final consonant)
- the rule that English words don't end in *v*
- the rule that *q* is followed by *u* in English spelling

(Gentry, 1987, 31)

5. **Help students find meaning-based connections between words.** If students know how to spell *compete*, the word *competition* is easy. Likewise *muscular* helps them figure out *muscle*.

6. **Alert students to pattern errors.** If a student makes similar spelling mistakes—like *naping*, *kiding*, or *faning*—you may want to plan a special presentation lesson (in this case, on doubling the final consonant before adding a suffix). Invite students to search for patterns of error themselves. Collect several misspellings from one piece of writing and ask students to determine what information this writer needs.

7. **Create individual spelling lists from errors in each student's writing.** Even second graders can be taught to test each other on short spelling lists, so individualized lists don't have to be time-consuming for the teacher.

Spelling errors offend readers and often interfere with the writer's message. Learning to spell in the context of one's own writing is important on the journey to successful, effective writing.

Handwriting

Since decisions about handwriting are usually made by the elementary school staff as a whole or by a committee for the entire school system, most teachers cannot decide for themselves which particular program they use. Variables in the commercial programs currently available include how they break individual letters into discrete graphic components and how students are instructed to connect those components to make the letters of the alphabet (as "balls and sticks" or "slides, glides, and monkey tails"). Attention to slant, spacing, and uniformity are also part of these programs. Each publisher includes guides for their particular writing system and suggestions for which year the students should move from manuscript to cursive printing.

Teachers have the responsibility of teaching the handwriting system adopted by their district. They should examine the particular program in light of the following:

1. **Are writers helped to recognize situations in which neat, careful handwriting is highly desirable and other situations when less careful writing is more practical?** Few adults hold high expectations for their writing on shopping lists or on notes they write in birthday cards. During writing workshop, for example, careful, neat writing is only expected on final copies, not rough drafts.

2. **Does the program provide developmentally appropriate practices in handwriting instruction?** Expectations for any handwriting program should be checked against what is known about fine-motor development. The Northeast Foundation for Children (1991) offers the guidelines below, based on the developmental characteristics of children at the ages listed.

Five-year-olds
- "Manuscript printing can be introduced, but children should not be expected to stay within lines."
- "Spacing of letters and numbers will be inconsistent." (14)

Five-and-one-half-year-olds

- "Reversals of letters and numbers are at their peak; reading and writing tasks can be extremely difficult." (15)

Six-year-olds

- "Children should do little copy work from the board. Although they will comply if asked, this is a difficult task at this age."

- "Spacing and the ability to stay on the line are difficult and performed with great inconsistency." (17)

Seven-year-olds

- "Children's printing, drawing, and number work tends to be small, if not microscopic. Children work with head down on desk, often hiding or closing one eye. Copying from the board can be harmful. Inappropriate time to introduce cursive writing."

- "Children will anchor printing to bottom line; find it difficult to fill up space."

- "Children work with pincer grasp at pencil point and find it difficult to relax their grip." (19)

3. **Can writers who do not yet have adequate fine-motor skills participate in handwriting activities without damaging their self-esteem?** In every classroom there will be children who cannot write neatly, despite sincere efforts on their part to do so. Although frustrating for teachers and parents as well as the students themselves, make every effort to focus on what they can do rather than on what they cannot. If computers are available, these students should be the first to "write" on the computer.

4. **Does this program give adequate consideration to left-handed writers?** Left-handed writers require different alignment of their paper. Check to see that they hold their pencils so they can see their work as they proceed.

■ **IDEAS TO LEARN**   Spend some time observing adults and children actually writing. Look at how they hold the pencil, pen, or crayon; notice the placement of the paper, the formation of each letter, the regularity of the slant and the spacing, and finally the overall neatness of the final product. All the individuals you observe were taught in school how to correctly hold a pencil, form each cursive or printed letter, and produce a neat final product. How would you rate the success of the nation's handwriting programs? What might account for the variations evident in your observations? Share your own experiences with handwriting with your peers.

Assessment

There is good news and bad news concerning assessment in writing. Since writing is relatively new to the list of "basics" in the elementary classroom, there is no nationally used, standardized test of writing; that is the good news. The bad news is that after the early, developmental stages of writing, there is little information on how to evaluate the writing of writers who have begun to use relatively standard conventions and spelling.

Observation checklists are readily available for the early stages of writing. First grade teachers in Mt. Pleasant, Michigan, developed the form shown in Figure 4.21 to collect information on fledgling writers. Such checklists generally focus on the look of the writing, as children learn to manage symbols and two-dimensional space.

Within the classroom writing community, students and teachers must build their own criteria for judging writing: What makes a piece of writing *good?* Fledgling writers can begin this process as they contribute to a classroom chart that asks, "What do we like to hear in our friends' writing?" Older students can begin more sophisticated lists.

Rather than looking at all aspects of a piece of writing and giving one holistic response, Vicki Spandel and Richard J. Stiggins (1990) suggest *analytic scoring*, which is "an attempt to define the main traits or characteristics of writing (*e.g., ideas, organization*) and to specify criteria that describe each of these traits in terms of the relevant strengths and weaknesses that we are likely to see in real samples of student writing" (7). Using the list of traits and criteria shown in Figure 4.22, students and teachers can discuss and compose their own list, which reflects their understanding of what makes writing *good.*

The Writing Portfolio

The use of portfolios is an attempt to link the curriculum to day-to-day instruction and to assessment; to view students' work over time; and to treat evaluation as an ongoing activity that looks at individual behavior and performance rather than abstract scores on standardized tests. Although some teachers have been using portfolios for years, recently portfolios have gotten much greater attention as an "alternative assessment" to traditional numerical assessments. In some cases portfolio assessment has been used in conjunction with standardized tests to provide a much more precise and detailed picture of children's work (Tanner-Cazinha, Au, and Blake, 1991).

A portfolio's contents vary according to its purpose. Some school districts and individual schools mandate portfolios as a means of demonstrating children's exit skills in writing. But they are used more beneficially as a

Emerging Writing Skills K-1

Name _____ School _____
Teacher _____ Year _____ Grade _____

Monthly Observations	Sept	Oct	Nov	Dec	Jan	Feb	Mar	Apr	May
Pictures only									
Invented symbols									
Random letters									
Letter name spelling									
Initial and final consonants									
Vowels in most words									
Leaves spaces									
Writes labels									
Writes single sentences									
Writes 2–3 sentences									
Writes stories									
Mixes capitals and lower case									
Some use of capitals									
Some use of punctuation									
Some standardized spelling									
Writes without drawing									
Name and date on work									
Reads back writing									
Shares writing with others									

D = Developing   S = Secure

FIGURE 4.21 A form for assessing the writing of young elementary students.

WRITING CHECKLIST

Trait 1: Ideas and Content

Strengths

____ Interesting
____ Well focused
____ Clear
____ Detailed, complete, rich
____ Written from experience

Weaknesses

____ Lacking in purpose or theme
____ Rambling
____ Unclear, muddled
____ Broad, general, vague
____ Not believable
____ Boring

Trait 2: Organization

Strengths

____ Good introduction
____ Good placement of details
____ Strong transitions
____ Smooth, easy pace
____ Reader doesn't have to think about organization
____ Strong conclusion
____ Starts somewhere: goes somewhere
____ Builds in tension: creates interest

Weaknesses

____ Details seem out of place
____ Introduction boring, predictable
____ Transitions absent, weak, or too obvious
____ Doesn't go anywhere
____ Wanders aimlessly
____ Stops abruptly
____ Drags on too long
____ Bogs down in trivia

Trait 3: Voice

Strengths

____ Individual
____ Honest
____ Natural
____ Expressive
____ Unusual, unexpected
____ Appealing
____ Written to be read and enjoyed

Weaknesses

____ Trite
____ Flat
____ Writer sounds bored
____ Phoney
____ Written to please others
____ Blends with others
____ Mechanical, lifeless

Trait 4: Word Choice

Strengths

____ Precise language
____ Strong verbs

Weaknesses

____ Language vague, abstract
____ Mostly *is, are* verbs

FIGURE 4.22 A checklist of writing traits and characteristics (Spandel and Stiggins, 1990, 153–155).

Trait 4: Word Choice

Strengths

_____ Specific, concrete nouns

_____ Natural

_____ Words used in new ways

_____ Strong imagery

Weaknesses

_____ Hard for reader to picture anything

_____ Redundancy

_____ Too many clichés

_____ Words used incorrectly

_____ Words used to impress

Trait 5: Sentence Fluency

Strengths

_____ Fluid

_____ Musical, poetic in sound

_____ Easy to read aloud

_____ Interesting word patterns

_____ Good phrasing

_____ Varied sentence length

_____ Varied sentence structure

_____ Varied sentence beginnings

_____ Fragments used well

Weaknesses

_____ Awkward

_____ Jarring word patterns

_____ Hard to read aloud

_____ Short, choppy sentences

_____ Long, rambling sentences

_____ Repetitious patterns

_____ Fragments awkward (sound accidental, tacked on)

Trait 6: Conventions

Strengths

_____ Correct or phonetic spelling

_____ Punctuation works with sentence structure

_____ Some sophisticated punctuation attempted

_____ Correct grammar

_____ Sound usage

_____ Paragraphing enhances organization

_____ Informalities in punctuation or usage handled well

_____ Attention to details (i.e., dotted i's, crossed t's)

_____ Effective title

_____ Good margins

_____ Easy to read

Weaknesses

_____ Spelling faulty, not phonetic

_____ Punctuation doesn't work well with sentence structure

_____ Grammatical problems

_____ Faulty usage

_____ Lack of subject-verb agreement

_____ No paragraphing

_____ Paragraphs start at wrong spots

_____ Careless, hasty errors

_____ No title

_____ Misleading title

_____ No margins

_____ Hard to read

*For the sake of consistency, we've based our checklist on the same six analytical traits that were used in the scoring guide; however, your list of traits might be quite different.

FIGURE 4.22 *continued*

> How I write a book is I think of stuff I like (TVshows, sports, Video games). If I can't think of anything I ask around, or read and get an idea. When I have a good idea I write it down on paper. Then I do anter draghts and put in the stuff I like and take out the stuff I don't like.
>
> Jeff chapman

FIGURE 4.23 A young writer's self-assessment.

collection of children's work over time that allows teachers and students to see and understand students' development in reading and writing. One central purpose for many who use the portfolio is to provide student ownership of his or her writing. It is the student who determines what goes into the portfolio, and student self-assessment is an important ingredient in helping children become independent, critical thinkers about their own work. The portfolio also provides parents with information about their children's growth and learning.

Once you as a teacher decide how you want to use the portfolio, you can decide what goes into it. If you want to use the portfolio for final evaluation or as a "showcase" of students' work, then students' final, polished pieces will go into their portfolios. In that case students and teacher together discuss what the students think is their best work and how they might best represent themselves; students have the final say on what the portfolio contains. In addition, the final evaluation portfolio may also contain a self-evaluation, a metacognitive piece in which students demonstrate their understanding of their progress and growth. In fact one of the most valuable aspects of the portfolio is children's opportunity to look back at their work and assess their own development. Their self-assessments are often as powerful as their best polished piece (see Figure 4.23) and provide "a window into the students' heads, a means for both staff and students to understand the educational process at the level of the individual learner'' (Paulson, Paulson, and Meyer, 1991, 61).

In their work on portfolios, Lamme and Hysmith report that children's self-evaluations are often highly thoughtful and perceptive. They provide this example:

> A kindergarten teacher placed the scale of children's writing on a bulletin board. Using the scale, she showed the children how writing develops and suggested they might want to determine where they were on the scale so that they could see where they had been and where they were going. The children came up and identified the level of their own work. The teacher was amazed to see that the children accurately placed themselves on the scale of development. She found that understanding the development of writing helped her children be more satisfied with where they were as writers and take more risks with their writing.
>
> (Lamme and Hysmith, 1991, 632–633)

Although the portfolio may be used for final assessments, it's also valuable as an overview of children's work, demonstrating such things as their writing processes, their interests and concerns, and their growth in thinking and in skills. This collection of work might include such things as:

- Pictures and drawings
- Brainstorming efforts (freewrites, clusters, etc.)
- Checklists (of skills, topics)
- Note cards
- Logs
- Journals
- Drafts
- Revisions and notes for revisions
- Published pieces (books, newspapers, cartoons, bulletin board pieces, etc.)
- Self-evaluations and reflections

The portfolio allows teachers to see not only their students' growth in the structural and mechanical aspects of writing but also to learn about their growth as thinkers, the subjects they care about, and the knowledge they build on. The portfolio, then, can become a holistic means of looking at children's development in language and thinking.

Setting up and maintaining portfolios require time and attention. They need to be kept where they are easily available to students and where they have room to grow. Plastic milk cartons or office supply boxes that are color coordinated with the folders themselves or with colored tabs help children find and put away their folders. The teacher and students should talk about what belongs in the folder and what doesn't, so that the portfolio doesn't become the storage space for miscellaneous bits of paper. Periodically the teacher needs to devote class time to organizing, updating, and cleaning out the portfolios, so that only what is relevant and valuable is kept there. The folder itself may be used for record keeping: Students can use the covers to write information about the portfolio's contents; they can use checklists that are taped or stapled to the folder to help them keep track of their work. Maintaining the folder may be a significant part of helping children learn to become responsible for their own work.

Once portfolios are in place and children are busily writing and maintaining their writing, teachers need to develop a way of assessing the children's work. Lamme and Hysmith (1991) report that the teachers in their study gathered three kinds of data: "observational data, checklist data, and interview or conference data" (634). Teachers observed children at work and developed various ways of keeping track of their observations. You can use notebooks, journals, or note cards to keep track of children's classroom work not covered by other means of assessment (such as checklists). Asking children about what they are doing and how they work also provides insight into their language and thinking. Checklists for children's skills, behaviors, and activities provide another way to assess children's patterns of growth (see Figure 4.24).

Portfolio assessment may seem daunting—and it *is* time-consuming, especially when you are not accustomed to doing it. Teachers who have found the process worthwhile are excited about the insights they have gained into children's learning. However, it is certainly helpful to have the support of your administrator as you put portfolio assessment in place. Inviting teachers who are familiar with portfolios to do an in-service workshop at your school and working with others who share your interests in alternative assessment are two ways to ease into using portfolios. The greatest reward you'll receive from using portfolios will be the deeper understanding of children's minds and hearts that you gain when you look closely at their work.

Educating Parents

As we learn more about how elementary students learn to write, it is critical that we share our new understandings with parents so that they can support their children's efforts. We can educate parents through personal letters and

Level 11: Child uses a variety of strategies for revision and editing.
Child uses writing techniques to build suspense, create humor, etc.

Level 10: Child willingly revises and edits.
Child writes creatively and imaginatively.
Child writes original poetry.
Child writes clearly. The message makes sense.
Child uses commas, quotation marks, and apostrophes.

Level 9: Writing includes details or dialogue, a sense of humor, or other emotions.
Child retells a familiar story or follows the pattern of a known story or poem.
Spelling becomes more conventional.
Child willingly revises.

Level 8: Child writes a short story with a beginning, a middle, and an end.
Child writes for several different purposes (narrative, expository,
and persuasive).
Revision involves adding to the story.
Child begins to use punctuation.

Level 7: Child writes the start of a story.
Child uses both phonics and sight strategies to spell words.
Child writes several short sentences.

Level 6: Child invents spellings.
Story is a single factual statement.
The message is understandable.

Level 5: Child labels drawings.
Letters have some connection to sounds.
Child writes lists.
Child separates words with a space or marker.
Child writes a message.
Child writes familiar words.

Level 4: Child repeats message.
Child has a message concept and tells you what the message is.
Letters don't match sounds.
Child writes alphabet letter strings.

Level 3: Child copies words he/she sees around the room.
Alphabet letters and mock letters are in a line across the page.

Level 2: Child writes alphabet and mock letters scattered around the page.
Child writes mock letters.
Child pretends to write.

Level 1: Child attempts to write in scribbles or draws patterns.

FIGURE 4.24 A scale of children's writing development (Lamme and
Hysmith, 1991, 631).

with professionally prepared pamphlets. The following pamphlets help explain children's development of written language:

How to Help Your Child Become a Better Writer
National Council of Teachers of English
1111 Kenyon Road
Urbana, IL 61801

Writing: Parents Can Help
NEA Professional Library
P.O. Box 509
West Haven, CT 06516

You Can Help Your Child Connect Reading to Writing
International Reading Association
800 Barsdale Road
P.O. Box 8190
Newark, DE 19714-8139

Final Reflections

Theories and practices concerning writing in the elementary school have changed dramatically in the past ten years. Those changes include:

- A new **conceptualization** of the writing process itself, which demands that we slow down and give more attention to what happens before and after we write.

- A new **commitment of time** to the actual process of writing rather than practicing the numerous subskills that are part of writing (handwriting, spelling, mechanics, etc.).

- Increased **choices** for the students in what they want to write about and how they want to present their ideas.

- Extensive **conferring and collaborating** with peers and teachers throughout the process.

- Continual **connecting** of the development of speaking, reading, writing, and listening.

- Regular **celebration** of what a child can do rather than what he or she cannot do.

Harvey Daniels and Steve Zemelman (1985), authors of *A Writing Project: Training Teachers of Composition from Kindergarten to College*, make these observations about writing:

- Writing is important. It is a highly practical and useful skill; more important, it enriches and empowers individual human beings.
- Writing is magic. It partakes of the primitive, deeply felt human need to make and share stories. Writing always holds the opportunity for joy.

(Daniels and Zemelman, 1985, 13)

The joy and empowerment described by these authors is not just that of the writers, but also of the writers' teachers. Recently Mary Lou, a first grade teacher for twenty years who had just completed her first year of using the writing process in her classroom, shared a comment made to her by one of her students at the end of the year. The child observed, ''You really like being a teacher, don't you?'' Mary Lou, who has always been an outstanding teacher, said that was the first time that a child said that about her. She felt confident that the joy and magic that had been created during their year of writing, sharing, and celebrating was responsible for the accuracy of her student's comment—it had indeed been a joyful year.

5

Bridges:
Language Across the Curriculum

The Language Across the Curriculum Movement

Before they begin school, children are natural learners. Almost from the time they can talk, children have questions about their environment, their world. They ask why, how, where, when, what in an effort to understand how the world works and to get some control over what happens around them. Children's natural curiosity seems to be just that: natural. They ask about where the water goes when it runs out of the bathtub, why water looks blue in a lake but when you hold it in your hand it doesn't, what crayons are made of, what's in space, what's inside a cloud, why cats kill cute little birds and bunnies, what makes cars go, how planes get off the ground, and why kids have to eat vegetables. What they see in their environment and what's happening in their lives inspires their questions.

Children's care givers may or may not have answers to those questions. Most parents do their best, but some questions are too profound to answer easily, if at all. Some parents, with resources and patience, refer to dictionaries and encyclopedias, which can encourage their children to seek answers and ask yet more questions. Other parents may not have the time or patience to answer their children's questions. Nevertheless, children's curiosity persists.

I know a [kindergarten] teacher who asked her youngsters soon after they had arrived in the school, to draw for her anything they could see in the classroom which they thought had energy in it. Christine, the teacher, was part of a small group of teacher researchers who were interested to find out more about how children systematized the world to themselves, before anyone had told them how to do it and what to look for. These children had received no formal teaching about energy—this invitation to draw may have been the first time she had actually used the word "energy" with them. Nevertheless, between them they drew pictures which represented energy in all its conceivable forms: the sun of course, clothes or trees blowing in the wind, people panting and puffed out, light bulbs, television sets, cookers and so on. They could also talk about their pictures and explain to their teacher when she asked them, why they had drawn a particular object: the sun gives us light, the wind is strong, the people are panting because they have used up all their energy and so on.

FIGURE 5.1 An example of how children make meaning of their world (D'Arcy, 1989, 17).

A central tenet in an integrated language arts classroom is that language is the means by which children learn about and gain control over the world. Before they start school children observe, ask questions, form hypotheses, and test those hypotheses on the basis of more and more experience. In observing my own and my friends' children over the years, I have heard many "cute" stories about the kinds of "silly" mistakes children make when they begin figuring out the world, beginning with their question "What dat?" and their early creation of categories. As they refine the categories (separating, for example, dogs and cats, horses and cows, milk and juice, apples and oranges, babies and kids), their questions become more complex; they begin to examine interrelationships and causes and effects.

Before they come to school, then, oral language is the means through which children construct an entire theory of the world in which they live, a theory based on good "scientific" principles of observing, hypothesizing, questioning, gathering data, and confirming their hypotheses. Sometimes, of course, they're wrong. Their observations were based on too few instances or someone misinformed them or they misunderstood the information they received. Nonetheless, if children have been encouraged to ask questions and been helped to find answers—if someone hasn't told them that they have no right to ask or seek answers to their questions—children come to school with some excellent resources for learning—they have been through a "life across the curriculum" learning experience. (See Figure 5.1.)

It is often the case when children come to school that their questions become less important than the questions posed in curriculum guides and textbooks. And often there is not time in the classroom to focus on children's questions because there is too much work that has to be "covered" before the end of the school year. Certainly the good teacher hears and answers children's "I'm curious" questions, but he or she often does this on an ad hoc basis rather than as a primary activity.

Moreover, the means by which children have been building their theories—oral language—becomes less valued. Schools emphasize written language instead. In addition, they place priority on answering the questions in the textbook, not on the children's prior knowledge, interests, or questions. Many textbooks still have a list of questions at the end of each chapter that simply asks children to restate facts, not to relate their reading to anything they know or care about. Mere "coverage" and rote learning seems to be the goal of this sort of curriculum.

Finally, in elementary school the curricula are not connected. Each subject area has a different curriculum, a different agenda. So even though social studies and literary and scientific questions may be closely tied together in real life (and usually are), there is little if any attempt to tie those issues together in elementary school studies.

A number of trends in recent years point to a new direction in schooling that provides more developmentally appropriate ways to help children learn about the world:

- Developers of textbooks and curricula in science, math, and social studies have begun to create materials that take into consideration how children learn and what subjects engage them.

- Teachers are placing new emphasis on trade books (as opposed to textbooks), many of which are more lively and interesting than those books written specifically for the classroom.

- More important, language across the curriculum (variously called writing across the curriculum, learning across the curriculum, interdisciplinary learning, or writing to learn) has begun to take hold in schools across the country (and indeed in many places around the world). This approach emphasizes the need for children to be active in their own learning, to engage in questioning, researching, thinking, talking, reading, and writing about what they want to know and to share and display what they have learned.

The language across the curriculum approach has three major goals: The first is to improve students' communication skills by integrating language more fully in all subject areas. The second is to develop students' critical thinking by considering "whys" and "hows" not just "whats" of subject matter. And the third is to help students become more actively engaged in learning—to develop concepts, processes, and information that will make them more knowledgeable and give them a fuller understanding of a subject area or topic. I want to emphasize that language across the curriculum is not

The claims of writing in the content areas to be part of the curriculum are many, but those that follow articulate some of the most persuasive reasons for all teachers to attend to the teaching of writing as well as to the teaching of content or subject matter.

1. *Writing about a subject helps students learn better.* The outcome of content writing programs is not simply improved language skills (an important end in itself), but improved learning of subject matter. If writing provides opportunities for students to play with ideas and concepts, then students will come to understand the subject more richly and deeply than before.

2. *Writing about content has practical payoff.* Perhaps the biggest reason Johnny and Jane do not write well is that they have not had enough practice doing it. Teachers whose students write frequently on content-area topics are providing a great service to those students, including short-term payoff (better writing of school papers) and long-range rewards (becoming successful writers at higher levels of education and in the real world).

3. *Content writing often motivates reluctant writers.* English compositions are often badly written because the topics are bland and banal: "My Summer Vacation," "The Most Unforgettable Character I Ever Met." Many so-called nonwriters are merely writers waiting for an engaging content-area topic to come along: *computers, science, history, futurism.* Writing about content gives substance to student writing and helps inspire many inexperienced and previously unmotivated writers.

4. *Content writing develops all language skills.* Although the principal concern here is writing, language skills are so tightly interwoven that a better title for this publication might be *Teaching Literacy in the Content Areas: Reading, Writing, Listening, Speaking.* The model units demonstrate this by including supplementary reading, questions for talk and discussion, and even opportunities for drama and media composition.

5. *Teaching writing teaches thinking.* According to an old, but accurate, cliché, one does not understand an idea fully until one can write about it. We do not believe that one can teach thinking the same way one can teach the multiplication tables, but it is clear that a student who is a good writer is generally perceived by his or her teachers as an effective thinker as well. Learning to write involves learning to think, and writing is unique in allowing students not only to think, but to display the products of their thinking in a form that invites further contemplation.

FIGURE 5.2 Why we use writing to teach content (Stephen Tchudi and Susan Tchudi, 1983, 6–7).

to be seen as an add-on to the many curricular responsibilities that a teacher already has but as a means of teaching subjects already in the curriculum (see Figure 5.2). Reading, writing, speaking, and listening in social studies, science, mathematics, literature, and even physical education, art, and music involves students in active learning rather than simply filling in blanks.

To explain the new direction that language across the curriculum is taking, Stephen Tchudi (1986) describes his experience in a writing across the curriculum workshop in which a teacher observed, "You're not just asking me to add more writing to my course. You're asking me to change my whole style of teaching. . . . To include good writing in my class I'd have to change from deductive teaching to inductive teaching, from covering the textbook to letting students do more figuring out for themselves" (22).

Tchudi agreed. "When we invite colleagues in other disciplines and fields to teach writing, we are in fact calling for nothing less than a revolution in most of education. For despite all the evidence gathered in this century that learning is experiential, that it requires learners to make connections for themselves, a majority of school and college teaching still follows the old deductive pattern of instructors presenting concepts and having students show mastery of them" (22). Consensus seems to be developing in all disciplines that students' engagement in learning, their connecting with and pursuing their interests, is basic to their success not only in school but after they leave.

The November 1989 issue of *Educational Leadership* was devoted to a discussion of the need for changes in the curriculum by a number of leaders in science, mathematics, social studies, and the arts. All of them advocate students using language to understand their subject areas.

For example, to improve science education says Thomas P. Sachse (1989) from the California State Department of Education, "factoids" have to go. Sachse defines factoids as "every person's favorite scientific tidbit." The focus on scientific terms, definitions, facts, and trivia "wastes students' time and destroys their motivation" (18). Instead, to develop scientific literacy, students need to learn scientific concepts by engaging in activities that are relevant to their daily lives. Sachse sees value in the Science, Technology, and Society movement, a curricular trend that makes connections between science and its technological applications. In addition, students are encouraged to see the connection between science and aesthetic concerns—for example, the loss of animals and natural beauty with the loss of the tropical rain forest. Sachse also sees the need to "integrate the disciplines of science and to integrate science with other areas of inquiry (19). He outlines three aspects to instructional reform in science that are having an impact on the development of materials and teacher training programs: "(1) thematic science teaching, where concepts are built upon a structure of the major ideas that connect the science disciplines; (2) constructivist science teaching, where teachers take account of students' prior experience to build rigorous conceptual models; and (3) interactive science learning, where students converse and collaborate about an issue or event" (19). All three models have language at their center. All engage students in asking questions, posing hypotheses, testing assumptions, and working collaboratively to come to conclusions. Moreover, rather than following the linear textbook design, students are encouraged to follow different routes, to find multiple solutions, and to pursue an interest in depth.

Leaders in mathematics education, too, are eager to see children develop their understanding of mathematics by building and testing their own hypotheses, as evidenced by the goals and directions set by the National Council of Teachers of Mathematics (NCTM) in their publication, *Curriculum and Evaluation Standards for School Mathematics*. John Dossey (1989), professor of mathematics at Illinois State University, captures the experience of many elementary school children when he says that "the teaching of mathematics has taken place in an atmosphere of rigidity and student fear, as the accumulated knowledge of past generations has been transmitted to anxious students in classrooms void of active, engaged investigation" (22). The NCTM (1989) encourages change: "The *Standards* calls instead for a curriculum that provides for students' participation, across the grades, in *constructing* their conception of mathematics. This construction must involve students in 'doing mathematics' with manipulatives, discussing the results of their investigations, and writing the results of their experiences. Such experiences, at each grade level, allow students to build on their extant knowledge by inventing new methods of assaulting problems" (22). Clearly language is significant to such an approach to teaching mathematics. Rather than telling students to do "all the odds" or "all the evens" in a textbook, this approach requires a change in the way teachers teach, calling on them to guide small group work and manage group discussions.

Students—their questions, their guesses, their working out not only of the answers but of the procedures—are at the center. The teacher becomes a coinvestigator rather than a transmitter of facts. Recommendations from the NCTM include giving attention to "recent and relevant applications of mathematics . . . to illustrate the value of mathematics, as well as to provide motivation for the study of mathematics" (24). Teachers, then, also help students explore the usefulness of mathematics by demonstrating its applications in the real world.

Teachers of history and geography are also reviewing both their curriculum and their instructional techniques. "Because social studies is lobbied by many interest groups to include their specialized contents, curriculum guidelines typically include so many topics that superficial instruction is practically guaranteed," according to Walter Parker of the University of Washington. "*Covering*," says Parker, "is a euphemism in social studies for teaching by mentioning; it implies superficial instruction. Covering typically means the teacher tells students a few facts about a person or event and then moves on to telling a few facts about another person or event. This parade-of-facts approach to social studies misrepresents the curriculum plan and undercuts authentic learning" (Parker, 1989, 40–41).

Parker agrees with other leaders in curriculum reform. Students need to be more actively engaged, and they need activities that involve them more fully. "More on less means that students will go into greater depth on a limited number of important topics. When topics are studied in depth, lessons can challenge students to perform near the ceiling of their abilities, going beyond the facts gathered to form durable and flexible understandings" (40). Parker believes that the "all-too-familiar cycle of teacher talk, worksheets, and tests are difficult to justify" (41). He provides another metaphor for the teaching/learning relationship, that of the teacher as a contractor, contracting out the sorts of labor that will get a house built. Teachers provide students with materials—readings, films, charts, maps, speakers—and students working cooperatively research, talk, dramatize, and construct learning to share with others. Again we see student reading, student writing, student speaking, student listening, student thinking, and student learning as the core of what happens in the classroom.

Clearly there is consensus, though not unanimity, among the leadership in professional organizations about the need to place students at the center of the curriculum and to develop an in-depth, inquiry-based educational system.

Textbook Limitations

The changes being advocated today emphasize the importance of actively involving students in their own learning. A growing number of educators believe that overreliance on textbooks often stands in the way of this involvement. In many classrooms the textbooks *are* the curriculum. In fact, according to Harriet Tyson and Arthur Woodward (1989), "Textbooks structure from 75 to 90 percent of classroom instruction. In most subject areas, textbooks define the scope and sequence of instruction, and the accompanying teacher guides (especially at the elementary level) provide a road map from which few teachers make major detours" (14).

One problem with texbooks is that in order to meet the needs of a diverse audience, they try to include everything. According to Tyson and Woodward (1989), textbooks "have become compendiums of topics, none of which are treated in much depth." In fact, "the material is compressed to the point of incomprehensibility," so that "only a small percentage of highly motivated students would be able to learn from available books." A study of science textbooks for grades 6–9 found that they "contained as many as 2,500 new and unfamiliar words—double what could be expected in a foreign language text for the same grades." Another study of K–12 science texts found "that one 6th grade text contained 3,400 specialized or technical words, a junior high text contained 4,600, and a high school biology textbook contained 9,900." The problem is similar in social studies texts, where the "emphasis on coverage means that almost every major topic receives short shrift. With so much material omitted, students gain little sense of the development of democracy and the principles on which it is based. (15)''

Among textbooks' shortcomings are the following:

- The usual goal of the textbook is to provide information. Of course no one objects to children (or anyone) getting information. But the problem is that often the information is valued over children's experience. Because children learn primarily through experience rather than through abstractions about experience, textbooks do not provide appropriate learning opportunities for children. They provide conclusions but they usually don't explain how those conclusions came about or what the information is based upon.

- Textbooks put forth a pretense of objectivity, because their ostensible purpose is to *provide* information, not to *interpret* it. But in fact they do select and interpret information in order to present it. It would be better for textbook writers to simply admit that they are *interpreting evidence* rather than *presenting truth*.

- As a result of the pose of objectivity, the writing in textbooks is often voiceless and wooden. The style is dry, dull, remote, and uninteresting. When children say their textbooks are boring, we ought to listen—they are letting us know that they don't value what they are being made to read.

- Textbooks often focus on issues and ideas in which children have no interest. Or the information presented is so compressed or generalized that children, with their limited background in the area, find it baffling and even incomprehensible.

- Textbooks often value rote learning over interaction or action on the part of the learner. Questions at the end of the chapter emphasize recall over interpretation and give children few opportunities to do or make something with the information they have received.

■ **IDEAS TO LEARN**   Choose a topic of interest to you in science, social studies, or some other area of the curriculum. Review how that topic is covered in a number of textbooks. What does each textbook emphasize? How is the topic introduced? What sort of pictures or graphics accompany the text? Are students asked to interact with the text or make judgments about what they read? How? What sorts of questions, projects, writing ideas, and the like are included in the text? Which text would you prefer to use and why?

If textbooks are so horrible, should we throw them out altogether? If so, what would replace them? How would we organize the curriculum without them? First of all, although textbooks present problems as the sole source of learning in the classroom, they are not worthless (after all, this is a textbook, and I certainly wouldn't want you to ignore it). They often provide a way to focus or organize the curriculum. They can provide a reasonable sequence of activities and a valuable content for learning. They simply cannot be the *sole* source for learning and understanding in a subject area. Second, all good teachers provide experiences outside the textbook to help their students understand its concepts and information. And many of the best teachers simply use the textbook as background material, to which children can go to confirm their own experiences in learning and to connect it to other related issues. The language across the curriculum movement has provided support and a conceptual framework for teachers who use language to engage students more fully in learning.

Tyson and Woodward (1989) think that textbooks can be better. Since publishers say that they publish what sells, teachers and textbook selection committees need to be clear and aggressive in letting publishers know what they want—books that are memorable, literate, well written, engaging; books that cover fewer topics in more depth by authors who want to share what they know with the young. But even if the textbooks are ideal, teachers shouldn't rely on them solely; they should augment them with trade books to enrich their classrooms.

Developing and organizing a unit of study is one of the basics in the life of a teacher. For many teachers—particularly those in more well-to-do school districts—the job is made "easier" by a curriculum centered on the textbook series that the school district adopts. Social studies units, then, are the chapters in the social studies textbook; the science units are prescribed by chapters one through twelve of the science book; the mathematics curriculum is spelled out in the mathematics book. Some teachers rely on the textbook alone; they have children read the chapters and write the answers to the questions at the end. In the following section I will present ways to use language that involve students more deeply in subject matter than a textbook alone ever can.

Practicing Language Across the Curriculum

Both the shortcomings of curricula and of textbooks point to a need to engage children more fully in their own learning. Children need to become more deeply involved in the ideas and concepts that they encounter, so that their learning is meaningful, lasting, and of interest to them. This section will help you develop a plan for a classroom that integrates students' experiences, language, and school subjects.

In *The Young Learner's Handbook*, Stephen Tchudi (1987) describes a model of learning that puts the interests and questions of the young learner at

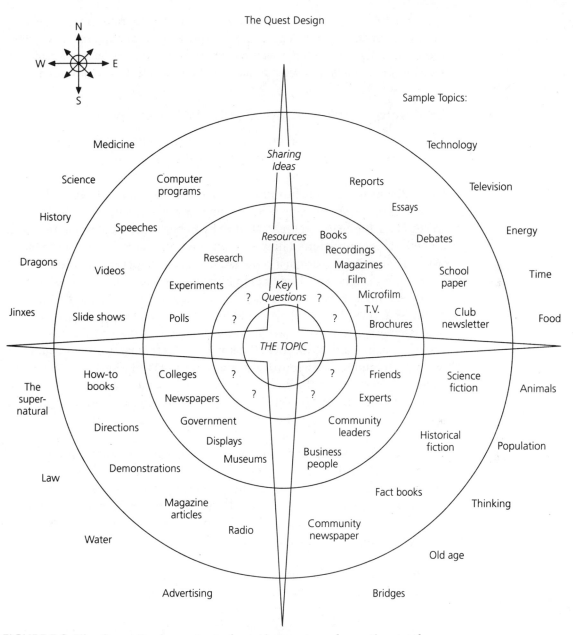

FIGURE 5.3 The Quest Design puts students' interests and questions at the center of their learning (Stephen Tchudi, 1987, 11).

the center of their "questing" process. Figure 5.3 shows Tchudi's "Quest Design," which includes topics, questions, resources, and sharing ideas. Although designed for the independent learner, this provides an excellent model for school quests as well.

The following practices in language across the curriculum demonstrate that children and teachers share responsibility for what happens in the classroom. Although the teacher acts as expert guide and resource person, the students are always involved in making choices, selections, and judgments.

Exploring a Topic Through Students' Experiences

You can use a variety of ways to get children to think about what they already know about a subject and what they would like to find out.

Class discussions   The introduction of a unit may simply begin with a discussion of the topic. To begin a discussion of jobs and occupations in a kindergarten class, for instance, I read *Owliver* by Robert Kraus, a story about a little owl whose mother wanted him to be an actor or a dancer and whose father wanted him to be a doctor or a lawyer. Owliver participates in all the activities his parents designed for him to help him achieve their goals. But when Owliver grew up, he became a fireman. After I read the book, I talked to children about what they thought they would like to be when they grew up. We then discussed other jobs we knew about and I listed all the possibilities on the board to begin a unit to discover the kinds of jobs that people do. In a unit on amphibians and reptiles, fourth grade teacher Ted Drake began by tacking up sheets of newsprint on the board, one for a list of what children already knew about the topic and one for what they wanted to know. The children used the second list to look for specific answers to the questions they raised.

Learning logs   Many classroom goals can be achieved through the use of journals and learning logs. There are probably as many kinds of journals and logs as there are teachers who use them. Two important elements about them need to be emphasized: First, students use them to think, explore, question, ponder, and reflect in language that is close to their thinking processes and their oral language, what James Britton (1970) calls "expressive language." Second, teachers use them to learn what their students think, understand, and feel. Logs and journals can help teachers discover what their students need, what confuses them; teachers can then respond to each student as an individual. In writing in content areas, learning logs allow children (and teachers) to keep track of questions, thoughts, hypotheses, and ideas as these develop. The learning log, then, is a good place to start an individual exploration. Joan LaMoyne Martins, a teacher in Postville, Iowa, demonstrates a wide variety of uses for the journal, from a place to express feelings to a record of academic responsibilities to a reflection on classroom activity (see Figure 5.4).

When introducing a unit, the first thing teachers might have students do is to make entries in their learning logs. For example, to begin a first grade

1. Color code your journals. Use five cover colors. In a class of twenty-five students use five yellow notebooks, five green ones, five blue, etcetera. This provides an easy way to divide up your written responses. You can ask for yellow journals to be handed in on Monday, green ones on Tuesday and so forth.

2. Each time the journals are used, the student should enter the current date in the margin (4-18-88). It is often handy to know when an entry was made.

3. The teacher should keep a dated list in which each student-assigned entry is recorded. Example: 3-17-88 Predict Chapter Seven science test questions.
   3-18-88 Tell me how you and the class behaved for the sub. Use "someone" in place of names.

   These short topic listings will be a handy teacher reference when responding to a journal entry written a week or two before.

4. Respond to journals as often as possible. If you let too much time pass, it will be hard to force yourself to catch up.

5. There are a variety of ways to respond to journals. Some people respond every five or ten pages. Others use stickers. I prefer to make personal responses to each entry. I never correct or criticize. I do praise, console, congratulate, comment, or just repeat, using as much humor as possible. I look on responding as my practice writing time.

6. In journals, the flow and the exploration of ideas are the important things. Therefore, students are not held responsible for spelling, punctuation, usage, or even neatness. Journals never go beyond first draft. If you give students the unencumbered freedom to write, they will tell you what you want to know.

7. Expect that there will be some tough entries to respond to. Also, expect some debris. When you open the floodgates and release writers' feelings for the first time, you must take what you get. Persevere! Muddy water soon clears.

8. Respond in the margin next to each entry. It allows you to draw arrows to something you are commenting on. The student also knows exactly what you are referring to.

9. Finally, when students write, you should write. That way your students know that writing is important to you, too. (You may want to instruct your most trusted friend to, in case of your unexpected death, find your classroom journal and burn it UNREAD!)

FIGURE 5.4 Useful hints for the implementation of working journals (Joan LaMoyne Martins, Postville Community Schools, Iowa, 1988).

unit on the family, ask students to write a list in their learning logs of what they like best about their family or what is the best thing about being part of a family. In a fifth grade unit on the American Revolution, ask students to write about some of the central issues; for example, what they would be willing to go to war for or what their definition of justice is; or simply ask them to list everything they know about the reasons for the American Revolution. After giving children a chance to reflect, discuss what they've come up with. Another option is to introduce a unit with a whole class discussion, generating ideas and questions. Then ask students to use their learning logs to record their own particular ideas and questions and the particular areas they would like to pursue further. Your students can use learning logs throughout a course of study, providing you and them with a clear pattern of their development of information, ideas, and concepts.

Brainstorming Brainstorming can be done by the whole class, small groups, or individuals. Its purpose is to help students explore the connections, associations, feelings, thoughts, and ideas related to a subject. You begin by introducing a topic: newspapers, the Civil War, slavery, Peru, constellations, ecology, the seasons, the moon. Your students then free associate, contributing any thoughts about the topic that occur to them. No one attempts to organize or categorize thoughts, but simply to get them down on paper. In doing this with the whole class or with small groups, it's important that students do not judge or censor one another's contributions. After the brainstorming list is complete, students discuss the connections they see among the responses and why they make the connections they do. Their discussion may lead them to past childhood experiences and fears, old movies, books they have read, places they have visited, stories they have been told, previous school experiences. The interesting thing about prior knowledge is its complexity, the diversity of its sources, and the emotional connections that affect knowledge.

Individuals can also brainstorm. The learning log is a good place for students to do their brainstorming or to make notes of anything they found interesting in the brainstorming of others.

Freewriting   Students use freewriting to explore a topic by uncovering past connections, learning, feelings, and anything else associated with it. Because they write in sentences and paragraphs, rather than phrases or lists, they can elaborate easily. Freewriting is done by individuals rather than in small groups or whole class sessions.

Clustering   In clustering, students create a web of related ideas, placing their main topic in the middle and linking related topics to it with radiating lines; they then develop ideas around the subtopics (see Figure 5.5). Students can use clustering at various stages in the development of a topic. At the beginning, they can use it to become aware of and organize what they already know. Once they've done some research, they can use it to help organize the information.

Clustering gives students some organizational principles to work with, which the students themselves develop as they create the cluster. If you want, you can have students base their cluster on organizational principles from the start. The subjects radiating from the central idea can be organized chronologically, or the subtopics can be steps in a process. Or students can use the

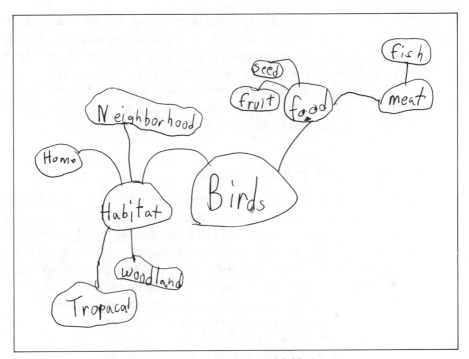

FIGURE 5.5 A cluster on birds by nine-year-old Chris.

cluster that journalists use—"5Ws plus one"—Who? What? Where? When? Why? How? (Tompkins, 1989, 52), with each subtopic answering one of those questions.

Including Students in Goal Setting

When children are involved in goal setting, both as a class and as individuals, they have a clearer sense of the reasons for exploring a topic and what they might learn and pursue during its study. Goal setting can proceed in several ways. After students have written about and discussed what they already know about a topic, they can decide what more they want to know. Have them first develop a list of collective questions, which you write on the board. The whole class can generate an extensive list and then work together to edit it down to the questions students find most important. Have students transfer the edited list to a more permanent location.

Involve students as individuals in setting personal goals and raising personal questions. They can make a list in their learning logs of questions they would like to answer (questions can come from the group list or from their own interests).

Once you have the class's edited list, you can design a variety of projects for students to choose from to pursue the answers to their questions. You may want to have older students (fourth through eighth grade) write contracts (which we'll discuss later in the chapter) or fill out forms for projects as part of exploring and reporting on their topic. You will need to be much more involved with younger children to help them answer their questions and develop a format for reporting on their findings.

Using Oral Language

Because children sometimes seek answers to individual questions, they occasionally will work alone, especially in the upper grades. But children are social beings, and the process of sharing their ideas with others helps them to articulate what they have discovered, to see the significance of what they have found, and to refine their understanding. In addition, students can help each other by sharing their resources and ideas. Children engaged in writing workshop several times a week (as we recommended in Chapter 4), will be learning how to respond and help one another. They will have the opportunity to discuss their learning with the whole class, in small groups, and in pairs. With the teachers' guidance they will learn how to give feedback to and ask more questions of one another, which will spur on the learning process.

Writing to Learn

Have students write throughout their exploration—using notes, journals, diagrams, reports, questions, hypotheses—for themselves and for others. In his quest model, Stephen Tchudi (1986) describes how young learners can use "Filing Systems" to seek answers to their questions. Tchudi suggests a variety of journal keeping activities that students can adapt for the learning log. Since much of students' research involves books, Tchudi suggests that students keep records of what they read in a variety of ways: First they can keep a clipping file of "Paper Artifacts," cutting out articles from magazines and newspapers that relate to the topics they are exploring. Students can also photocopy important parts of books to keep in the clipping file. The file can be a scrapbook-like collection, a series of envelopes, or boxes brought from home (shoe boxes or cereal boxes). Or students can include clippings in the learning log, where the teacher and student make them a part of their ongoing dialogue.

Notetaking is another important learning method. For many young learners, notetaking often simply involves writing down bits and pieces of information copied out of the encyclopedia. But upper elementary children can learn to take reading notes that are more than a collection of facts. Help and encourage them to write why they think the information they've copied is important or how it connects to something else they've learned. Notes can become a part of the learning log and the teacher-student dialogue; or students can keep them in a separate notebook or on index cards. The advantage of index cards is that they are portable, and students can rearrange them easily as necessary.

Both primary and upper elementary students who are involved in scientific projects (observing nature or experiments) or sociological projects (learning about people's eating habits or family interactions) can keep observational notes, using careful descriptions of what they see, hear, smell, and perhaps taste and touch to chart the progress of their study. Students must use their firsthand experience when taking observational notes, which helps them to develop their ability to focus on details and to keep track of what they notice. As with reading notes, students should record not only what they observe but their reactions and ideas as well. This is what Tchudi (1986) calls "Notes Plus."

Notes Plus helps students recognize that their own knowledge, their own experience, and their own ideas are an important part of the process of making meaning and coming to understanding. To make this clear one student mentioned by Tchudi used two different-colored pens, to distinguish between what she took from other sources and what her own reactions were. Another way to get students into the habit of recording and responding is to have them use the double-entry journal. Students divide their writing paper into two columns. In the left column they take notes from other sources (observations, books, talks, TV, radio, magazines, and newspapers); in the right column they write their interpretations and reactions and the connections they make.

Writing things down is only one of the ways that students can collect and record their learning, although it is probably the most important. Nevertheless, you should encourage students to use other data-gathering methods as well. They can draw or sketch to record observations, describe processes, explain designs, or chart chronology. They can use a tape recorder to record field notes and observations or their reactions to information from the media or their reading.

Providing a Wide Range of Materials

Although textbooks can provide a good summary of a topic, additional materials provide depth, richness, variety, multiple perspectives, and divergent interpretations. Give students a range of resources so they can choose, question, categorize, and synthesize, rather than just reproduce or copy. Another benefit of such materials is that students can draw on the variety of modes, ideas, topics, styles, and approaches for their own writing.

Trade books   Bibliographies of good trade books abound. Libraries and professional organizations have bibliographies on many different topics. The National Council of Teachers of English and the International Reading Association publish journals that include bibliographies of good trade books as a regular feature. (See Chapter 7 for specific information on these professional organizations.) In addition, journals often feature articles that provide updates of bibliographies for a particular area. The *Reading Teacher*, for example, recently published a bibliography of books relating to the natural sciences—a list of riches including fiction, nonfiction, and poetry about the earth and the animals that inhabit it.

Interviews   Interviews provide hands-on data-gathering experience and involve children in a variety of language activities. Shirley M. Haley-James and Charles David Hobson (1980) describe several advantages to interviewing:

1. "In an interviewing program children assume language roles that all too often are allowed only adults" (497). Given the opportunity to do practice interviews, children learn how to ask questions that yield answers (see Figure 5.6).

2. "When children take on the role of the interviewer of a person who brings some of the dynamism of the real world into the school, a drive to communicate is released within them. In addition to asking intelligent questions, they become willing writers and readers of their own writing" (497). Children are interested in the real world of jobs and people and real-life events. The drive to understand and communicate takes place in classrooms only when children see the topics as meaningful.

3. "In an interviewing program of the type described here, students are in control" (497). It is the children who ask the questions and listen for the answers rather than the teacher. The children also decide whom they want to interview and what questions they want to ask.

4. "In an interviewing program, children have the freedom to abandon any image of being failures in school" (498). I know of a first grade student, behind in his reading and writing development, who was filled with new life when he interviewed someone about a topic in which he, too, was interested and knowledgeable. This experience motivated him to read and write about what he was learning.

5. "Our fifth observation about what happens to children and their language learning during an interview program is that interviewing unifies

1. Specific suggestions for preparing children to participate in an interviewing program include:
   a) Conduct a practice interview. Bring in a person, or have the students interview you about an interest of yours. Have an object to show related to this interest.
   b) Tell the students that you will give them only as much information as they ask for, and do so. If they ask yes-no questions, give yes-no answers.
   c) After the interview, ask students what questions produced the most information. List them. Repeat practice interviews as needed until the students have learned to ask good interview questions.
   d) Have the students interview each other. Have younger students bring in favorite toys for other students to interview them about. Have older students bring in objects related to hobbies or special interests.
   e) Discuss, again, kinds of questions that produce more information.

2. Once children have learned the structure of the interview process teachers should ask questions about their interests and follow their interests in scheduling further interviews.

3. Teachers should observe their children's writing and listen to their comments for cues about what language lessons the children are ready for.

4. Rather than correcting them for what they are not employing in their writing, teachers should encourage and support students by approving their efforts. Teachers encourage their children by showing them that they knew what they were trying to communicate and asking them questions that would help them clarify their meaning.

5. Teachers should provide an audience for children's writing by reading their work as a reader, not a critic, and by encouraging children to read their stories to their classmates and other teachers and friends.

6. Teachers should structure at least some learning experiences so that students are first speakers, listeners, and writers, and then readers. Their active participation in communicative processes leads not only to additional personal expressive experiences, but to motivation to read and to increasing communicative competence. Through their oral and written communication and their reading, students will reveal their instructional needs.

FIGURE 5.6 Teaching students how to interview (Haley-James and Hobson, 1980, 501–502).

the communcative process of listening, speaking, writing, and reading, with one process leading naturally to another'' (498). The children asked questions, listened for answers, put those answers down, and wrote about what they discovered.

6. ''When children use the conventions of written expression regularly, they discover rules about language that are based on experience and observation. The rules that they acquire are more functional and permanent than rules learned from exercises in boxes'' (499). It is in real-life situations, when children are actively involved in using language, that the conventions of language become important and teachable.

A beneficial aspect of using interviews in the classroom is that they demonstrate for students that people are one of the most important resources for getting answers to questions. As adults we often go to an authority when we need information. We can encourage children to do the same by having them conduct interviews. In addition, when planning interviews, it's important that children choose what they want to know and whom they want to ask. Older children could even arrange a classroom interview themselves, setting up the dates and times. A bit later I will discuss some of the voices of authority available to schools, even in the smallest communities.

Surveys   Surveys are another way for children to draw on people as resources. Instead of the in-depth knowledge of one person that an interview provides, surveys provide an overview of a group. They give students the opportunity to poll a number of people on their knowledge, attitudes, opinions, and beliefs. For example, students can use surveys to find out how people celebrate various holidays, what people's favorite TV shows or movies are and why, what people eat for breakfast or what their favorite foods are, what activities people engage in to keep fit, what they know about various subjects (animals, electricity, historical events, etc.), what family traditions they uphold, and so forth. Surveys have three parts:

1. Information about the person answering the survey: age, sex, grade in school, and the like.

2. Yes/no or multiple choice questions that give respondents general choices about the subject.

3. Open-ended questions that give respondents an opportunity to explain or describe their answers.

Children can conduct surveys by mail (surveys of grandparents, aunts, and uncles might require this), by phone, or in person. Or they can make copies of their surveys and hand them to people to fill out and return. Young children will probably have only three or four questions on their survey while older children might be able to handle as many as ten. After children have gotten the results of their surveys, they will need to sift through the information, perhaps making charts and graphs to display the numbers and discover the significance of the responses. Math immediately becomes a part of this process as students count which answers received the most responses. Upper elementary students can also calculate percentages and display these with a bar graph or a pie chart.

Media   With the diversity of radio and television cable programming now available, the media have become a rich source for multidimensional information gathering. Both television and radio abound with programs that teach us about our worlds: about our own culture and the cultures of others throughout the world; about strange and wondrous animals and insects and birds that thrive or face extinction; about climates and crops and survival techniques in various topographies and terrains; about historical events and their impact on current movements both political and cultural; about music and art and dance; about the technology and science of everything from the clothes we wear to the places we'll live in the next century; about the lives of the rich and famous and the poor and downtrodden. Alerting children to these resources can help turn the villain (of television, in particular) into a helpmate.

In addition, many children receive magazines and newspapers in their homes. Encouraging them to look for relevant information will not only inform them about what's in the newspaper but help them involve their parents as well.

Inexpensive and free materials   Your local library or bookstore has a number of books on free and inexpensive materials. In addition, the classified sections of many magazines contain information about such materials. Although these are often produced by companies for commercial reasons, they are nonetheless sources of all kinds of information, from nutrition to energy-saving to pet care. In addition, junk mail sometimes provides information on political and community issues.

Giving Students Options

The "report"—often a dry rehash of an encyclopedia entry—has been a conventional means for imparting information. But if children base their reports on subject matter that really engages them, their reports will be much more interesting than a mere rehash. (See Chapter 4 for ideas for other writing formats besides the report.) Figure 5.7 displays a list of writing possibilities for a unit on American women in history. The list demonstrates the range of possible forms (from diaries and journals to letters and conversations to articles and speeches) that students can use and issues about which they can write after exploring a topic.

TEACHING IDEAS

Choose a topic or a unit that you hope to teach to children. Develop a list of writing ideas in different genres and for different audiences that children could use to guide and express their discoveries in the topic or unit. (Refer to Figure 5.7.)

1. Pretend you are Harriet Tubman. Create a mini-drama about an incident in your life. Write your script.

2. Write a conversation that Pocahontas and John Smith might have had after she saved his life.

3. Write and illustrate a book jacket for the book *Sojourner Truth*, the African-American woman who traveled in Michigan, Ohio, and Indiana.

4. Pretend you are Annie Sullivan. Keep a journal about your work with Helen Keller.

5. You are Patsy Jefferson. Write an editorial about why your father did not free his slaves.

6. Rewrite the ending to the Amelia Earhart story. No one knows what really happened to her.

7. Pretend that Maria Mitchell returns to life. Bring her up-to-date on astronomy and space. Tell her about our space explorations, our movies and television shows on space, and about the flying saucer mania.

8. You are Jane Addams. Write a letter to your parents about your successes at Hull House in Chicago.

9. Write your diary for a week as Clara Barton might have while she worked for better and cleaner hospitals during the Civil War.

10. You are Laura Ingalls Wilder's niece or nephew and are visiting her at her "little house on the prairie." Write a letter home telling what you see, eat, hear, play, visit, and so on.

11. If Nancy Hanks could return to life, what would you tell her about her beloved son, Abraham Lincoln?

12. Interview Elizabeth Blackwell about how people are accepting her as a woman doctor. Write or tape your questions and her answers. Have her tell how she wins people's confidence.

13. Write a letter to Louisa May Alcott telling her about your brothers and sisters. Try to contrast the ways in which you live with the ways in which the "little women" lived.

14. Write the letter that Mary McLeod Bethune might have written to Harriet Tubman about her work to secure an education for African-Americans.

15. In a letter to Dorothea Dix tell her how you feel about her encouragement to Americans to stop hiding mentally ill patients and to begin curing them.

16. Write your opinions of what might have happened if Elizabeth Cady Stanton, Susan B.

FIGURE 5.7 A list of writing possibilities for a unit on American women in history (created by Phyllis Jeppeson, former sixth grade teacher in Mt. Pleasant, Michigan).

Units That Use Language Across the Curriculum

Creating learning units is a central activity of teachers. Sometimes a unit may be based on a single subject—a chapter in the math textbook on percentages, a section in the curriculum guide on nutrition. Sometimes a unit will connect several subjects—a language arts–social studies unit on families, for example. Increasingly teachers are finding ways to make connections among subjects that are not written into the curriculum guides. Common to all of the following units is the importance of using language as a way to help children deepen and extend their learning. Consider the following ways to construct units:

Anthony and others had not worked for women's rights.

17. Write the speech that Sarah Winnemucca might have given about her destitute Paiute tribe in Boston in 1882.

18. Interview Deborah Sampson, Revolutionary War soldier. List the questions you plan to ask. Have a friend who has also studied Sampson try to answer as Sampson might have.

19. Try to write a poem as Phillis Wheatley might have during the Revolution.

20. You are Abigail Adams. Write a letter to your husband John Adams asking him to remember women and rights for them in the Constitution.

21. You are Sacajawea. Write a diary of your trip with Lewis and Clark.

22. List the duties that Susie King Taylor had in one week for her Civil War regiment.

23. You are Kate Wiggins. Write a letter to your mother about your job as the first kindergarten teacher in your town.

24. Write a speech against drinking such as Carrie Nation might have given.

25. You are Anne Hutchinson and you dare to disagree with the minister in your church. Write an article for an underground newspaper for women in the Colonies.

26. You are Juliet Lowe. Write an essay on why you founded the Girl Scouts.

27. Describe your friend, Annie Oakley.

28. Read about Harriet Beecher Stowe. Write your own story about a slave family sold away from each other.

29. Try to write a poem (any form you wish) about one of the following: Harriet Tubman, Pocahontas, Laura Ingalls Wilder, Helen Keller, Martha Washington, Deborah Sampson, Clara Barton, Carrie Nation, or Annie Oakley.

30. Create a cartoon or cartoon strip about a famous American woman in history.

FIGURE 5.7 *continued*

Units That Use Language to Explore a Subject

Because the textbook provides an overview, it is a helpful jumping-off point for classroom explorations and individual projects. It makes some sense to use the textbook as an outline for the year and as a resource for children's projects. Units, then, can be centered around the sequence of the textbook, but the teacher and students actually create the curriculum.

Mathematics

For most students mathematics has been a matter of receiving an explanation of a concept at the beginning of a chapter and then doing a bunch of problems that illustrate the "concept." Many children, however, do not understand the concept and simply use the rote operations that have been shown to them. As educational leaders in mathematics have indicated, however, this does not result in sufficient understanding. Mathematics educators want to deeply engage children in the use of mathematical concepts so that students grasp their meaning and understand their application. New math programs are beginning to involve children in manipulatives and other sorts of applications that allow them to "experience" the concept and to see it working.

The math book is a good starting place for the introduction of concepts, but from there teachers should make it possible for students to conduct in-depth explorations. For example, Leah Richards's (1990) mathematics program engages children actively throughout, from setting goals to evaluation. The students' work is divided into three parts: *pretheme work*, in which children brainstorm topics and set goals and Richards organizes resources; *investigation*, in which children work on individual projects and collaborate with the teacher and each other as needs arise; and *tie-up*, in which children find ways to prepare and share their findings with others and in which both children and teacher assess what they have learned during the unit. Whether they are learning about time, decimals and fractions, or angles, children put their learning into words: They "share, question, evaluate, and clarify their work through talk" (17). They read extensively: books produced by other children ("instructions, explanations, definitions, applications, summaries, reports, rules, facts, and questions" [17]); mathematics dictionaries; goals, problems, and discoveries posted on the bulletin board; mathematical information on charts and labels in the classroom; feedback and response sheets; newspapers.

Because they are required to keep a record of their learning, Richards's students fill their mathematics logs with many different kinds of writing (see Figure 5.8). Writing involves diverse tasks in Richards's class: Shaun recorded what he knew about the decimal system; Peter wrote an argument defending an answer he arrived at using the protractor; Philip wrote a diagram with notes on how to find percentages; Ermini compiled a brainstorm list of what she knew about decimals and then wrote a summary of it to see how she could build on her knowledge. Richards provides models through her own language and approach to mathematics: "I think out loud, pose questions, show strategies, summarize ideas, explain processes, etc. I demonstrate my own ways of recording" (25). Modeling the use of language for mathematics issues and problems is important to students' development.

Science

Many science texts include experiments that take children beyond reading about science to practicing it, a method strongly advocated by leaders in science education, who recognize the importance of hands-on experiences for children. Science educators emphasize that even first and second graders can observe, experiment, and record what they see in simple activities that promote scientific thinking. Many scientific lessons are cheap—for example, states of change can be learned by feeding caterpillars and observing the

Summaries	of findings, processes used; learning done
Translations	of definitions, information; concepts and how they are applied
Definitions	of terms used; mathematical areas
Reports	on an area of mathematics; their work and what they've done
Personal writing	feelings; conversational reports and responses; letters of response
Labels	for diagrams accompanying explanations; numerical representations
Instructions	for solving a problem (steps involved)
Notes	from books; from other children's books; from peer tutor sessions; from teacher tutor sessions; ideas to follow through
Lists	of findings, knowledge; words; symbols/terminology; ideas; questions; goals; content
Evaluations	feedback sheets; comments about work
Descriptions	of procedures; conversations
Predictions	for outcomes; strategies; meanings of terms; results; methods
Arguments	to persuade others and give their point of view
Explanations	of learning processes; findings; terms; strategies; answers; where challenges come from; applications; procedures; how they came to beliefs/interpretations; rules or patterns

FIGURE 5.8 The kind of math writing done by students in an innovative math program (Richards, 1990, 18).

results or boiling water to make steam—and don't require teachers to have a technical background (Begley, 1990). Although the textbook can be the source for ideas and experiments, the questions should be the students' own, ones that they explore in language—to ask, to observe and record, and to answer in their learning logs or lab notebooks.

Social Studies

Social studies teacher William Bigelow (1989) uses the textbook in yet another way. Concerned about the authority that the textbook has in the classroom, Bigelow gets his students to question any textbooks they encounter. He teaches a unit on textbooks to "present a whole new way of reading, and ultimately, of experiencing the world. Textbooks fill students with information masquerading as final truth and then ask students to parrot back the information in end-of-the-chapter 'checkups.' . . . Students are treated as empty vessels waiting for deposits of wisdom from textbooks and teachers. We wanted to assert to students that they shouldn't necessarily trust the 'authorities' but instead need to be active participants in their own learning, peering between lines for unstated assumptions and unasked questions" (642–643).

Bigelow and his coteacher Linda Christensen began by juxtaposing students' prior knowledge of Christopher Columbus and their textbook material about him with other information from Columbus's own writing and from detailed historical accounts of his activities. Most students had rosy views of Columbus discovering America, befriending the Indians, and showing that the world was round. By his own account and others, however, Columbus enslaved Indians (sending many of them back to Spain), became dictator of the new lands he found, and pressured Indians to find gold for him, thus revealing the true, mercenary nature of his goals. Bigelow and Christensen lead their students to question the language used in the text (such as the use of the term *discovery* to describe what Columbus did to the *New World*) and what that reveals about the values and opinions of the writers of the accounts. After providing alternative materials and doing simulations of Columbus's activities, students began a project, which was to find a textbook and write a critique of its account of the story of Columbus. Bigelow provides the following guidelines:

- How factually accurate was the account?
- What was omitted—left out—that in your judgement would be important for a full understanding of Columbus? (for example, his treatment of the Indians, slave taking, his method of getting gold; the overall effect on the Indians.)
- What motives does the book give to Columbus? Compare those with his real motives.
- Who does the book get you to root for, and how do they accomplish that? (For example, are the books horrified at the treatment of Indians or thrilled that Columbus makes it to the New World?)
- What function do pictures in the books play? What do they communicate about Columbus and his 'enterprise'?
- In your opinion, *why* does the book portray the Columbus/Indian encounter the way it does?
- Can you think of any groups in our society who might have an interest in people having an inaccurate view of history?

(Bigelow, 1989, 639)

After students have done their individual critiques, they join small groups to share their papers and make notes toward "collective texts," to discover areas of agreement and disagreement. Then students share the papers with the whole class and each student has the chance to respond to the whole class's collective text. Students then discuss what implications their discoveries have for other representations of historical events and the social/political implications of those events in today's world. Bigelow's goal is not to encourage an "'I-don't-believe-anything' cynicism, but rather to equip students to bring a writer's assumptions and values to the surface so students can decide what is useful and what is not in any particular work'' (639–640).

Units That Connect Subjects

Because each subject in the curriculum is taught separately in the classroom, many of the natural connections among subjects are sometimes overlooked or ignored. It's too bad, because elementary school education provides the perfect opportunity for helping children see how one subject relates to another. This section suggests ways to organize your teaching to show relationships between disciplines. You may use one subject—say, science—as the central element in creating your interdisciplinary unit, or you may choose a topic—like airplanes—to organize your curriculum materials and activities.

The purposes of the interdisciplinary unit are (1) to help children connect learning across disciplines; (2) to individualize activity so that students can choose the areas they want to work in; (3) to give students opportunities to engage in active experiences with a subject, instead of simply relying on the textbook; and (4) to provide opportunities for students to do in-depth work. In order to create an interdisciplinary unit, the teacher needs to go outside the classroom to draw on a diverse range of resources and activities.

An Interdisciplinary Unit

To show you how to organize an interdisciplinary unit, let's begin with life science, a subject that is commonly taught at various grade levels in the science curriculum in elementary school. At different grade levels a number of subtopics are considered: Children learn about animals (how they live and move); they learn about plants and their uses; they learn about ecosystems and how they are constructed. So although the subject is science, children also learn about the social system of animals, how they live together and how they are affected by people (social studies); they learn about sizes and shapes (mathematics); they have aesthetic responses to nature (art and literature). A topic in one area of the curriculum, then, has connections with other areas of learning; in organizing a unit, you can demonstrate these connections.

TEACHING IDEAS

Choose a textbook unit that you want to teach (in math, social studies, science, etc.). Design some classroom activities that give children hands-on, language-based work to help them thoroughly understand the concepts being presented.

Do not plan to create an interdisciplinary project all by yourself. Involve your students in planning, setting goals (both as individuals and as a class), finding and organizing materials, developing ideas for projects, and uncovering resources that they can share with the class (artifacts, postcards, magazines, books, parent experts, records and tapes, posters, etc). You will need to provide more support for younger children; older students will be able to contribute a great deal. In either case you will need to have a structure, an organization, and a time frame for students to complete their work.

A good starting point is to organize the reading materials. The librarian or media center director is a great resource, perhaps even willing to provide a cartful of books for the duration of the unit. The public library is another tremendous resource for enrichment (I sometimes check out twenty or more books on a topic for students to read, study, and research).

Although most of the printed materials are intended for individuals or small groups to use, you will want to share certain materials with the whole class, perhaps choosing outstanding nonfiction trade books, or stories or novels that build on the topic, or poetry that illuminates or vivifies the subject. Lee Galda (1990) describes the value of using various kinds of literature in a unit on science:

> Every year hundreds of nonfiction books are published. They cover topics ranging from the moon to turnips, from computers to medieval feasts. Some of the most beautiful illustrations in all of children's literature, as well as some of the liveliest prose, can be found in informational books. A good informational book is as artistically arranged as a good picture book, with text and illustrations working together to explain information, to distinguish between fact and opinion, to illuminate concepts, and to inspire young readers to explore some facet of their world. . . .
>
> In addition to nonfiction, [there are] examples of fiction and poetry that could accompany a study of the natural world. One of the nice results of building a topic-focused unit with children's literature is that you get the opportunity to approach the topic in a variety of ways. You can read about the ecology of a meadow in a nonfiction text, share some poems about its inhabitants with your students, and visit a meadow through a story. Your students' sense of what a meadow is like certainly will be expanded by this multigenre approach to the topic.
>
> (Galda, 1990, 322)

In addition to reading about the natural world, give children some direct experience with what they find in the books. When reading about insects or seasons, children can do a hands-on project to see nature in detail. For example, to help your students learn about ecology, have them stake out a piece of land (say, one foot by one foot) in their own yard for observation. You can also do this in the school playground or a nearby park. If you do it at school, you can take students outside with their notebooks to record what they observe. In a four-season climate spring is an excellent time for this, because children will see many changes taking place on their piece of land—changes in color, moisture, new growth, new insects. Have them record and describe what they see in their patch of ground, share their findings with other children, chart what they discover on graph paper, and do a class project—using both art and words—that illuminates the minute changes they have observed.

Animals in the classroom also provide many opportunities to observe, to record, and to share. Robert W. Smith (1986) says that "at last count, my classroom contained 30 children, 4 lizards, 3 toads, 2 crayfish, 1 frog, 24 crickets, 35 snails, 43 guppies, several hundred mealworms, and 1 grasshopper. No, I'm not crazy. These insects and other small creatures provide a dynamic program of science enrichment for my students" (82). Pet stores have everything you need to keep insects and animals of various sorts. Insects are especially easy to care for once you set up their homes—which you can do with everyday items. You can make an ant farm, for example, with a glass jar or bottle, sandy soil, a mesh cover, a few seeds, and a little bit of candy. Insect-loving children can provide the ants (or you can simply buy an ant farm). Smith's students keep a chart to record observations, feedings, and general maintenance activities. His students vary the ants' diet to see how they respond; one child brought in a dead beetle and everyone enjoyed watching the ants disassemble it. Children also enjoy watching ants' cooperative efforts in building and providing for the whole group. Smith occasionally lets children destroy a tunnel in the colony so that they can watch how the ants rebuild it. His students draw and write about their observations of the lives of the ants.

As students engage in their explorations of the natural world, they will make observations, keep records, read about what they see, and informally share what they know with one another. Formal opportunities to share may involve both oral and written presentations with visual as well as verbal art

TEACHING IDEAS

Choose one to three pieces of literature (fiction, nonfiction, or poetry) about the natural world that you would like to share with your students. Develop some ideas for hands-on projects related to the literature that will help your students extend their observations of the topic. (Make sure that your ideas require them to use language to understand or share their findings.)

for a variety of possible audiences—parents, other classrooms, younger children. Here are some ideas for insect projects:

- Create a poster of the life cycle of a particular insect.
- Write a story from an ant's point of view about the frustration of rebuilding or the importance of working together.
- Write a story in which the lives of ants (or crickets) have an impact on the story's events.
- Write a collective description of "small changes" or "things you didn't know about our playground."
- Write and illustrate insect poems.
- Create a bulletin board display for the rest of the school of "nature observations" or "insect observations" with illustrations.
- Write "information books" for children in younger grades to be read to them and/or to become part of their classroom library.
- Write and illustrate "small things" poems.
- Create an insect world newspaper with pieces written by various insects about events in their communities.

Media Units for Older Elementary Students

Children's hobbies—bicycling, stamps, baseball cards, pet care, video games, travel—can provide the basis for interesting explorations into history, geography, the sciences, and mathematics. Consider such wonderfully fun units as Fast Foods; Chocolate; Ice Cream; Dragons; The Loch Ness Monster, Big Foot, and Other Famous Creatures; The History of the Comic Book; The World of Cartoons. All these topics have the potential for students to learn more about history, science, geography, mathematics, and even literature and art.

Children's home experiences are another valuable way to connect school and home learning, and we can't afford to ignore them. One significant home experience is television. A recent newspaper article (Elias, 1990) reported that the American Academy of Pediatrics sees television viewing as a major influence on children. Children "ages 2 to 5 see about 25 hours of TV

TEACHING IDEAS

Choose a topic for an interdisciplinary unit, perhaps using a textbook as the starting point. Develop a list of resources, activities, and writing projects that you would like to include in the unit.

TEACHING IDEAS

Do you have an interest or some expertise that you can share with your students? Develop a short unit on it. What reading, writing, and hands-on activities can you use to engage children in the topic?

per week; 6- to 11-year-olds, 22 hours; 12- to 17-year-olds, 23 hours'' (1). Recent research findings indicate that there are twenty-five violent acts per hour on children's weekend daytime shows and that TV viewing promotes both violence and obesity in children.

It is vital that community leaders like educators and doctors continue to speak out against inappropriate use of television. But it is also important to recognize that changes will be slow in coming and that we must continue to deal with the fact that many children come to school with much of their behavior and understanding shaped significantly by television.

In a 1984 meeting of the International Federation for the Teaching of English, a group of educational leaders from around the world studied the influence of media on children and came up with a number of recommendations. One of them was the following: "English teachers must be encouraged, supported, and even directly trained in media literacy. They must learn to view literature (both print and non-print) as a representation of the human condition open to private and public interpretation which leads to the personal/social growth of the individual. They must come to respect their students' delight in various electronic media and commit themselves to exploring in the classroom the *students'* world of media'' (England, 1985, 156).

Students should not be simply passive receivers of television and movies, both so prevalent in their lives. Instead they should have opportunities to think critically and creatively about what they watch. The intent should not be to put down children's TV viewing and to pit the world of print against the world of electronics. Rather we should be helping them to put into their own words what their TV ''literature'' means to them.

Violence on television   Help students become aware of this issue by having them chart or count the number of violent acts that they witness on TV, on everything from cartoon shows to murder mysteries. Precede the TV count with a discussion about what they consider to be violence and whether they think watching it influences their behavior. Children can also survey or interview their friends and family members about their opinions of violence on television, which can again lead to classroom discussion. Children may wish to write letters to newspapers, television stations, or television production companies expressing their opinions on these issues. Magazine and newspaper articles frequently address the issue of TV violence and its influence on young people. Use these sources to develop children's critical reading and research skills.

What's funny?   Cartoon shows, zany kids' quiz shows, situation comedies, and comic movies are also part of children's viewing world. Have children explore what they find funny on television. Have them compare their own views of what's funny with the views of their peers, the views of older and younger siblings, the views of adults. Interviews and surveys are good first-hand research techniques for this project, giving children plenty of evidence to share with the class. A class chart can give them experience in measuring, graphing, and comparing findings.

Images of . . .   Television puts us in contact with all kinds of people. Upper elementary students especially can learn more about the depiction of stereotypes and of realistic characters by describing the kinds of people they find on television. Students can focus on a group or type of character—women, men, children, different ethnic groups (African-Americans, Asians, etc.), different occupational groups (doctors, policemen, factory workers, etc.); document their appearance on television; and then describe how they are characterized. Students may wish to write a critique or create a new type of character or program to offset or augment what they find on television.

Behind the scenes   Children can also learn a great deal about science, technology, advertising, writing, and marketing by doing a behind-the-scenes project on movies and television. Children enjoy learning about how movies are made, how special effects are shot, what goes into creating a finished product. Students will also have their eyes opened by learning more about how television shows are either chosen to continue or are dropped from a network's offerings. Finally children can and should be taught to be alert to the effects of advertising in order to become discerning consumers. Much of television is about marketing products. Children should become analytical about what techniques and appeals are used to sell products. Learning more about how children's toys and TV shows have been developed in order to sell products is a starting point.

■ **IDEAS TO LEARN**   Create and conduct a survey of what children watch on television. How much television do they watch? What are their favorite shows? Why? What don't they like on television? Why? What other activities do they engage in while they are watching television?

The interdisciplinary unit also extends children's range of experience and satisfies their curiosity about the larger world. With its influence on direct and multidimensional experience, children truly can take a vicarious trip to other times and places.

A Winter Unit for Kindergartners

Taiwan kindergarten teachers prepared a unit for their students at the American School in Taipei (Stephen Tchudi, 1991b). Although Taipei has a subtropical climate, teachers Karen Kirk, Virginia Rogers, and Clarene Tossey chose the theme of winter to give their students a larger, global view. Their five-week unit included not only mainstream subjects (literature, social studies, science, math, and geography) but also dance, drama, art, computers, sports, and astronomy. Each week they focused on a different topic or theme: Winter Season, Animals in Winter, People in Winter, Winter Activities, and Winter Holidays. In addition to regular curricular materials, the teachers included a variety of materials and resources from the community and the library. Figure 5.9 details the day-by-day schedule of the unit.

A Community Unit

Several years ago the well-known child psychologist David Elkind (*The Hurried Child; All Grown Up and No Place to Go*) addressed a group of parents and teachers in the Okemos, Michigan, public schools about the importance of children engaging in learning that is developmentally appropriate. That is, children should pursue knowledge and understanding that relates to their interests, needs, and thinking abilities as 5-year-olds, 8-year-olds, 11-year-olds. Elkind said that too often this is not the case; he cited as an example first grade classrooms where there are models of the solar system for children who don't even know what comprises their own community.

Although I wouldn't discourage models of the solar system (children are intrigued by space), activities that help children learn about their own spheres can often bridge the gap between home and school, between direct experience and vicarious experience. When children begin to explore their own community, they also learn about communities in general.

The list in Figure 5.10 only begins to demonstrate the rich possibilities available in neighborhoods. Rural, urban, and suburban neighborhoods will have different lists, but in all of them you will see the same potential for studying history (through museums, antique stores, newspapers, taxidermists, even the zipper repair shop), geography (through museums, airports, newspapers, the exotic plants found in the florist shop), science (flowers, food, gas, electricity, the technology that the community uses to function), and mathematics (of running a business, of determining how much to buy and sell for a profit, of planning space and time in the world of work). Writing

Topics and Disciplines	Monday	Tuesday	Wednesday	Thursday	Friday	Field Trips and Other Resources
"Winter Season" Science Geography Math Literature Art Music Computers	"Why does it snow?" Filmstrip: "The Changing Seasons" Lit: A Book of Seasons and The Season Collection	"Where does snow come from?" Field trip: Weather station Photo display of winter photographs	"Where does it snow?" Class discussion and roleplaying Journal writing and illustrations	"What do snowflakes look like?" Drama: Roleplay Art: Cutting snowflakes	"What happens when snow melts?" Sequence lesson, cutting and pasting Sing: "Frosty" Computer: Melting snowman	Weather station Snowman video Science teacher Encyclopedia Filmstrips Globe and maps Childcraft materials
"Animals in Winter" Literature Art Math Dramatic Play	"What animals like the snow?" Read "The Rabbit and the Turnip" (Chinese fairy tale) Lit: The Big Snow	"What happens to animals in winter?" School science teacher will discuss colors, hibernation, etc. Lit: The Snow Parade	"How do animals protect themselves?" Film on animal survival Game: Survival in wintertime	"How do Taiwanese farmers protect their animals?" Field trip: Taipei farm Lit: Winter Magic	"How can people help animals?" Craft: Make birdfeeder Lit: Deer in the Snow	Farm field trip Science teacher Videos National Geographic video: Bears
"People in Winter" Social Studies Art Health Math Literature	"What do people wear in winter?" Filmstrip: "Winter on the Farm" Photos: Winter wear Lit: White Snow	"How do you dress when it snows?" Bring in family photos from U.S. Lit: Over the River and Through the Woods	"Where do people live in winter?" Lit: The Little Igloo Crafts: Marshmallow models	"Why do people get colds in winter?" School nurse discusses health care Lit: The Winter Noisy Books	"What do people eat in winter?" Cook: Chicken soup with rice, cocoa Lit: Sugar on Snow, Chicken Soup with Rice	School nurse Parents Film Audio cassettes Childcraft materials Library books
"Winter Activities" Sports Music Dance Astronomy Computers Social Studies Art	"What happens when it snows so much you can't get out?" Lit: The Day Daddy Stayed Home	"How do people get around in winter?" Bring in snowshoes Crafts: Make snowshoes Lit: Cross Country Cat	"What do the stars look like?" Field trip: Observatory, winter sky Lit: Mole's Family Christmas	"What are some good winter sports?" Video: Winter sports Computer game: Olympics	"What can you do at home in a snowstorm?" Popcorn plus journal writing Lit: Popcorn Book	Outdoorsman P.E. teacher Observatory Videos Maps Parent helpers Library books
"Winter Holidays" Social Studies Geography Music Dance Drama Arts and Crafts	"How do people celebrate?" Swedish mother to visit class Lit: Holly and Ivy	"How can we help?" Crafts: Making gifts Clustering: Ways to help out	"What are special holiday foods?" Jewish mother talks of Hannukah Poem: "Eight Days"	"What are family traditions?" German mother discusses Lit: Night Before . . .	"How do you get ready for a party?" Set up for class party; program for parents; visit from St. Nick	St. Nick Home ec. teacher Parents Music teacher

FIGURE 5.9 The day-by-day schedule of an interdisciplinary unit on winter (Stephen Tchudi, 1991b, 88).

Airport	Newspaper
Bookkeeper	Office Supply Store
Collectors' Shops	Pancake House
Detective Agency	Quick Printer
Electric Power Company	Radio Station
Florist	Salvage Store
Gas Station	Taxidermist
Hardware Store	Upholstery Shop
Ice Cream Shop	Vacuum Cleaner Store
Jukebox Distributor	Waste Removal Service
Key Maker	X-Ray Laboratory
Laboratories: Medical, Dental or Scientific	Yacht Club
Museums: Art, Historical, Scientific	Zipper Repair Shop

FIGURE 5.10 The A to Z of Writing Around Town (Susan Tchudi and Stephen Tchudi, 1984, 119–122).

about the community is especially significant in children's development of oral language: They observe and listen to what happens in a particular place, they ask questions (the interview again becomes important), and they listen for answers.

In units on the community, parents and other local people can become extremely valuable contacts and resources. Children can visit people where they work—either with their families or on a class trip—or invite community members, including parents, into the classroom to talk about their work or area of expertise.

A community-based project that investigates jobs can be much more than that. Students researching the telephone company can explore history: Who invented the telephone? When? How did it come into wide usage? What did people do before its use? Science: How does the telephone work? How

TEACHING IDEAS

Choose a business in your community as a basis for an interdisciplinary study. Call or write to the company to discover what resources it could make available to your class—perhaps speakers and printed materials or (in the case of big companies) materials prepared especially for schools. What school disciplines might be relevant to understanding the "business" of this company? List some projects students might do related to the company's business.

has it changed over the years? What recent technology will influence the telephone? Why might you get a shock if you talk on the phone during a thunderstorm? How do systems in different countries differ? Mathematics: What determines the cost of using the telephone? How much does it cost to call coast to coast? to call Jamaica? England? Ethiopia? Moscow? How are costs calculated? The telephone company—and almost all major businesses and industries—can provide educational materials on the industry and consultants to talk about the work.

As in all other learning projects, children can share their discoveries in a variety of ways: interviews and feature articles describing the place of business and the people who work there; an opinion piece that discusses the contributions or negative aspects of the service or product; a story in which the place of business is the setting; or a poem that captures the physical nature or the uses of the service or product. Students can share their work in a class newspaper or one that goes home to parents or on a school or classroom bulletin board.

Units That Promote Multicultural Understanding

The United States has always prided itself on its multicultural and multiethnic nature. In schools we continue to experience a growth in population from a variety of cultures, both immigrant children (particularly Asian and Hispanic) and children from various ethnic American cultures (including African-American, Chinese-American, Eskimos, Native Americans, Japanese-Americans, and Puerto Rican–Americans). Some of these children come into our classrooms with little or no English, others with different cultural values and expectations. Teachers must make sure that the culture and experience of these children are represented in the life of the classroom and in its language activities. Such an atmosphere is enriching for all children and for the teacher as well.

Children's literature is an excellent place to learn about and value other cultures. Bernice E. Cullinan, a distinguished children's literature expert, says the following about the importance of multicultural literature for children:

> The image of a melting pot once used to characterize the United States when millions of immigrants came from various lands and supposedly were homogenized into Americans is no longer accurate. . . . The image of a salad bowl or a hearty stew in which diverse elements blend together but each retains its distinctive flavorings is a more appropriate metaphor. Each group blends with the larger society, when such is demanded for the common good, but preserves its own cultural traditions in the home and community in the multicultural society we live in today. . . .

It is important to have multicultural literature in schools and libraries because stories do shape readers' views of their world and of themselves. If some children never see themselves in books, then that absence subtly tells them that they are not important enough to appear in books. Even more harmful are the negative or stereotypic images of an ethnic group in children's books; they not only damage the children of that ethnic group but give others a distorted and unfortunate view of self-importance. Children's literature that accurately reflects cultural values can be a potent force in the socialization, acculturation, and personal and moral development of children.

(Cullinan, 1989, 575)

The following units are just a few of the ways we can bring a multicultural perspective into our classrooms.

A Folklore Unit

Cullinan (1989), who says that folklore reflects "the beliefs, rituals, and songs of a group's heritage" (588), suggests using folk tales from many cultures. Asian, African, Caribbean, Hispanic, and Native American tales reflecting the traditions of these cultures are readily available in books for children (see Chapter 6).

In a unit on folk tales, children may begin by reflecting on their own traditions and experiences. Children can talk about familiar stories—stories they have heard again and again—either from their parents' storytelling or from traditional books that have been read to them. In addition, television and movies have created other versions of traditional stories—Johnny Appleseed, Little Red Riding Hood, Sleeping Beauty, Robin Hood, Paul Bunyan, Cinderella, Puss in Boots, Hansel and Gretel, Snow White. Begin by having children talk about their favorite old stories, perhaps listing them on the board and giving children an opportunity to tell their version. In this way children get a sense of traditional stories as a part of their culture along with the recognition that these stories have many versions. Then expose children to folk tales from other traditions, by reading to them, by displaying books around the classroom, by making a classroom library available, by having them read stories on their own.

Activities for Using Folk Tales
- Discuss the various kinds of relationships between humans and animals in the stories. Compare them with other familiar stories.
- Discuss the use of magic in the stories. Compare the use of magic in various cultures.
- Discuss the force of evil in the stories. What form does evil take? Are there any similarities among cultures? Any common symbols of evil?

- Discuss the role of nature in the stories. Is nature a friend or an enemy or both? Do humans use it or vice versa?
- Read different versions of the same story and then compare and contrast them.
- Create and perform readers theater scripts based on the folk tales.
- Create puppet shows complete with costumes and scenery that reflect the culture and environment of the story.
- Create a diorama. Use a shoe box to create a three-dimensional view of a scene from the tale. Use cardboard cutouts or clay.

A Biography/Autobiography Unit

In an autobiography or biography unit, include famous Americans of varied ethnic and cultural backgrounds. Encourage children to learn about one important American, beginning first with the reading of a biography or an autobiography. Then try to help children locate other sources through which they can learn more about their person. What does the encyclopedia emphasize about this person's life? What does the history book say about him or her? Take a trip to the library to look at magazines and newspapers for a new perspective on a contemporary person. If you are in a large city or a college town, you might have access to archives for older historical documents. Are there any recorded speeches or video tapes of this person? In short, get your students to move beyond the autobiography or biography to discover other sources for learning about people. Do they find different emphases in different materials? Do they find contradictions?

After students have found and recorded information about their person, help them organize it. Set aside a day or two so children can present their information publicly. Encourage them to become their person, dressing and, if possible, talking like their character to parents, students in other classes, and their own classmates to tell about their lives.

An International Fair Unit

The fifth graders at Edgewood Elementary School in Okemos, Michigan, spend the month of May working on their International Fair. Each child chooses a country and researches it. Children are required to use a wide variety of sources—books, magazines, interviews, newspapers, encyclopedias—to do their research and write their papers. Travel agents, travel businesses, and travel magazines come in handy here. Well in advance of beginning their research, have children decide what country they want to learn about, so they can write away to sources listed in magazines and travel sections of newspapers. Not only is this a way to get some attractive and detailed (if romanticized) information, but children get to write letters and receive something in return. Older children can take this exploration one step further—they can compare the glossy brochures with real-life newspaper accounts of the country, which may contain information about financial problems, civic unrest, or political infighting.

Studying countries is an ideal interdisciplinary subject, because children learn the natural connections between geography, mathematics, economics, sociology, anthropology, history, art, music, dance, and literature. Often projects like this emphasize the "facts" about a country, but children should get a feel for the culture of the country as well. Literature is an excellent source for this. In addition to folk tales, children can look at the country's poetry and fiction for yet another window into its culture.

Students present the results of their research at the International Fair— they display pictures (from books, magazines, brochures), maps, food, and in some cases, artifacts (parents and other teachers may help here). They can display poems, book reviews, and artwork they've created that reflects all the kinds of reading and research they've done on their countries. Of course parents and other classes should be invited to view the results.

Evaluation and Assessment

The Curriculum

Many teachers are worried that changing the curriculum means giving them even more things to do and new areas to teach. But the real task is to reorganize curriculum, not to add or subtract from it. Essential questions should be the basis of the curriculum. Like many others, educational consultant Grant Wiggins (1989) suggests using themes to get children to pursue questions and seek answers. For Wiggins, "The issue is ultimately not which great book you read but whether any book or idea is taught in a way that deadens or awakens the mind, whether the student is habituated to reading books thoughtfully, and whether the student comes to appreciate the value of warranted knowledge (as opposed to mere beliefs called 'facts' by someone else)" (48).

Although things are changing dramatically in education, many teachers still find themselves in school systems where the curriculum guides are isolated from one another and teachers are expected to cover the concepts in isolation. In such a situation teachers will gradually find ways to make connections between the various curricula; to develop children's experiences beyond the list of facts into individualized projects that will take them on indepth explorations; to find room for short units in areas of interest outside the curriculum guide; to discover and integrate supplementary materials and human and institutional resources outside the school to bring the school subjects to life. The new teacher—without years of experiments and files of materials—will need to start these projects one step at a time.

Perhaps your first step will be to concentrate on multicultural materials to combine a history unit with a language unit; and maybe your second step will be to develop a short interdisciplinary unit on rain forests, which you will focus on for a small part of each day for three weeks; and perhaps your third step will be to bring animals into the classroom to combine math and science in a unit that observes animal behavior and measures their food and growth. And then there will be another step and another step and another step. In a classroom where the teacher's and children's creativity is combined with the structure of a curriculum guide, teachers will find ways to teach so that children will learn and even enjoy the process.

The Students

When teachers revise their curriculum so that children create pieces of writing and artifacts that reflect their learning, new forms of assessment are needed. "Objective" tests and tests that ask students to fill in the blanks or provide short "factual" answers will need to be replaced with a more inclusive and broadly based form of assessment. According to Wiggins (1989), as teachers we are guilty of reinforcing our students' undesirable habits by paying attention to the trivial, by emphasizing coverage, and by relying on short-answer tests. Authentic assessment needs to take the place of the trivial kinds of assessments that dominate the educational scene today. The problem is not only one of teaching to the test, a common problem when the textbook is the core of the curriculum. The more significant problem is the statement we make about what is important when we give tests that ask students to supply "factoids," unrelated and undigested and unassimilated bits of information. If "thoughtfulness" is a goal in our teaching, then we need to emphasize thoughtfulness as the means by which we assess students' learning.

There is a recurring hue and cry in education that we need to maintain standards to show that we are doing our jobs and students are doing theirs. But the use of *standards* as a rallying cry is really a distortion of the term. Wiggins describes standards by describing their original use: a flag that soldiers rallied around as the "source of self-orientation and loyalty; it represented what mattered, what one was willing to fight for. To speak of high standards is to invoke images of pride in one's work, a loving attention to detail, an infusion of thoughtfulness" (45). Pride, craftsmanship, attention to detail are difficult to muster when what one is asked to do is trivial and unconnected to anything one knows or cares about. The test of our teaching, then, becomes whether students are actively engaged. How can we evaluate this? According to Wiggins, "Craftsmanship and pride in one's work depend on 'tests' that enable us to confront and personalize authentic tasks'' (58). He goes on to say that students, then, should write, speak, present, demonstrate, and perform knowledge that is based on the learning they have done, on the understandings they have reached.

Consider the following assessment tools as ways to record and demonstrate children's progress in learning across the curriculum.

Learning Logs

I have mentioned the learning log throughout this chapter. Its most important use is to demonstrate students' work throughout the unit or term. Students' work, then, is the centerpiece of the learning log (which may take the form of a file folder, an accordion folder, a shoe box, etc.). It includes their final products—stories, poems, plays, readers theater scripts, reports, results of interviews and surveys, graphs, charts; it also includes notes, hypotheses, drafts, false starts, lists of sources, clusters, and jottings. In addition, you may want students to include feedback from you and their classmates, so you and your students can see how they've revised or developed their work in response to others.

Start a new log with each new project or unit and store the completed ones in a box in the classroom. You may want to give students a method for keeping track of the items in their learning log; you may also want to have occasional "let's get our stuff organized" days, so students can go through their learning logs to make sure they know what they have, that they are storing all that they need, and that it's in some sort of order. Provide plenty of paper clips on these days.

■ **IDEAS TO LEARN**   One assessment tool that teachers find useful for a variety of purposes is the learning log. Make a list of the items you might have students keep in their logs to help you assess their growth. What other classroom performance or behavior might you use to assess students' learning? Make a list of observable traits that you can use as indicators of students' growth and understanding.

Checklists

In units that move beyond the textbook to reading/writing/speaking/listening activities, you will want to provide evidence that students are learning, that they are fulfilling the goals in the curriculum guide. To do so, create a checklist of objectives (taken from the curriculum guide) for each subject area that you cover in a unit and make a copy for each child. As children engage in projects—researching; creating hypotheses; testing and questioning their findings; creating charts and graphs to show relationships; keeping notes on their reading; creating displays and giving oral presentations to demonstrate their knowledge—the checklist will help you keep track of the skills they use from the various content areas. Children may also keep their own lists of the skills they are developing and those they have mastered. Research skills, questioning skills, reporting skills, as well as content-based information may all be part of the checklist system. You may wish to jot anecdotal information on the checklist to substantiate your observations (as suggested in Chapter 3). In addition, students' learning logs will illuminate the evidence provided on the checklist. Use the checklists to describe students' progress in conferences with parents and students, when reporting to the administration, and when filling out report cards.

Contracts

Especially useful with upper elementary and junior high/middle school students, the contract can help you plan and evaluate. In the contract system, the teacher provides various activities that students can fulfill to achieve the goals of the course, starting with minimum requirements (to receive a grade of C) and progressing through more extensive projects (to receive a B or an A). Students choose the projects they would like to complete and know in advance the grade they will receive. For example, in a five-week unit on biography/autobiography, in order to receive basic credit for the unit (a C), students may be required to read five different sources about the person they are studying (e.g., at least one book, an encyclopedia, magazine and newspaper articles, the textbook); keep notes in their learning logs on their reading; share at least one of the things they have read with their peer/response group; take one piece of public writing (a story, a play, a mock interview, a diary entry, a report) on the person they are studying through the writing process to final product.

To receive a B, students may choose to do an additional project involving community-based research—interviewing someone who knows a lot about the person being studied; visiting a museum that contains artifacts or information about the person or the times in which he or she lived; writing away for additional information about the person. Students at this level may prepare some sort of public display to demonstrate the additional information they have collected (a poster, a diorama, a collage). Students who wish to achieve at the highest level may prepare a class presentation that combines all the information they have collected, such as a readers theater presentation; a dramatization of the person or some event from the person's life; a radio program with a mock interview of the person.

In preparing contracts, the teacher and student should work together to realistically assess what the student would like to accomplish. Give students options so that they can find projects that will interest them and will help them synthesize and extend their learning (rather than simply provide them with busy work). Make progress reports part of the contract, so you can be sure that students complete what they've set out to do. Most important, keep the focus on the activity and the learning, rather than on the grades. The purpose of contracts is to take emphasis off grades and place it on learning. As students progress through school, they place increasing emphasis on the grade rather than the substance of their learning; as teachers, we need to refocus their attention.

Speaking of Grades

I have never heard teachers at *any* level of teaching, kindergarten through college, say they enjoy giving grades. And yet grades seem to be a fact of most teachers' lives. Some teachers have tried—and some even succeeded—in changing the reporting system. But those of us still stuck with grades face a number of knotty problems. What do I grade on: effort, growth, competence? Do I grade children by some absolute standard or should grades reflect their individual ability—and how do I know what that ability is? Am I responsible to the fifth grade teacher when I encourage a slowly blossoming fourth grader with a B in reading when he's still struggling with word calling? Am I fair to other students when I give a child whose native language is Spanish an A in language when she is still using only a few words of English in her writing?

There are no hard and fast rules and no easy answers to these questions. However, if one has to err (and there's probably no way to be right), then I prefer erring on the side of the child. We can't expect all children to be at the same place at the same time. We can't expect writing to be easy for all children. We can't expect an ESL student to have the same fluency in reading English that a native speaker has. For me, the most educationally sound as well as the most ethical way to handle grades is to grade students so they are encouraged rather than discouraged; that is, to base grades on evidence of the strengths and the progress of each individual child.

In addition, having students and parents participate in the process of evaluation—through self-assessments, conferences, and contracts—not only helps children become responsible for their own learning but provides substance and evidence for our own assessments as teachers. Most teachers who have used self-assessments have found that children are amazingly accurate about their own levels of achievement; teachers are often able to use these self-assessments in the grading process. Children who are involved in assessment have a much more highly developed sense of its uses, which tends to minimize the impact of the grade and maximize what's really important—children's progress and control over their development of literacy (in the broadest sense of the word).

6

Literature:
Language and the Imagination

by Janet Culver

My book and heart
Shall never part.
Old Rhyme

The relationship of a reader to a special book is unique and bonding. How young readers develop a closeness to certain kinds of books and for what reason is not clearly known, but it *is* clear that books provide children with a variety of rewarding experiences. Books take children to other times, other places, other cultures, allowing them to imagine what it is like to live there and broadening and deepening their sense of the world and their place in it. Books help children build their own identities, as well as giving them pleasure that can continue throughout their lives.

In this chapter we will see that literature provides many opportunities for learning throughout the lives of young readers, both in school and at home. These days one hears that "real" books (as opposed to *text* books) lead to "real" learning. This will be tested as schools build meaningful programs using literature for learning. Charlotte Huck, well known in the field of children's literature, has long held a vision that literature should be the heart of the elementary and middle school curriculum (in Hickman and Cullinan, 1989). In Australia Johnson and Louis (1987) have also described the ideal that "real" books can be widely used throughout the school's literacy program. They feel that since language is used to communicate, literature will *involve* children in language rather than simply teaching them about its rules and abstractions.

Teachers can count on literary works to provide models of language from the simple to the complex, from the applied to the creative. We know that students' capacity for listening, speaking, reading, and writing increases through contact with literature. Comprehension grows as well through the use of multiple information sources. Teachers can reduce traditional textbook drudgery by making the world of books available.

But the value of literature is far greater than simply displacing or supplementing textbooks. Teachers who use literature as a major part of instruction must look beyond the information provided by books to appreciate their aesthetic value as well. Those who would use literature successfully must immerse themselves in it. They will want to visit libraries and bookstores to see all that is available; they should study reviews in current periodicals. (Some teachers even fall victim to the disease of overindulgence in children's books, a malady that finds them spending too much time and money in bookstores, always reading and seeking something brand-new or just right for a particular child or classroom.) Once teachers have a broad-based knowledge about books, old and new, they can pass on their love of reading to their students.

Historically Speaking

Recent publications and scholarship supporting the use of literature in the classroom may lead one to think that this is a new trend, untried. However, the use of children's books in the classroom goes well back in this century. My Aunt Marvel obtained her first teaching job with the Detroit Public Schools in the 1930s as a teacher for the younger grades. Her greatest success with children occurred in her read-aloud sessions: Her students sitting near her on the floor would creep closer and closer to more intimately share what she read. Aunt Marvel had students keep folders for their own poetry and stories; she had them dramatize, illustrate, and supply new endings for the stories they read; she displayed their art, illustrating literature and their own writing, on the bulletin board. But when parents came to visit, they told Aunt Marvel that the children said hers was the room where they "don't do any work." When children are involved in the learning process, they certainly do not feel that they are "working." Aunt Marvel's students enjoyed the early works of Dr. Seuss and were fond of the story of Babar, the elephant. She recalls using *The Silver Pennies: A Collection of Poems for Modern Boys and Girls* by Blanche Thompson, as well as work by A. A. Milne and Rachel Field. She went on to teach at the junior high level, where she continued to enjoy success with literature, using thematic units and even the works of Shakespeare to encourage her students to think and make connections. She certainly was a teacher ahead of her time.

Although some books for children appeared prior to the twentieth century, the modern era begins around 1920, when a number of notable books appeared, many of them still used lovingly today. Margery Williams's *The Velveteen Rabbit*, published in 1922, has been illustrated and reissued over the years in many different forms. A. A. Milne published his *Winnie the Pooh* stories about this time, and Wanda Gág gave readers *Millions of Cats* followed by *The ABC Bunny*. In 1929 Rachel Field wrote *Hitty, Her First Hundred Years* for older readers. Teachers who have a fondness for old-time favorites and classics will include these books in their repertoire.

In the 1930s, stories with sequels made their appearance, beginning with the work of Laura Ingalls Wilder and the *Little House* stories. Talking animal stories became popular with the adventures of Babar and Celeste. And the hilarious and bizarre also made inroads with the appearance of Dr. Seuss and his wonderfully imaginative *And to Think That I Saw It on Mulberry Street*. He was prolific, entertaining young readers for almost sixty years—so much so that upon his death, my students created a tribute to him. They each brought in their favorite Seuss stories and then created wonderful imaginary vehicles that could only have been seen on Cornell Road, where our school is located (see Figure 6.1).

The 1930s also saw an increase in illustrations by artists using different styles and media. Artists from that time include Arthur Rackham, Kurt Wiese, Marguerite deAngeli, Robert Lawson, Paul Ardizzone, Robert McCloskey, Paul d'Aulaire, and Garth Williams. Who cannot recognize deAngeli's soft pictures from *Copper-Toed Boots* or *Yonie Wondernose*, the expressive faces of Lawson in *Wee Gillis*, Wiese's *The Story About Ping*, or McCloskey's fresh pictures in his *Make Way for Ducklings*? The latter, a Caldecott award–winning book, has recently celebrated its fiftieth anniversary.

With the evolution of radio and drama during the 1940s, 1950s, and 1960s, children became more sophisticated. As fathers and husbands returned from World War II, family life was held in high esteem, and parents and writers took a new interest in children and their antics. Books were written to reflect the contemporary if idealized family. Young readers were introduced to McCloskey's Homer Price and his famous doughnut machine and to Atwater's Mr. Popper and his notorious performing penguins from the Antarctic.

In more recent times the range and imaginativeness of literature for children and young adults has expanded a thousandfold. Children are treated seriously as readers, and books are written about real homes and real parents, siblings, peers, people and places, and a wide range of young people's concerns and problems. What was once viewed somewhat contemptuously as

FIGURE 6.1 A well-loved author like Dr. Seuss is an inspiration to students. My students at Cornell Elementary School in Okemos, Michigan, recently created a tribute to him.

■ **IDEAS TO LEARN**   Interview a person who went to elementary school in the 1930s, 1940s, 1950s, or 1960s about books they remember from school. Ask them about their favorite characters, selections, and settings. Consider inviting this adult into your classroom to share favorite books with your students, perhaps reading sections or entire books to the class.

"kiddie lit" now has a respected list of authors and a distinguished body of scholarship surrounding it.

Prior to 1955 there were few college courses available in children's literature. At Ohio State University, Charlotte Huck was influential in establishing coursework for undergraduates and graduates alike. Early classes offered at major universities and liberal arts colleges merely gave surveys of children's literature, maybe including a few teaching strategies. Now a master's degree program typically includes course titles such as the Roots of Fantasy, History of Children's Books, Children's Poetry, Informational Books, Critical Reading Using Children's Literature, and the Art of the Picture Book.

Doctoral programs include research into such topics as narrative theory and reader response.

Keeping Current with Children's Literature

We now know that children can learn through exposure to various kinds of books and print. Andrea Butler and Jan Turbill from New South Wales, Australia, Kenneth and Yetta Goodman from Arizona, and Jane Hansen from New Hampshire have published research supporting this view. Marie Clay, a researcher from the University of Auckland, has shown that children go through various stages of growth and development and that their growth is paralleled by the development of reading skills.

Above all we now know that children need to have an abundance of literary materials around them through which they can experience emotions and explore possibilities and potentialities, all in relation to what they know and can do already.

There are a number of ways teachers can keep up with what's available in children's literature:

1. Read publications like *Language Arts, Reading Teacher, Horn Book, Book List,* or *The New Advocate*.
2. Attend local, state, or national conferences of different professional groups like the International Reading Association, the National Council of Teachers of English, or their affiliates.
3. Enroll in a nearby university class.
4. Attend workshops and in-service programs prepared by your local or intermediate school district.
5. Enroll in summer forums (usually offered at a campus or resort area).
6. Use a professional visitation day to visit a model classroom in another building or district.
7. Hang out at bookstores; watch for sales and markdowns.
8. Share ideas with your colleagues and ask questions.

What Literature Is

Those of us who pursue literature as an integral part of each day have developed a sense of great personal resource. I attended a large urban elementary school in the 1940s, where I was an avid reader. I became part of the student library staff, which allowed me to enter school early after lunch to reshelve books and help with the end-of-the-year inventory. Just being able to look at and handle all of those wonderful books was exciting. I paid attention to my teachers and their selection of materials for the classroom. I spent my baby-sitting money in the book department of a large downtown department store. I couldn't get enough of books and of reading.

I had a sense of what literature was through the classics of Lewis Carroll and Robert Louis Stevenson and Carol Ryrie Brink's *Caddie Woodlawn* along with all the Laura Ingalls Wilder books. I was thrilled to be asked to read to a younger class Dr. Seuss's *To Think That I Saw It on Mulberry Street*, a new purchase for the library. Marguerite Henry's *Misty of Chincoteague* and Caro-lyn Bailey's *Miss Hickory* were gifts from the Junior Literary Guild. Books and reading gave me immense pleasure. I discovered on my own what Ber-nice Cullinan says:

1. That literature informs the imagination,
2. pushes one to wish to read more,
3. provides language models,
4. helps stimulate the intellect,
5. reflects the heritage of mankind and
6. is the key to our literary and cultural heritage.

(Cullinan, 1987)

■ **IDEAS TO LEARN**   Write about your favorite childhood books. Who were your favorite characters? Did any books scare you? Inspire you? Influ-ence your thinking? How? Who read to you? Teachers? Parents? What are your favorite memories of being read to? Share some of these experiences with your students.

What is literature? Patricia Cianciolo, Michigan State University, offers this view:

> The subject of literature comprises aspects of the human condition. It may per-tain to any human experience, everything which has to do with people—their actions, their needs and desires, their strengths and frailities, their response to the world in which they live. Writing literature, be it fiction, poetry, or drama, is not the same as writing a script for a documentary movie or television report or writing a newspaper article. The writers who view them as comparable will make little use of their imagination. And imagination is the human faculty that lends the writer (or illustrator) to create a literary work of art, art at its finest and most memorable.
>
> When literature is viewed as one of the humanities, one tends to read a literary selection to find out how the author interprets people's responses to certain

social issues or to aspects of the human condition. Literature is used as a source through which one gains an understanding of oneself and one's relationship to other people and things. It is used to find out what an author offers the reader in relation to the perpetual and universal human questions common to people of all ages: ''Why am I like I am?'' ''Who am I?'' ''What is my world?'' ''What else might it be?'' This approach to literature is justified if one remembers that literature, as an art form, should not be read on the literal level for actual or even partial answers to these persistent human concerns, nor should it be read as a source for factual information. No attempt should be made to read into these stories or poems or even to judge them on terms of eternal standards, such as ''truth,'' as though they were factual or informational writings.

(Cianciolo, 1990, 10–11)

We experience literature in more than one dimension. The literary experience can be affective, cognitive, aesthetic, or any combination of these (Figure 6.2 on page 246 shows the elements of literature more explicitly). Let's look more closely at the various ways in which readers respond to the things they read and examine separately the affective, cognitive, and aesthetic domains of reading.

After reading, successful students respond in many ways that include talking about what they have read, doing something to interpret the work, writing their own stories, or making recommendations to others. Students will reflect upon that which they have read or written. They will feel success and want to read and write again (Butler and Turbill, 1987).

■ **IDEAS TO LEARN**   Expand your aesthetic awareness of literature by doing at least one of the activities suggested here.

1. Write a narrative in the style of or on the topic of a particular author or illustrator. *The Man Whose Name Was Not Thomas* by M. Jean Craig, written in the negative, is particularly challenging.

2. Draw a scene from a book that you have just read. An example would be a scene from Frances Hodgson Burnett's *The Secret Garden*, say, the heather and moors or the various stages of the garden.

3. Perhaps working with others, create a puppet show using puppets made from sticks, paper bags, gloves, socks, or papier maché.

4. Create a mural or large paper collage to reflect your response to reading a children's book.

5. Make a tissue paper collage in the style of Eric Carle, who first painted his tissue paper with random brush strokes.

6. Don't let children have *all* the fun. Try construction paper sculpture yourself!

7. Tomie dePaola's *Grouchy Ladybug* doesn't always have to be grouchy! Get children involved in the experience of a book by having them retell the story with a different ending, say, happy instead of sad. Putting the characters into another time and place will do the same.

The **affective** domain of literary response refers to emotion and feeling. Readers of literature will especially enjoy such books as the humorous *Daddy's Whiskers* by Steve Charney; Lawson's *Rabbit Hill*, in which the bonding of animals to humans is evident; the story of survival in the gutters of New York City in George Selden's *Cricket in Times Square*. They will appreciate language and the elements of literature that demonstrate enduring quality. Since its publication in 1952, E. B. White's *Charlotte's Web* has become a modern-day classic. Its multiple plots—about Fern the farm girl, Wilbur the pig, Templeton the rat, and A. Cavatica the spider who could spell—have survived thousands of readings and should be examined carefully to determine why. Literature enables readers to experience an array of human emotions, including fear, anger, sadness, and humor. *The Secret Garden* introduces us to Colin's lonely nighttime fears, Mary's curiosity and haughtiness, and Dickon's gentleness with animals and humans alike. The meshing of these three personalities brings readers to an exciting and emotional ending as the master of Misselthwaite Manor returns from a world trip to a home unlike the one he left in his own sorrow.

More recent books also tap into young emotion, such as Eve Bunting's *The Wednesday Surprise* or Mem Fox's *Wilfred Gordon McDonald Partridge*. In the first book young readers come to understand that a nonreading adult can learn to read. In the second book they are moved by the young man who helps nursing home residents connect with their memories. Although these are both picture books about the elderly, they can be used for all ages.

Children's emotional impact is swift and intense, and teachers must remember that individual children respond differently to the same selection. A child who reads Carol and Donald Carrick's *The Accident* and has had a similar experience will certainly be more touched by the story than a child whose pet has never been endangered.

In the **cognitive** domain, readers reflect on universal and diverse knowledge. They learn about things removed from their direct experience. Paddington the bear takes his readers to present-day England, beginning with his arrival at Paddington Station. Book characters and readers experience abandonment and solitude like Karana felt in Scott O'Dell's *Island of the Blue Dolphins* or Pippi Longstocking in Astrid Lindgren's book of the same name. How do these young people care for themselves and survive against the odds? What was life like for Young Fu who lived in Chunking, China, or for Little Pear from the same era? For cognitive learning, children can look at maps or

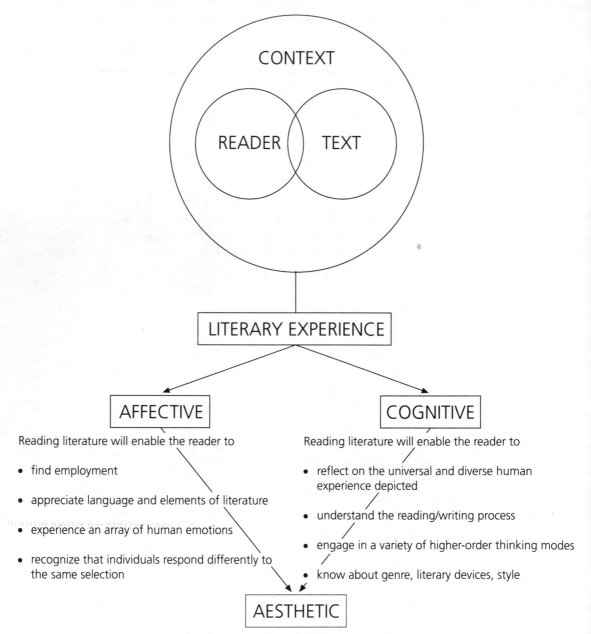

FIGURE 6.2 The elements of the literacy experience (Cianciolo & Culver, 1991, unpublished).

globes and relate a story's adventures to their own world. In addition, they will see how authors write. They will learn that writings can be grouped into different genres or themes. And as our society and our schools become increasingly multicultural, diversity in literature will give children a deeper knowledge and understanding of one another.

When children read books for an **aesthetic** experience, they are sensitive to the art and beauty of the image and the language. Words will be made beautiful with figurative language such as alliteration, simile and metaphor, and onomatopoeia. Description will conjure up beautiful and imaginary places in ancient or future times. Stories of conquest, mystery, or adventure will create emotional experiences for readers (Norton, 1987). We can use picture storybooks for children of all ages. For second graders, Alice and Martin Provensen's *Shaker Lane* is a story of a changing community; for fifth graders, it's a story of urban sprawl. When we use *Shaker Lane*, we can bring in other Provensen books so that children can look at the art work and at the variety of topics about which the Provensens have written. Their story of Leonardo daVinci is a magnificent, three-dimensional book for older students, who can handle such a book carefully and with respect.

Reading fine literature allows readers to recognize and appreciate literature as an art form. We always want our students to listen to how words are put together and how the illustration enhances those particular words. Students will value beautiful words in the poetry of Myra Cohn Livingston, in *Worlds I Know and Other Poems* or *A Circle of Seasons* (illustrated by Leonard Everett Fisher).

Jane Yolen gives her readers a unique experience with her poetry book *Ring of Earth: A Child's Book of Seasons*, illustrated by John Wallner. She also uses poetic language in her award-winning narrative book *Owl Moon*; readers will long remember time spent out on the cold, crisp snow late at night "owling." Young readers will have another memorable experience with *Stopping by the Woods on a Snowy Evening*, illustrated by Susan Jeffers—a single edition

TEACHING IDEAS

Extend literature throughout your curriculum. Choose a unit from a social studies or a science textbook and find literature that will expand on it and demonstrate its aesthetic and personal dimensions. Look for:

- Nonfiction trade books
- Short stories or novels
- Poetry or drama

of Robert Frost's poem perfect for sharing on one of winter's first snowy days. Some books have to wait on teachers' desks for just the right moment!

Literature and Very Young Children

Teachers of very young children—in preschool, Head Start, or the lowest elementary grades—interact with students regularly and in short time segments. Learning occurs at a fast clip. For beginning listeners and readers, meaning dominates in literature. Early books are highly predictable: Words are familiar and outcomes are easily guessed from text and illustration. Books for the very young are easy to talk about; they make great sense. Although literature in the primary classroom concentrates on the growth of readers

TEACHING IDEAS

The imaginative re-creation of literature allows children to think about what they read by remaking it in some way—which extends their knowledge of how literature works and enhances their own ability to make literature themselves. Consider giving children a number of options for writing from, rather than about, literature:

- Rewrite the ending of a story according to your own desires and explain why you did so.
- Add a new character to a scene. How does this character develop, change, or influence the interactions in the scene?
- Write a scene from a different character's point of view. How does he or she view the events differently?
- Rewrite the scene in script form. How do you portray people's thoughts and feelings in dialogue?
- Have characters in the story write letters to one another five, ten, or fifteen years after the story has ended.
- Keep a diary for a character in the story.
- Write a description of the character's life ten years after the story has ended.
- Write a poem as a character in the story might.
- Rewrite a scene or event in the story as a character might tell it to his or her grandchild.

rather than on the development of skills, skill learning is an obvious outgrowth of early reading. In fact children often begin to read before school by exploring the words on the backs of cereal boxes, grocery shopping lists, fast-food restaurant signs, and especially from cherished books that have been read aloud time and again. What is called the *lap method* in educational jargon is merely the time-honored method of learning to love literature by sitting in a parent's or grandparent's lap and hearing and seeing books read aloud.

Many children come to school having seen adults model reading behavior. At home or in small intimate relationships, they have had positive and meaningful interactive responses (Routman, 1988, 1991). Even if children haven't had the good fortune to experience the lap method at home, teachers can quickly help to bridge the gap by using the same approach. Research shows that children who have books in their hands and hearts from the very beginning of school think of themselves as readers right away. And such an attitude has been shown to carry over into other curricular areas as well.

Teachers of the very young should keep favorite books around and bring in new books as well so that children have something to look forward to each day, something new or an old standby.

Literature in the Integrated Language Arts Classroom

As we begin to discuss more formal approaches to literature in the integrated language arts classroom, I want to stress the need for patience with how young people learn.

Years ago in one of my classes, a little fellow named Greg was struggling to learn to read. Although he had gone through kindergarten and most of first grade, he clearly wasn't making a great deal of progress. But one April afternoon (it was a Thursday around two o'clock, I remember clearly), the light dawned and Greg shrieked, "Hey, I can read!" This was a turning point for this little boy. He began to read daily, and he became more attentive to read-aloud stories. As his teacher I had had a hard time waiting. But my patience paid off, and eventually Greg really could read on his own.

It's also important to stress that we need to respect children's own intellectual and emotional development and start from there. There is no room for a lockstep curriculum in the integrated language arts classroom. Although it is difficult to provide the sort of individual attention required by this approach, the strategies discussed here should help you get started. Perceptive and observant teachers will guide and nurture children, provide them with many and various materials, explain, . . . and wait. Children need to be shown, have things pointed out, have things explained to them, and be allowed to wonder about the world of print and picture. Pieces will fall into place when the time is right (Hansen, 1987).

We need to recognize that the approach of integrated language arts draws on a natural manner of learning, the same way children learn at home and in the community. Children ask questions and they get answers. They read aloud when they can. The lap method really works, and many teachers even get grandparents or other senior citizens to come to school to help out. Parent and grandparent volunteers do not admonish young readers for their errors but instead supply words and phrases for them. These adults are full of praise and look forward to the next scheduled visits. Parents and grandparents have long been recognized as quality teachers for youngsters. We could do worse than to imitate them. (See Figure 6.3).

The Classroom Library

Elementary teachers have the world at their fingertips—the worlds of time, place, and experience. Books are central to expanding that world. Most elementary teachers know the importance of building a classroom library. One well-known teacher, Vera Milz, has nearly four thousand books in her classroom. I don't want to scare off the new teacher, but I myself have about seven thousand children's books, which I've collected over many years. I move portions of this library back and forth regularly between home and school. My collection is built around favorite topics, well-loved authors and illustrators, and genres. Among the subcollections I have developed are:

Land, Sea, and Sky	Fall Ball Games
Mistress Mary	Whoo-oo-o-o!
Long, Long Ago	War Stories
Beautiful Books	Trucks and Boats
The First Snow	Places We've Been
The Wild West	Alone, All, All Alone
Family Life	In Days of Old
Grandmas and Grandpas	Sports Heroes
Best Friends	Fly Away
Anno's Math Books	Woof, Woof
Once Upon a Time	The Good Egg
Monet's Garden	We Love Tomie dePaola
Across the Ocean	Fritz Knows a Lot
Alice and Martin Provensen	Hot, Hot Deserts
Surprise Cinderella	B is for Betsy
Encyclopedia Brown	Eric Carle
ABC and 123	On the Trail
Mew, Mew	Roald Dahl

FIGURE 6.3 Adult volunteers in the early elementary classroom can be invaluable in helping the teacher integrate literature with the rest of the curriculum.

Building a personal collection of books can be very costly—but you can do it very slowly. Although you can spend a lot of money for books, you can find inexpensive sources with a little effort. My own collection has come from such sources as

- Local bookstores
- Children's book clubs
- Publishers' samples at state or national conferences
- Outlet distributors
- Requests for holiday or birthday gifts
- Antique shops
- Garage sales
- Library discard sales

You can also work with the school librarian in order to learn about and *influence* the holdings in that collection. Many librarians fully welcome suggestions from teachers who are willing to keep up-to-date in children's literature and make recommendations. Before discussing how to use these materials—whether fifty or five thousand books, whether from your own collection or the school's—I want to review the principal categories of children's books and some of the more notable titles one is likely to encounter there.

The Finest in Children's Books

The number of children's books in print and in circulation is so vast that it becomes necessary to sort and classify them into meaningful categories. Libraries themselves are arranged according to formal classifications using the Dewey decimal system or the Library of Congress system. Bookstores group together and display specific types of books. My own personal system only works for me—it is neither of the library systems mentioned.

Before we look at books by category, let's look at *art in children's books*. Artists use many different media to illustrate texts and extend story lines or concepts. Line and wash illustrations are soft and regular. Pen and ink drawings are bolder and simpler, as are images from woodcuts and linoleum blocks. Watercolors produce soft, graceful pictures, such as Beatrix Potter's illustrations in her little animal stories. Painters also use acrylics or oils. Other media include pastels, chalk, charcoal, and pencil.

Some artists combine media, as did Leo and Diane Dillon, who used watercolors, pastels, and acrylics in their award-winning book *Ashanti to Zulu*, written by Margaret Musgrove. Brian Pinkney uses scratchboard (a white board covered with black ink upon which the design is "scratched" off with a sharp tool to create the image). He then adds color with oil pastels. His Afro-American tale *Sukey and the Mermaid* uses this technique. Lynne Cherry is another artist who combines techniques. In *A River Ran Wild*, the seven-thousand-year story of a river, she used watercolors and colored pencils. Other illustrators make collages out of tissue paper, fabric, wallpaper, or craft paper. Best known for this work is Eric Carle, including the well-loved *Very Hungry Caterpillar* and a more recent publication, *Dragons, Dragons and Other Creatures That Never Were*, illustrated by Carle and compiled by Laura Whipple (see Figure 6.4).

When you share books with these different media, you can teach your students about artists and their contributions to literature. You can also use the artists as models for making art in the classroom. I like to have my students try on different artists' styles in their art projects. Applying paint all over tissue paper before cutting it out for a collage, in the style of Eric Carle, is certainly enriching. Sharing *Bear's Picture* by Daniel Pinkwater lets every budding artist know that it is the individual who matters.

In addition to reading some type of topic-related story or part of a chapter in a book each day, I present a picture book. Illustrations in children's books range from the realistic or representational, which is comfortable and

FIGURE 6.4 Sometimes teachers can entice a professional author to visit their class. Eric Carle, the noted writer and collage artist, helped my class celebrate his book *Dragons, Dragons*.

familiar, to the surrealistic, impressionistic, expressionistic, naive, and folk art. I use illustrations to judge children's books, to assess the overall quality of excellence. I want to examine how the artistic techniques are executed in relation to the text and how well the pictures interpret the story. I also must consider who the audience is for a particular book—different types of illustrations appeal to different ages of children (for instance, Leon Garfield's *The Wedding Ghost* illustrated by Charles Keeping is definitely not for young children). Overall, determining what is best is highly subjective and very personal, for adults and children alike (Cianciolo, 1990).

Picture Books

Years ago picture books were produced for very young readers only. Nowadays picture books exist for all ages, and they have wide appeal. Books in this category include alphabet books, number books, concept books, beginning-to-read titles, storybooks, and brief glimpses into other times and places. Single poem editions have become popular and include Harry Behn's *Trees*,

Lear's *The Jumblies*, Longfellow's *Paul Revere's Ride* (both the latter illustrated by Ted Rand), and Coleridge's *Rime of the Ancient Mariner* (illustrated by Ed Young). All these provide quick and easily presented models for writing, learning, and enjoyment.

There is a wide variety of **alphabet books**. A collection of these will include Duke's *The Guinea Pig ABC*, Hague's *Alphabears*, Merriam's *Halloween ABC*, and Sloane's *ABC Book of Early Americana* for older readers. These expose children to the richness of language within a theme and the elusive letters Q and X. **Number books** for young children are plentiful and have many of the same characteristics as alphabet stories. Some are merely numeric with a picture on the page representing the quantity, as in Thornhill's *Wildlife 1.2.3.*, which has vivid illustrations of numbers to 20, then 25, 50, 100, and finally 1,000 (tadpoles!). Another such book is *Numblers* by Suse MacDonald. The number itself transforms into the picture. Number books have also been used with the very young for chanting and finger games. It's no wonder that young school children still rely on their fingers for early math skills.

Many picture books demonstrate **concepts**. The visual presentation cements the information provided in the text. Overlapping with the number books mentioned above are David Schwartz's book *How Much Is a Million?* (illustrated by Steven Kellogg) and the Annos' *Mysterious Multiplying Jar*. Both present fantastic clues about large numbers. Other concept books deal with scientific data. All of Maria Rius's *Let's Discover* books (about the seaside, the city, the mountains, and the countryside) are presented with simple illustrations and words but include full explanations at the back of the books for adults to extend the concepts. These books have been translated from Spanish and were printed in Spain. Ruth Heller has produced many beautifully illustrated concept books, including *Plants That Never Ever Bloom*.

As children are beginning to learn to read, familiar stories or rhymes or stories with patterns support them in their efforts to match what they know with what is on the page. Familiar Mother Goose rhymes in print allow them to see the words they can say "by heart." In addition, children who have stories read over and over to them begin to match the words that they have memorized with what they see. Helpful **beginning-to-read books** include those books which build on patterns. ABC and counting books use children's knowledge of numbers and letters as reminders of what comes next in the story and encourage children to join in as someone reads to them. Other predictable books include those which have repeated questions, phrases, or words throughout the story, such as Bill Martin, Jr.'s *Brown Bear, Brown Bear, What Do You See?* (which uses a repeated question), Maurice Sendak's *Chicken Soup with Rice* (which uses the months of the year), Eric Carle's *The*

Very Hungry Caterpillar (which uses the days of the week), and Eve Sutton's *My Cat Likes to Hide in Boxes* (which uses a repeated sentence pattern).

Picture storybooks have flooded the market during recent years as publishers strive to meet the demand for such materials. Many talented illustrators and writers have joined forces to produce stunning books. Teachers are finding that their students can read materials that are not necessarily written with a controlled vocabulary, short pages, or overly simple sentences. Teachers and parents also find that children are eager to reread favorite stories or try books on their own based on their interest in beautiful or arresting illustrations. Wordless storybooks appeal to children across the grades.

Books about **other places and times** have become significant, such as Ivan Gantschev's *The Train to Grandma's*, Arthur Dorros's *Abuela*, and Masako Hidaka's *Girl from the Snow Country*. Generational stories have appeared, like Cynthia Rylant's *When I Was Young in the Mountains* and Gloria Houston's *My Great Aunt Arizona* (both semiautobiographical stories about mountain life in different parts of this country). Toshi Maruki's World War II story *Hiroshima No Pika*, presented with touching surrealistic art, is definitely for mature readers who can understand the atrocity of atomic destruction and the prospect of nuclear war.

■ **IDEAS TO LEARN**   Clearly picture books are not only for beginning readers. Many, many of these books appeal to older children and to adults as well. Go on a picture book hunt to find books that you feel would appeal to the more sophisticated reader and thinker. What do you think the appeal is for older readers? Describe how you might use picture books with children in upper grades. Develop a lesson or activity to use in conjunction with a picture book.

Picture books can provide insight into literary styles and aspects of life not experienced by the readers or listeners. In the context of sharing materials with a caring and loving adult, children establish positive attitudes and experience warm feelings. Even adults can be strongly affected, say, by Byrd Baylor's *I'm in Charge of Celebrations* or *Guess Who My Favorite Person Is* (anyone can play that game!). On an even lighter note, rules for school are taken care of in Cazet's *Never Spit on Your Shoes*.

Picture books can provide new meanings for familiar words, new synonyms for known words, and new vocabulary and concepts for students ready to learn. You can extend a picture book's story by interpreting for your students and sharing related experiences. As we've seen, picture books come in a wide variety: They can be highly structured as in cumulative tales, very funny as in humorous tales, or full of magic or explanations as in tales that tell how or why something occurs.

Historical and Realistic Fiction

These stories reflect life as experienced now or in the past and have an enduring fascination for readers. Such books can carry youngsters beyond the threshold of their own worlds into other times and places. Before the turn of this century Louisa May Alcott's books captured the imaginations of young readers. Laura Ingalls Wilder's fictionalized accounts of her family's many new homesteads in the woods and Great Plains were equally gripping. Historical fiction provides a look at the world from different perspectives. Two notable books, *Adam of the Road* by Elizabeth Janet Gray and *A Door in the Wall* by Marguerite deAngeli, give insight into the lives and times of young people during the Middle Ages and their struggles for survival (including a search for a lost parent in the former and a physical handicap in the latter). Other stories dealing with survival give older readers a sense of adventure, as in Scott O'Dell's *Island of the Blue Dolphins*, Theodore Taylor's *The Cay*, and Robert O'Brien's *Z for Zachariah*. Robinson Crusoe and his man Friday were certainly the forerunner of this type of story. Many contemporary realistic fiction for children deals with survival against social ills. Stories describe complex social problems, like divorce, alcoholism, desertion, adoption, foster care, poverty, prejudice, death, aging, war, dissolved friendships, and separation, showing young readers that they aren't the only ones to experience such difficulties.

Titles that reflect the nature of modern living include Bette Greene's *Philip Hall Likes Me I Reckon Maybe* on friendship in rural Arkansas and her *Summer of My German Soldier* about the friendship between a German prisoner of war and a young Jewish girl during World War II. Prejudice is dealt with forthrightly in Mildred Taylor's *Roll of Thunder, Hear My Cry*, as it is in *The Cay* mentioned above. A different type of problem is revealed in the story of a family that decides to care for a so-called tough kid in Walter Dean Myers's *Won't Know Till I Get There*. This first-person narrative written as a journal describes what happens to one "regular kid" and his friends when the newcomer arrives.

Death and aging are a part of every child's life, too. Children often establish strong ties with grandparents on whom they rely for very special relationships. They enjoy their company in many different ways, defend their possessions, and worry about them when they fall ill. *The Hundred Penny Box* by Sharon Mathis tells the tender story of a grandmother's significant memories, represented by the pennies saved over the years. Aliki's *The Two of Them* is the story of give and take, when a little girl and her grandfather change roles following his illness (Tomie dePaola's *Now One Foot, Now the Other* tells a similar story). Friendship is another popular topic that winds its way through children's literature. Of note is the award-winning book that has almost become a modern-day classic, Katherine Paterson's *Bridge to Terabithia*. Not only is friendship a strong theme but the abrupt ending and the response to the very permanent loss of a friend is well portrayed. For younger readers *Ira Says Good-bye* by Bernard Waber realistically tells the story of one family's move to a new community. Readers and listeners will recognize the false bravado that masks the feelings about losing a friend.

African-American culture in metropolitan settings is portrayed in Helen King's *Willy* and in Walter Dean Myers's recent Newbery honor book *Scorpion*. Similarly *Tar Beach* by Faith Ringgold received a Parents' Choice award and is lovingly illustrated. On a lighter note for school-age children is Mary Hoffman's *Amazing Grace*, a young African-American child's story of ambition and determination. Publishers are taking advantage of a new interest in the multicultural by supplying books for today's children that more directly reflect the diversity in American society, its different races and ethnic groups.

Writers of realistic and historical fiction must take into account many factors. First, they must develop a story line that is believable. Second, their young readers must be able to identify with it: Strong family relationships, like those in Eloise Greenfield's *Grandmama's Joy* and *Grandpa's Face* and in Karen Ackerman's *Song and Dance Man*, reflect life as children know it. Third, characters and settings must accurately reflect the particular time and place. Finally, conversations, clothing, speech, mannerisms, and physical geography must be consistent with the main idea and support the theme or the purpose for which the book was written. Readers always want to know what it was like then or there. Many books in this field can provide additional information to support textbook learning in content areas (social studies, science, mathematics).

■ **IDEAS TO LEARN**   Choose a historical period or a social or political issue that you think will be of interest to children. Read and review three to five books on that topic. Which are appropriate to read to the whole class? Which might you recommend that all children read? Which might you recommend for individual readers? Support your recommendations. Or choose a particular culture, in the United States or elsewhere, to explore through literature. Recommend books for classroom and individual use.

Human relationships and understandings can be broadened by reading the wide range of materials that deal with cross-cultural issues and ethnic groups. When children have a better understanding of their counterparts in other parts of this country or in other parts of the world, they will be more accepting, better informed, and more aware of likenesses and differences. As children become more globally aware, they can appreciate different language patterns, home lives, socioeconomic variations, and cultural origins. Their worlds will expand when they read Rabe's *Girl Who Had No Name* (in which the main character is determined to find out why she had no name and why she was unwanted), Henry's *Misty of Chincoteague* set on the eastern sea-board, Paterson's *Of Nightingales That Weep* set in ancient Japan, or Hender-shot's *In Coal Country* set in the mining areas of Pennsylvania. These glimpses through windows into other lives and times empower young readers to explore the world of books. Readers can also learn to make their own judgments when they read different books about the same topic with opposing points of view. Sometimes one book will deal with different viewpoints: *My Brother Sam Is Dead* by James and Christopher Collier presents different perspectives on the American Revolution, as family members are torn apart by opposing loyalties (Hickman and Cullinan, 1989).

Poetry

It is very hard to define just what poetry is. One's experience largely feeds one's attitude toward poetry. *Webster's* says that a poem is an arrangement of words expressing experiences, ideas, or emotions in a style more concen-trated, imaginative, and powerful than that of ordinary speech or prose. Al-though this is not an exact formula, it does suggest that some type of emotional response will occur. From a very young age, children can respond to poetry, especially poems aimed at small children, such as nursery rhymes. (It has been found that many children enter school not knowing who Peter, Peter, Pumpkin Eater or Little Polly Flinders are. How sad!) Early experiences with rhyme and rhythm set the stage for further enjoyment of verse, and reading poetry at home to very young children expands and enriches their vocabulary (Cullinan, 1987). Children will repeat, chant, supply missing words, add new endings, and want to hear a favorite verse again and again. Marguerite deAngeli, Tomie dePaola, Tasha Tudor, and Gyo Fukijawa all have colorfully illustrated collections of nursery and Mother Goose rhyme books for young listeners. Primary teachers can find time every day to share a few poems with children. In the elementary school schedule, too, there are brief periods when a poem can be shared . . . each day! Impromptu readings or recitations bring joy and unity to a classroom. I think books of rhyme and verse should be a staple for every classroom throughout the grades. I hope teachers will remember old favorites, keep looking for new poems or old standbys in new forms, and keep abreast of other new publications.

There are many ways to share poetry in the classroom. Impromptu choral reading, creative movement, tapping out rhythms, and interpretations in drawing, painting, and cut paper all extend the poems shared by children or adults. In my classroom I set up the poetry center around themes. For instance, I'll bring in my collection of poetry about cats and then extend it to include poetry about other animals (by reading to children from Eric Carle's *Animals, Animals*, Arnold Adoff's *Birds*, and Myra Livingston's *Dog Poems*). Some authors, like Adoff and Livingston, write their own poetry while others—anthologists—compile unique and topic-centered poems for books illustrated by a certain artist. Seven- and eight-year-olds show a particular interest in poetry about familiar pets and animals (Arnstein, 1962). Aileen Fisher has written many books for that age group about the creatures found in children's neighborhoods (she provides facts, both well-known and obscure, that strive to answer questions and dispel doubts). Her work includes *Rabbits, Rabbits* and *A Cricket in a Thicket*, in which she describes how insects listen and ''speak.'' Byrd Baylor uses lyrical prose to tell about desert life in many of her books, including *Hawk, I'm Your Brother* and *Everybody Needs a Rock*.

Poetry anthologies range from early childhood nursery rhyme collections, books for young readers, humorous and zany volumes, to larger, family-treasure books. You can turn poems from these collections into creative drama or pantomime, set them to music, or use them for recitation. Some collections are built around a very narrow topic, like Lee Bennett Hopkins's *Still As a Star—A Book of Nighttime Poems* and *Munching—Poems About Eating*. Many adults have fond memories of poems from large anthologies read to them during some part of their elementary school education. Favorites include ''Little Orphan Annie,'' ''Animal Crackers,'' ''Paul Revere's Ride,'' and ''O, Captain, My Captain.'' Large volumes like Frances Parkinson Keyes's *A Treasury of Favorite Poems* are intended for young and old alike. Books like these are usually indexed by title, author, topic, and first lines so that readers can reminisce, reread, and enjoy or share with their own students or family members.

It's inspiring to use books of the collected poetry of an individual poet, like Karla Kuskin, Valerie Worth, Paul Fleischman, Shel Silverstein, and Jack

TEACHING IDEAS

Choose some vivid poems for children that are *active*, that lend themselves to dramatic presentation. Have the children prepare individual readings, choral readings, a readers theater presentation, or a puppet show. (See Chapter 2 for ideas on preparing dramatic activities.) Or choose vivid poems that are *concrete* in their images. Have children illustrate the poems for display in the classroom. (Having lots of illustrated poetry in the poetry center provides children with ideas and inspiration for their work.)

Prelutsky. These poets write from a variety of perspectives and bring to their work a breadth of talent, knowledge, and imagination that will astonish and inspire your students.

Poetry gives children pure enjoyment that they will never forget. It extends children's knowledge of concepts, expresses mood, expands vocabulary, and gives insight into self and others (Norton, 1987). You don't need to overpower students with analyses about why the poet said or wrote what he or she did; rather you can simply share poetry, just for the satisfaction of doing so. It is not necessary to break a poem apart to get a feeling for the whole. I like to read poetry to the children regularly, and I often ask a student to find a poem for me to share. Some days I ask each child to find a poem to read aloud and tell why he or she chose it.

Fantasy and Folk Tales

A complex body of stories has been handed down through oral tradition in all parts of the world. These now appear in print with illustrations. Large anthologies of fairy tales by the brothers Jacob and Wilhelm Grimm include over two hundred tales from Germany. These familiar tales (like Cinderella, the Wolf and the Seven Little Kids, Hansel and Gretel, and Jorinda and Joringel) are found in single printings and in small collections. Recent publications have altered some familiar tales to meet current demands for less violence and less antagonistic family relationships (like cruel stepparents).

The most common stepparent story is Cinderella. It is found in every country in one form or another, and comparing the different versions makes a good classroom project. The French version attributed to Charles Perrault is commonly marketed in the United States, including his *Cinderella and Other Tales from Perrault* (illustrated by Michael Hague), Amy Erhlich's *Cinderella by Charles Perrault* (illustrated by Susan Jeffers), and Charlotte Huck's *Princess Furball*. International versions, with colorful illustrations, include *The Egyptian Cinderella* by Shirley Climo and *Yeh-Shen—A Cinderella Story from China* by Ai-Ling Louie. As with the Cinderella story, every country has its versions of traditional stories. Travelers who spoke the language of the countries they visited no doubt had some impact on this phenomenon.

Libraries and bookstores are full of well-illustrated fairy tales. Fairy tales are important to children for their universal appeal. They reflect the traditional values of the times even though today many are criticized for their sexism and violence. They are commentaries on humanity's dreams, aspirations, emotions, and frailties. Others reflect morals, traditions, or the humor of the culture in which the stories originated (Cianciolo, 1990). Some are published in single editions, like *Snow White and Rose Red*, retold and illustrated by Bernadette Watts, and *Lon Po-Po: A Red Riding Hood Story from*

China, translated and illustrated by Ed Young. (This won him the Caldecott Medal for 1989. He also illustrated the Chinese Cinderella story mentioned in the above paragraph.)

Original stories written by Denmark's Hans Christian Andersen are now accepted as fairy tales. However, the overriding mood in many of his stories is one of sadness and despair, so you will have to think about how to present his work to children. Eric Carle has retold and illustrated a collection of these Danish tales in *Seven Stories by Hans Christian Andersen*. Demi created a uniquely illustrated Andersen tale, *The Nightingale*, in which she used traditional Chinese paints and brushes made of animal hairs on Wu silk to achieve the artistic impression she wished. Lisbeth Zwerger used watercolors to illustrate traditional Grimms' tales, such as her *Hansel and Gretel*, which students can read at the same time as Adrienne Adams's version and Joan Walsh Anglund's *Nibble, Nibble Mousekin*, to discover similarities and differences. In addition, they can compare the art media used in each book and tell how it enhances the story.

Certain characters like Baba Yaga and Vasilisa appear regularly in Russian tales. Stories of simpletons who overcome greedy siblings with absurdity and humor also recur, as in *Tales from Atop a Russian Stove* by Janet Higgonet-Schnopper. Wanda Gág's *Three Gay Tales from Grimm* includes three lesser known stories, all of this type as well.

Fables, legends, and folk tales have been written down from oral history over the centuries. Greek and Roman myths were used to explain religious and natural events. The gods and goddesses had supremely powerful characteristics that defied human law. Their stories and names linger in the English language, which has many derivatives from the ancients. Children often hear references to ancient stories in the modern world. *Demons, Monsters & Abodes of the Dead* by Robin Palmer is an easy-to-use reference book that explains the origins of golden cities and of magical rivers and countries where every wish could be fulfilled.

More recently Native American tales and legends have been written and published. These tales were also passed on to modern writers and illustrators through the oral tradition. A Hopi folk tale *The Mouse Couple* was written by Ekkehart Malotki and illustrated by Michael LaCapa, himself a Native American. Paul Goble has concentrated his publications on books about the Southwest. The brilliant colors and distinct lines of his unique, stylized art capitalizes on old stories in *Buffalo Woman* and *The Gift of the Sacred Dog*. Steptoe's *The Story of Jumping Mouse* speaks to the dreams and aspirations of one of the smallest creatures on the vast northern plains. Native American tales have endured for centuries and are now being read and enjoyed by an even wider audience. Likewise African-American literature has moved out of the shadows and into the pages of books for today's children. How things came to be appears in books by Yarbrough, such as *Cornrows*, which tells the story of the intricate hair-braiding patterns.

School children can increase their knowledge of and appreciate the heritage of their peers when teachers share these kinds of books and then expand on and explore the information that the books presented in story form. Some books are about the country of origin while others are about families in America. *The Boy of the Three Year Nap* by Dianne Snyder and *The Village of Round and Square Houses* by Ann Grifalconi explain how customs developed in Japan and central Africa respectively. Children can begin to look at themselves in a different perspective when they realize that there are common characteristics that all children share: the need for love and family, the need for protection against the elements, and the need to be recognized.

Modern Fantasy

In a literature-based, integrated language arts classroom, there will always be an abundance of modern fantasy stories, in which one or more elements of reality are altered, and animals, people, and nature itself act differently than in the world as we know it (Norton, 1987). Classic fantasy stories include the ever-popular writings of Lewis Carroll about Alice's adventures in a strange underground world. James Barrie's story of a little boy named Peter Pan who could fly through the air and who never wished to grow up has been transformed into an enduring stage production. Little people have been written about in Mary Norton's *The Borrowers*. Pinocchio, carved out of wood in Collodi's story, has been famous for many years and reminds us all to be ever truthful.

Fantasy stories are written about friendly and frightening spirits, time warps, personified objects, and talking animals. Themes are built around universal truths in regard to values, struggles, desires, and emotions. Good versus evil prevails in many of these stories, (as in fairy tales and myths and legends of origin). Obstacles are overcome with faith and determination. Love and friendship are strong elements as well as personal and social relationships. At some point in each story young readers suspend disbelief and become involved enough in the text to nearly believe and to wish that certain elements were really true (Norton, 1987).

A wide variety of fantasy stories are written for young readers. **Low fantasy** stories include an element of magic. These are mostly set in the natural, *primary world* known and familiar to children. Many low fantasies are filled with talking animals. Children have long loved the works of Beatrix Potter and her many familiar animals like Peter Rabbit and Aunt Jemima Puddle Duck, as well as the animal stories of A. A. Milne. Animals of the countryside in Robert Lawson's *Rabbit Hill* and the little animals of the New

York sewer system in George Selden's *Cricket in Times Square* give insights beyond the activity of the characters. Jon Scieszka provides a modern explanation of an old tale in his *True Story of the Three Little Pigs*, which explains the wolf's motivation for doing what he had to do! Humor abounds in the simple nature of the well-loved Mr. Popper, who explored the North Pole vicariously until the pole came to him, in Atwater's *Mr. Popper's Penguins*. Older readers are put in touch with the super intelligence of usually disdained animals, the rats, in O'Brien's Newbery award-winning book *Mrs. Frisby and the Rats of NIMH*.

High fantasy, on the other hand, is written for the more sophisticated reader in the middle or upper grades. The stories are complex and more serious, about high adventure, quests, self-discovery, and good versus evil. Settings are not the familiar, primary world but an unknown, *secondary world*. The laws of nature are altered but believable. The topography of the land is unique, and flora and fauna are strange. The writers develop mystical realms to meet the value-laden overriding themes of basic human relations and attitudes (Hickman and Cullinan, 1989). Ursula LeGuin writes about supernatural elements and nonrational phenomena in her *Earthsea Trilogy*. Other writers of high fantasy include Lloyd Alexander, who wrote a five-book series set in the land of Prydain. The complexity of these writings appeals to the more sophisticated reader. However, some readers may not understand or be able to interpret all of the messages and meanings buried in the plot and action of the story without some help from teachers (Cullinan, 1987). No matter how far removed from reality, the stories are internally consistent and logical.

Teachers generally introduce the books just mentioned at the middle school level (or above). Upper elementary grade teachers select high-fantasy books like C. S. Lewis's *The Lion, the Witch and the Wardrobe* and Bill Brittain's *The Wish Giver*. Another popular author is Madeleine L'Engle, who bases many of her stories on science and the mysteries of the universe; she looks forward to the time when the light barrier will be broken and people will be free from the restraints of time (Norton, 1987). Her stories are good for reading aloud to a class. Other flights into fantasy were written by George Mac-Donald in *The Princess and the Goblin* and *At the Back of the North Wind*. His stories are allegorical, and the characters move in and out of dreamlike states.

How young readers deal with the art of fantasy is difficult to know. Some people really believe that adults should be ever truthful with young children to avoid confusion. But writers of books for the very young have kept the fictitious nature of their stories alive. The wise teacher who reads a book of high fantasy to students can alert them to departures from reality, encouraging them to look for such divergences and to think about them. Although it is not our responsibility to tell students what to think, we do *want* them to think!

Information Books

Information books are essential to the book collection of an integrated language arts classroom. In my classroom these books comprise the largest section of the classroom library. They are grouped according to broad topics, such as biblical books, fairy tales and legends, mammals, fish, birds, landforms, water, crafts, art, photography, music, and poetry. One very large section is devoted to biography and autobiography, which introduce children to the life and times of people in history or in the modern worlds of sports, medicine, art, performance, or politics.

Informational reading satisfies children's curiosity. Books for the very young in this category are heavily illustrated, whereas books for older readers contain more text and are usually divided into sections for easy reference. Students recognize that many of these texts are not intended to be read from beginning to end but can be dipped into for either general or specific information. Some nonfiction books are clearly works of art, such as the Provensens' *Leonardo daVinci*. Its unique format and beautiful pictures appeal to all ages. Ruth Heller has written poetic and colorfully illustrated science books, such as *Animals Born Alive and Well* and *Chickens Aren't the Only Ones*.

Sharing nonfiction materials with young readers gives them the opportunity to

- Look at the world in a new way
- Discover the laws of nature and society
- Identify with people different from themselves

I like to use literature to stretch social studies and science textbooks. The world of living things is broadened by reading Susan Bonners's *Panda* and Jennifer Dewey's *Can You Find Me? A Book About Animal Camouflage*. *Who's Hiding Here?* by Yoshi is another camouflage story, beautifully illustrated with batik images on silk. Kathryn Lasky's *Sugaring Time* tells the story of maple syrup, complete with photographs of the entire process.

When I bring informational books to the classroom, I expect several things to happen. First, as my students gain knowledge about the world, they will develop critical reading and thinking skills. Second, their minds will be stretched as they put information into perspective according to their level of development. Third, they will learn to compare one book about a topic with another. Factual accuracy is a must for informational books, but some discrepancies do appear. Children can learn to check for this. Finally, children will increase their vocabularies and have their search for information stimulated (Norton, 1987). Their future life work may depend on what captures their minds at a very young age with a special writer or book.

Jean Fritz brings historical events right down to the level of children in such books as *Can't You Make Them Behave, King George?* about the American Revolution. Ann McGovern writes biographical books for young readers like *The Runaway Slave—The Story of Harriet Tubman*. Through the pages of a book, you can put children in touch with any historical period. Nancy Smiler Levinson's *I Lift My Lamp—Emma Lazarus and the Statue of Liberty* explains how the young writer Lazarus's words came to be inscribed on the base of the Statue of Liberty. The Newbery award-winning *Lincoln—A Photobiography* by Russell Freedman, written for middle graders, is accurate and pictorial.

Endless are the books in the nonfiction category and seemingly endless are the topics. If a reader wants to learn more about skipping rope, there's Skolnick's *Jump Rope*, which explains how to jump for joy, how to jump with chants and jingles, and how to jump for health. Sports and games and their performers (such as Olympic medalists) are popular reading for all grades. Students can develop their skills for advanced research and writing with specific classroom work related to informational books: how to gather information and decide what is relevant, how to organize notes, and how to actually write a report or research paper. (You can ask young children to work in groups to share information and to plan projects.)

Third grade teachers in my school have an annual Biography Party. Children read about and report on their characters in an oral presentation. They dress in the clothing of the person and speak in the first-person narrative. Parents and local school dignitaries attend the party, which is complete with refreshments and a printed program. Video tapes are made of these impressive renditions. Authenticity is a key (one student borrowed a wheelchair for his impersonation of F.D.R.). A gallery of large, hand-painted portraits lines the hallway on the day of the big event.

How to Integrate Literature into the Curriculum

Organizing the Classroom

Obviously, if you organize an integrated classroom around a large collection of books, you must keep track of materials, and students must be able to easily find what they need. There is no rigid pattern or model that must be followed; in fact you will probably want to develop your own plan.

In my classroom I like to arrange the furniture so that there are a lot of open spaces where children can be comfortable alone or with others. I always expect the noise level to be a productive, moderately quiet hum of activity. Figure 6.5 is a sample floor plan that allows flexibility for many types of

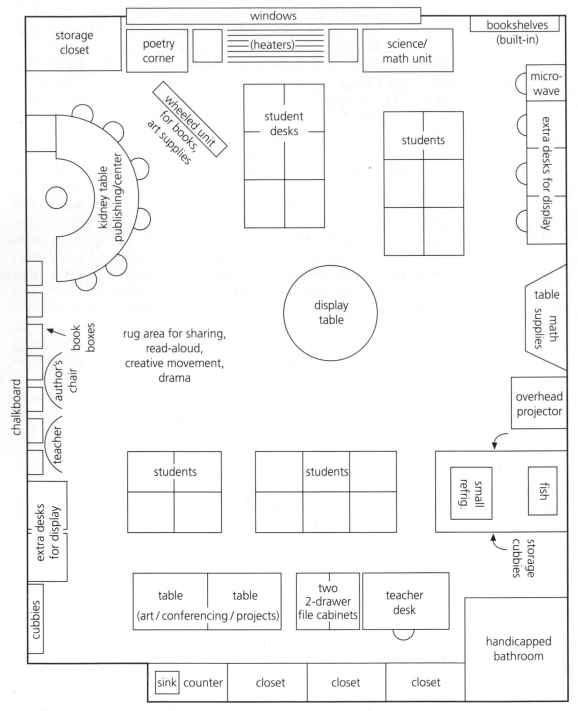

FIGURE 6.5 A sample floor plan for an integrated language arts classroom.

FIGURE 6.6 Small cardboard storage boxes are clearly labeled so students can find and return books easily.

projects. I use small cardboard file-type boxes to store small collections of books. Some of these boxes sit on the floor around the perimeter of one or two of the classroom walls. Others dot specific tables or display areas (see Figure 6.6). There is a permanent poetry section. I display books there with their covers visible so that students can easily select them. A colorful poster or two dominates the wall with a large (six-inch) caption made from letters cut out of bright construction paper. The captions vary. Most recently the poetry corner was entitled, "A Poem for Your Pocket" (a large denim pocket held poems that had been read aloud on 8½ by 11 inch paper). I try to keep thirty or more revolving titles in the poetry section. Another section (next to the windows) is where we keep special collections, like alphabet and number books, pioneer stories, animal stories, or Raggedy Ann and Andy books with the children's assorted dolls from home (see Figure 6.7). Bears—Real and Make Believe is another collection, which we do in the fall. There is hardly room for all the teddy bears that attend a Teddy Bear's picnic (from the book of the same name).

No matter how you arrange the room, your classroom library will demonstrate to students that reading is a very special activity, especially if you establish times for children to read and to interact with the books and with each other.

FIGURE 6.7 Special collections of books can lead to a variety of projects. The Raggedy Ann and Andy stories by Johnny Gruelle inspired my class to make rag dolls (with the help of parent volunteers) and to write and present ''autobiographical'' sketches for them.

Choosing and Discussing Literature

I have relinquished some of my responsibility for choosing reading materials for my students so that they can choose for themselves. Some teachers are afraid to do this. Jane Hansen (1987) wonders why this is the case when there are so many benefits for doing so. When teachers give children choices in what they read and write, the children develop some responsibility for their own learning and thereby develop their skills even further. Hansen goes on to explain that teachers should encourage students to read more than one book at a time: one that is easy for fun and rereading, one that is just about right to solidify reading skills, and one that is a challenging book to grow on. These options give children new outlooks about their own reading.

How children choose books to read depends on taste, time, place, and circumstance. Eventually they will discover that not all books are of equal literary value. However, the reserved and knowing teacher allows children to make some mistakes, because young readers don't automatically choose the best, since they don't yet know what constitutes literary merit or how to recognize hallmarks of excellence (Hickman and Cullinan, 1989). (Of course teachers themselves sometimes make mistakes. If you haven't had time to preview a story that you've begun to read aloud to the class and find that, for whatever reason, it isn't working, feel free to discontinue reading it.)

When children have time to discuss what they read, several things happen. They learn from one another. They build up a list of "I want to read . . ." books. They become intent listeners and analyzers. They learn to ask meaningful questions. They make suppositions and comparisons with their own previous book experiences. They encourage their friends to exchange book information with them. They decide if a book is worthy of a project (a chart, a poster, a play, a puppet show, a diorama, or a readers theater presentation).

A rich language environment encourages children to "try on" language. After hearing *Winnie the Pooh*, children want to "queue up" for lunch and recess. In first grade, my daughter, Martha, invented her own word, *brr.r.r.y*, to mean very cold. When children experiment with language and form, it's clear that language is taking root, actually getting inside them. In the upper grades students write fantasy and war stories, mysteries, and adventure stories after reading and hearing selections from those genres. Their vocabulary is enriched with words from earlier times. They become mindful of interpersonal relationships unlike their own. They gain an understanding of the world, its boundaries and people. They venture into unfamiliar times and spaces. Literature provides the means for writing and the knowledge to grow.

Scheduling Daily Activities

In an integrated language arts classroom—where there are no basal reading groups and where structure gives way to curiosity—all day long is the time for reading and sharing literature. Of course some special time is reserved for pure enjoyment, but the day lends itself to many opportunities for fitting in an appropriate piece of literature for learning.

You may wonder how a day proceeds in an integrated language arts classroom, how a teacher keeps track of what is going on, and how subject matter is controlled. Following is a schedule of a typical day in my class, although each day is subject to change because the children bring new challenges and questions. Rigidity is not part of my plan—flexibility is key.

9:00–9:10   Welcome, pledge, attendance, lunch count. Change "jobs" on Monday.

9:10–10:00 Group meeting on floor. Discuss yesterday's events; sharing; read aloud one or more selections; discuss books (author, style, art work); student authors read from their published works from the Author's Chair. Feedback is welcome.

9:15–10:00   Thursday: art.

10:00–10:15   Seat work: handwriting practice, skill work lessons. On Monday, the spelling pretest is given.

10:15–10:30   Recess.

10:30–10:45   Finish seat work, check it together, put it away. On Monday, find spelling words for individualized list to replace words correctly spelled on pretest.

10:45–11:30   Independent reading and conference time, alone, in pairs, or small groups, with parent volunteers in the hallway or with the teacher. On Friday, posttests are given individually by a parent volunteer.

11:30–11:50   Meet in a large circle to share latest reading material for impressions and recommendations.

11:50–12:00   Clean-up; prepare for lunch.

12:00–12:50   Lunch.

12:50–1:00   Review the morning; share new information.

1:00–1:30   Gym/music, twice each during the week.

1:30–2:10   Writing workshop (writing and publishing).

2:10–2:50   Math: textbook, manipulatives, read aloud.

2:50–3:15   Science/social studies alternating in two-week cycles. Use literature books when applicable (frequently).

2:10–3:10   Friday: library/computer lab.

3:20   Dismissal.

Literature for the Curriculum

The curriculum in a school district sets forth guidelines and objectives for learning. In social studies the topics often begin with those close to home and gradually expand as children get older: from self, family, home, community, city, state, and nation to the world. Students study how people function in regard to food, shelter, occupation, and personal time. They study regional areas to see how people are alike and different depending on their natural resources. In my school, for example, third graders study the Everglades, the desert, the forest, and the grasslands to examine different landforms and vegetation. They also learn about the building of cities, from ancient Tenochtitlán to modern Washington, D.C. and Chicago. Integrated with literature, their work is tied together by *Tales of the American West* by Neil and Ting Morris and *Chicago—A Picture Book to Remember Her By* by David Gibbon and Ted Smart. Students represent the different topics in various ways: by making a mural, doing small group reports, making small wooden Kachina dolls (for one of the Native American groups studied).

In the same building fourth grade teachers base social studies on regional parts of the United States and finish with regions of the world. Many fiction stories fit into those topics, particularly in the development of communities during the last century. *Sarah, Plain and Tall* by Patricia MacLachlan and the Laura Ingalls Wilder books come to mind. Another is *Long Ago in Oregon* by Claudia Lewis.

Upper grades usually study the development of the United States as a nation, beginning with the Revolutionary War (for which there are many stories), the Civil War, the Industrial Revolution, and Westward expansion to the modern country we know today. Young adult novels and easy-to-read stories alike give background and detail and help children experience as well as learn about historical events. For instance, Robert Lawson (with tongue in cheek) credits a great many historical events to Paul Revere's horse and to Benjamin Franklin's mouse in *Mr. Revere and I*, and *Ben and Me. Obadiah the Bold* by Brinton Turkle, an easy read, gives a glimpse into the family life and language of an early eastern seaport town.

In addition, teachers at my school sprinkle map and globe skills throughout the social studies units, and use literature to provide several levels of understanding. For example, lively accounts of mountain life are found in Cynthia Rylant's *When I Was Young in the Mountains* (for all ages), Judith Hendershot's *In Coal Country*, and Michelle Dionetti's *Coal Mine Peaches*. I help children understand the concept of an island by reading several books about islands, including Golden MacDonald's *The Little Island*, which has a philosophical statement all its own; *The Big Island* by Julian May, a true account of the ecology of Isle Royale; *Island Boy* by Barbara Cooney, the three-generational story of a developing community; and the provocative *Rabbit Island* by Jörg Steiner, an account of a debate about freedom and security.

Thematic collections of material provide a good focal point for inquiry, which helps break down rigid time schedules. You can also combine resources and efforts while monitoring your students' reading and comprehension (Hancock and Hill, 1988). This particularly helps with evaluating what your students are actually learning.

I use fairy tales in the classroom for different levels of thinking and response. I reinforce learning in connection with those stories and their settings: Information about medieval times, in which fairy tales are set, is covered in picture books like *Anno's Medieval World* and Aliki's *A Medieval Feast*. Older children can learn about knighthood from Lasker's *Tournament of Knights*. All ages can enjoy the smugness of the negative language used in Craig's picture book *The Man Whose Name Was Not Thomas*, a charming peasant love story set in early times. You can use fairy tales to teach about superstition, ancient customs, and trading and bartering, while getting to read hundreds of tales.

Science is another wonderful topic to explore with literature. Elementary students study plant and animal groups, simple organisms, the universe, rocks and fossils, matter, electricity and magnetism, landforms and the changing earth, the senses, and light and sound. For my science units I first find out what students know and what misconceptions they have by brainstorming, recording what they say either on large chart paper or a transparency on an overhead projector. I also ask them what they want to know (Hansen, 1987). Then I know what informational and fiction books to look for, keeping in mind that the illustrations in picture books supply unwritten information about relationships, life cycles, and habitats. When my students are learning about the characteristics of fish, for instance, they enjoy stories like Clement's *Big Al* illustrated by Yoshi and Lionni's *Swimmy*, both about food chains and survival. Their knowledge of sea life is enriched by reading Carle's *House for Hermit Crab*. Their study of rocks is certainly more meaningful with Baylor's *Everybody Needs a Rock* and its ten special rules for finding just the right one. Carle's well-known *Very Hungry Caterpillar* helps children understand the concept of metamorphosis.

Following is my favorite thematic unit of study. It floats in and out of our school day throughout the year but intensifies in the spring. It allows us to explore the Impressionist painters, biology, gardening, construction, geography, and cooking—combining a lot of learning with a lot of fun and enthusiasm.

Water Lilies and Beyond

A fictitious little girl, Linnea (named after the woodland flower of the same name) gives us information and adventure throughout the year via four delightful books by Christina Bjork and Lena Anderson. I introduce Linnea to the children in the fall with *Linnea's Almanac*. We meet her neighbors, Mr. Bloom, a retired gardener, and Mr. Brush who rents a little home in the country. Three to five pages in the book are devoted to each month of the year. On the first of each month we read the almanac to see what we can expect in nature. Although the stories are set in Sweden, the climate and natural effects

TEACHING IDEAS

Choose a topic from the curriculum and find as many books related to it as you can. Be sure to include picture books, short story books, novels, and informational books. Decide how you will introduce them to your class and discuss how you would like them to be used. Try to pinpoint a narrow topic rather than one that is too broad; for example, tiny bugs, smugglers, war heroes, birds, stories written in dialect, the Caribbean, river towns, and the like. What kind of art projects or written tasks would be appropriate for your topic?

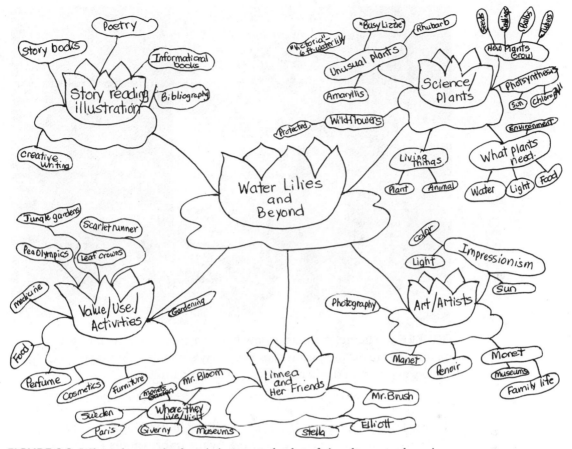

FIGURE 6.8 When the curriculum is integrated, a lot of simultaneous learning takes place. The thematic Water Lilies and Beyond unit that I use with my class branches off into science, art, and hands-on activities.

are similar to the region where we live. I plan about three months of extended reading and activities for the end of the school year, beginning that unit of study with *Linnea in Monet's Garden*. I check my own curriculum guides to be sure that what I teach the children is appropriate for their age and what they need to have from me as a teacher (I don't want time with Linnea to take away from other topics that I need to cover). The integration of studies works well because a lot of learning occurs simultaneously (see Figure 6.8).

In the Monet book, Linnea and Mr. Bloom visit Paris. From there they take the train to Giverny to visit Monet's garden. While the two of them stroll through the gardens (which have been lovingly replanted as a tourist attraction), Linnea learns about impressionistic painting and about particular flowers. Using a camera and a sketchbook, she examines flowers and compares

FIGURE 6.9 Thematic units not only help teachers integrate the curriculum but can lead to exciting student projects. My students enjoyed growing a variety of plants in the Water Lilies and Beyond unit.

them to the renderings of Claude Monet. Back in Paris Linnea and Mr. Bloom visit museums to look at other art work by the Impressionists.

My class usually spends February and part of March with *Linnea in Monet's Garden*. My students paint a wall-sized mural of the garden, creating large flowers that overlap. (This made a big impression on Andrew, a second grader who wrote on the last day of school that he never knew that Monet had painted with globs [of paint]!) To see how the various flowers look, we examine seed catalogs, library books, and artists' paintings. Students paint pictures of the Japanese bridge over the water lily pond as they learn about Monet's life and family from Linnea. In time Linnea almost seems like a member of the classroom. My students want to know whether she is real and whether they can write to her.

In the Linnea books we learn that the kitchen is a great place to find things to plant. We sprout sweet potatoes and avocados; we plant seeds from oranges, apples, grapefruit, and cucumbers. We plant beans of all kinds and the children bring in seed packets from home to add to our "garden" (see Figure 6.9). Children take cuttings from houseplants and learn how to plant and care for plants germinated in different ways. They learn about the water cycle and how plants grow, about photosynthesis and chlorophyll. The classroom begins to look like a greenhouse in the springtime. The almanac book also teaches us what happens to plant life in winter and how the seasons affect plant growth and nearby animals.

Linnea and Mr. Bloom teach us that all plants have Latin names, from the work of the Swedish botanist Carolus Linnaeus (after whom a special flower and a special little girl were named). We make cardboard flower presses with newspaper pages for springtime flowers and leaves. The children become observant and knowledgeable about all aspects of plant life. The picture book *The Rose in My Garden* by Arnold and Anita Lobel, which tells the story of the life of a rose, adds to their knowledge about common garden flowers; and *Monet's Passion* by Elizabeth Murray shows how Monet worked diligently to create his gardens. Ethne Clark's *The Flower Garden Planner* (which I found at a local nursery) contains 140 pages of press-outs, so the children can plan their own gardens on paper. They also draw plans for jungle gardens with paths and ponds and then add small plastic figures.

The latest Björk and Anderson book, *Elliot's Extraordinary Cookbook*, gives us new ideas about how to appreciate food. We enjoy fixing and eating ''Earth Apples in Field Jackets'' (boiled potatoes in their skins). This book is full of information about nutrition; it discusses the basic qualities of meat from cows and chickens, of bread, fruits, and vegetables, and of snack foods. It also contains easy, child-pleasing recipes.

Books about gardening fill two sections of the Monet table, where several plants grow. The children particularly enjoy the panoramic fold-out book *When the Root Children Wake Up* by Helen Dean Fish. Children learn about home gardening in Skelsey and Huckaby's *Growing Up Green*. The library yields a whole armful of books about trees, leaves, and plants; other books introduce the children to other Impressionist painters like Renoir.

Each day I read one or more stories or selections from books during the morning oral language time. During reading instructional time before lunch, I encourage children to read on their own from the many selections. During science time in the late afternoon, we read some more and do all our planting, labeling, observing, and comparing.

All in all, the school year ends too soon. The children are busy all day long with hands-on experiences: reading, writing, doing research, observing, planting, recording, comparing, analyzing, creating artistic impressions— and waiting for things to grow. They come to school excited to see how high an amaryllis has gotten or what has sprouted overnight.

I wove the strands of this unit together on the loom of literature in its many forms. I had to be a master planner and researcher in order to integrate science, art, and literature. I had to be a master organizer to structure the daily activities—but I could not be inflexible: I had to respond to the children's input and adjust my schedule accordingly, in what I call *spontaneous teaching*. It is a richly rewarding experience for me and my students.

TEACHING IDEAS

Using the Water Lilies and Beyond unit as a model, choose one of the books recommended in this chapter or one of your own favorites. Develop a list of spin-off activities that are suggested by the ideas and events in the book. In addition to reading and writing activities, be sure to include many hands-on activities: constructing, observing, feeding and nurturing, painting, drawing, interviewing, modeling, and the like.

Assessment and Record Keeping

Teachers need to know how literature helps their students learn. They must keep track of and evaluate their students' reading—not only the range of difficulty but also the amount, variety, comprehension, and word knowledge of what students read. Below are some suggestions for doing this (also see Chapter 3, "Assessment in Reading"):

1. Have students keep reading logs in a notebook or file box.

2. Make a "bookworm": Add a four-by-six-inch worm segment with the title and reader's name for each book read. My class's bookworm consists of segments for each mini-report completed. Our bookworm winds around the room and all the way down the hallway to the principal's office.

3. Set aside a sharing time for students to respond aloud to what they have read. Get them to try to influence others to read the book.

4. Ask students to complete a book report form for each book read informally, or establish a regular book report schedule.

5. Use frequent conferences to keep track of what students are doing.

Figure 6.10 lists the questions I use in conferences with students. I also use it with adults and volunteers who participate in my reading program.

Assessment is a key issue in a classroom that doesn't use basal readers, workbook pages, multiple drill sheets, or paper-and-pencil tests to determine report card grades. Some teachers use a three-ring notebook with a page for each child. On it, they record dates, titles chosen, fluency or "voice" notations, difficult vocabulary (reviewed after the reading), impressions, predictions, or notes on the selection. Other teachers use four-by-six-inch cards to keep these notes, an easy way to keep records (just store them in a file box) and to share with parents at conference time. Some teachers have students

I'm curious. Why did you choose this book?

Have you read this before?

Do you know any other books by this author?

Do the pictures help you read this book?

What do you think will happen next in this story? (Come back and let me know.)

What is the hardest word on this page? How did you figure it out? Or, How could I help *you* figure it out? It's all right to skip a word unless it is absolutely necessary. Then tell it.

What do you know about reading that enables you to read this?

What do you know about reading this week that you didn't know last week?

What would you like to read next?

How could I help you choose your next book?

Would this be a good book to read with a friend? Would you recommend it to someone? Why or why not?

Why do you suppose: (point out skills here):
. . . all these words have capitals?
. . . these words are indented a little?
. . . these little marks are here (quotation marks)? Also point out hyphens, compounds, question marks, exclamation marks, contractions, plurals, etc.

Give praise and positive feedback:
I see you enjoyed this book.
This book seemed easy (difficult) for you.
I can't wait to read with you again.
You're working really hard on your reading.

FIGURE 6.10 Questions to use in reading program conferences with students.

keep their own reading records in pocketed folders or spiral notebooks (teachers must establish the criteria for what to include in each entry).

It is impossible to read individually with and to conference with each student each day. Reading in small groups or as a whole class can keep teachers in touch with each student. Teachers can move among small clusters of children or call the class together for a large group, brief response from each child. Either way gives teachers the opportunity to make brief entries on the children's forms.

It is extremely important that you keep careful records in the integrated, literature-centered classroom. At the same time it is important that you do not drive "good" literature into the ground by overassessing and overanalyzing it. In the end, engaged and active reading on the part of youngsters makes assessment a relatively easy task, although one that requires careful organization and disciplined record keeping.

The Value of Literature

The value of literature is that children come to realize that books are not cameras taking snapshots of the world but are interpretations of all that is possible. Books enable readers to realize their humanity while delighting in the souls of all (Cullinan, 1987). The long-range goal of teaching literature is to develop readers who not only know how to read but will want to read throughout their lives. A teacher who reads aloud and talks about books will model for children the identity of a reader, as he or she explains, interprets, and adds to the story, chapter, or poem.

To paraphrase Mem Fox (in *Wilfred Gordon McDonald Partridge*), literature offers something warm, something from long ago, something that makes you laugh, and something as precious as gold. It provides insight, satisfies curiosity, expands knowledge, and extends thinking. There is nothing else to be said for the value of literature in its many forms.

7

On Being a Professional

The resources required by teachers are many because the demands placed on them are great. They must maintain a vital, interesting, and stimulating classroom. They must produce successful students according to the expectations of administrators (this varies a great deal from administrator to administrator—some care about standardized tests, others about parents' reactions; some want to see quiet classrooms, others to see activity). They must meet the demands of parents, who want their children to be successful, happy, challenged, and nurtured. And many of them must also meet their own internal demands, which may require them to reach and teach every child. It is no surprise that many teachers experience burnout.

To respond to all these demands, teachers need support—support for continued professional growth, support for locating and evaluating new ideas, support for taking risks in the classroom, support for obtaining classroom materials to create a rich learning environment. In this chapter I will describe the organizations and the human and material resources that can provide the support you need in order to maintain a vital and interesting classroom and a vital and interesting career as a teacher.

Some research indicates that burnout is not the result of working too hard but of working unproductively. There's no doubt that many teachers put in long hours, not only in the classroom but at home, responding to children's work and preparing classroom activities and materials for use in school.

Many of these teachers stay vital and energetic despite the extra hours. Others leave teaching tired and discouraged, to find a new profession. What can help? Staying "centered" and feeling and being "professional" can make a difference. You may feel tired by the end of the week but not burned out and unprepared to return. What follows is a discussion of resources that will supply not only new ideas and materials for maintaining a vigorous classroom but also personal and professional support for you as a teacher.

This chapter offers you a wealth of materials, available through professional, government, business, and community organizations and services. The intent is not to overwhelm you—though the number of resources may indeed be overwhelming—but to demonstrate the riches available, which you can access to the benefit of yourself and your students.

Note: In some cases, I provide addresses and prices for materials. This information was accurate when this book went to press, but please check prices before ordering.

Professional Organizations

Involvement in professional organizations can add imagination, energy, and intelligence to your teaching life. Through their journals and other publications, national conferences, and local meetings, professional organizations not only keep you up-to-date in your profession but also bring you into contact with others who share your concerns. This is especially important nowadays, because of the tremendous growth in knowledge in the field of children's learning and language acquisition. In addition, many new resources for teaching language and literature throughout the curriculum are continually becoming available.

Some major organizations that focus on children, language, and language education are discussed below.

National Council of Teachers of English

NCTE publishes two journals of interest to teachers of language arts from the elementary to the junior high levels. *Language Arts* is intended for teachers of kindergarten through junior high. Eight issues a year include columns on research on children's language and learning; reviews of children's books; descriptions and reviews of professional materials; information on how to use computers; reports on issues of interest to administrators and supervisors; and articles on teaching language and literature in elementary school. The journal also includes occasional reports from the Center for the Study of Reading, the Center for the Study of Writing, and the Center for the Study of

CONTENTS

A Publication of the National Council of Teachers of English

Cover by Victoria Martin Pohlmann

Language Arts
Volume 70, Number 4
April 1993

FIGURE 7.1 A table of contents from *Language Arts*, published by the National Council of Teachers of English.

Learning and the Teaching of Literature (see Figure 7.1). The editor is eager to hear from teachers in the form of articles or letters responding to the journal's contents.

William H. Teale, Editor
Language Arts
Division of Education
The University of Texas at San Antonio
San Antonio, TX 78285-0654

The *English Journal* includes articles, features, and reviews for teachers of English at the secondary level (including middle school through junior high).

In addition to these journals and others, NCTE publishes books on the teaching of English/language arts. A few of its many popular titles of interest to elementary school teachers are:

Adventuring with Books, by Shelton L. Root, Jr.

Counterpoint and Beyond: A Response to Becoming a Nation of Readers, edited by Jane L. Davidson

Focus Units in Literature: A Handbook for Elementary School Teachers, by Joy F. Moss

Learning to Spell, by Richard E. Hodges

Literature in the Classroom: Readers, Texts, and Contexts, edited by Ben F. Nelms

Response Guides for Teaching Children's Books, by Albert B. Somers and Janet Evans Worthington

Writing Is Reading: 26 Ways to Connect, by Eileen Tway

In addition, NCTE publishes pamphlets and information sheets to help teachers and parents support the development of literacy in children. For example, the pamphlet partially reproduced in Figure 7.2 is intended for parents but can help teachers as well.

NCTE holds its annual conference the weekend before Thanksgiving, with sessions on many topics of interest to teachers, K–college. The conference also features a meeting of the Children's Literature Assembly, of special interest to language arts teachers since it features prominent children's authors as speakers. The weekend conference is followed by half-day, full-day, and two-day workshops, which allow teachers to participate in more intensive study of particular issues. The annual conference moves from city to city throughout the United States in an effort to be accessible to as many regions as possible.

NCTE also holds a spring conference, in March or April, at cities in different areas of the country, with a focus on teaching in the schools. Conventions are an excellent way to learn more about the profession as well as to make new friends and enjoy tours and cultural events in the various cities.

How to Help Your Child Become a Better Writer

**Suggestions for Parents
from the National Council of Teachers of English**

NCTE National Council of Teachers of English
1111 Kenyon Road, Urbana, Illinois 61801

Dear Parent:

We're pleased you want to know how to help the NCTE effort to improve the writing of young people. Parents and teachers working together are the best means for assuring that children and youth will become skillful writers.

Because the situation in every home is different, we can't say when the best time is to pursue each of the following suggestions. In any case, please be aware that writing skill develops slowly. For some, it comes early; for others it comes late. Occasionally a child's skill may even seem to go backwards. Nonetheless, with your help and encouragement, the child will certainly progress.

The members of the National Council of Teachers of English welcome your involvement in your child's education in writing. We hope you will enjoy following these suggestions for helping your child become a better writer, both at home and at school.

Sincerely,

Executive Director

Things to Do at Home

1. Build a climate of words at home. Go places and see things with your child, then talk about what has been seen, heard, smelled, tasted, touched. The basis of good writing is good talk, and younger children especially grow into stronger control of language when loving adults—particularly parents—share experiences and rich talk about those experiences.

2. Let children see you write often. You're both a model and a teacher. If children never see adults write, they gain an impression that writing occurs only at school. What you *do* is as important as what you say. Have children see you writing notes to friends, letters to business firms, perhaps stories to share with the children. From time to time, read aloud what you have written and ask your children their opinion of what you've said. If it's not perfect, so much the better. Making changes in what you write confirms for the child that revision is a natural part of writing—which it is.

3. Be as helpful as you can in helping children write. Talk through their ideas with them; help them discover what they want to say. When they ask for help with spelling, punctuation, and usage, supply that help. Your most effective role is not as a critic but as a helper. Rejoice in effort, delight in ideas, and resist the temptation to be critical.

4. Provide a suitable place for children to write. A quiet corner is best, the child's own place, if possible. If not, any flat surface with elbow room, a comfortable chair, and a good light will do.

5. Give the child, and encourage others to give, the gifts associated with writing:
   —pens of several kinds
   —pencils of appropriate size and hardness
   —a desk lamp
   —pads of paper, stationery, envelopes—even stamps
   —a booklet for a diary or daily journal (Make sure that the booklet is the child's private property; when children want to share, they will.)

   —a dictionary appropriate to the child's age and needs. Most dictionary use is for checking spelling, but a good dictionary contains fascinating information on word origins, synonyms, pronunciation, and so forth.
   —a thesaurus for older children. This will help in the search for the "right" word.
   —a typewriter (even a battered portable will do), allowing for occasional public messages, like neighborhood newspapers, or play scripts.
   —erasers or "white-out" liquid for correcting errors that the child wants to repair without rewriting.

6. Encourage (but do not demand) frequent writing. Be patient with reluctance to write. "I have nothing to say" is a perfect excuse. Recognize that the desire to write is a sometime thing. There will be times when a child "burns" to write; others, when the need is cool. But frequency of writing is important to develop the habit of writing.

7. Praise the child's efforts at writing. Forget what happened to you in school and resist the tendency to focus on errors of spelling, punctuation, and other mechanical aspects of writing. Emphasize the child's successes. For every error the child makes, there are dozens of things he or she has done well.

8. Share letters from friends and relatives. Treat such letters as special events. Urge relatives and friends to write notes and letters to the child, no matter how brief. Writing is especially rewarding when the child gets a response. When thank-you notes are in order, after a holiday especially, sit with the child and write your own notes at the same time. Writing ten letters (for ten gifts) is a heavy burden for the child; space the work and be supportive.

9. Encourage the child to write for information, free samples, and travel brochures. For suggestions about where to write and how to write, purchase a copy of the helpful U.S. Postal Service booklet *All about letters* (available from NCTE @ $2.50 per copy; class sets of 20 or more, $1.50 each).

FIGURE 7.2 Selections from a pamphlet from the National Council of Teachers of English.

Figure 7.3 contains a program from one of NCTE's spring conferences. Figure 7.4 shows a sample of the kinds of conference sessions you find at the annual meetings.

NCTE also sponsors regional meetings (Southwest, Southeast, Northwest, etc.). These are hosted by the state affiliates and usually include participants from three to five states, which makes these conferences a bit smaller and more intimate.

Finally, NCTE's state affiliates (e.g., Michigan Council of Teachers of English, Nevada State Council of Teachers of English) sponsor a variety of publications and activities—newsletters, journals, state publications, state conferences, in-service workshops, dinners, and social events. NCTE is eager to include student members in its organization, and both the national organization and many of the affiliates have student membership rates that are considerably reduced from the standard membership.

1992 Spring Conference March 26-28

Washington Hilton Hotel

SPONSORED BY
ELEMENTARY SECTION
SECONDARY SECTION
CONFERENCE ON ENGLISH EDUCATION
DISTRICT OF COLUMBIA COUNCIL OF
TEACHERS OF ENGLISH

Conference Calendar

Tuesday and Wednesday, March 24 & 25

9:00 a.m.–5:00 p.m.	Preconference Workshops

Thursday, March 26

8:30 a.m.–9:45 a.m.	A Sessions
10:00 a.m.–11:00 a.m.	Opening General Session
10:00 a.m.–5:00 p.m.	L. Ramon Veal Seminar on Research in Language
11:30 a.m.–12:45 p.m.	B Sessions
11:30 a.m.–1:30 p.m.	CEE Luncheon
1:45 p.m.–3:00 p.m.	C Sessions
3:30 p.m.–5:00 p.m.	D Sessions
5:00 p.m.–6:00 p.m.	Social Hour in the Exhibits
8:30 p.m.–Midnight	Conference Cabaret

Friday, March 27

8:30 a.m.–9:45 a.m.	E Sessions
10:00 a.m.–10:45 a.m.	Coffee and Conversation
11:00 a.m.–12:15 p.m.	Secondary Section General Session
11:00 a.m.–12:15 p.m.	F Sessions
12:30 p.m.–2:30 p.m.	Elementary Section Luncheon
1:30 p.m.–2:30 p.m.	*G Sessions
2:45 p.m.–4:00 p.m.	H Sessions
2:45 p.m.–5:30 p.m.	CEE General Session and Business Meeting
4:15 p.m.–5:30 p.m.	I Sessions
7:00 p.m.–11:15 p.m.	Friday Night Out

Saturday, March 28

9:00 a.m.–10:15 a.m.	J Sessions
10:30 a.m.–3:45 p.m.	Idea Exchange
10:45 a.m.–Noon	Elementary Section General Session
10:45 a.m.–Noon	K Sessions
12:15 p.m.–2:15 p.m.	Secondary Section Luncheon
1:00 p.m.–2:15 p.m.	*L Sessions
2:30 p.m.–3:45 p.m.	M Sessions

*These sessions are scheduled to begin during the last half of the preceding luncheon time.

FIGURE 7.3 A schedule for one of NCTE's Spring Conferences.

To find out more about the National Council of Teachers of English and their affiliate in your state, write to the address below. National membership with a subscription to your choice of one journal (eight issues) is $35 per year.

The National Council of Teachers of English
1111 Kenyon Road
Urbana, IL 61801

Concurrent Sessions

A SAMPLE OF TOPICS FROM THURSDAY, FRIDAY, AND SATURDAY

The NCTE Spring Conference has three program strands, one for each of the professional interests represented in the audience: elementary language arts, secondary school English, and teacher education (preservice as well as inservice education). Running through all three strands are several research-based sessions of interest to practitioners and researchers alike. Each of the parallel program strands extends from Thursday morning, March 26, through Saturday afternoon, March 28, with four time periods on Thursday, five time periods on Friday, and four time periods on Saturday. Registrants can choose from among five to eight sessions offered at their own teaching level each time period, or they can attend sessions in either of the other strands. Among the topics to be discussed are those listed below.

Elementary Strand

THURSDAY

Featured Speaker: Dorothy Strickland (E)
Portfolio Assessment: Emerging Issues (E, JH/MS)
Moving into Poetry (E)
Skits for Collaborative Problem Solving and Language Use (E, JH/MS)
Reliving History through Story and Bringing Culture Shock into the Classroom (E, JH/MS)
Sharing Pleasure, Excitement, and Understanding through Folktales (E, JH/MS)
Talking about the Business of Writing (E)
Why Are School Buses Yellow?: Models of Collaborative Inquiry in Elementary Schools (E)
Enhancing Reading Instruction through Selected Strategies (E, JH/MS)
The Book Report Pizza, or Greatest Lessons Ever Taught (G)
Beginning Readers: What Their Writing Tells Us (E)
Collaboration, Reflection, and Inquiry: Children, Teachers, and Institutions as Co-Learners in Process (E)
Featured Speaker: Bernice Cullinan (E)
Children as Historians: Challenges, Formats, Results (E)
The Spelling Dilemma: Addressing Spelling Instructional Concerns in the 90s (E)
America's Melting Pot: Advancing Multicultural Relationships through Literature and Media (E, JH/MS)
Workshop in Reaching and Responding to Literature for Elementary School Teachers (E)
Using Drama in the Classroom to Promote Language Development and Thinking Skills (E)
Collaborative Language Arts Learning: Primary, Middle Grades, and College Students Working Together (E, JH/MS, TE)

FRIDAY

Featured Speaker: John Pikulski (E)
Assessing Writing: Who? What? Where? When? Why? How? (E, JH/MS)
Concerns about Collaborative Learning (E, JH/MS)
Tangibles and Techniques: Activities to Expand Children's Responses to Literature (E)
Variation and Experimentation in Children's Picture Book Design (E)
The Faculty Lounge: Reflecting on the Way We Teach (G)
Portfolios: Assessment and Evaluation in K–5 Reading/Writing Classrooms (E, JH/MS)
The Right Connections (E)
Gender Concerns in Education (E)
Cultural Perspectives: Using Multicultural Literature across the Curriculum (E)
The Role of Writing in a Literature-based Reading Program: Multiple Possibilities (E)
Candid Comic Comments on the Contemporary Scene (E, S)
How a Picture Book Is Made: History, Technology, Creativity, and Magic (E)
Keeping the Arts in Language Arts (E)
Featured Speaker: Pat Cianciolo (E)
Report Card on Basal Readers Revisited (E)
The Circle of Literacy: Creating Writers (E)
Children's Books: Springboards to Writing (E)
Authenticity, Image, and Pedagogy in Multicultural Children's Literature (E)
Gender: A Hidden Agenda in Literacy, Learning, and Teaching (G)

SATURDAY

Creating Look-and-Listen Stories: Aladdin's Magic Overhead Projector and Tape Recorder (E)
Featured Speakers: Diane Lapp and Jim Flood (E)
Selecting the 1992 Caldecott Awards (E)
Links across the Curriculum (E)
A Conversation with Lucy Calkins (E)
Featured Speaker: Richard Allington (E)
When Politics Come between Teachers and Teaching (E)
Once More . . . with Filling: A Practical Approach to Overcoming the "I'm Outta Here" Revision Aversion Mentality (E, JH/MS)
Outstanding Nonfiction Choices Nominated for the 1992 Orbis Pictus Award (E)
Teacher Research Fair and James Britton Award Winners (G)
Promoting International Exchanges of Teachers: The Fulbright Scholar Program (G)
Tomorrow Begins Today: Language Arts for the Future (E, JH/MS)
Stories as Bridges: Establishing a Multicultural, Literature-based Model in the Classroom (E)

Initials in parentheses indicate level of instruction addressed: (E) Elementary, (JH/MS) Junior High/Middle School, (S) Secondary, (TE) Teacher Education, (G) General, (R) of particular interest to Researchers.

FIGURE 7.4 A sample of conference sessions at an NCTE annual meeting.

International Reading Association

IRA publishes the *Reading Teacher*, a journal for those interested in teaching reading at the preschool and elementary school levels. It contains both practical articles on the teaching of reading as well as articles on the theory and research that supports the teaching ideas. Also included are regular columns on reviews of children's books and instructional and professional resources; on new technological advances in computers and audiovisual materials; and on issues of importance to teachers, such as assessment and working with parents.

> James F. Baumann, Editor
> *Reading Teacher*
> School of Education
> Purdue University
> West Layfayette, IN 47907

IRA also publishes the *Journal of Reading* for secondary school teachers. It contains theoretical and practical articles as well as reviews of materials for children and teachers.

Like the National Council of Teachers of English, the International Reading Association publishes many books that can keep the practicing teacher up-to-date. Some recent, useful titles include

Beginning to Read: Thinking and Learning about Print, by Marilyn Jager Adams

Children's Choices (published yearly)

Young Adults' Choices (published yearly)

Teachers' Choices (published yearly)

Creating Readers and Writers, by Susan Mandel Glazer

How Children Construct Literacy: Piagetian Perspectives, edited by Yetta Goodman

Toward Defining Literacy, edited by Richard L. Venezky, Daniel A. Wagner, and Barrie S. Ciliberti

IRA's pamphlet series for parents can help teachers promote literacy development in their classrooms. Figure 7.5 shows the front and back covers of a pamphlet that discusses how to select books for children. The back cover lists other IRA pamphlets.

The International Reading Association holds its annual conference the first weekend in May at different sites around the country to provide access to members in different geographic locations. Among the highlights of the conference are presentations by authors and illustrators of children's literature. The IRA World Congress meets in places around the globe to offer teach-

This brochure may be purchased from the International Reading Association in quantities of 100 at a cost of US$5.00 per 100, prepaid only. Single copies are free upon request by sending a #10 self-addressed, stamped envelope. Requests for four or more titles should be accompanied by first class postage for two ounces. (Requests from outside the U.S. should include an envelope, but postage is not required.) Brochures in this series include:

Eating Well Can Help Your Child Learn Better
*Good Books Make Reading Fun for Your Child
Studying: A Key to Success...Ways Parents Can Help
*Summer Reading Is Important
**You Can Encourage Your Child to Read
*You Can Help Your Child in Reading By Using the Newspaper
**You Can Use Television to Stimulate Your Child's Reading Habits
**Your Home Is Your Child's First School
You Can Prepare Your Child for Reading Tests

*Also available in French
**Available in French and Spanish

International Reading Association
800 Barksdale Road
PO Box 8139
Newark, Delaware 19714, USA

FIGURE 7.5 The front and back covers of a pamphlet from the International Reading Association.

ers everywhere access to understanding reading and literacy from a global perspective.

IRA has active and large affiliates throughout the United States that sponsor conferences, workshops, and in-services for teachers. IRA is also interested in bringing student members into the organization and has student membership rates. To find out more about the services offered by the IRA, write them at the address below. Membership with a subscription of nine issues to the *Reading Teacher* is $30 per year.

> International Reading Association
> 800 Barksdale Road
> P.O. Box 8139
> Newark, DE 19714-8139

Association of Childhood Education International

ACEI publishes *Childhood Education*, a journal "For Those Concerned with Children from Infancy Through Early Adolescence to Stimulate Thinking Rather Than Advocate Fixed Practices." The journal is intended for parents as well as teachers and covers such things as curriculum, issues surrounding children with handicaps, child care centers, the gifted, and literacy issues. It includes columns on books for children and recent research into children's learning.

ACEI holds regional, national, and international conferences. It also has a number of state and student affiliates. For information on publications, conferences, and memberships write

> ACEI
> 3615 Wisconsin Avenue, N.W.
> Washington, DC 20016

■ **IDEAS TO LEARN**   Find out which NCTE, IRA, or ACEI conferences are being held in your local area, state, or region. Write for information about the programs. Research whether there are any campus resources for sending students to professional meetings.

Teachers & Writers Collaborative

Teachers & Writers Collaborative publishes *Teachers & Writers* magazine and a number of publications by creative writers and artists. It is best known for its publications by practicing poets and writers of fiction and its history of "real" writers working with children in the schools.

For more information write

> Teachers & Writers Collaborative
> 5 Union Square West
> New York, NY 10003

National Writing Project

The National Writing Project is "teacher-centered with teachers, from the primary grades through the university, working together as colleagues in a collaborative university-school program to improve student writing and the teaching of writing in our nation's classrooms." (Gray, n.d., 1) The basic assumptions of the National Writing Project are as follows:

1. The university and the schools must work together as partners. The "top-down" tradition of past university-school programs is no longer acceptable as a staff development model.

2. Successful teachers of writing can be identified, brought together during university Summer Institutes, and trained to teach other teachers in follow-up programs in the schools.

3. Teachers are the best teachers of other teachers; successful practicing teachers have a credibility no outside consultant can match.

4. Summer Institutes must involve teachers from all levels of instruction, elementary school through university; student writing needs constant attention and repetition from the early primary grades on through the university years.

5. Summer Institutes must involve teachers from across the disciplines; writing is as fundamental to learning in science, in mathematics, and in history as it is in English and the language arts.

6. Teachers of writing must also write: Teachers must experience what they are asking of their students when they have students write; the process of writing can be understood best by engaging in that process firsthand.

7. Real change in classroom practice happens over time; effective staff development programs are on-going and systematic, bringing teachers together regularly throughout their careers to test and evaluate the best practices of other teachers and the continuing developments in the field.

8. What is known about the teaching of writing comes not only from research but from the practice of those who teach writing.

9. The National Writing Project, by promoting no single "right" approach to the teaching of writing, is now and will always be open to whatever is known about writing from whatever source.

(National Writing Project: Model and Program Design, 2)

For more information about the National Writing Project, write

James Gray, Director
National Writing Project
School of Education
University of California
Berkeley, CA 94720

Other Professional Resources

Horn Book

The *Horn Book* is considered a basic item in the library of any expert in children's literature. Its book reviews are more detailed than those in more general publications. It also includes articles by writers on their own work, profiles of authors and illustrators, and information on how to use books in the classroom. The July issue regularly features profiles and the acceptance speeches of the Caldecott and Newbery award winners. There is also a very useful column, "The Hunt Breakfast," that lists book awards, conferences and meetings, and publications important in the world of children's literature. Write

> *Horn Book*
> 14 Beacon Street
> Boston, MA 02108

Instructor

Instructor is a general magazine for teachers and includes articles on math, science, literature, the arts, technology, research, professional development, and the like. It also provides a monthly planner and a poster, as a kind of "fun" bonus. Although it's not sufficient for keeping up with the field of language and literature teaching, I do like its emphasis on cross-curricular hands-on activities for children.

> *Instructor*
> Scholastic, Inc.
> P.O. Box 2039
> Mahopac, NY 10541-9962

Learning

Learning is a general magazine describing teaching ideas, recent research, trends and issues in education, social problems affecting education, opinion surveys, teacher tips and hints—a kind of *Ladies' Home Journal* of the teaching field. The articles are short and easy to read, and the magazine is filled with pictures and other graphics. Posters and calendars are also included. For more information write

> *Learning*
> P.O. Box 2589
> Boulder, CO 80321

New Advocate

The *New Advocate* announces that it is "For Those Involved with Young People and Their Literature." The journal includes book reviews, sources for teachers, articles about and by writers and illustrators about their work, teaching ideas, and articles on literacy issues.

> *New Advocate*
> Christopher-Gordon Publishers, Inc.
> 480 Washington Street
> Norwood, MA 02062

Reading Is Fundamental

Reading Is Fundamental (RIF) is a national nonprofit organization that sponsors local projects to support literacy and the joy of reading in young people. In addition to providing free books for children and conducting activities that increase children's pleasure in reading, RIF helps parents to help their children with reading. Some of their pamphlets include *TV and Reading; Choosing Good Books for Your Children: Infancy to Age 12; Reading Aloud to Your Children; Upbeat and Offbeat Activities to Encourage Reading; Children Who Can Read, But Don't; Building a Family Library;* and *Family Storytelling.* Pamphlets are fifty cents apiece and can be ordered at reduced rates in quantities of one hundred. You can obtain information about booklets and brochures by writing

> Reading Is Fundamental, Inc.
> Publications Department
> 600 Maryland Avenue, S.W., Suite 500
> Washington, DC 20024-2520

Teaching preK–8

The publication *Teaching preK–8* features one curriculum area per month for a close-up view of what's new in that area and presents teaching ideas to put the new theories into practice. In addition, it includes teaching ideas in various disciplines, reviews of books and teaching materials, news items relevant to teachers, and articles for parents. Write

> *Teaching preK–8*
> P.O. Box 912
> Farmington, NY 11737-9612

■ **IDEAS TO LEARN**   Choose a popular children's book and compare reviews of it in the various journals we just discussed. How do the reviews compare? Which journal formats do you find most appealing? Which journals are you most likely to consult again to learn about children's literature?

In addition to the book review sections we mentioned in the journals and publications above, the following sources provide reviews of children's books and should be available in your college or university library:

Kirkus

Booklist

School Library Journal

Publishers of Professional and Children's Literature

There are scores of publishers that publish professional materials for teachers and classroom materials and literature for children. The following are some of the largest and best known. Write to them to receive catalogues containing specific information about their publications.

Ballantine/Del Rey/Fawcett Ivy Books
201 East 50th Street
New York, NY 10022

Bantam Doubleday Dell Publishing
  Group, Inc.
666 Fifth Avenue
New York, NY 10103

Christopher-Gordon Publishers
480 Washington Street
Norwood, MA 02062

Farrar, Straus & Giroux
19 Union Square West
New York, NY 10003

Harcourt Brace Jovanovich
Children's Book Division
1250 Sixth Avenue
San Diego, CA 92101

School Department
6277 Sea Harbor Drive
Orlando, FL 32887

HarperCollins Publishers
10 East 53rd Street
New York, NY 10022

Heinemann-Boynton/Cook
361 Hanover Street
Portsmouth, NH 03801

Holt, Rinehart and Winston
1627 Woodland Avenue
Austin, TX 78741

Houghton Mifflin
2 Park Street
Boston, MA 02108

Little, Brown and Company
34 Beacon Street
Boston, MA 02108

McDougal, Littell & Company
P.O. Box 1667
Evanston, IL 60204

Macmillan Publishing Company
866 Third Avenue
New York, NY 10022

National Textbook Company
4255 West Touhy Avenue
Lincolnwood, IL 60646

Putnam & Grosset Book Group
200 Madison Avenue
New York, NY 10016

Random House
225 Park Avenue South
New York, NY 10003

Rigby
P.O. Box 797
Crystal Lake, IL 60014

Scholastic, Inc.
730 Broadway
New York, NY 10003

Scott Foresman
1900 East Lake Avenue
Glenview, IL 60025

Silver Burdett & Ginn
250 James Street
Morristown, NY 07960

Simon & Schuster Children's
  Books
1230 Avenue of the Americas
New York, NY 10020

Teachers College Press
1234 Amsterdam
New York, NY 10027

Wadsworth, Inc.
10 Davis Drive
Belmont, CA 94002

■ **IDEAS TO LEARN**   Distribute the list of educational publishers among your fellow classmates. Write to various publishers to find out what resources and materials you would like to put on your wish list for your future teaching.

Periodicals That Publish Work by and for Children

Most public and elementary school libraries subscribe to some if not all of the publications listed below. These magazines cover a wide range of subjects, provide children with leisure reading, and are sources for classroom activity, discussion, and research.

Chickadee   "The Discovery Magazine for Children," published by the Young Naturalist Foundation and intended for children up to nine years old. It contains pictures, articles, stories, and activities on the environment and the world.

> *Chickadee*
> P.O. Box 11314
> Des Moines, IA 50340

Cobblestone   "The History Magazine for Young People" includes stories about famous people and events and a section for children's work (poems, drawings, and letters).

> *Cobblestone*
> 30 Grove Street
> Petersborough, NH 03458

Cricket   This magazine contains a variety of articles, stories, and poems of interest to children.

> *Cricket*
> Box 51144
> Boulder, CO 80321-1144

National Geographic WORLD   Published by National Geographic for young people, this magazine contains colorful pictures, articles, and stories about people and lands around the world.

> *National Geographic WORLD*
> P.O. Box 00889
> 17th and M Streets, N.W.
> Washington, DC 20036

OWL   "The Discovery Magazine" for older children (over eight) is also published by the Young Naturalist Foundation and is intended to help children become more aware of the world around them.

> *OWL*
> P.O. Box 11314
> Des Moines, IA 50340 .

Penny Power   This "Consumer Reports Publication," published by Consumers Union, will be of interest to older elementary school children for its evaluation of products used by children (games, movies, fast food, etc.).

> *Penny Power*
> Subscription Department
> P.O. Box 51777
> Boulder, CO 80321-1777

Ranger Rick   Published by the National Wildlife Federation, this magazine contains articles, fiction, and activities about plants, animals, and natural events and about caring for the natural world.

Ranger Rick
National Wildlife Federation
8225 Leesburg Pike
Vienna, VA 22184-0001

Shoe Tree   This magazine publishes stories, poems, art, and book reviews by and for children, ages six to fifteen.

Shoe Tree
215 Valle del Sol Drive
Santa Fe, NM 87501

Stone Soup   Another publication of children's writing, *Stone Soup* seeks fiction, poetry, book reviews, and art by children through age thirteen.

Stone Soup
Children's Art Foundation
Box 83
Santa Cruz, CA 95603

Community Resources

The Public Library

In addition to making good use of your school librarian/media consultant, you should also be aware of the many resources, both human and material, that are available at your public library. Some are available to you as background and source materials for developing teaching units. Some are available for your students—either through them going to the library or you bringing things to them.

Community information   Many libraries have an information center (a bulletin board, rack, or table) where they provide information about

TEACHING IDEAS

Visit your local library to see what magazines are available for children. Choose one that you might use profitably in your classroom. Develop a list of writing and project ideas based on the contents of the magazine.

community events (art festivals, lectures, movies, cultural fairs, etc.). The booklets, notices, and brochures available here are free to the public.

Public service information   The library is also often the clearinghouse for information for the public put out by local city, county, state, and federal government agencies and by nonprofit or service-oriented organizations. These brochures and bulletins may provide information on such issues as health, fitness, government services, animal care, plant care, and other kinds of how-to's. The library usually has tables or stands filled with free information for consumers.

Current periodicals   The library has a wide variety of magazines and journals, some of a specialized nature to which you wouldn't subscribe but from which you might need information. There are magazines on current events, historical periods, the arts, cats, plants, cars and other vehicles, stamps, records, jewelry, vacation spots, the occult, religion, and so on. Some larger libraries may have professional journals, such as *Instructor*, *Learning*, or *English Journal*. The children's librarian may subscribe to the *Horn Book* or *Kirkus* and is usually more than willing to share his or her resources and expertise. Current periodicals, then, can provide resources for the teacher and for the students. In addition, many of the children's magazines mentioned earlier (and perhaps others that weren't mentioned) can be found in the children's section of the library.

New releases   Of special interest to you in keeping up with what's new in children's literature (and in finding the latest titles of your students' favorite authors) is the new releases section of the library, which is devoted to new acquisitions. Sometimes these circulate for a shorter period of time than the other books, but for an eager reader, that short time will be sufficient. In addition, the children's librarian is an excellent source of what's new.

Seasonal books   Many children's librarians set aside a shelf for books that are appropriate to the season (Thanksgiving, Halloween, Christmas, Hanukkah, New Year's). These may include fiction or nonfiction. Again, these books may circulate for a shorter period of time than the regular books.

Other special collections   Libraries may also set aside collections of books, like fairy tales and nursery rhymes, Caldecott and Newbery award winners, ABC and counting books, and the like. Be sure to ask the librarian about special categories.

Audiovisual resources   Bringing literature alive through the voices of professional actors and actresses or the authors themselves can give children a new way to experience literature. Libraries' collections include records and tapes of literature, music, historical events, and speeches to enrich and enliven your class.

Primary teachers can use the read-along books in the children's library (popular children's books accompanied by tapes). Children's resource centers can be enriched and children's reading supported by taped stories, which allow children to read along (see also Chapter 3 on reading).

Some libraries have videotapes of outstanding children's works, like *Anne of Green Gables*, the *Ramona* series, and *Charlie and the Chocolate Factory*. Many charge nothing or a minimal fee for use of videotapes. I expect that the videotape sections in libraries will continue to expand.

Book lists   Many children's librarians prepare book lists for specialized interests (or reproduce them from other sources). The children's section in the Reno, Nevada, public library reproduces the list of Caldecott and Newbery books, in addition to thematic lists of books for children at various grade levels. The second and third grade list, for example, includes eighty-six fiction and nonfiction titles under the categories Mystery and Adventure; Olden Days; Family and Friends; Funny Stories; Fantasy; Animals and Nature; and Sports, Hobbies, and Poems. The East Lansing, Michigan, public library has a number of pamphlets arranged by interest, theme, or issue—Time Travel, African-Americans, Understanding Death and Dying, Adventure into Sports, Find Adventure in Historical Fiction, Puppetry, Folklore of Michigan's Native Americans, Science Fiction, Modern Realistic Fiction, Parents and Children and Divorce, Frontier and Pioneer Life, Children's Classics, and more. Many librarians also make available articles and information sheets about selecting books for children.

Reference books   As a rule the books in the reference section cannot be checked out, so if you want your students to use this section, you will have to get them to the library. However, you can use the reference section yourself to discover and expand upon your knowledge of topics for your students. In addition to good old encyclopedias for compendiums of information, a quick perusal of the reference section reveals these titles:

What's What: A Visual Glossary of Everyday Objects—From Paper Clips to Passenger Ships (This book provides hundreds of pictures of common and not-so-common objects, with labels identifying the various parts. You find yourself saying, "So that's what it's called!")

Famous First Facts ("More than 9,000 first happenings, discoveries and inventions that have occurred throughout American history . . .")

Reader's Digest: *Facts and Fallacies: Stories of the Strange and Unusual*

How Did They Do That? ("Wonders of the Far and Recent Past Explained")

Writer's Market: Where and How to Sell What You Write

Oxford Illustrated Encyclopedias: *The Natural World; The Physical World*

World Almanac

Mysteries of the Bible

Dog Law: A Legal Guide for Dog Owners and Their Neighbors

The History of Beads: From 30,000 B.C. to the Present

Everyday Dress: 1650 to the Present

Festivals U.S.A. ("The 1000 Best Festivals!")

Do's and Taboos Around the World

Mythical and Fabulous Creatures

The Birds Around Us

The Weather Book

Color Encyclopedia of Gemstones

Dinosaurs and Prehistoric Animals

Color Atlas of Anatomy

The Oxford Dictionary of Art

The Encyclopedia of Superheroes

The Encyclopedia of Toys

World Coin Encyclopedia

The Great Song Thesaurus

The World Sports Record Encyclopedia

The Home Book of American Quotations

Cultural Atlas of China

Great Lives of the 20th Century

Encyclopedia of the Civil War

Dictionary of Names

Harvard Encyclopedia of American Ethnic Groups

The reference section for children's materials can provide you with more ideas for using books with children. For example:

A Multimedia Approach to Children's Literature, compiled and edited by Ellin Greene and Madalynne Schoenfeld, American Library Association,

1977. Although this selective list of films, filmstrips, and recordings based on children's books is somewhat old, it has many outstanding titles for bringing oral literature into the class.

Book Sharing: 101 Programs to Use with Preschoolers, by Margaret Read MacDonald, Library Professional Publications, 1988. Although this book is intended for use by librarians in preschool story programs, it provides wonderful ideas for structuring story time for primary age children. It offers suggestions for books to read as well as how to use poetry, music, rhythm instruments, art, films, creative dramatics, puppets, flannel boards, and dress-up as a part of storytelling.

The World's Best Poetry for Children, prepared by the Editorial Board of Roth Publishing, Poetry Anthology Press, 1986; in two volumes including over five hundred poems in nine thematic sections. The compilers have sought to include traditional poetry "from a wide range of different time periods and national literatures."

The children's reference section also includes book lists of specific interests or genres, including regional literature (Midwest, South, West, etc.), fantasy, award winners, sports literature, historical literature, literature about single-parent families, literature to help children deal with loss and death, fairy tales, folklore, and so on.

Children's librarian Whenever you want to know something, go to the children's librarian. I have met few who didn't know answers or want to help people find answers. If possible, take your children to the public library on a field trip. Make sure the librarian knows you are coming, and be sure that you have a specific purpose in mind for your visit—things that you want the children to know, understand, discover, get involved in. Once the children's librarian knows whether you are coming to work on projects, or to discover the reference section, or to check out books for fun reading, he or she will be able to help you plan and execute your agenda.

Children's librarians are usually involved in children's programs offered by the library. They may provide story hours for preschoolers through upper elementary students, they may operate summer or school-year book clubs or reading clubs, they may bring in authors to talk to children about their books. Find out what children's programs are available in your public library and help your students take advantage of them.

■ **IDEAS TO LEARN** Discover your local library! Choose a topic (goldfish, bicycling, ballet) and locate all the resources in the library that tell you about it.

Museums

We are probably not exaggerating much when we say that no matter where you live there will be some kind of museum within thirty miles. Of course all large cities are filled with museums—museums of science and industry, planetariums, arboretums, art museums, geological or geographical museums, ethnic museums, cultural museums that describe a part of our history (mining, cars, dance, theater, the military, farming), and regional historical museums that describe the history of a town, a section of a state, or the entire state. Even very small towns have historical societies that have saved and described artifacts for the next generation.

Whenever possible, take your students on field trips to these museums. If you can't get to a museum, see if the museum can come to you. Find out whether speakers or materials can be made available to you and your students. Many museums have outreach programs and are eager to come to schools. Some even have traveling collections for this purpose.

■ **IDEAS TO LEARN** Using the telephone directory or library resources, make a list of what's available in your community that you could use to enliven and enlighten topics you would like to teach in history, geography, science, the arts, and other curriculum areas.

Artists/Poets in the Schools Program

Funded by the government, these programs are available throughout the country. Your media specialist/librarian should be able to get you a list of artists in the schools in your area. You will need to apply in advance for someone to come to your school for a day or several days to work with both children and teachers. The more specific your plan for using the artist/poet, the better your chances of a positive reply.

Performing Arts Groups

If there are any theater or puppet companies in your area, contact them to see whether they have special programs for schools. Some community groups and most professional groups have some sort of provisions for students, perhaps allowing school children in free for dress rehearsals or having special "preview" programs that come to the schools.

Businesses

Chambers of Commerce   To learn more about what your city (or a city you are studying) has to offer, write to its chamber of commerce. The chamber can provide information about the city's history, economy, and cultural offerings.

Travel agents   Travel agents are often willing to provide free brochures, posters, booklets, and travel information about historic and scenic sites around the world. If you give them advance notice, they can save their out-dated materials for you (in this business this happens fast).

Newspapers   Most newspapers of moderate size have an education program. For a modest fee you can receive a class set of the newspaper in addition to teaching materials that provide you with lots of ideas for ways to use the newspaper to enrich your curriculum and for teaching students about news-papers. Of course with only your imagination and a copy of the newspaper in your classroom, you can help children widen their view of the world, learn about their own community, and expand their knowledge of types of reading and writing.

Other businesses   Big businesses (department store chains, for example) and industry very often have educational wings that they maintain as a ser-vice to the community (and for good public relations with consumers). Call or write to find out what services may be available.

In addition, both small and large businesses may be willing to make donations for a school project. I've had good luck, for example, getting home-improvement businesses to donate wallpaper samples and carpet squares for classroom publishing and reading centers. The local nursery may be willing to donate a bag of dirt and a few seed packets for a project on growing things.

Many magazines have classifieds or write-away sections in which com-panies offer free information and sometimes free samples. When planning a

TEACHING IDEAS

Select a unit that you hope to teach. Develop a list of write-away addresses that you and your students might use for classroom resources related to the unit.

project, alert kids to this resource. Be sure to start early enough so that materials reach the classroom in time.

Summer Possibilities

Many universities sponsor special summer workshops for teachers, some on site and some overseas (England and Australia are especially popular). New York University, Michigan State University, Northeastern University, the University of New Hampshire, and the University of Nevada, Reno, all operate outstanding summer programs for teachers. Professional journals (*Language Arts, Reading Teacher*) contain announcements and advertisements of summer programs. In addition, check with your local university (both the college of education and the English department) to see what special programs are available to teachers of English/language arts. Also, the National Writing Project has many summer workshops on the teaching of writing. Write your local project to find out what's happening in your area.

Government Resources

Extension services   Counties or universities (sometimes cooperatively) often operate a local extension service, an agency that seeks to help citizens live more productively. Extension services cover such areas as farming, land care and development, child rearing, health, human services, and home care. They provide printed material and advice from experts to anyone living in the county who requests it, usually for free.

State department of education   State departments of education have a wide variety of responsibilities from state to state, some useful and some not so useful. Often they are the government body that develops procedures to implement statewide policies such as state objectives and state testing. They may also provide in-service workshops for teachers; sponsor state conferences to discuss important issues or to implement new research findings; and provide materials to support creative teaching.

Federal Government Publications

The federal government has many resources available to citizens on a wide variety of topics. Some publications are extremely specialized and some are a bit expensive, but many are free or inexpensive and can be used to augment classroom activities. Having your students write to the government for materials will increase their involvement in the life of the classroom.

The *Guide to Popular U.S. Government Publications* (available from your reference librarian) contains eighty-four categories of publications covering 2900 titles. Among those most interesting to elementary school children are aeronautics and space sciences, birds and wildlife, climate and weather, food and nutrition, geology, history and biography, minorities and ethnic studies, oceans, pets and animal care, and television and radio. The section on posters includes some of the following deals:

America the Beautiful: 52 posters representing each state, plus Puerto Rico and the Virgin Islands ($20).

Portfolio of American Agriculture: 20 posters of agricultural scenes and landscapes ($11).

Soldiers of the American Revolution: 10 posters representing famous battles of the American Revolutionary War ($7).

Wildlife Portrait Series: Birds and Mammals, 10 for $6.50; Sports Fish, 10 for $6; Host of Sea Birds, 6 for $6; Alaska Birds and Mammals, 10 for $7.50. The sets include a booklet or sheet that describes each poster.

In addition, the federal government publishes small catalogues. The *Summer 1990 Consumer Information Catalog* includes both free and nominal-fee publications, including the following titles:

Becoming a Nation of Readers: What Parents Can Do (50¢)

Growing Up Drug Free (Free)

How to Create a Kidsummit Against Drugs (Free)

Summertime Favorites (400 titles for K–12 readers) (50¢)

Help Your Child Learn to Write Well (50¢)

Helping Your Child Use the Library (50¢)

The Grazing of America: A Guide to Healthy Snacking (Free)

Some Facts and Myths About Vitamins (Free)

Eating Better When Eating Out ($1.50)

Making Bag Lunches, Snacks, and Desserts ($2.50)

Chew or Snuff Is Real Bad Stuff (Free)

The Common Cold (Free)

Family Folklore ($1)

A Guide to Your National Forests ($1)

A Look at the Planets ($1)

Stars in Your Eyes: A Guide to the Northern Skies ($1.50)

Our Flag ($2)

To receive more information about federal government publications or to receive a catalogue, write

The Consumer Information Center-R
P.O. Box 100
Pueblo, CO 81002

■ **IDEAS TO LEARN**   Choose one of the many resources listed here and write off for materials. In addition to adding to your supply of teaching ideas, you can get some idea of how long the turn-around time is for receiving materials after you have written.

Scavenging

More than any other teachers I've ever met, elementary school teachers are scavengers. I don't mean this derogatorily. Elementary school teachers know that their students need lots of ideas, lots of stimulation, and lots of resources as part of expanding and controlling their world. Since school resources are often limited, creative teachers venture out on their own, looking for resources throughout the community, including parents, who are great sources of materials. Instead of throwing away old fabric, egg cartons, and magazines (among all of the other things you can use in your classroom), ask them to give the stuff to you. In addition, go to rummage and garage sales to collect things for the classroom; they are an excellent source for second-hand books (for ten cents to a dollar!) to build your classroom library. "Scavenge" at state and national conferences. You always know who the elementary school teachers are—they're the ones loaded down by shopping bags (supplied by publishers) full of posters, pencils, balloons, and free books (also supplied by the publishers).

We aren't suggesting that you fill your room with junk. We are suggesting that the world can be much bigger than the textbook series provided by your school system. Have fun!

Peers

When this book was in draft form, my editor sent it to a number of language arts teachers for review. One comment on this chapter was that it ignored one of the main resources for teachers: their peers. It's amazing to me that I could have overlooked this source, because my peers have been among my most important teachers and supporters. The teachers whose ideas are included in this book—Linda Dinan, Janet Culver, Mike Gazaway, Diane Olds, and Ann Urie—have described their students to me, invited me to their classes, led workshops on teaching and learning, and taught me about children through their eyes and experiences. Most of my best friends are teachers and when we get together we talk about kids and school—knotty problems, kids we're having trouble helping, kids' accomplishments, ideas we tried that worked and ideas we tried that didn't. Sometimes we argue—about theory, about approaches, about the way to handle a classroom situation. Sometimes we commiserate about particularly tough problems. We share the titles of professional books and articles and new findings in children's literature. (I have three books on my desk by Will Hobbs that one of my teacher friends said I had to read.) We come home from conferences still talking about the things we learned, what we liked and what we didn't.

Your colleagues will become a major source of your support and growth. Forming a community of kid watchers, teacher researchers, and children's literature readers will be one of the most satisfying experiences in your professional life—and perhaps your personal life as well. Moreover, together you can develop insights on learning that will not only enhance your theory and influence the creation of your classroom but will provide the basis for a coherent, collaborative curriculum that will serve the students and the teachers.

8

Orchestrating an Integrated Language Arts Classroom

Throughout the book I have provided lots of ideas and suggestions for ways to integrate reading and writing in the classroom, make oral language a major part of children's language learning in school, use reading and writing to learn throughout the curriculum, and include more literature to enliven and enhance children's understanding of themselves and their world. Linda Dinan and Janet Culver's more than forty years of combined teaching experience provided other sources for ways in which you can create a lively, whole, integrated learning experience for your students through language.

Recently I was talking with a classroom teacher who had given a conference presentation on "whole language" and was bombarded with questions about the "method" to use to integrate students' learning. This presenter was rightly frustrated at the attempt to pin down *the* approach. We've tried to demonstrate throughout this book the importance of understanding how children's language and understanding grow (even while presenting you with lots of classroom practices that illustrate how to integrate children's experiences in school). We believe you should make children's development and understanding the basis for deciding how and what to teach.

The following interviews further illustrate the process of creating a language curriculum. Here three successful and enthusiastic teachers demonstrate that learning to help learners involves a good deal of decision making and creative thinking on the part of the teacher. All three were students in a class I taught on the relationship between reading and writing at the University of Nevada, Reno. I decided to interview them because of the thoughtful way they all view teaching and learning and because of their ongoing quest to help each and every child reach his or her potential.

Interviews with Teachers

Ann Urie

Ann Urie is a new mom and a third grade teacher in Reno, Nevada. She received her undergraduate degree in elementary education at Towson State University in Maryland and recently completed a master's degree in reading and language arts at the University of Nevada, Reno. She resides in Reno with her husband, Michael, and their daughter, Elizabeth.

ST: Tell me how you teach reading and writing to your third graders.

AU: I use all literature to teach.

ST: You don't use the basal at all?

AU: I use the *Impressions* series because I do a lot with folk tales, and for third grade it has a lot of really nice folk tales from everywhere. But basically I do use literature.

I think my reading program is in constant flux. I do not have groups that are stable. And I definitely do not have kids grouped by ability. I pair kids that are good readers with kids who can't read as well. And most of the time I have my reading time set up—it's actually my favorite part of the day—where we have an hour and a half block and I can make it shorter or longer, depending. I don't have any interruptions at all during that time. That's when I feel I get the most out of the kids. I also use it sometimes for writer's workshop.

ST: So what do they do during this hour and a half that you call reading time?

AU: It depends, but generally speaking I find that kids need a routine, so I start them off at the very beginning of the year to do a circle/seat/center rotation. I have the centers set up where the kids are with a partner, I have circle time set up where they're with me, and then seat time set up where they're either working on writer's workshop or they're responding to the literature they're reading. As I said, we're in a constant state of flux, but I do keep it regimented in the sense that I want my kids to have a feel of where they're going next as well as a little bit of diversity.

ST: Who chooses what they read?

Ann Urie listens to her student read during circle time.

AU: It depends. Sometimes I like to do whole group reading. Most recently we have been doing this, where we took about four weeks to get through one book.

ST: What book?

AU: *Dear Mr. Henshaw* by Beverly Cleary, which is a high book for third graders. Each child had a book and sometimes we would read whole group, when I would read and the class would be reading along with me in the book. Some days instead of meeting with me in circle time I would hold reading conferences.

ST: Now circle time is when everybody is together?

AU: No. Circle time is specifically with me in a small group situation.

ST: Oh, a small group comes to you.

AU: Uh-huh.

ST: And you address things specific to them?

AU: Right. We would read, say, ten pages, and then we would all write about what we read. I would write too. I'd sit with my little book that looked just like their little journal and I would write with every group. Then we would share what we wrote. So they were reading within our circle and then they would be writing and then they would read what they'd written. Some kids always wanted to share what they'd written and some kids never wanted to share.

ST: Now while you're with this group, what are the other kids doing?

AU: I'd have a third of the kids at centers.

ST: Now what are they doing in centers?

AU: I try to keep a math center set up where they're working with a game that reinforces something that I've been teaching; I try to have an art center where they're just kind of experimenting with something that we've been working on—colors or lines or whatever. And a listening center and usually something else related to our study; usually it's a thematic thing we've been working on. I also sometimes have a reading center with books on a theme or from a featured author.

The third group of kids can be either looking back in their reading journals—their logs that they've been keeping with *Dear Mr. Henshaw* and writing something more in there—or they can be working on a piece in their writer's workshop folders and that includes responding with each other, going to a peer for editing or whatever they want to do, as long as I feel like they're being productive. And they kind of know how I feel about that. Every once in a while I need to look up and give that *G r r r r* coming out of my mouth, but most of the time I don't. I will not have them doing seat work just for the sake of doing seat work. I can't do that.

ST: No busy work.

AU: Yes, right.

ST: Do they ever meet in peer groups or pairs?

AU: Yes. Instead of circle time, about once a week what I like to do is set them on their own. I'll say, "This side of the room is just for you guys that need to be in circle at this time. When it's your circle time, come over here, read with your partner, go back, read your favorite letters; you can write about them if you want; you can share any writing that you've done." And that's when I get to conference with all of my kids. I can get through all of my kids in an hour and a half, listening to everybody read, asking questions about the story. I feel like I really pick up a lot right here. I have my little notebook with me and I write their name and I write, "Joel's reading rate is really improving." "Tiffany's expression is incredible with this story." "So-and-so is still reading word by word." They're actually reading to each other so I just kind of quietly pull up my chair and stick my nose in and listen. Then I'll ask a couple of questions.

ST: And then does that become a part of your evaluations? How do you use the notes that you take?

AU: I use them more as a diagnostic tool, I think. And I ask: Do I have this child paired with the right person? If this child is still reading word by word and this child is reading with such lucid expression, yes, I think I do have this child paired with the right person. If I have one kid that's really improved so much in the last couple of months, then maybe I need to think about putting him with someone else who needs improvement.

ST: Do you see advantage for the kids who are really accomplished readers to working with kids who are maybe still struggling with reading or reading word by word? Do the accomplished readers gain anything from that?

AU: Oh, I think so. I think those are the kids that always love to play teacher. Definitely. The other day I was listening to Megan. She's a very accomplished reader, but I wouldn't say she's reading at an eighth or ninth grade level like some of my kids, but she's a high fourth, maybe fifth grade. She's reading with a little boy who I just cannot figure out where he is having problems. I have really, really struggled with him. Megan will be reading along just beautifully and she'll miss a word and he'll pick up on it. It's just incredible. That's one of the reasons why I can't figure out what he's doing when he reads. He'll be struggling with every fifth or sixth word and she's right there for him, not as a crutch; it's like she's got the right pause.

ST: She listens to what he's saying.

AU: Yes, absolutely. She doesn't interject, she just helps him along when he needs it; otherwise it would be totally frustrating, and that's my reason to have them paired that way.

ST: How do they balance out how much who reads? Is it a certain amount of time and then they switch?

AU: Generally speaking. The nature of that book [*Dear Mr. Henshaw*] is a series of letters and journal entries. One child reads a favorite letter and then they switch. I specifically like that book because of the brevity of the letters. It's easy to chop up like that.

ST: And so during reading time you work with them in small groups, they work in pairs. What else? Any other things happen during that time?

AU: When we get back into the whole group, we still may have twenty minutes before lunch and we'll talk about what we've been reading, if anybody heard something that someone else wrote that they want to share. And I think that's the best time of our morning. Especially after reading Hansen [*When Writers Read*, 1987], I really started to step back and let them take control of the reading discussions and what was going on. That's why I felt it was very important for me to read to them from that book [*Dear Mr. Henshaw*], because there are some things that I think they would miss otherwise. But if they're listening to the book, they pick up on some really important issues. I heard some of the most fascinating conversations! The things they would discuss . . . wow, I never would have thought of some of their observations.

ST: What are the kinds of things that they write after they've read?

AU: I think that book lends itself so well to letter writing. They picked up on the letter form and on all the signature closings—"your disgruntled reader"—and they just loved that. They started writing "Dear Mrs. Urie" or "Dear Mrs. Pretend Urie" in their response logs. Or they'd write at the top, "I am Leigh," and then they'd write "Dear Mr. Henshaw" as if they were Leigh, or they would write another part of the story as if they were Leigh. So they are picking up many of the literary elements from the book.

　　So when they're writing in their journals, they can respond to me— what I have written to them on the previous day, they can respond to any character in the story, or they can just write. I had some kids that would say, "I'm tired of writing letters; now I'm going to be just writing." They always felt compelled to tell me.

ST: How did you establish that at the beginning of the year? How they would write back to or respond to what was written. Did they know how to do that already?

AU: I think our second grade teachers did some of that last year. I saw something by Bleich [1978] about using prompts: What did you notice in the story? How did the story make you feel? He suggested that you do this in a Language Experience form at the beginning of the year. I didn't get this info until October or November, but I felt like I really had started that way with them. From the very first day of school I read to them and had them respond; now looking back I would certainly do it in a chart form.

ST: You mean in chart form like Language Experience?

AU: Yes, and just putting up the responses that were more viable for different avenues of articulation: "That's really nice that you told me about the story. But did it remind you of anything else?" Bleich would say just write down the responses that were more in-depth and intuitive and associative.

ST: So that you're not just getting retellings, but you're getting ways of interpreting and understanding through their own experiences.

AU: Exactly. What I did instead of the Language Experience was the modeling:

"I really like the way so-and-so said that. Can you repeat that so everybody can hear it again?" I would have them write and then the next day we would put everybody's up and I'd read three or four that were especially good and say, "What do you think about the way so-and-so described what she liked about the story or what they thought about the story?" I want them to feel like whatever they say is going to be OK, but I want to keep prompting.

ST: Lots of possibilities. Do they read some things independently or individually? How do you manage that?

AU: I do four units a year with folk tales, which I break up into different continents. In Washoe County at third grade they have to know the seven continents. I started this last year, for a paper to put social studies and reading together. What I found was the folk tales were just so rich with incredible vocabulary and different cultural aspects for the kids to learn. I just absolutely love them. The stories are so great and because of the brevity you can teach so many literary elements. I have now probably fifty different folk tales from Asia in my classroom. It's incredible what you can find. When I introduce the unit I go through the books and say this one might be harder and this one might be easier. We'll talk about how a story might look too hard. If you can't figure out five words on a page that book might be too hard for you. We talked about that from the beginning of the year.

I started with African folk tales and then I went into North American folk tales with Native Americans, and now Asian. And I did Europe as well. That's the four that I go through. I think Asian folk tales are probably the richest. There's so much there to explore. Each child has an individual folk tale. That wasn't my main premise when I started this last year, to individualize. But it works, as long as you have enough books for everybody with a few extras for those who finish quickly. Here's what I hear from the kids all the time: "You should read this. This is the most incredible story." The talk goes back and forth. I say to them, "Recommend a book to a friend if she's stuck for something." Or they'll go back and read a story that I know they've read ten times before; I've seen them check it out or their mom bought it on the last book order. But that's OK; they're still reading it and then they're responding to the story in writing.

ST: Now where do you get all these books?

AU: Most of them I've either gotten through book orders, or I go to the public library on Saturday and take a stack of books to school. The LRC [Learning Resource Center at the University of Nevada, Reno] has a lot of them. And the teachers that I work with are really great in lending books.

ST: So you're just very imaginative about getting to all of the sources that are available to you to put together a library that will work for your . . .

AU: . . . for that unit. The hardest part is collecting them all afterwards and getting them back where they belong. But that's just a part of it. The librarians are really helpful and the kids are really helpful. What I find more than anything is parents love it; they just absolutely love all the stories that I send home. I send them home for homework in an envelope with my name on it. And I always get things back. Also *Impressions* has a couple that I'll send home for reading homework, which I think parents appreciate.

ST: And what do children do with these books after they have read them? They share them with one another; they talk to one another about them. Do they do any writing, any projects?

AU: Yes, they have a log where they keep the name of the book and the author and maybe the country that they think it comes from and any words that they think might be particular to that country or any customs that are particular. We'll talk about motif; we'll talk about theme. Is there a lesson to be learned from this story? Does this sound like any other stories you know that you've heard before? We read Ed Young's book *Yeh Shen*, the Cinderella story from China, and do comparisons with this and the Cinderella story they have grown up with, using a Venn diagram. A couple of books I do whole group like *The Funny Little Woman*. I have multiple copies of *Yeh Shen* so I'll do that in my group time next week. I will read aloud to them because some of that is really difficult to get through. But the richness of the language I find really sticks in their minds. And they start using it. Have you ever seen the book *Abi Yo Yo*? The giant that falls down. It's an American folk tale adapted from an African folk tale. It's so funny. It's hysterical. James Earl Jones does the narration on tape and the kids absolutely love it. But one of the words in it is *ostracize* and it even says in the book, ''that means, they sent him to the edge of the town.'' And the children start using words like that in their writing. Of course it's not spelled right but, wow, who cares? That's a nice word. Of the things that I do all year long, I've found that the folk tales are the richest thing I do.

ST: You mentioned writing workshop and that sometimes it's a part of your reading time and sometimes it's not a part of your reading time. When do you do writer's workshop?

AU: The writer's workshop time I've had a struggle with from the very beginning as a teacher. My sister-in-law gave me *Lessons from a Child* [by Lucy Calkins]. I mean, I had not even heard of Donald Graves before I started teaching and then all of a sudden everyone says, ''Well, here you have to do this and you have to do that.'' I do? Well, what shall I do? So that's where my weakest point is, although I've come to the conclusion that my kids get a lot more out of it than I think they do. Number one, I have my kids write in journals in the morning and I don't give them any topic. Sometimes I really give them a lot of time and what I found was these incredible stories emerging first thing in the morning that are continuous and episodic—these soap operas—and I'm wondering, "Where did you come up with this?" I only respond to those once a week—everybody's on a different day so I'm not inundated. But for my writer's workshop I'll say, "Look at something from your journal that you've been doing. If there's something else that you want to start on, then go and work with that." If we don't get to this during reading time, then it will be in the afternoon when we have a spare twenty or thirty minutes. It was hard for me and I felt like I wasn't getting anything published. But if you avoid it it's not going to go away. They really need to write these stories and it doesn't matter to them that they don't get published. They love to sit and write and read to each other what they are writing, and isn't that the point?

ST: So you've had to come to terms with the fact that you may not be doing it according to the "bible," but you're doing it in a way that works in your classroom with your children and other things you're trying to accomplish. Do children like reading to one another things that they've written?

AU: They love it. I find that this writing will get them more involved than anything. And air time is a commodity. If you can get some when you're an eight-year-old, you are really producing something, and this is the most wonderful thing in the world. Constantly they come up to me, "Could I please read this in class?" They don't want just two people, they want everybody. Because I felt like I wasn't getting these things into publication, I just recently asked some mommies to help, and they said, "We'd be willing to help out with that, sure." After the children have responded with a couple people [in the class] and answered their questions, then they work it over with a mommy, who says, "I'm not sure what you're trying to say here . . ."

ST: So their revision help happens primarily with another adult rather than with one another.

AU: Right. And it's more one-on-one. Then I'll send it home with another mommy who's volunteered to type it up and I'll get it back on Monday and we're ready to roll. But then I really need to roll. So now I'm kind of sitting there with all these typed things saying, OK, let's roll.

ST: So how are you publishing them? In a class book or individual books?

AU: Individual books. We've done a lot of class books, which I think are really valid. In silent reading time those are strong picks. They are what they want to read. It's just incredible. The problem is they breeze through them and then they have to get back up and grab another one so I suggest that they take three.

ST: Tell me about your class books a little bit. How do you go about putting those together and what are some of them about?

AU: I like to use a book as a model, like Ruth Heller's books on nouns or verbs. I'll go through the book with them and we'll list as many as we can on the overhead and then I'll say, "Now choose something that strikes you that you think you can create just one sentence about, or two, or three, and then just a picture. Do something with your verb to make it look special in your sentence like she does with hers." We also do books on special events, things like visiting the planetarium: What your favorite thing was and draw it. They love to see what each other thought was interesting, and everything's so varied—it makes for a wonderful book. One of my favorite books that I did last year and this year as well is Margaret Musgrove's *Ashanti to Zulu*, which is an alphabet book with twenty-six tribes and the kids redo the tribes. They have to decide from the description what the custom is in the tribe and with that I teach main idea. I also teach syllabication and accent marks; the pronunciation is underneath the name of the tribe. I think they learn a lot from that. And we publish this as a big book.

ST: And then you're working on trying to get the individual publications done.

AU: Yes. And I'm having them write a "dummy book" beforehand to set it up. I want it to be something that they are really proud of when it is finished and that they can show to people. I think a lot of their writer's workshop writing is just wonderful, but let's just take one thing at a time and take it to a really fine product.

ST: You mentioned with the folk tales that you were working in the social studies connection. I wondered if there were any other ways in which you saw reading and writing activities useful in other areas of the curriculum. If they write at other times of the day or if they read things other than textbooks in other areas.

AU: I think it's really fun to write with math. I remember even at the beginning of the year I'd ask them some question like, "Tell me everything you know about addition." They have a learning log, which is just a notebook where when you need a piece of paper just take out your learning log—so they don't have fifty thousand papers stuck in their desk that should be in the trash or something. It's not of any big significance, but I want something where everything is together and I can look at it if I need to and I know where it is and they're accountable for it.

So for their learning log I ask them: "Tell me what addition means to you or tell me what subtraction means to you." And some kids really know the process. I really learn a lot about where kids are and how they're looking at math. I use a lot of writing in science. Whenever we do anything, like an experiment related to something we're working on in class, or a film that they've seen, I say, "Please take about three or four minutes and write about it in your science log." I put lots of little books together, like with six pages in them, and then at the end of the unit I'll just send it home. That way I have everything together. I don't have to go searching. It works well for the kids too. I don't feel like I'm giving them a crutch or anything, but I'm showing them how to keep things organized. I have them put the date and skip a line here. I model how to write a definition of a word. I give gentle suggestions. I'm not real didactic in saying, "You have to do this in your log! You must write fourteen lines!"

ST: How have you learned to do the things you are doing? Actually I have two questions. The first one is, how did you come to teaching in the way that you teach? And the second one is, what are some directions you think you'd like to take with your teaching in the future?

AU: I graduated from undergraduate school ten years ago, and I think I had a really strong program. I told you before about the creative expression core program I was in before I did my student teaching, where I had six university professors that we were with all day from six different disciplines. It was just wonderful. There were twenty or twenty-five of us in the class in an experimental program, and they showed us how to teach using an interdisciplinary approach. Then when I got out into the school district I was so disillusioned because nobody was doing this. People were stabbing each other in the back for jobs, and I just said, "Gee, I don't think I need to work eighty hours a week for this $13,000-a-year salary when I'm twenty-two years old." So I stayed away from it. Then I got to the point where I was really ready to go back into education—because I missed it—and I had had all that education and I wasn't applying it. Here in Nevada I got my feelers out and felt like people were doing things that I had learned as an undergraduate and went back to the university to get my credential and found that people were definitely doing these things. So being at UNR really helped me a lot. I took the reading clinic with Dr. Bear [Donald Bear, professor], and Tamara [Tamara Baren, teaching fellow, at UNR's College of Education] was one of the graduate assistants and she really turned me on to so many great things that helped me.

ST: Part of it is that there's a network, it seems, that really supports you in what you're doing and a safety net as well as a network.

AU: I really felt like I needed to find a place for myself in the district and a friend said well you've got to see Diane Olds's class at Lenz and she just kept talking it up and talking about the principal. I knew I wanted to be at Lenz—I'd heard about a couple of other teachers there. I had been subbing and looking for a job. Two weeks before school started, an opening became available at Lenz and I went down there and interviewed. I somehow convinced Roberta Lawson (who's the principal) and she called me the next day. Being with Diane and the other third grade teachers there is just wonderful. Everyone is so literature oriented. Everyone shares with everyone, and it's a great feeling to be there. The teachers really enjoy teaching. Everyone's always going into each other's room with something a kid's done saying, "You have to see this." That's what you want. You want it to be exciting. And that's the way it is every day.

ST: What are some goals or plans that you have for yourself?

AU: I hate to keep sighing. [Ann's intensity requires her to release her tension with some frequency.] It's just that when you finish a unit of study with the kids—wow, I really did a great job with that, wasn't that great? wasn't that wonderful? And now here you go! And now here's the next one. And is it going to be great? And is it going to be wonderful? Am I going to be just as exhausted? But it's always great and it's always wonderful. I don't know. I want to apply more of what I'm learning at the university as a graduate student. I feel like I really don't have time to nurture and really encourage the kids to do things that I know they could do if I did have the time. It's not that I don't have the inclination. I really want to rearrange my schedule a little bit. I just want to take a look at what I'm doing. And I want to write about what I'm doing and put it down on paper and say, "This is working; this is not working; how can I make this work?" It's difficult to find the time to do this.

Mike Gazaway

Mike Gazaway has been teaching fourth through sixth grade for eleven years. Currently he teaches fifth grade at Lincoln Park Elementary School in Reno, Nevada. Mike, with his teaching partner Fran Terras, is one of a number of teachers in the Reno area involved in a research project on team teaching.

ST: Tell me how you teach reading and writing to your fifth graders.

MG: Every morning I have writer's workshop. I break my first period into two thirty-minute blocks where we may talk about some specific topic in the language area; we have to cover so many items on district and curriculum objectives sheets that the school district distributes each year. So, if I'm going to talk about nouns or verbs or adjectives, we'll talk about it, do exercises, think about it, but then I carry that into the next thirty minutes and look for real live examples in the writing.

As far as the writing is concerned, generally I have the kids choose their own topics. What I do at the beginning of the year is to give everybody a journal and have them put across the top ''Idea Bank,'' and then we talk about banks. What is a bank for? A bank is a place where you keep your money. Good. This is an idea bank. What are you going to keep in here? Ideas. All right. When you go to the bank with mom or dad what do they do? Well, they put money in or they take money out. Oh. OK. So if you put something in you have it on deposit and when you want to use it you withdraw it, take it out. OK. So, what happens if you overdraw your account? You get these little notices from the bank. So think of the idea bank this way, when you take an idea out, you can add ideas too; in fact, if you really want to build up a big bank account or a big idea account, add ideas as you think of them. This is very effective in eliminating the ''I don't know what to write about'' syndrome.

I tour them through the writing process. We talk about the writing process and I have it up on my board. I have all the stages. Prewrite, compose, revise, and we end with evaluation. What I find [in their process] is prewriting and composing, and that's as far as they go. I ask them how many of them, before they came to this room, have been through this entire writing process. Most of them said they have never gone beyond the composing process until they got to my room. I can see why this happens, because the hardest part for kids—and I think for teachers, too, I know it was for me—was to hurdle that revision process. Revision. Thinking, looking at it again, getting somebody's response to it; getting a different viewpoint, looking at it differently, putting it away for a while and coming back to it.

In the beginning I show them the entire process. We work together through the entire process. I have these big sheets of paper two feet by three feet that I put up so I have all the prewriting processes displayed. I say, ''These are five different ways to get yourself into prewriting''— starting with clustering all the way to using the Venn diagram. I might say, ''Today we're going to talk about this prewriting activity,'' mapping, for example, and use the state of Nevada. I say, ''This is how you use the mapping/cluster prewrite. Now I'm going to show you what happens.'' We take the outline drawing of Nevada and I draw all these lines out on a big map, and the kids generate ideas about Nevada. ''When you think of Nevada what do you think about?'' They say, ''Well, there's Lake

Mike Gazaway reviews a student's journal.

Tahoe and there's Las Vegas, and there's Reno, and the desert and the mountains." We put all of these ideas around the map, the central figure, and that is their prewriting activity.

A lot of them use clustering for prewriting. That's all right; I don't have any problem with that. I do ask them to do at least one prewriting activity before jumping into composing. I go through these for a few weeks. We reach a point where I say, "You choose a prewriting activity. It's now your choice."

I don't use [prewriting activities] in just one particular subject. I may use a Venn diagram, say, as a way to [compare] a film with a book and use that as an activity to write about. We've used it with math; we've used it to compare and contrast subjects; I've asked them which subject they liked the most and which subject they liked the least and then compare and contrast them using the Venn diagram.

ST: Do your kids publish their writing?

MG: Yes. We publish an anthology every year.

ST: Do they all get copies of it?

MG: Yes, they do. Last year I taught all the language arts for sixth grade. We had sixty-six students. A parent volunteer transcribed their writing on the word processor, and I sent it to the print shop. It was all very rushed due to the end of the school year. My last principal, Steve Kaylor, bought a book binder. This year I have been binding books. I will be binding this year's anthology.

ST: How do your fifth graders do at revision?

MG: This is a major hurdle. At the beginning of the year I do it with each paper. In all honesty, when I ask the kids what we mean by revision they say, "Well, I write it over in neater handwriting and correct the spelling." And I say, "Well that's part of it, but there're some other things." I show them what re-vision means—to look at again—and we talk about movability: how you can take a pair of scissors and cut this thing apart and rearrange it.

We have a computer lab. I want the students to learn keyboarding skills. I had a student who was one of the best oral presenters I've ever met, but the physical act of handwriting was terribly painful. He was embarrassed; he couldn't spell. This kid could sit and listen. He could pick out those little minor points and details in a novel and had excellent recall. Now, if he'd had access to a word processor, I can imagine what he could have produced.

ST: Can you explain a little bit more about how you set up your literature program?

MG: A colleague, Fran Terras, and I started our current program four years ago. We were doing, instead of a "pull out" program, a "push in" program where we combined the remedial teacher and the regular classroom teacher with a designated low-reading group. We work together as a team. First of all we start with a book that we know is at least a grade level book. For example, this year we started with *Charlotte's Web*. We didn't just read it. We did research on spiders. We learned about different types of spiders and the fact that some spiders have webs and some don't have webs. We had the kids get in their groups and they made paper spiders. They went to the library for books and read about spiders. We do what we call "lateral movement." Instead of a straight reading from cover to cover, we explore subjects in the text, to give us a greater understanding of the text.

We ask students to make up quizzes. We say, "OK, we want you to read the next five pages and form groups. Then each person must think up a question—make up what we call 'on-the-page' questions and 'off-the-page' questions. We want every person to contribute at least one on-the-page question; you must have a page number that tells where the answer can be found when you turn it in to us. We're going to go home and type it up, because tomorrow we're going to have a quiz." We say, "We'd like you to also include one off-the-page question." We explain,

"This is called inferential thinking if you ever see this written somewhere; it's reading between the lines: 'What do you think?' We'd like you to always preface these questions with 'Why do you think . . . ?' Because that way it's not something that we're going to find exactly on the page." We take the questions home and we type them exactly as they are written, spelling errors and all. We type the questions that don't make any sense. We use no names. We make a collection of duplicated questions. We put the questions together and give them back to them.

The students say, "Wow, I can't read this; I don't understand it."

We say, "Well, do the best you can." At the end of it we have a good discussion. "What'd you think about it?"

"I had a problem."

"What was your problem?"

"I couldn't even figure out what a certain word was." "This question didn't make any sense."

"What was the problem?"

"Well, they didn't spell it right," or "The question wasn't written so I could understand it."

"What do you learn from that?"

"If you're going to write questions, you gotta make sure that the person that's going to read them can understand them."

Ding! That's worth ten thousand lectures on writing clear questions. The quality of questions escalates, because they now see the purpose to writing clear questions.

ST: How have you changed over the years?

MG: My first teaching assignment was in a very small rural school in Montana. The elementary school at that time had about ninety students, K–6. My first year I taught a combination fifth/sixth grade. I had nine sixth graders. I used a basal. I didn't know any better; that's what I'd been through in school.

I literally taught two separate classes. I used to liken it to this: Remember on the old Ed Sullivan show? The guy that used to have the wooden rods and plates? He'd take the plates and spin them on top of the rods—he'd have about twelve to fifteen—and he'd get them all spinning all the way down to the end of the line; then he'd have to run back because the first one would start to wobble and he'd have to keep it going. That's what I did all year. Kept students going. Back and forth.

But my methods of teaching are really different now. As I taught literature, I began to get more and more dissatisfied with what I was teaching and they were learning. I began to question myself and the reading curriculum. I began to doubt that what I was doing was beneficial. I vowed when I left there I wasn't going to teach anymore—that was it.

When I came here I put in my name with the school district to sub part-time while I hunted for another type of job. Two weeks after I arrived I was hired full-time at Lincoln Park School. It was here I met Fran Terras, who has been my mentor for the past four years. The first year we did not teach together. But we began to interview each other and talk about philosophies of teaching literature with the basal reader. Finally I found someone else who said, "You know, you're right. I've been teaching twenty-five years and I don't like the basals." We wanted to teach without them. We tried it and it's been very successful.

My methods of teaching are different now. I now do a lot more writing across the curriculum. [For example], we talk about the flag and the pledge of allegiance. We write it out and [ask]: What does this mean to you? [After we discuss it] they write up their own opinion and we make a big bulletin board.

Science writing: we pick a topic and write about it. I just turn my students loose. You know I'm not going to sit here and methodically go through the science book lessons. We go through the first unit. I say to them, "I want you to look at what the book thinks is important; I want you to look at what the tests think is important. I'll show you the teacher's book. Did you think I knew all the answers to all these questions? Nah-uh; they're right here. Do you think I think up all these questions? No, they're written right here, complete with answers." So I say, "Now, I'm going to break you into five groups, six students in each group. You pick a person and decide who comes up and draws from a hat." "OK, you're going to do unit number such-and-such."

Then I tell each group, "You are to do the following: You choose a taskmaster, someone who's going to make sure everything works; you choose a scribe, a person who's going to write down what you discuss. You all will be responsible for reading the entire unit: You are going to read the unit, you are going to discuss it. You are welcome to look at the teacher's book; whatever you want to do, let me know. Then what we're going to do is figure out how you're going to present your unit: I will be your resource person and you are going to teach the rest of the class your unit. Everybody has to read it and everybody has to have a job. You can come to me and ask for suggestions. If you need things like library materials, I can get those. I need to know what you need."

I say to them, "You know something, you need to have an assessment. You have to figure out if the people out there understand what you say. You can do it anyway you want. It can be a test; it can be a project; it can be a play; it can be anything you want to come up with to find out if they are listening and understand you, whether you've gotten it across." Basically the two assessment tools groups have chosen so far have been tests, and I think after this one I'm going to say, "Is there any other way you can think of for assessment?"

And then I say, "We also need to do one more thing. Everybody in here: we need to look at evaluation." We cluster as a group evaluation. What should we be evaluating? Participation, cooperation, attitude? I list what they say and type it out. They all sit and listen to the presentations. Then they do their evaluation and share them with the presenters. After a presentation, I hear comments about what a teacher must feel like up there. I feel this gives them a good experience in taking charge of their education.

Diane Olds

Diane Olds has been teaching fifth and sixth grade for fifteen years. Currently she is working on an E.Ed. in elementary education with a specialty in reading; at the same time she teaches in the Washoe County, Nevada, school district. Diane is currently teaching a multigrade class of fourth, fifth, and sixth graders.

ST: Tell me how you teach language arts.

DO: My students read novels. We do not use the basals. When I first started using novels with them, I used some of the basal and gradually moved away so that now my students read nothing but novels. And except for two novels that I choose for doing with the whole class, their novels are all self-selected during the year. Sometimes they're reading them by themselves; sometimes they choose to read them with a group of other students. They write every day about their reading in a response log and sometimes I give them prereading topics, sometimes a specific idea to write about, and many times they just do free response. I collect their journals after every assignment and I respond to them and give them back—usually before they have to read and write again, but not always.

ST: Is there a prescribed period of time that they are reading a particular novel? Are they meant to finish a novel in a week or two weeks? What about the kids that go slower or faster?

DO: The kids that go faster read at their own pace. The kids that go slower read at their pace too. So a student, for example, might start out reading *From the Mixed-up Files of Mrs. Basil E. Frankwiler* with five other children, might finish the novel, complete a project about it, and go on to read another book while their friends are still back there reading that

book. Sometimes what they'll do then is go back to that group to participate in their small group discussions.

ST: Are these novels the ones that are chosen by you or are they the ones
students pick in small groups?

DO: Small group. When we read a novel together, we finish it at a certain
time and that way I'm sure that everybody gets to the same point at the
same time and doesn't read ahead or fall behind as we read it together. I
read orally and they read silently so that some of the children who aren't
such good readers can still participate in the literature experience, because even though they read at perhaps below grade they can often
comprehend the ideas of a complex novel. It also allows me to guide
what I want response to be and what I want them to find out about
literature, so we begin the year with a group novel—*The Bridge to Teribithia* is the one I've used most frequently—and then we end the year,
or shortly before the end of the year, with another group novel. I frequently use *The Cay* because it ties into our ocean week. We do an all-
school study of the ocean for a period of time in the spring and the novel
The Cay connects with that all-school project.

ST: And then in the middle, they can work individually, in pairs, in small
groups, however they want to handle reading their novels. Now where
do all of those books come from? Are they library books or . . . ?

DO: These are books that I've managed to collect in small sets. I have, for
example, sets of six of a great number of titles, and they've been collected in different ways. A lot of them have been bought out of my own
pocket; some of them have been provided by the school. We usually get
a hundred dollars at the beginning of the year that we can choose to
spend any way we want, and about the last three years I've chosen to
spend that money on novels. When my students order from the book
clubs, I use all my bonus points to get books rather than get some of the
junk that they offer, like the free prizes. So I've built them up in that
way. Or I go to the bookstore and I'll say, ''Well OK, I'll buy six copies of
this, and then next month I'll buy six copies of another novel.''

Sometimes the kids are really interested in reading a particular
book that they either have at home or they've gotten in the library. For
example, I had a boy last year who wanted to read *Huckleberry Finn*,
which nobody else was interested in reading, so he read that by himself.
Of course he didn't have anybody to meet with in small groups, so
through his log and a dialogue between the two of us, I could monitor
his reading, and then we would meet to talk about the book.

ST: Do they seem to like the group projects more than the individual or do a
lot of kids do individual?

DO: It depends. Sometimes they want to be part of a group and sometimes they want to be alone. The year before last I had about ten boys who decided they wanted to read *The Whipping Boy*, but I broke them into two groups for discussion purposes. So it just varies.

ST: Now, do you give them guidance in how to handle the discussion?

DO: When they're going to do literature discussion, the first few times I do give them some guidance, and we've already read one novel together, and I have modeled the kinds of questioning I think is appropriate in discussing literature. I also have them at the end of that first novel get into groups and generate the kinds of questions that should be—or that could be—asked about a novel. And then we come back together as a group and we've got all the different kinds of questions that they could do and we pick some of those for their final writing assignment on the book. So they've had some practice already, and I have found they never ask literal questions—even the lowest and slowest come up with meaningful, inferential kinds of questions, analyses, generalizations, comparisons to other books. It's amazing.

So when they get into their literature groups, they know what to do. But to help them get started, I say, "Here are some things that you could talk about. However, if you'd like to talk about other things, that's all right too." Eventually, then, they control their own discussions, because I don't know what's going to be meaningful to them. Sometimes there are certain points that I want to be sure come out of a book and I can guide them to discuss those, but they have a pretty good sense of what ought to be talked about in a book.

And I have books at a lot of different levels; for example, at sixth grade I have copies of *Charlotte's Web*, but at the same time I have *Tuck Everlasting* to accommodate the different reading levels the children have.

ST: Do the children move among various difficulty levels? Do kids who are fairly sophisticated go back to the easy books? Or the kids who aren't really big readers sometimes choose books that are challenging to them?

DO: I have found that. And I know from my own personal reading that sometimes if I've read something that's very taxing I need to take a break and read something in the mind-candy area. And I think we need to let students do that too. They don't always need to be reading something that is taxing them. Some children will choose books ahead of their reading level too.

ST: Do you read everything they read?

DO: No, I do not. And I don't think a teacher needs to have read everything. Because I'm not interested in the exact details of the plot. I'm interested in them making analyses, generalizations, evaluations, and I can ask general kinds of questions, and when I read their logs I know whether they're doing their reading or not without knowing the exact plot or details.

ST: What would be the kind of question that you would ask?

DO: "Tell me about the book." Begin with that. "What do you think about . . . ?"—the name of a particular character. I might pull cues from their journal, like, "I noticed you said that this person acts like John in our class. Can you tell me more about what you mean there?" Or, "Does this book remind you of other books that you have read?" "Have you ever had these kinds of experiences in your life?" Usually if you just ask some very general kinds of questions—the kinds of things that you and I would ask each other if we'd been to see a movie or we'd read the same book—usually that's all that they need to get started And I let what they want to tell me guide the discussion.

ST: And so sometimes the journals that you have them write in every day provide the basis for the discussions that they have with you?

DO: Yes.

ST: So they are always thinking and writing and using writing to talk and talk to write.

DO: Yes, so they all support each other there.

I ask that they respond at the end of every chapter, because many of them would race through the book and not stop to respond. I think that the response that you have at the end of the book is very different from that ongoing response. What usually happens with the students who really have taken control of their learning is at some point one will say to me, "There's not enough to respond to in this chapter. Is it all right if I wait and respond after two chapters?" Or might even say, "This chapter is very long and there's really a lot to say; is it all right if I stop and respond in the middle of the chapter?" I don't give them that option at first, but once they ask I'm thrilled, because they're in control then and they respond at the points that are meaningful to them.

ST: About how much of your class time is involved in reading, responding, doing projects in response to literature? How long do you spend each day? And do you have trouble finding time fitting it in?

DO: Sometimes it is really hard. I always think of Donald Graves and Lucy Calkins' comment about the cha cha cha curriculum, which is why I'm working to build a totally integrated thematic curriculum. My students—probably in the actual reading/literature/responding phase of our language arts day—spend an hour or less. But we also do a lot of writing and reading of literature that goes with our science and social studies curriculum.

ST: Can you talk a little more about that?

DO: Well, for example, if we were studying Greece, I would bring in books that deal with the history of Greece, the culture of Greece, the geography, etcetera. We would also be reading Greek myths at the same time. So that we would maybe have an hour and a half or a two-hour block where they might do some reading of myths, they might look at some information in their social studies books, and then they might pick up some of these trade books, which they also have to do some kind of writing about. So they do some responding just the same way they do with literature and also do some writing of nonfiction, because the text of nonfiction is very different from what they find in fiction. And so I have to teach them how to read nonfiction as well as how to read fiction.

ST: What do they discover about how nonfiction is different?

DO: That you have to pay much closer attention to the text, for one thing, because what comes out of expository text—you need to be very aware of what the details and the information are. Even though your own background influences what you bring away from it, there are some things that you need to know when you put that down. A lot of the information is imbedded in a different way. It's not a story; it's often just a series of facts and they need to learn how to pay attention to what might be important facts and what are just interesting facts, ones that it's OK if you don't remember afterwards. And how to write about that to get some of that information in place so that they remember it and how to use subheadings and chapter summaries and things like that.

ST: You said you do some reading and writing with science. Can you give an example of that?

DO: Well, like when we're studying the ocean. There are lots of wonderful books out there that are not just written from a scientific perspective. But they're exciting; they have beautiful pictures. And the kids might respond to that. Sometimes we might create poetry out of factual things that they have read. Or they might take those facts and try to include them in a story that they have written. And the students really do that a lot. They frequently would run down to the library to check something because they don't want an incorrect fact even though they may be writing a piece of fiction. Or when we're studying Japan I have them keep a travel log as if they were really going through the country.

ST: Is there time in the day when they can write whatever they want?

DO: We usually do writer's workshop twice a week, and it's total free choice

Diane Olds helps a student with his paper.

of topics. In fact, I refuse to supply children with any topics. We begin the year by having them generate things that they think they could write about and then I encourage them to keep adding to that list in their folders. And they go through the writing process. Some days maybe all they get to is the prewriting; and some days maybe they just kind of sit and think. But eventually, then, after composing they meet with response groups and they have to revise their pieces and do some editing. I only evaluate four major pieces of writing from the writing workshop every year. That's at the end of every quarter. A lot of what they write they want to abandon or they've explored something and they've decided that it's not worth continuing or they're tired of it—I just want them writing for that fluency—so they can put those away.

But they have to choose something that we can take through the whole process and then it's published. And if you've done everything—and you have to turn in all your drafts, you have to show me evidence that you tried to grow and do some changing and self-evaluation—it's basically an A. And I give some progress grades along the way. The first time they turned in that first draft you just get a grade of an A because you did that part. Then if you do that second draft and meet in a revision conference, you get another A. So there's some A's along the way and because it's a nine-week project I weigh that very heavily. And that becomes probably a third to a half of their English grade for the entire quarter.

ST: How do you publish?

DO: Whatever your finished project is, that is what we call publishing, because it's really nice; you've made it so other people can read it. The kids usually like to do a picture or a series of illustrations, or they make a cover; sometimes they get really elaborate. I had a little girl who did a book of poems, and she covered it with cloth and did this beautiful lettering all over it. Other kids who aren't so much into it, or maybe they're not quite as competent, will just put a construction paper cover on it and draw a simple picture.

As we go along we often have things on the walls; they haven't gone necessarily through the entire process but maybe we've written ocean poems and we publish them by putting them on display in the hallway. And I firmly believe that when you do a project, every student's work goes up, not just the ones that I've decided are the best. I encourage them to do a good job because people are going to look at them, but if they choose not to, that's their decision, and those go up too.

We do class books. When we've written on a common theme, once again, maybe I'd take those ocean poems after they come down, laminate them, put them in a book and that stays as part of our classroom library; some things too I send over to the printing department and we have bound, so that every student can then take a copy home.

I do an anthology at the end of the year with pieces of writing they've done the whole year, and once again every student has several things in there and those go home as a bound book. They think it's so exciting when it's bound like that, and they'll frequently say, "Oh couldn't we get these printed? These are really good. We would like to take these home and show them to our parents." It makes it so official for them. And sometimes we publish by standing up and reading to the whole class, because that's a form of publishing too.

ST: Do you see them drawing on literature when they do their independent writing or drawing on their experience as writers when they read literature?

DO: Yes. Year before last I had several boys who got into reading Stephen King, unfortunately. And I was having a writing conference with one of the boys and I noticed very short what he was calling chapters, and I just asked him what was going on, and he said, "I'm trying to write like Stephen King." Also you'll see them taking characters from literature and writing new stories about them, such as Maybelle in *Bridge to Teribithia* or trying to copy stylistic devices.

On the other hand, when they're doing their reading and writing in their logs, they'll make reference to themselves as writers. One girl Marisa, who's a very sophisticated writer, said that she thought that the reunion in *The Cay* was very fake and very stilted and then she said, "But I have the same problem when I write in trying to write reunions too." They also become very aware of the writer's craft. They'll comment on things that they notice: foreshadowing, hints that the author drops, or they'll say, "[The author] probably put in this character, so they can show the change in the other character." They're very aware of what real writers do.

ST: There's a lot of concern about whether children are learning their basic skills. How do you manage the teaching of skills in your classroom?

DO: I try as much as possible to do it in context. For example, if we need to find out about adjectives, let's look at how writers have used adjectives, carefully and clearly, by taking a look at a piece of writing and begin by looking at the concept and then giving it a label. Quotation marks the same way; let's look at dialogue, see what we can notice about it, see if we can figure out what some of these rules are.

ST: You mentioned something about how you evaluate in writing workshop; you give them kind of guideposts and grades along the way. And in your system your children get A's and B's. So how do you grade their responses to literature and their projects in literature?

DO: That's the hard part. I tend to keep changing and playing around with different ideas, because the idea of evaluating process learning is just really hard for me. I've tried different things. I've tried giving them a set number of points with all kinds of ranges. I started out with twenty-five points for a response, then I found that twenty-five points is just too many, and I was ending up giving kids too few points because I'd think, well, they should have said this and they should have said that; so I scaled that down to ten and I still wasn't happy with that.

I came up last year with a five-point system that seemed to work pretty well. I discussed with the kids when we started the logs what was a zero, what was a five; kind of like what they do when they holistically evaluate for our state and county writing tests. A five was that you probably had stretched a little bit, that you had tried to have something unique to say, that you tried to think about something just a little bit different, and maybe gone beyond yourself a little bit and shown me an idea that I maybe had never heard before in relation to this piece of literature. And a four was really good, but maybe you could have just pushed a little bit; a three was just fine; there's nothing wrong with it but you probably could have done a little more; and a two, you really didn't think you put much into this; and a one was basically you put your name on it and maybe wrote one quick sentence; and a zero was you just didn't do it or you were totally off the topic. Sometimes I use a system of plus, check, and minus, for above average, average, and below average.

ST: Do the literate kids get all the fives and the children who don't have books at their house get all the zeros?

DO: No. Because I try to do it in terms of what I think their developmental level is. Some of my special ed kids often get fives and my top students who've never really had to do anything except be [obedient] students might be threes and fours, which is hard for some of them because they haven't quite figured out how to play this new educational game. It's hard to be fair. I was looking at some folders the other day and I thought, ''Well, why did I evaluate it that way? I don't think I was probably very fair to that kid.'' And if the projects they do are hands-on kinds of projects, it's very hard to get less than an A because I'm judging creativity and I just want them to do it. A lot of the projects they do have to do with writing, and most of those get A's too. I am interested in them doing something at the end of a book to extend their learning a little bit. It might be something like making a diorama, painting a mural, making a model. It might be turning a scene from the book into play dialogue, writing a letter to a character, writing an extension of the story, or writing an analysis paper. In sixth grade a lot of the students are very sophisticated thinkers and they begin to try and do some analysis of what's in a piece of literature.

ST: I know you have standardized tests somewhere along the way.

DO: The California Test of Basic Skills is what we use now. It used to be the Stanford Achievement Test. And we are required to give those.

ST: How does what you do relate to that and what do you do with that?

DO: I treat them disdainfully for one thing. During the year we have some time when I teach children about how to do worksheets and about how to fill in bubbles and fill in the blanks because I think that that is a skill that they need as they go through the educational system. But we really don't call that part of our reading time. Right before the test I just try to be sure we've seen a few of those. However, I do not pull things out of the test and teach specifically that. Standardized tests are not meant to reflect your curriculum; they are not criterion referenced, they are norm referenced; if too many children are getting the right answer, they rewrite those tests. They are made to—I think—separate the wheat from the chaff—and they want them to miss a fair number of things. I just refuse to let my curriculum be dictated by the results of standardized testing.

ST: And yet your administrators say, "Omigosh, our scores are down in our school, we need to do this." So they aren't really used properly by the administration.

DO: No, they aren't. And I've just decided that I'm not going to be one of those teachers who's going to get all upset about what these scores might mean or how it might reflect what they are doing. And since I've started teaching more of a literature-based writing process curriculum, my children are scoring just as well as they ever did; their scores have not gone down, so I've decided it's nothing that I'm going to get all upset about.

ST: I have one final question. You've been teaching for quite a long time—fifteen years—and apparently you've changed in that time. How did that come about?

DO: It came about from a dissatisfaction that children didn't seem to be learning and applying. They could do worksheets and then they didn't seem to be able to use those skills in their reading and their writing. I started out thinking that curriculum was the most important thing that kids had to learn, and it really didn't matter where they were when they came to me. I got tired of saying, "How come they don't seem to be learning it? I've taught it and I know I taught it really well," instead of thinking maybe there's something wrong with what I'm teaching. Watching other teachers get excited about things that were happening. One of the biggest changes was when I went to a workshop given by Dr. Gabrielle Rico here in Reno in 1978 when she was first talking about clustering, and I thought this is so exciting and this makes so much sense and began to experiment with my kids. And the more I moved away from the traditional curriculum, the more excited I got about what kids were doing. I found them thinking at a high level; I found them being excited about school. And we tend to think that sixth graders don't get very excited about school.

It's not a panacea. And I wish it were. We still have children who are not buying into our curriculum, who are not doing well in school, but those kids weren't making it under a traditional system either. But I find more students who are trying in school with this kind of a learning system. At least I have one or two kids who say "I like to read now" or when a child says, "You know, I've never finished an entire book before and now I finished this one, and look what else I'm reading." That's pretty exciting.

■ **IDEAS TO LEARN**   Interview a teacher about his or her classroom, philosophy, the way he or she creates a schedule, and the activities, books, and other materials he or she uses. Compare with your own philosophy and goals or with the philosophy and goals of the teachers interviewed here.

Teachers as Decision Makers

In my years of visiting and participating in classrooms and working with teachers, I have found that the happiest and most successful teachers were those who saw themselves as decision makers in their own classrooms. Sure, they had tests to contend with, and skeptical administrators, and curriculum guides that they often felt were at best unhelpful and at worst unrelated to children's growth and needs. But the best of teachers were those who learned for themselves—through experience and through participation in professional activities and courses—what children need, and then conducted their classrooms in such a way that they could begin to meet those needs. Ann, Diane, and Mike are three such teachers. Although they each conduct their classes differently from the other, and view their successes differently, and struggle with different aspects of teaching, I see several common elements in their approaches.

All three view their students as thinking, growing, capable human beings. All three see children as meaning makers and recognize the need to allow children to have control over the meanings they make. Children do not come to them as empty vessels waiting to be filled or with identical interests or experiences to which the same treatment can be applied in order to prepare them for the next rung on the educational ladder. All three of these teachers celebrate the uniqueness of the students in their classes and strive to provide appropriate and engaging experiences to encourage that uniqueness.

All three view langauge learning as an integrated, holistic process. Their students are engaged in meaningful activity: reading books that are interesting and enjoyable and writing about those books in personal and creative ways. Children grow and develop when they see learning as personal and satisfying. Language that is fragmented, isolated from context, and unrelated to children's interests and needs is not only boring and useless—it becomes alienating. Students come to see school as unrelated to anything they consider of worth. Not so in these teachers' classrooms.

All three strive to give over responsibility for learning to the students. In Jane Hansen's (1987) words, each teacher provides *choice, time,* and *structure*. Teachers are not the ones who hold the answers, the proper interpretations, the truth. Teachers are facilitators, collaborators, resources, and cheerleaders. Students come to have more and more control over their time, over the things they choose to read and write, and over the ways in which they choose to read and write. This does not mean that these teachers are passive. Hardly. They question, they challenge, they suggest, they help . . . and they often exhaust themselves. Even (or especially) in a child-centered classroom, the teacher has plenty to do.

All three characterize their classes as having structure and flexibility. Figure 8.1 shows Ann Urie's daily schedule for one of her two-week folklore units. But as she talks about what she does in each of the time slots, one sees very quickly that the subjects are not as distinct as they look. For example, the word study part of the morning will include individualized study of words and word patterns but will also include words that have come up during the study of folklore. The math time may integrate the study of numbers with counting systems in other cultures. The language arts part of

9:00–9:15	Journal Writing (Ann writes, too, or gets organized for the day.)
9:15–9:40	Word Study (Individualized spelling; children work with words on cards—their "writing words"—in groups; may include words from folklore unit.)
9:40–10:15	Math (Ann integrates math with folklore study, "when it works.")
10:15–10:30	Recess
10:30–12:00	Language Arts (The main time of day devoted to the folklore unit; includes geography, social studies, writing on folklore, response writing, small group work, silent reading time.)
12:00–1:00	Lunch
1:00–2:00	Read-Aloud Time Writer's Workshop (Children choose their own topics in writer's workshop, but it is "a natural thing" for them to focus on folklore.)
2:00–2:15	Recess
2:15–3:00	Science (Related to the study of folklore—seeds, the weather.)

FIGURE 8.1 Ann Urie's daily schedule in a two-week unit on folklore for her third grade class.

the day will include geography, social studies, and writing about folklore during small group work and silent reading time. It's natural, Ann says, but not required that some of the themes and ideas that students are reading about during the folklore study will come up during students' work in writer's workshop. And such topics as weather, crops, and animals of the culture they are studying may be a focus during science. Although the day has a predictable schedule, the topics and activities in those times shift, and Ann adapts to the interests of the children and the possibilities in the subject areas.

■ **IDEAS TO LEARN**   Interview some teachers about the process of creating a daily, weekly, and unit plan. How do they decide how to structure a day? How do they plan a week? *How ever* do they plan a whole unit? Ask, too, about how flexible they are once the plan is set.

All three work on creating a classroom environment that reflects their ideas of teaching and learning. In the materials they choose, the patterns of communication they set up, the classroom's physical arrangement (see Figure 8.2), these teachers demonstrate their desire for children to have a rich, interesting, vital classroom where students have plenty of choice and where the emphasis is on learning from one another as well as from the teacher.

■ **IDEAS TO LEARN**   Design the "perfect" classroom. If you had unlimited resources, what sort of classroom would you have? What sort of materials would you include? How would you organize all this great stuff? Now create Plan B. Given more limited resources, what would your classroom contain and how would you organize it?

All three have found and continue to seek ways to meet language objectives in a holistic and integrated way. Although they may question the administration's view of learning (as we can see most clearly through their responses to standardized tests), none of these teachers ignores nor discounts the school district's aims and objectives. However, knowing how students learn has led them to teach meaningful language, through which children learn the skills that help them succeed in expressing themselves and understanding the world around them.

All three struggle with grades and evaluation. Once teachers observe that growth in children occurs gradually over time, idiosyncratically according to children's previous experience and individual learning patterns, and with support from people who encourage and extend their learning, it is

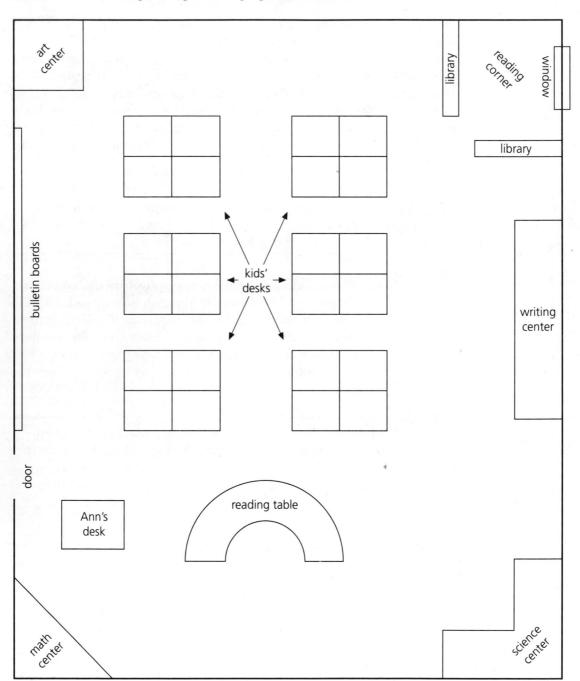

FIGURE 8.2 The floor plan of Ann Urie's classroom.

very difficult to set rigid standards by which to measure a child. The effort to seek ways to fairly reflect what a child is doing while supporting a child's learning are—for these teachers and many others—ongoing and frustrating. Most good teachers I know would prefer not to give grades, believing that the process of evaluation could be better done without them.

All three—with from three to fifteen years experience—engage in an ongoing process of self-evaluation and change. Some changes involve fine-tuning and refining; others involve revamping, say, an entire way of handling a unit or even the whole school day. All of it is initiated by observing the children—their enthusiasm, their growth, their successes, their struggles. As Diane said, she started out thinking that it was the curriculum that needed to be taught and then realized that what was really important was what the kids were doing.

■ **IDEAS TO LEARN**   Throughout this book in a variety of ways you have been asked to think about your goals for teaching, your goals for learning. As you finish, create your tentative credo. What are your central goals for yourself as a teacher (and learner) and your students as learners (and teachers) of the English language arts?

Writer and educator Donald Murray has a book entitled *Learning by Teaching: Selected Articles on Writing and Teaching*. I really like that title. It reflects the vitality, the collaboration, and the continuous nature of the teaching process. Each of the students we encounter—whether just beginning the education process or with years of both positive and negative experience of school—has something to teach us, not only about how to be better teachers but about the nature of learning, which is central to our humanness.

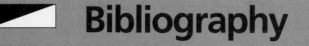

Bibliography

Allen, Elizabeth Godwin, Jone Perryman Wright, and Lester L. Laminack. 1988. "Using Language Experience to ALERT Pupils' Critical Thinking Skills." *Reading Teacher* (May): 904–910.

Allen, R. R., and Robert W. Kellner. 1984. "Integrating the Language Arts." In *Speaking and Writing K-12* by Christopher Thaiss and Charles Suhor. Urbana, Ill.: National Council of Teachers.

Alvermann, Donna E., Deborah R. Dillon, and David G. O'Brien. 1987. *Using Discussion to Promote Reading Comprehension*. Newark, Del.: International Reading Association.

Arnstein, Flora J. 1962. *Poetry in the Elementary Classroom*. New York: Appleton-Century-Crofts.

Atwell, Nancie. 1985. "Writing and Reading from the Inside Out." In *Breaking Ground: Teachers Relate Reading and Writing in the Elementary School*, edited by Jane Hansen, Thomas Newkirk, and Donald Graves. Portsmouth, N.H.: Heinemann.

———. 1987. *In the Middle: Reading, Writing, and Learning with Adolescents*. Portsmouth, N.H.: Boynton Cook.

Babbitt, Natalie. 1975. *Tuck Everlasting*. New York: Bantam.

"Baby Talk." 1987. *Nova*. Boston: WGBN.

Bailis, Pamela, and Madeline Hunter. 1985. "Do Your Words Get Them to Think?" *Learning* (August): 43.

Begley, Sharon. 1990. "RX for Learning." *Newsweek* (April 9): 55–57, 61, 64.

Berliner, David. 1983. "The Executive Functions of Teaching." *Instructor* (September): 29–38.

Bigelow, William. 1989. "Discovering Columbus: Rereading the Past." *Language Arts* (October): 635–643.

Bissex, Glenda. 1980. *Gnys at Wrk: A Child Learns to Write and Read*. Cambridge, Mass.: Harvard University Press.

Blatt, Gloria. 1978. "Playing with Language." *Reading Teacher* (February): 487–493.

Bleich, Robert. 1975. *Readings and Feelings: An Introduction to Subjective Criticism*. Urbana, Ill.: National Council of Teachers of English.

Bohning, Gerry, and Lynn Cuccia. 1990. "Fold-a-Books (in the Classroom)." *Reading Teacher* (March): 525–527.

Brandt, Ron. 1987. "On Cooperation in Schools: A Conversation with David and Roger Johnson." *Educational Leadership* (November): 14–19.

Britton, James N. 1970a. *Language and Learning*. Middlesex, England: Penguin Press.

———. 1970b. "The Student's Writing." In *Explorations in Children's Writing*, edited by Eldonna Evertts. Champaign, Ill.: National Council of Teachers of English.

Burchby, Marcia. 1988. "Literature and Whole Language." *New Advocate* (Spring): 114–123.

Busching, Beverly A. 1981. "Readers Theatre: An Education for Language and Life." *Language Arts* (March): 330–338.

Busching, Beverly A., and Judith I. Schwartz. 1983. *Integrating the Language Arts in the Elementary School*. Urbana, Ill.: National Council of Teachers of English.

Butler, Andrea, and Jan Turbill. 1987. *Towards a Reading and Writing Classroom*. Rozelle, New South Wales, Australia: Primary English Teaching Association.

Butler, Lynn. 1992. Interview with Susan Tchudi. Reno, Nevada, September 1991.

Calkins, Lucy McCormick. 1983. *Lessons from a Child*. Portsmouth, N.H.: Heinemann.

———. 1986. *The Art of Teaching Writing*. Portsmouth, N.H.: Heinemann.

Calkins, Lucy McCormick, and Shelley Harwayne. 1991. *Living Between the Lines*. Portsmouth, N.H.: Heinemann.

Cambourne, Brian. 1988. *The Whole Story: Natural Learning and the Acquisition of Literacy in the Classroom*. Auckland, New Zealand: Ashton Scholastic.

Candal, Patricia. 1988. "As the Teacher Researches, the Student and the Teacher Grow." *Carolina English Teacher* 1–6.

Cariello, Matthew. 1990. "'The Path to a Good Poem, That Lasts Forever': Children Writing Poetry." *Language Arts* (December): 832–838.

Carlsen, G. Robert, and Anne Sherrill. 1988. *Voices of Readers—How We Came to Love Books*. Urbana, Ill.: National Council of Teachers of English.

Cazden, Courtney. 1988. *Classroom Discourse: The Language of Teaching and Learning*. Portsmouth, N.H.: Heinemann.

Chomsky, Carole. 1971. "Write First, Read Later." *Childhood Education* (May): 296–299.

Chomsky, Noam. 1957. *Syntactic Structures*. The Hague: Mouton.

———. 1972. *Language and Mind*. Enl. ed. New York: Harcourt Brace Jovanovich.

Church, Susan, and Judith M. Newman. 1985. "Danny: A Case History of an Instructionally Induced Reading Problem." In *Whole Language: Theory in Use*, edited by Judith M. Newman, 169–179. Portsmouth, N.H.: Heinemann.

Cianciolo, Patricia J. 1990. *Picture Books for Children*. 3rd ed. Chicago and London: American Library Association.

Clark, Roy Peter. 1987. *Free to Write: A Journalist Teaches Young Writers*. Portsmouth, N.H.: Heinemann.

Clay, Marie M. 1975. *What Did I Write?* Portsmouth, N.H.: Heinemann.

Cleary, Beverly. 1983. *Dear Mr. Henshaw*. New York: Morrow.

Coleman, Ike. 1988. "Research Is Power." *Carolina English Teacher* 81–85.

Collerson, John. 1988. *Writing for Life*. Rozelle, New South Wales, Australia: Primary English Teaching Association.

Comber, Barbara. 1988. "Any Questions? Any Problems? Inviting Children's Questions and Requests for Help." *Language Arts* (February): 147–153.

Cook, Wayne D. 1993. *Center Stage: A Curriculum for the Performing Arts*. Palo Alto, Calif.

Cranston, Jerneral W. 1991. *Transformations Through Drama*. Lanham, Md.: University Press of America.

Craven, Jan. 1991. "Conferencing and Record Keeping in Fifth/Sixth Grade." Presentation at the National Council of Teachers of English Spring Conference, Indianapolis, Indiana.

Cullinan, Bernice E., ed. 1987. *Children's Literature in the Reading Program*. Newark, Del.: International Reading Association.

———. 1989. *Literature and the Child*, 2nd ed. San Diego, Ca.: Harcourt Brace Jovanovich.

Dailey, Sheila. 1985. *Storytelling: A Creative Teaching Strategy: A Curriculum Guide to Storytelling in the K–8 Classroom*. P.O. Box 2020, Mt. Pleasant, Mich.

Daniels, Harvey, and Steven Zemelman. 1985. *A Writing Project: Training Teachers of Composition from Kindergarten to College*. Portsmouth, N.H.: Heinemann.

———. 1991. "Writing to Learn." Handout for Whole Language/Integrated Learning from K to 12, July, at the Walloon Institute, Petosky, Michigan.

D'Arcy, Pat. 1989. *Making Sense, Shaping Meaning: Writing in the Context of a Capacity-Based Approach to Learning*. Portsmouth, N.H.: Boynton Cook and Heinemann.

Denman, Gregory. 1991. *Sit Tight and I'll Swing You a Tail: Using and Writing Stories with Young People*. Portsmouth, N.H.: Heinemann.

Devine, Thomas G. 1982. *Listening Skills Schoolwide: Activities and Programs*. Urbana, Ill.: National Council of Teachers of English.

Didion, Joan. 1968. "On Keeping a Notebook." In *Slouching Toward Bethelem*. New York: Farrar, Straus & Giroux.

Dillon, David A. 1981. "Perspectives: Drama as a Sense of Wonder—Brian Way." *Language Arts* (March): 356–362.

———. 1988. "Dear Readers." *Language Arts* (January): 7–9.

Dillon, J. T. 1984. "Research on Questioning and Discussion." *Educational Leadership* (November): 50–56.

Dinan, Linda L. 1976. Unpublished paper. University of Massachusetts.

———. 1980. "Viewpoints." *Language Arts* (October): 724–725.

———. 1985. "Writing Pamphlets." *Livewire: Classroom Ideas K–7* (August): 7–9.

Donaldson, Margaret. 1978. *Children's Minds*. New York: W. W. Norton.

Dossey, John A. 1989. "Transforming Mathematics Education." *Educational Leadership* (November): 22–24.

Dunn, Sonja. 1987. *Butterscotch Dreams*. Portsmouth, N.H.: Heinemann.

Dyson, Anne Haas. 1986. "Staying Free to Dance with the Children: The Dangers of Sanctifying Activities in the Language Arts Curriculum." *English Education* (October): 135–146.

Educational Resources Information Center (U.S.). 1983. *National Assessment of Educational Progress: 1983–84*. Microform. Princeton, N.J.: Educational Testing Service.

Elbow, Peter. 1981. *Writing with Power: Techniques for Mastering the Writing Process*. New York: Oxford University Press.

Elias, Marilyn. 1990. "Doctors Say TV Helps Make Kids Fat, Violent." *Lansing State Journal* (April 17): 1.

Elkind, David. 1990. Talk on child development, Spring, Okemos Public Schools, Okemos, Michigan.

England David A. 1985. "Language and the New Media." In *Language, Schooling, and Society*, edited by Stephen N. Tchudi. Montclair, N.J.: Boynton Cook.

Erickson, Karen L. 1988. "Building Castles in the Classroom." *Language Arts* (January): 14–19.

Evans, Christine Sobray. 1984. "Writing to Learn in Math." *Language Arts* (December): 828–835.

Farnsworth, Kathryn. 1981. "Storytelling in the Classroom—Not an Impossible Dream." *Language Arts* (February): 162–167.

Fields, Marjorie V. 1989. "Talking and Writing: Explaining Whole Language Approach to Parents." *Reading Teacher* (May): 898–903.

Fitzgerald, Jill. 1988. "Helping Young Writers to Revise: A Brief Review for Teachers." *Language Arts* (November): 124–129.

Five, Cora Lee. 1988. "From Workbook to Workshop: Increasing Children's Involvement in the Reading Process." *New Advocate* (Spring): 103–113.

Fleischman, Sid. 1968. *The Whipping Boy*. New York: Greenwillow.

Flower, Linda, and John R. Hayes. 1981. "A Cognitive Process Theory of Writing." *College Composition and Communication* (December): 365–387.

Fox, Mem. 1984. *Teaching Drama to Young Children*. Portsmouth, N.H.: Heinemann.

Galda, Lee. 1990. "Children's Books: Our Natural World." *Reading Teacher* (January): 322–326.

———. 1987. "Teaching Higher Order Reading Skills with Literature: Primary Grades." In *Children's Literature in the Reading Program*, edited by Bernice Cullinan. Newark, Del.: International Reading Association.

———. 1987. "Teaching Higher Order Reading Skills with Literature: Intermediate Grades." In *Children's Literature in the Reading Program*, edited by Bernice Cullinan. Newark, Del.: International Reading Association.

Gates, Dale D. 1983. "Turning Polite Guests into Executive Readers." *Language Arts* (November–December): 977–982.

Geller, Linda Gibson. 1981. "Riddling: A Playful Way to Explore Language." *Language Arts* (September): 669–674.

———. 1982. "Linguistic Consciousness-Raising: Child's Play." *Language Arts* (February): 120–125.

———. 1983. "Children's Rhymes and Literacy Learning: Making Connections." *Language Arts* (February): 184–193.

———. 1984. "Exploring Metaphor in Language Development and Learning." *Language Arts* (February): 151–161.

Genishi, Celia, Andrea McCarrier, and Nancy Ryan Nussbaum. 1988. "Research Currents: Dialogue as a Context for Teaching and Learning." *Language Arts* (February): 182–191.

Gentry, J. Richard. 1982. "An Analysis of Developmental Spelling in GYNS AT WORK." *Reading Teacher* (November): 192–200.

———. 1987. *Spel . . . Is a Four Letter Word*. Portsmouth, N.H.: Heinemann.

Ginott, Hiam. 1972. *Between Teacher and Child*. New York: Macmillan.

Goldenberg, Claude. 1991. "Learning to Read in New Zealand: The Balance of Skills and Meaning." *Language Arts* (November): 555–562.

Goodman, Kenneth. 1986a. "Basal Readers: A Call for Action." *Language Arts* (April): 358–363.

———. 1986b. *What's Whole in Whole Language?* Portsmouth, N.H.: Heinemann.

Goodman, Kenneth, Patrick Shannon, Yvonne Freeman, and Sharon Murphy. 1987. *Report Card on Basal Readers*. Report of the Commission on Reading. Urbana, Ill.: National Council of Teachers of English.

Goodman, Yetta M. 1983. "Beginning Reading Development: Strategies and Principles." In *Developing Literacy: Young Children's Use of Language*, edited by Robert P. Parker and Frances A. David. Newark, Del.: International Reading Association.

———. 1985. "Oral and Written Language Development." In *Observing the Language Learner*, edited by Angela Jaggar and M. Trika Smith-Burke. Newark, Del.: International Reading Association.

Goodman, Yetta M., M. Haussler, and D. Strickland. 1982. *Oral and Written Language Development Research: Impact on the Schools*. Urbana, Ill.: National Council of Teachers of English.

Goodman, Yetta M., Dorothy J. Watson, and Caroline L. Burke. 1987. *Reading Miscue Inventory: Alternative Procedures*. New York: Richard C. Owen Publishers.

Graves, Donald H. 1983. *Writing: Teachers and Children at Work*. Exeter, N.H.: Heinemann.

———. 1984. *A Researcher Learns to Write: Selected Articles and Monographs*. Exeter, N.H.: Heinemann.

Gray, James. N.d. *The National Writing Project: Model & Program Design: The Fifteenth Year 1973–1988*. The National Writing Project.

Haley-James, Shirley M., and Charles David Hobson. 1980. "Interviewing: A Means of Encouraging the Drive to Communicate." *Language Arts* (May): 497–502.

Halsted, Isabella. 1975. "Putting Error in Its Place." *Journal of Basic Writing* (Spring): 72–86.

Hancock, Joelie, and Susan Hill, eds. 1988. *Literature-Based Reading Programs at Work*. Portsmouth, N.H.: Heinemann.

Hansen, Jane. 1983. "Authors Respond to Authors." *Language Arts* (November-December): 970–976.

———. 1987. *When Writers Read*. Portsmouth, N.H.: Heinemann.

———. 1992. "The Language of Challenge: Readers and Writers Speak Their Minds." *Language Arts* (February): 100–105.

Harp, Bill. 1988. "When the Principal Asks: 'Is All of That Drama Taking Valuable Time Away from Reading?'" *Reading Teacher* (May): 938–940.

———. 1991. *Assessment and Evaluation in Whole Language Programs*. Norwood, Mass.: Christopher-Gordon.

Harris, Violet J. 1992. *Teaching Multicultural Literacy*. Norwood, Mass.: Christopher-Gordon.

Harste, Jerome C., Kathy Short, and Carolyn L. Burke. 1988. *Creating Classrooms for Authors: The Reading-Writing Connection*. Portsmouth, N.H.: Heinemann.

Harste, Jerome C., Virginia A. Woodward, and Carolyn L. Burke. 1984. *Language Stories and Literacy Lessons*. Portsmouth, N.H.: Heinemann.

Hayes, Curtis W., and Robert Bahruth. 1985. "Querer Es Poder." In *Breaking Ground: Teachers Relate Reading and Writing in the Elementary School*, edited by Jane Hansen, Thomas Newkirk, and Donald Graves, 97–108. Portsmouth, N.H.: Heinemann.

Heard, Georgia. 1989. *For the Good of the Earth and the Sun: Teaching Poetry*. Portsmouth, N.H.: Heinemann.

Heath, Shirley Brice, and Leslie Mangiola. 1991. *Children of Promise: Literate Activity in Linguistically and Culturally Diverse Classrooms*. Washington, D.C.: National Education Association.

Heller, Ruth. 1988. *Kites Sail High: A Book about Verbs*. New York: Grosset and Dunlop.

Herman, Joan L., Pamela R. Arschbacher, and Lynn Winters. 1992. *A Practical Guide to Alternative Assessment*. Alexandria, Va.: Association for Supervision and Curriculum Development.

Hickman, Janet, and Bernice E. Cullinan. 1989. *Children's Literature in the Classroom: Weaving Charlotte's Web*. Needham Heights, Mass.: Christopher-Gordon.

Hillocks, George. 1987. "Synthesis of Research on Teaching Writing." *Educational Leadership* (May): 71–82.

Holdaway, Don. 1979. *The Foundations of Literacy*. Exeter, N.H.: Heinemann.

Holt, John. 1983. *How Children Learn*. Rev. ed. New York: Delacorte/Seymour Lawrence. First published in 1967.

Jackson, Jacqueline. 1974. *Turn Not Pale, Beloved Snail*. Boston: Little, Brown.

Jaggar, Angela. 1981. "Viewpoints: Listening and Talking." *Language Arts* (February): 151–152.

Jagger, Angela, and M. Trika Smith-Burke. 1985. *Observing the Language Learner*. Newark, Del.: International Reading Association.

Jenkins, William A. 1978. "Theory into Practice circa 1978." *Language Arts* (September): 693–698.

Jensen, Julie, ed. 1983. *Language Arts* [A Sixtieth-Year Retrospective Issue] (January): 1983.

Jeppeson, Phyllis. N.d. "American Women in History." Course handout, Central Michigan University, Mt. Pleasant, Michigan.

Johnson, David W., and Roger T. Johnson. 1975. *Learning Together and Alone: Cooperation, Competition and Individualization*. Englewood Cliffs, N.J.: Prentice-Hall.

———. 1986. "Cooperative Learning: The Power of Positive Goal Interdependence." Presentation at the Association for Supervision and Curriculum Development Annual Conference, San Francisco.

Johnson, David W., Roger T. Johnson, Edythe Johnson Holubec, and Patricia Roy. 1986. *Circles of Learning: Cooperation in the Classroom*. Rev. ed. Alexandria, Va.: Association for Supervision and Curriculum Development.

Johnson, Terry, and Daphne R. Louis. 1987. *Literacy Through Literature*. Portsmouth, N.H.: Heinemann.

Johnstone, Velerie M. 1990. "Writing Back: Revising and Editing." *English Journal* (September): 57–59.

Jones, Richard-Lloyd. 1988. "Division and Synthesis: Implications of the Aspen Coalition Conference." *Language Arts Journal of Michigan* (Spring): 1–14.

Judy (Tchudi), Stephen. 1980. *The ABCs of Literacy*. New York: Oxford University Press.

Judy (Tchudi), Stephen, and Susan Judy (Tchudi). 1982. *Putting on a Play: A Guide to Writing and Producing Neighborhood Drama*. New York: Scribner's.

Kehl, Delmar G. 1983. "How to Read an Ad: Learning to Read Between the Lies." *English Journal* (October): 32–38.

Kennedy, X. J. 1981. "Go and Get Your Candle Lit: An Approach to Poetry." *Horn Book* (June): 273–279.

Kohl, Herbert. 1981. *A Book of Puzzlements: Play and Invention with Language*. New York: Schocken Books.

———. 1982. "What Does It Take to Be a Real Teacher?" *Learning* (March): 30, 33–34.

Konigsburg, E. L. 1967. *From the Mixed-up Files of Mrs. Basil E. Frankwiler*. New York: Atheneum.

Krashen, Stephen D. 1982. *Principles and Practice in Second Language Acquisition.* New York: Pergamon.

Kukla, Kaila. 1987. "David Booth: Drama as a Way of Knowing." *Language Arts* (January): 73–78.

Lamme, Linda Leonard, and Cecilia Hysmith. 1991. "One School's Adventure in Portfolio Assessment." *Language Arts* (December): 629–640.

Lehr, Fran. 1983. "ERIC/RCS Report: Developing Critical and Creative Reading and Thinking Skills." *Language Arts* (November-December): 1031.

———. 1984. "ERIC/RCS Report: Student-Teacher Communication." *Language Arts* (February): 200–203.

Lemke, Jay L. 1989. *Classrooms and Literacy.* Edited by David Bloome. Norwood, N.J.: Ablex.

Lindfors, Judith Wells. 1980. *Children's Language and Learning.* Englewood Cliffs, N.J.: Prentice-Hall.

———. 1984. "How Children Learn or How Teachers Teach? A Profound Confusion." *Language Arts* (October): 600–606.

———. 1988. *Children's Language and Learning.* Rev. ed. Englewood Cliffs, N.J.: Prentice-Hall.

Louie, Ai-Ling. 1982. *Yeh-Shen: A Cinderella Story from China.* New York: Philomel.

Luce, William. 1978. *The Belle of Amherst.* Boston: Houghton Mifflin.

Lucking, Robert. 1985. "Just Two Words." *Language Arts* (February): 173–174.

Lundsteen, Sarah W. 1979. *Listening: Its Impact at All Levels on Reading and the Other Language Arts.* Urbana, Ill.: National Council of Teachers of English.

Madden, Lowell. 1988. "Do Teachers Communicate with Their Students as if They Were Dogs?" *Language Arts* (February): 142–146.

Martins, Joan LaMoyne. 1988. "Using Journals in Elementary School Classrooms." Handout at the annual meeting of the Iowa Council of Teachers of English, November, Des Moines, Iowa.

Marzano, Robert. 1992. *A Different Kind of Classroom: Teaching with Dimensions of Learning.* Alexandria, Va.: Association for Supervision and Curriculum Development.

McClure, Amy. 1990. *Sunrises and Songs: Reading and Writing Poetry in the Elementary Classroom.* Portsmouth, N.H.: Heinemann.

McCord, David. 1977. *One at a Time.* Illustrated by Henry B. Kane. Boston: Little, Brown.

McTighe, Jay, and Frank T. Lyman, Jr. 1988. "Cueing Thinking in the Classroom: The Promise of Theory-Embedded Tools." *Educational Leadership* (April): 18–24.

Meek, Margaret. 1982. *Learning to Read.* Portsmouth, N.H.: Heinemann.

Merriam, Eve. 1992. "Inside a Poem." *Writer* (April): 18–19.

Michigan State Board of Education. 1985. *Michigan Essential Goals and Objectives for Writing.*

Moffett, James, and Betty Jane Wagner. 1976. *Student-Centered Language Arts and Reading K-13.* Boston: Houghton Mifflin.

Morgan, Norah, and Juliana Saxton. 1988. "Enriching Language Through Drama." *Language Arts* (January): 34–40.

Morrow, Lesley Mandel, and Muriel K. Rand. 1991. "Promoting Literacy During Play by Designing Early Childhood Classroom Environments." *Reading Teacher* (February): 396–402.

Mosel, Arlene. 1972. *The Funny Little Woman.* New York: Dutton.

Murray, Donald. 1982. *Learning by Teaching: Selected Articles on Writing and Teaching.* Montclair, N.J.: Boynton Cook.

———. 1987. *Write to Learn.* 2nd ed. New York: Holt, Rinehart and Winston.

———. 1990. *Write to Learn.* 3rd ed. Fort Worth, Tex.: Holt, Rinehart and Winston.

Musgrove, Margaret. 1976. *Ashanti to Zulu.* New York: Dial.

National Council of Teachers of Mathematics. 1989. *Curriculum and Evaluation Standards for School Mathematics.* Reston, Va.: National Council of Teachers of Mathematics.

Nelson, Pamela. 1988. "Drama Doorway to the Past." *Language Arts* (January): 20–25.

Newkirk, Thomas, and Nancie Atwell. 1986. *Understanding Writing: Ways of Observing, Learning and Teaching.* Portsmouth N.H.: Heinemann.

Nilsen, Alleen Pace. 1983. "Children's Multiple Uses of Oral Language Play." *Language Arts* (February): 194–201.

Northeast Foundation for Children. 1991. *A Notebook for Teachers: Making Changes in the Elementary Curriculum.* Rev. ed. Deerfield, Mass.: Northeast Foundation for Children.

Norton, Donna E. 1987. *Through the Eyes of a Child.* Columbus, Ohio: Merrill.

O'Callahan, Jay. 1980. "Storytellers in the Classroom." *Teacher* (November-December): 33–36.

Parker, Elaine. 1992. "The Writing Portfolio." Presentation at the Teaching Writing Workshops, University of Nevada.

———. N.d. Unpublished broadside. University of Nevada, Reno, Nevada.

Parker, Walter. 1989. "How to Help Students Learn History and Geography." *Educational Leadership* (November): 39–43.

Paterson, Katherine. 1977. *Bridge to Teribithia.* New York: Crowell.

Paulson, F. Leon, Pearl R. Paulson, and Carol A. Meyer. 1991. "What Makes a Portfolio?" *Educational Leadership* (February): 60–63.

Pearson, Craig. 1980. "Can You Keep Quiet for Three Seconds?" *Learning* (February): 40–43.

Pellowski, Anne. 1984. *The Story Vine: A Source Book of Unusual and Easy-to-Tell Stories from Around the World.* New York: Macmillan.

Petreshene, Susan S. 1988. "Ten-Minute Think Sessions." *Instructor* (January): 69–71.

Postman, Neil, and Charles Weingartner. 1969. *Teaching as a Subversive Activity.* New York: Delacorte.

Purves, Alan C., Theresa Rogers, and Anna O. Soter. 1990. *How Porcupines Make Love II—Teaching a Response-Centered Literature Curriculum.* White Plains, N.Y.: Longman.

Read, Charles. 1975. *Children's Categorization of Speech Sounds in English.* Urbana, Ill.: National Council of Teachers of English.

Reasoner, Charles F. 1975. *When Children Read.* New York: Dell.

———. 1979. *Bringing Children and Books Together.* New York: Dell.

Rhodes, Lynn K., and Curt Dudley-Marling. 1988. *Readers and Writers with a Difference: A Holistic Approach to Teaching Learning Disabled and Remedial Students.* Portsmouth, N.H.: Heinemann.

Ricento, Thomas. 1988. "The Framers Knew Best." *TESOL Newsletter* (April): 1, 3–5.

Richards, Leah. 1990. " 'Measuring Things in Words': Language for Learning Mathematics." *Language Arts* (January): 14–25.

Rico, Gabrielle. 1983. *Writing the Natural Way: Using Right-Brain Techniques to Release Your Expressive Powers.* Los Angeles: J. P. Tarcher.

Rief, Linda. 1992. *Seeking Diversity—Language Arts with Adolescents*. Portsmouth, N.H.: Heinemann.

Rietz, Sandra A. 1983. "Songs, Singing Games, and Language Play." In *Integrating the Language Arts in the Elementary School*, edited by Beverly A. Busching and Judith Schwartz, 102–119. Urbana, Ill.: National Council of Teachers of English.

Ritchie, Joy S. 1989. "Beginning Writers: Diverse Voices and Individual Identity." *College Composition and Communication* (May): 152–173.

Root, Robert L. 1985. "Marketplace and the Classroom: The Writing Process of Professionals and Students." *Language Arts Journal of Michigan* (Fall): 10–15.

Rosenblatt, Louise M. 1938. *Literature as Exploration*. New York: Appleton-Century-Crofts.

———. 1983. "The Reading Transaction: What For?" In *Developing Literacy: Young Children's Use of Language*, edited by Robert P. Parker and Frances A. Davis, 118–135. Newark, Del.: International Reading Association.

Routman, Regie. 1988. *Transitions: From Literature to Literacy*. 1988. Heinemann.

———. 1991. *Invitations: Changing as Teachers and Learners, K–12*. Portsmouth, N.H.: Heinemann.

Rowe, Mary Budd. 1986. "Wait Time: Slowing Down May Be a Way of Speeding Up!" *Journal of Teacher Education* (January-February): 43–50.

Sachse, Thomas P. 1989. "Making Science Happen." *Educational Leadership* (November): 18–21.

Sanborn, Jean. 1986. "Grammar: Good Wine Before Its Time." *English Journal* (March): 72–79.

Schickedanz, Judith A. 1978. "You Be the Doctor and I'll Be Sick: Preschoolers Learn the Language Arts Through Play." *Language Arts* (September): 713–718.

———. 1990. *Adam's Righting Revolutions*. Portsmouth, N.H.: Heinemann.

Sitton, Rebecca. 1989. "Spelling: Instruction Across the Curriculum Using Research-Based Activities." Presentation at the National Council of Teachers of English, Baltimore, Maryland.

Skean, Susan M. 1982. "The Pamphlet: A Successful Writing Project." *English Journal* (February): 85–86.

Slaughter, Helen B. 1988. "Indirect and Direct Teaching in a Whole Language Program." *Reading Teacher* (October): 30–34.

Sloan, Glenna Davis. N.d. *Good Books Make Reading Fun for Your Child*. Newark, Del.: International Reading Association.

Smith, Frank. 1973. "Twelve Easy Ways to Make Learning to Read Difficult." In *Psycholinguistics and Reading*, edited by Frank Smith, 183–196. New York: Holt, Rinehart and Winston.

———. 1979. *Reading Without Nonsense*. New York: Teachers College Press.

Smith, Robert W. 1987. "The Class Menagerie: Using Small Animals to Enrich Your Science Curriculum." *Learning* (January): 82–84.

Smith, Roy A. 1987. "A Teacher's Views on Cooperative Learning." *Phi Delta Kappan* (May): 663–666.

Sowers, Susan. 1986. "Six Questions Teachers Ask About Invented Spelling." In *Understanding Writing*, edited by Thomas Newkirk and Nancie Atwell. Portsmouth, N.H.: Heinemann.

Spandel, Vicki, and Richard J. Stiggins. 1990. *Creating Writers: Linking Assessment and Writing Instruction*. New York: Longman.

Suid, Murray. 1984. "Speaking of Speaking." *Instructor* (May): 56–58.

Sutherland, Zena, Dianne L. Monson, and May Hill Arbuthnot. 1981. *Children and Books*. Glenview, Ill.: Scott, Foresman.

Tanner-Cazinha, Diane, Kathryn H. Au, and Karen M. Blake. 1991. "Reviews and Reflections: New Perspectives on Literacy Evaluation." *Language Arts* (December): 669–673.

Taylor, Theodore. 1969. *The Cay*. Garden City, N.Y.: Doubleday.

Tchudi, Stephen. 1986. "The Hidden Agendas in Writing Across the Curriculum." *English Journal* (November): 22–25.

———. 1987. *The Young Learner's Handbook*. New York: Scribner's.

———. 1991a. *Planning and Assessing the Curriculum in English Language Arts*. Alexandria, Va.: Association for Supervision and Curriculum Development.

———. 1991b. *Travels Across the Curriculum: Model for Interdisciplinary Learning*. Richmond Hill, Ontario: Scholastic Canada.

Tchudi, Stephen, and Margie C. Huerta. 1983. *Teaching Writing in the Content Areas: Middle School/Junior High*. Washington, D.C.: National Education Association.

Tchudi, Stephen, and Susan Tchudi. 1983. *Teaching Writing in the Content Areas: Elementary*. Washington, D.C.: National Education Association.

Tchudi, Susan. 1985. "The Roots of Response to Literature." *Language Arts* (September): 463–468.

———. 1988. "A Readers Theater Performance." Presentation at the National Council of Teachers of English Spring Conference, Boston.

Tchudi, Susan, and Stephen Tchudi. 1984. *The Young Writer's Handbook*. New York: Scribner's.

Temple, Charles A., Ruth G. Nathan, and Nancy A. Burris. 1982. *The Beginnings of Writing*. Boston: Allyn and Bacon.

Templeton, Shane. 1986. "Synthesis of Research on the Learning and Teaching of Spelling." *Educational Leadership* (March): 73–78.

Thaiss, Christopher. 1986. *Language Across the Curriculum in the Elementary Grades*. Urbana, Ill.: National Council of Teachers of English/ERIC.

Thaiss, Christopher, and Charles Suhor. 1984. *Speaking and Writing K–12*. Urbana, Ill.: National Council of Teachers of English.

Thaler, Mike. 1988. "Reading, Writing and Riddling." *Learning* (April-May): 58–59.

Tierney, Robert J., Mark A. Carter, and Laura E. Desai. 1991. *Portfolio Assessment in the Reading-Writing Classroom*. Norwood, Mass.: Christopher-Gordon.

Tompkins, Gail, and David Yaden. 1986. *Answering Students' Questions About Words*. Urbana, Ill.: National Council of Teachers of English.

Tough, Joan. 1985. *Listening to Children Talking: A Guide to the Appraisal of Children's Use of Language*. London: Ward Lock.

Turbill, Jan, ed. 1982. *No Better Way to Teach Writing!* Portsmouth, N.H.: Heinemann.

———. 1983. *Now, We Want to Write!* Rozelle, New South Wales, Australia: Primary English Teaching Association; distributed in the United States by Heinemann.

Turner, Rebecca R. 1988. "How the Basals Stack Up." *Learning* (April): 62–64.

Tutolo, Daniel. 1981. "Critical Listening/Reading of Advertisements." *Language Arts* (September): 679–683.

Twain, Mark. 1888; 1986. *Huckleberry Finn*. New York: Penguin.

Tyson, Harriet, and Arthur Woodward. 1989. "Why Students Aren't Learning Very Much from Textbooks." *Educational Leadership* (November): 14–17.

Van Allen, Roach. 1976. *Language Experiences in Communication*. Boston: Houghton Mifflin.

Verriour, Patrick. "The Reflective Power of Drama." 1984. *Language Arts* (February): 125–130.

Vygotsky, L. S. 1962. *Thought and Language*. Cambridge, Mass.: M.I.T. Press.

Wagner, Betty J. 1983. "The Expanding Circle of Informal Classroom Drama." *Integrating the Language Arts in the Elementary School*, edited by Beverly A. Busching and Judith Schwartz, 155–163. Urbana, Ill.: National Council of Teachers of English.

———. 1988. "Research Currents: Does Classroom Drama Affect the Arts of Language?" *Language Arts* (January): 46–55.

Wason-Ellam, Linda. 1988. "Using Literacy Patterns: Who's in Control of the Authorship?" *Language Arts* (March): 291–301.

Watson, Dorothy, and Paul Crowley. 1988. "How Can We Implement a Whole-Language Approach?" In *Reading Process and Practice: From Socio-Psycholinguistics to Whole Language*, by Constance Weaver, 232–279. Portsmouth, N.H.: Heinemann.

Weaver, Constance, 1988. *Reading Process and Practice: From Socio-Psycholinguistics to Whole Language*. Portsmouth, N.H.: Heinemann.

White, E. B. 1952. *Charlotte's Web*. New York: Harper and Row.

Wiggins, Grant. 1989. "The Futility of Trying to Teach Everything of Importance." *Educational Leadership* (November): 44–59.

Wilde, Sandra. 1990. "A Proposal for a New Spelling Curriculum." *Elementary School Journal* (January): 275–289.

———. 1992. *You Kan Red This!* Portsmouth, N.H.: Heinemann.

Wilson, Marilyn, and Celeste Resh. N.d. *Reading in the Home*. Pamphlet. Department of English, Michigan State University.

Winn, Deanna. 1988. "Develop Listening Skills as Part of the Curriculum." *Reading Teacher* (November): 144–149.

Wiseman, Ann. 1975. *Making Things, A Book of Creative Discovery: Book 2*. Boston: Little, Brown.

Write Source 2000, Teacher's Guide. 1990. Burlington, Wis.: Write Source Publishing House.

Bibliography of Children's Books

Selections are arranged by genre. The interest level (I) and reading level (R), by grade, are indicated in parentheses after each entry.

Picture Books

Ackerman, Karen. *Song and Dance Man*. Illustrated by Stephen Gammell. New York: Knopf, 1988. (I: 2–5; R: 2–4)

Aliki. *A Medieval Feast*. New York: Crowell, 1983. (I: 2–8; R: 3–5)

———. *The Two of Them*. New York: Mulberry Books, 1979. (I: 1–3; R: 2–3)

Anglund, Joan Walsh. *Nibble, Nibble, Mousekin—A Tale of Hansel and Gretel*. New York: Harcourt, Brace & World, 1962. (I: 1–5; R: 2–4)

Anno, Masaichiro, and Mitsumasa Anno. *Anno's Mysterious Multiplying Jar*. New York: Philomel Books, 1983. (I: 3–10+; R: 3–10+)

Anno, Mitsumasa. *Anno's Medieval World*. Translated by Ursula Synge. New York: Philomel Books, 1979. (I: 2–8; R: 3–8)

Baylor, Byrd. *Everybody Needs a Rock*. Illustrated by Peter Parnall. New York: Atheneum, 1974. (I: 1–5; R: 2–5)

———. *Guess Who My Favorite Person Is*. Illustrated by Robert Andrew Parker. New York: Scribner's, 1986. (I: 2–8; R: 2–8)

———. *I'm in Charge of Celebrations*. Illustrated by Peter Parnall. New York: Scribner's, 1986. (I: 1–8; R: 2–8)

Bonners, Susan. *Panda*. New York: Dell, 1978. (I: K–3; R: 1–3)

Bunting, Eve. *The Wednesday Surprise*. Illustrated by Donald Carrick. New York: Clarion Books, 1989. (I: 2–4; R: 3–4)

Burton, Virginia Lee. *Mike Mulligan and His Steam Shovel*. Boston: Houghton Mifflin, 1967 (1939). (I: K–3; R: 2–3)

Carle, Eric. *Animals, Animals*. New York: Philomel Books, 1989. (I: K–5; R: 2–5)

———. *The Grouchy Ladybug*. New York: Crowell, 1977. (I: K–2; R: 1–2)

———. *A House for Hermit Crab*. Saxonville, Mass.: Picture Book Studio, 1987. (I: K–3; R: 2–3)

———. *Seven Stories by Hans Christian Andersen*. Illustrated and retold by Eric Carle. New York: Franklin Watts, 1978. (I: 2–5; R: 3–5)

———. *The Very Hungry Caterpillar*. New York: Philomel Books, 1987 (1969). (I: K–2; R: 1–2)

Cazet, Denys. *Never Spit on Your Shoes*. New York: Orchard Books, 1990. (I: 1–2; R: 2–3)

Charney, Steve. *Daddy's Whiskers*. New York: Crown, 1989. (I: K–3; R: 2–3)

Cherry, Lynne. *A River Ran Wild: An Environmental History*. San Diego: Harcourt Brace Jovanovich, 1992. (I: 2–5; R: 3–5)

Clark, Ethne. *The Flower Garden Planner*. New York: Simon and Schuster, 1984. (I: 2–5; R: 4–5)

Clements, Andrew. *Big Al*. Illustrated by Yoshi. Saxonville, Mass.: Picture Book Studio, 1988. (I: K–3; R: 2–3)

Climo, Shirley. *The Egyptian Cinderella*. Illustrated by Ruth Heller. New York: Crowell, 1989. (I: 2–5; R: 3–5)

Cohen, Barbara. *Gooseberries to Oranges*. Illustrated by Beverly Brodsky. New York: Lothrop, Lee and Shepard Books, 1982. (I: 2–6; R: 3–6)

Coleridge, Samuel Taylor. *The Rime of the Ancient Mariner*. Illustrated by Ed Young. New York: Atheneum, 1972. (I: 3–adult; R: 6–adult)

Cooney, Barbara. *Island Boy*. New York: Viking Kestrel, 1988. (I: 1–4; R: 2–4)

Craig, M. Jean. *The Man Whose Name Was Not Thomas*. Illustrated by Diane Stanley. Garden City, N.Y.: Doubleday, 1981. (I: 2–5; R: 2–5)

dePaola, Tomie. *The Kids' Cat Book*. New York: Holiday House, 1979. (I: 1–4; R: 3–4)

———. *Now One Foot, Now the Other*. New York: Putnam's, 1981. (I: 2–5; R: 2–3)

Dewey, Jennifer. *Can You Find Me? A Book About Animal Camouflage*. New York: Scholastic, 1989. (I: 1–3; R: 2–3)

Dionetti, Michelle. *Coal Mine Peaches*. New York: Orchard Books, 1991. (I: 2–5; R: 3–4)

Dorros, Arthur. *Abuela*. New York: Dutton Children's Books, 1991. (I: 1–3; R: 2–3)

Duke, Kate. *The Guinea Pig ABC*. New York: Dutton, 1983. (I: K–2; R: 1–2)

Ehrlich, Amy. *Cinderella by Charles Perrault*. Illustrated by Susan Jeffers. New York: Dial Books for Young Readers, 1985. (I: 1–5; R: 2–5)

Fish, Helen Dean. *When the Root Children Wake Up*. LaJolla, Calif.: Green Tiger Press, 1991 (1906). (I: 1–4; R: 2–4)

Fox, Mem. *Wilfred Gordon McDonald Partridge*. Brooklyn, N.Y.: Kane/Miller, 1985. (I: 1–4; R: 2–4)

Frost, Robert. *Stopping by the Woods on a Snowy Evening*. Illustrated by Susan Jeffers. New York: Dutton, 1978 (1923). (I: 2–8+; R: 3–8+)

Fujikawa, Gyo. *Poems for Children*. New York: Platt and Munk, 1969. (I: K–3; R: 2–3)

Gág, Wanda. *The A B C Bunny*. New York: Coward, McCann and Geoghegan, 1931. (I: K–2; R: 1–2)

———. *Millions of Cats*. Newbery Award. New York: Coward-McCann, 1977 (1928). (I: K–2; R: 1–2)

Gantschev, Ivan. *The Train to Grandma's*. Natick, Mass.: Picture Book Studio, 1987. (I: K–2; R: 1–2)

Garfield, Leon. *The Wedding Ghost*. Illustrated by Charles Keeping. Toronto: Oxford University Press, 1988. (I: 7–12; R: 7–12)

Goble, Paul. *Buffalo Woman*. Scarsdale, N.Y.: Bradbury Press, 1984. (I: 3–5; R: 3–5)

———. *The Gift of the Sacred Dog*. Scarsdale, N.Y.: Bradbury Press, 1980. (I: 3–5; R: 3–5)

Greenfield, Eloise. *Cornrows*. Illustrated by Carole Byard. New York: Philomel Books, 1980. (I: 2–5; R: 2–5)

———. *Grandmama's Joy*. New York: Philomel Books, 1980. (I: K–3; R: 2–3)

———. *Grandpa's Face*. New York: Philomel Books, 1988. (I: K–3; R: 2–3)

Grifalconi, Ann. *The Village of Round and Square Houses*. Boston: Little, Brown, 1986. (I: 2–4; R: 3–4)

Hague, Kathleen. *Alphabears*. Illustrated by Michael Hague. New York: Holt, Rinehart and Winston, 1984. (I: K–3; R: 1–3)

Heller, Ruth. *Animals Born Alive and Well*. New York: Grosset and Dunlap, 1982. (I: 2–8; R: 3–8)

———. *Chickens Aren't the Only Ones*. New York: Grosset and Dunlap, 1982. (I: 2–8; R: 2–8)

———. *Kites Sail High—A Book About Verbs*. New York: Grosset and Dunlap, 1988. (I: 2–8; R: 3–8)

———. *Plants That Never Ever Bloom*. New York: Grosset and Dunlap, 1984. (I: 2–8; R: 3–8)

Hendershot, Judith. *In Coal Country*. New York: Knopf, 1987. (I: 2–5; R: 3–5)

Hidaka, Masako. *Girl from the Snow Country*. Brooklyn, N.Y.: Kane/Miller, 1986. (I: K–3; R: 2–3)

Hoffman, Mary. *Amazing Grace*. New York: Dial Books for Young Readers, 1991. (I: 2–4; R: 2–4)

Houston, Gloria. *My Great Aunt Arizona*. Illustrated by Susan Condie Lamb. New York: HarperCollins, 1992. (I: 2–5; R: 2–5)

Huck, Charlotte. *Princess Furball*. Illustrated by Anita Lobel. New York: Greenwillow Books, 1989. (I: 1–5; R: 3–5)

Keller, Frances Ruth. *The Contented Little Pussy Cat*. New York: Platt and Munk, 1949. (I: K–2; R: 1–2)

Kennedy, Jimmy. *The Teddy Bears' Picnic*. La Jolla, Calif.: Green Tiger Press, 1983. (I: K–3; R: 2–3)

Lasky, Kathryn. *Sugaring Time*. Photographs by Christopher G. Knight. New York: Macmillan, 1983. (I: 3–5; R: 3–5)

Lawson, Robert. *Rabbit Hill*. Newbery Award. New York: Viking, 1972 (1944). (I: K–5; R: 2–5)

Leaf, Munro. *Wee Gillis*. Illustrated by Robert Lawson. New York: Viking, 1938. (I: 1–4; R: 2–4)

Lear, Edward. *The Jumblies*. Illustrated by Ted Rand. New York: Putnam's, 1989. (I: 2–8; R: 4–8)

Lionni, Leo. *Swimmy*. New York: Pinwheel Books, 1973. (I: K–2; R: 2–3)

Lobel, Arnold. *The Rose in My Garden*. Illustrated by Anita Lobel. New York: Greenwillow Books, 1984. (I: 1–5; R: 2–4)

Longfellow, Henry Wadsworth. *Paul Revere's Ride*. Illustrated by Ted Rand. New York: Dutton Children's Books, 1990. (I: 2–adult; R: 4–adult)

MacDonald, Golden. *The Little Island*. Illustrated by Leonard Weisgard. Caldecott Award. Garden City, N.Y.: Doubleday, 1946. (I: 1–4; R: 2–3)

MacDonald, Suse. *Numblers*. New York: Dial Books for Young Readers, 1988. (I: K–2; R: 1–2)

Maruki, Toshi. *Hiroshima No Pika*. New York: Lothrop, Lee and Shephard Books, 1980. (I: 5–8; R: 5–8)

McCloskey, Robert. *Make Way for Ducklings*. Caldecott Award. New York: Viking, 1969 (1941). (I: K–2; R: 2–adult)

Merriam, Eve. *Halloween ABC*. Illustrated by Lane Smith. New York: Macmillan, 1987. (I: K–5; R: 1–5)

Mori, Tuyosi. *Socrates and the Three Little Pigs*. Illustrated by Mitsumasa Anno. New York: Philomel Books, 1986. (I: 3–8; R: 3–8)

Musgrove, Margaret. *Ashanti to Zulu*. Illustrated by Leo and Diane Dillon. Caldecott Award. New York: Dial, 1976. (I: 2–5; R: 3–5)

Nozaki, Akihiro. *Anno's Hat Tricks*. Illustrated by Mitsumasa Anno. New York: Philomel Books, 1985. (I: 3–8; R: 3–8)

Pinkwater, Daniel. *Bear's Picture*. New York: Dutton, 1972. (I: K–2; R: 1–2)

Provensen, Alice, and Martin Provenson. *Leonardo DaVinci*. Paper engineering by John Strejan. New York: Viking, 1984. (I: 2–8; R: 4–8)

Ringgold, Faith. *Tar Beach*. New York: Crown, 1991. (I: 2–4; R: 3–4)

Rius, Maria. *Life Underground*. New York: Woodbury, 1987. (I: 2–5; R: 3–5)

————. *The Middle Ages*. New York: Barron's, 1988. (I: 2–5; R: 2–5)

Rylant, Cynthia. *When I Was Young in the Mountains*. Illustrated by Diane Goode. Caldecott Award. New York: Dutton, 1982. (I: 2–4; R: 2–4)

San Souci, Robert D. *Sukey and the Mermaid*. Illustrated by Brian Pinckney. New York: Four Winds, 1992. (I: 2–5; R: 3–5)

Schwartz, David M. *How Much Is a Million?* Illustrated by Steven Kellogg. New York: Scholastic, 1985. (I: K–5; R: 2–5)

Scieszka, Jon. *The True Story of the Three Little Pigs*. New York: Viking Kestrel, 1989. (I: 1–5; R: 2–5)

Seuss, Dr. *And to Think That I Saw It on Mulberry Street*. New York: Vanguard, 1964 (1934). (I: K–3; R: 2–3)

————. *The Cat in the Hat*. Boston: Houghton Mifflin, 1957. (I: K–3; R: 2–3)

Sloane, Eric. *ABC Book of Early Americana*. Garden City, N.Y.: Doubleday, 1963. (I: 3–8+; R: 3–8+)

Synder, Dianne. *The Boy of the Three-Year Nap*. Boston: Houghton Mifflin, 1988. (I: 2–5; R: 3–5)

Steiner, Jorg. *Rabbit Island*. Translated by Ann Conrad Lammers. New York: Harcourt Brace Jovanovich, 1978. (I: 3–8; R: 4–8)

Thornhill, Jan. *The Wildlife 1.2.3*. New York: Simon and Schuster, 1989. (I: K–2; R: 1–2)

Vining, Elizabeth Gray. *Adam of the Road*. Illustrated by Robert Lawson. New York: Viking, 1960 (1942). (I: 1–4; R: 2–4)

Waber, Bernard. *Ira Says Good-bye*. Boston: Houghton Mifflin, 1988. (I: K–4; R: 2–4)

Watts, Bernadette. *Snow White and Rose Red*. Retold and illustrated by Bernadette Watts. Faellanden, Switzerland: North-South Books, 1988. (I: 1–5; R: 2–5)

Whipple, Laura. *Dragons, Dragons and Other Creatures That Never Were*. Illustrated by Eric Carle. New York: Philomel Books, 1991. (I: K–5; R: 2–5)

Williams, Margery. *The Velveteen Rabbit*. New York: Holt, Rinehart and Winston, 1983 (1922). (I: 2–4; R: 3–4)

Yarbrough, Camille. *Cornrows*. New York: Coward-McCann, 1979. (I: 1–5; R: 2–5)

Yolen, Jane. *Owl Moon*. New York: Philomel Books, 1987. (I: 2–4; R: 2–4)

Yoshi. *Who's Hiding Here?* Natick, Mass.: Picture Book Studio, 1987. (I: K–3; R: 2–3)

Young, Ed. *Lon Po Po: A Red Riding Hood Story from China*. New York: Philomel Books, 1989. (I: 1–5; R: 3–5)

Poetry

Adoff, Arnold. *Birds*. New York: Lippincott, 1982. (I: 2–5; R: 3–5)

Baylor, Byrd. *Everybody Needs a Rock*. Illustrated by Peter Parnall. New York: Atheneum, 1974. (I: 1–5; R: 2–5)

——. *Guess Who My Favorite Person Is*. Illustrated by Robert Andrew Parker. New York: Scribner's, 1986. (I: 2–8; R: 2–8)

——. *Hawk, I'm Your Brother*. Illustrated by Peter Parnall. New York: Scribner's, 1972. (I: 1–5; R: 2–5)

——. *I'm in Charge of Celebrations*. Illustrated by Peter Parnall. New York: Scribner's, 1986. (I: 1–8; R: 2–8)

Behn, Harry. *Trees*. Illustrated by James Endicott. New York: Henry Holt, 1992. (I: 2–5; R: 2–5)

Carle, Eric. *Animals, Animals*. New York: Philomel Books, 1989. (I: K–5; R: 2–5)

Charney, Steve. *Daddy's Whiskers*. New York: Crown, 1989. (I: K–3; R: 2–3)

deAngeli, Marguerite. *Marguerite de Angeli's Book of Nursery and Mother Goose Rhymes*. New York: Doubleday, 1967. (I: K–3; R: 1–3)

dePaola, Tomie. *Tomie dePaola's Mother Goose*. New York: Putnam's, 1985. (I: K–3; R: 1–3)

Dunning, Stephen. *Reflections on a Gift of a Watermelon Pickle*. New York: Scholastic, 1966. (I: 4–8; R: 4–8)

Fisher, Aileen. *A Cricket in a Thicket*. Illustrated by Feodor Rojankovsky. New York: Scribner's, 1963. (I: 1–5; R: 2–5)

——. *Rabbits, Rabbits*. New York: Crowell, 1964. (I: 1–4; R: 2–4)

Fleischman, Paul. *Joyful Noise—Poems for Two Voices*. Newbery Award. New York: Harper and Row, 1988. (I: 3–8; R: 3–8)

Frost, Robert. *Stopping by the Woods on a Snowy Evening*. Illustrated by Susan Jeffers. New York: Dutton, 1978 (1923). (I: 2–8+; R: 3–8+)

Fujikawa, Gyo. *Poems for Children*. New York: Platt and Munk, 1969. (I: K–3; R: 2–3)

Gág, Wanda. *The A B C Bunny*. New York: Coward, McCann and Geoghegan, 1931. (I: K–2; R: 1–2)

Heller, Ruth. *Animals Born Alive and Well*. New York: Grosset and Dunlap, 1982. (I: 2–8; R: 3–8)

——. *Chickens Aren't the Only Ones*. New York: Grosset and Dunlap, 1982. (I: 2–8; R: 2–8)

——. *Kites Sail High—A Book About Verbs*. New York: Grosset and Dunlap, 1988. (I: 2–8; R: 3–8)

——. *Plants That Never Ever Bloom*. New York: Grosset and Dunlap, 1984. (I: 2–8; R: 3–8)

——. *The Reason for a Flower*. New York: Grosset and Dunlap, 1986. (I: 2–8; R: 3–8)

Hopkins, Lee Bennett. *I Am the Cat*. Illustrated by Linda Rochester Richards. New York: Harcourt Brace Jovanovich, 1981. (I: K–5; R: 2–4)

——. *Munching—Poems About Eating*. Boston: Little, Brown, 1976. (I: K–5; R: 2–5)

——. *Still As a Star—A Book of Nighttime Poems*. Boston: Little, Brown, 1989. (I: 2–5; R: 2–5)

———. *Surprises*. New York: Harper and Row, 1984. (I: K–2; R: 1–2)

Kennedy, Jimmy. *The Teddy Bears' Picnic*. La Jolla, Calif.: Green Tiger Press, 1983. (I: K–3; R: 2–3)

Keyes, Frances Parkinson. *A Treasury of Favorite Poems*. New York: Hawthorn Books, 1963. (I: All; R: 5–adult)

Kuskin, Karla. *Near the Window Tree*. New York: Harper and Row, 1975. (I: 2–5; R: 3–5)

Larrick, Nancy. *Cats Are Cats*. Illustrated by Ed Young. New York: Philomel Books, 1988. (I: 1–5; R: 3–5)

Lear, Edward. *The Jumblies*. Illustrated by Ted Rand. New York: Putnam's, 1989. (I: 2–8; R: 4–8)

Livingston, Myra Cohn. *Cat Poems*. Illustrated by Trina Schart Hyman. New York: Holiday House, 1987. (I: 1–5; R: 2–5)

———. *A Circle of Seasons*. Illustrated by Leonard Everett Fisher. New York: Holiday House, 1982. (I: 4–8; R: 4–6)

———. *Dog Poems*. New York: Holiday House, 1990. (I: 1–5; R: 2–5)

———. *Worlds I Know and Other Poems*. New York: Atheneum, 1985. (I: 2–5; R: 2–5)

Prelutsky, Jack. *Circus*. Illustrated by Arnold Lobel. New York: Macmillan, 1974. (I: K–3; R: 1–3)

———. *The Mean Old Mean Hyena*. Illustrated by Arnold Lobel. New York: Greenwillow, 1978. (I: K–5; R: 2–5)

———. *The Random House Book of Poetry*. Illustrated by Arnold Lobel. New York: Random House, 1983. (I: K–6; R: 2–6)

———. *Ride a Purple Pelican*. Illustrated by Garth Williams. New York: Greenwillow, 1986. (I: K–6; R: 1–6)

Seuss, Dr. *And To Think That I Saw It on Mulberry Street*. New York: Vanguard, 1964 (1934). (I: K–3; R: 2–3)

———. *The Cat in the Hat*. Boston: Houghton Mifflin, 1957. (I: K–3; R: 2–3)

Silverstein, Shel. *Where the Sidewalk Ends*. New York: Harper and Row, 1974. (I: 2–5; R: 3–5)

Szekeres, Cyndy. *A Child's First Book of Poems*. New York: 1981. (I: K–2; R: 1–3)

Thompson, Blanche J. *The Silver Pennies: A Collection of Modern Poems for Boys and Girls*. New York: Macmillan, 1925. (I: K–3; R: 1–3)

Tudor, Tasha. *Mother Goose*. New York: McKay, 1944. (I: K–3; R: 1–3)

Viorst, Judith. *If I Were in Charge of the World*. New York: Atheneum, 1981. (I: 2–5; R: 3–5)

Whipple, Laura. *Dragons, Dragons and Other Creatures That Never Were*. Illustrated by Eric Carle. New York: Philomel Books, 1991. (I: K–5; R: 2–5)

Worth, Valerie. *More Small Poems*. Illustrated by Natalie Babbitt. New York: Farrar, Straus, 1976. (I: 1–5; R: 1–5)

———. *Small Poems*. Illustrated by Natalie Babbitt. New York: Farrar, Straus, 1972. (I: 1–5; R: 1–5)

Yolen, Jane. *Ring of Earth: A Child's Book of Seasons*. New York: Harcourt Brace Jovanovich, 1986. (I: 4–8; R: 4–8)

Historical, Multicultural, and Realistic Fiction

Ackerman, Karen. *Song and Dance Man*. Illustrated by Stephen Gammell. New York: Knopf, 1988. (I: 2–5; R: 2–4)

Alcott, Louisa May. *Little Men*. New York: Macmillan, 1963 (1876). (I: 4–12; R: 6–12)

———. *Little Women*. New York: Macmillan, 1962 (1878). (I: 4–12; R: 6–12)

Aliki. *The Two of Them*. New York: Mulberry Books, 1979. (I: 1–3; R: 2–3)

Atwater, Richard, and Florence Atwater. *Mr. Popper's Penguins*. Newbery Award. Illustrated by Robert Lawson. Boston: Little, Brown, 1958. (I: 2–5; R: 3–5)

Brink, Carol Ryrie. *Caddie Woodlawn*. New York: Macmillan, 1935. (I: 4–6; R: 4–6)

Bunting, Eve. *The Wednesday Surprise*. Illustrated by Donald Carrick. New York: Clarion Books, 1989. (I: 2–4; R: 3–4)

Burnett, Frances Hodgson. *The Secret Garden*. Illustrated by Tasha Tudor. New York: Dell, 1962 (1911). (I: 5–7; R: 5–7)

Carrick, Carol. *The Accident*. Illustrated by Donald Carrick. New York: Clarion Books, 1976. (I: K–3; R: 1–3)

Carter, Forrest. *The Education of Little Tree*. Albuquerque: University of New Mexico Press, 1991 (1976). (I: 5–9; R: 5–9)

Clark, Margery. *The Poppyseed Cakes*. Illustrated by Maud and Miska Petersham. Garden City, N.Y.: Doubleday, 1924. (I: 1–3; R: 2–3)

Climo, Shirley. *The Egyptian Cinderella*. Illustrated by Ruth Heller. New York: Crowell, 1989. (I: 2–5; R: 3–5)

Cohen, Barbara. *Gooseberries to Oranges*. Illustrated by Beverly Brodsky. New York: Lothrop, Lee and Shepard Books, 1982. (I: 2–6; R: 3–6)

Collier, James Lincoln, and Christopher Collier. *My Brother Sam Is Dead*. New York: Four Winds, 1974. (I: 5–8; R: 5–8)

Cooney, Barbara. *Island Boy*. New York: Viking Kestrel, 1988. (I: 1–4; R: 2–4)

Craig, M. Jean. *The Man Whose Name Was Not Thomas*. Illustrated by Diane Stanley. Garden City, N.Y.: Doubleday, 1981. (I: 2–5; R: 2–5)

deAngeli, Marguerite. *Copper-Toed Boots*. Caldecott Award. New York: Doubleday, 1938. (I: 3–4; R: 3–4)

———. *Yonie Wondernose*. Caldecott Award. New York: Doubleday, 1938. (I: 3–5; R: 3–5)

dePaola, Tomie. *Now One Foot, Now the Other*. New York: Putnam's, 1981. (I: 2–5; R: 2–3)

Dionetti, Michelle. *Coal Mine Peaches*. New York: Orchard Books, 1991. (I: 2–5; R: 3–4)

Dorros, Arthur. *Abuela*. New York: Dutton Children's Books, 1991. (I: 1–3; R: 2–3)

Field, Rachel. *Hitty, Her First Hundred Years*. Newbery Award. New York: Macmillan, 1929. (I: 3–5; R: 3–5)

Fox, Mem. *Wildred Gordon McDonald Partridge*. Brooklyn, N.Y.: Kane/Miller, 1985. (I: 1–4; R: 2–4)

Gantschev, Ivan. *The Train to Grandma's*. Natick, Mass.: Picture Book Studio, 1987. (I: K–2; R: 1–2)

Goble, Paul. *Buffalo Woman*. Scarsdale, N.Y.: Bradbury Press, 1984. (I: 3–5; R: 3–5)

———. *The Gift of the Sacred Dog*. Scarsdale, N.Y.: Bradbury Press, 1980. (I: 3–5; R: 3–5)

Gray, Elizabeth Janet. *Adam of the Road*. Illustrated by Robert Lawson. New York: Viking, 1942. (I: 5–8; R: 5–8)

Greene, Bette. *Philip Hall Likes Me I Reckon Maybe*. New York: Dell, 1974. (I: 5–8; R: 5–8)

———. *Summer of My German Soldier*. New York: Bantam Books, 1988 (1973). (I: 5–8; R: 5–8)

Greenfield, Eloise. *Grandmama's Joy*. New York: Philomel Books, 1980. (I: K–3; R: 2–3)

———. *Grandpa's Face*. New York: Philomel Books, 1988. (I: K–3; R: 2–3)

Grifalconi, Ann. *The Village of Round and Square Houses*. Boston: Little, Brown, 1986. (I: 2–4; R: 3–4)

Hendershot, Judith. *In Coal Country*. New York: Knopf, 1987. (I: 2–5; R: 3–5)

Henry, Marguerite. *Misty of Chincoteague*. Illustrated by Wesley Dennis. Chicago: Rand McNally, 1947. (I: 2–5; R: 3–5)

Hidaka, Masako. *Girl from the Snow Country*. Brooklyn, N.Y.: Kane/Miller, 1986. (I: K–3; R: 2–3)

Higonnet-Schnopper, Janet. *Tales from Atop a Russian Stove*. Chicago: Albert Whitman, 1973. (I: 3–7; R: 3–7)

Hoffman, Mary. *Amazing Grace*. New York: Dial Books for Young Readers, 1991. (I: 2–4; R: 2–4)

Houston, Gloria. *Little Jim*. New York: Philomel Books, 1990. (I: 4–6; R: 4–6)

King, Helen. *Willy*. Illustrated by Carole Byard. Garden City, N.Y.: Doubleday, 1971. (I: 4–6; R: 4–6)

Lasky, Kathryn. *Sugaring Time*. Photographs by Christopher G. Knight. New York: Macmillan, 1983. (I: 3–5; R: 3–5)

Leaf, Munro. *Wee Gillis*. Illustrated by Robert Lawson. New York: Viking, 1938. (I: 1–4; R: 2–4)

Levinson, Nancy Smiler. *I Lift My Lamp—Emma Lazarus and the Statue of Liberty*. New York: Lodestar Books, 1986. (I: 5–8; R: 5–8)

Lewis, Claudia. *Long Ago in Oregon*. New York: Dell, 1987. (I: 3–4; R: 3–4)

Lewis, Elizabeth Foreman. *Young Fu of the Upper Yangtze*. New York: Bantam Doubleday Dell Publishing Group, 1990 (1932). (I: 5–8; R: 5–8)

Louie, Ai-Ling. *Yeh-Shen—A Cinderella Story from China*. Illustrated by Ed Young. New York: Philomel Books, 1982. (I: 2–5; R: 3–5)

Lowry, Lois. *Number the Stars*. Newbery Award. Boston: Houghton Mifflin, 1990. (I: 4–6; R: 4–6)

MacLachlan, Patricia. *Sarah, Plain and Tall*. Newbery Award. New York: Harper and Row Junior Books, 1985. (I: 3–5; R: 3–5)

Malotki, Ekkehart. *The Mouse Couple—A Hopi Folktale*. Illustrated by Michael Lacapa. Flagstaff, Ariz.: Northland Press, 1988. (I: 3–5; R: 3–5)

Maruki, Toshi. *Hiroshima No Pika*. New York: Lothrop, Lee and Shepard Books, 1980. (I: 5–8; R: 5–8)

Mathis, Sharon Bell. *The Hundred Penny Box*. Illustrated by Leo and Diane Dillon. New York: Puffin Books, 1986. (I: 4–6; R: 4–6)

McGovern, Ann. *The Runaway Slave—The Story of Harriet Tubman*. New York: Scholastic, 1965. (I: 2–5; R: 2–5)

Morris, Neil, and Ting Morris. *Tales of the American West*. New York: Derrydale Books, 1988. (I: 3–5; R: 3–5)

Musgrove, Margaret. *Ashanti to Zulu*. Illustrated by Leo and Diane Dillon. Caldecott Award. New York: Dial, 1976. (I: 2–5; R: 3–5)

Myers, Walter Dean. *Scorpion*. Newbery Award. New York: Harper and Row, 1988. (I: 5–8; R: 5–8)

———. *Won't Know Till I Get There*. New York: Viking, 1982. (I: 5–8; R: 6–8)

O'Dell, Scott. *Island of the Blue Dolphins*. Boston: Houghton Mifflin, 1960. (I: 2–6; R: 3–6)

Paterson, Katherine. *Bridge to Terabithia*. New York: Crowell, 1977. (I: 5–8; R: 5–8)

———. *Of Nightingales That Weep*. New York: Avon, Camelot, 1974. (I: 5–8; R: 5–8)

Provensen, Alice, and Martin Provensen. *Shaker Lane*. New York: Viking Kestrel, 1987. (I: 2–5; R: 3–5)

Rabe, Bernice. *Girl Who Had No Name*. New York: Bantam Books, 1979. (I: 5–8; R: 5–8)

Ringgold, Faith. *Tar Beach*. New York: Crown, 1991. (I: 2–4; R: 3–4)

Rylant, Cynthia. *When I Was Young in the Mountains*. Illustrated by Diane Goode. Caldecott Award. New York: Dutton, 1982. (I: 2–4; R: 2–4)

San Souci, Robert D. *Sukey and the Mermaid*. Illustrated by Brian Pinkney. New York: Four Winds, 1992. (I: 2–5; R: 3–5)

Snyder, Dianne. *The Boy of the Three-Year Nap*. Boston: Houghton Mifflin, 1988. (I: 2–5; R: 3–5)

Steptoe, John. *Mufaro's Beautiful Daughters*. New York: Morrow, 1987. (I: 2–5; R: 3–5)

———. *The Story of Jumping Mouse*. New York: Lothrop, Lee and Shepard Books, 1984. (I: 3–4; R: 3–4)

Taylor, Mildred D. *Roll of Thunder, Hear My Cry*. New York: Bantam Books, 1989 (1976). (I: 5–9; R: 5–8)

Taylor, Theodore. *The Cay*. Garden City, N.Y.: Doubleday, 1969. (I: 2–6; R: 4–6)

Waber, Bernard. *Ira Says Good-bye*. Boston: Houghton Mifflin, 1988. (I: K–4; R: 2–4)

Wilder, Laura Ingalls. *Little House* Series. Nine volumes. Illustrated by Garth Williams. New York: Harper, 1953. (I: 1–5; R: 3–5)

Yarbrough, Camille. *Cornrows*. New York: Coward-McCann, 1979. (I: 1–5; R: 2–5)

Young, Ed. *Lon Po Po: A Red Riding Hood Story from China*. New York: Philomel Books, 1989. (I: 1–5; R: 3–5)

Fantasy and Folk Tales

Alexander, Lloyd. *The Black Cauldron*. New York: Holt, Rinehart and Winston, 1965. (I: 3–8; R: 4–8)

———. *The Book of Three*. New York: Holt, Rinehart and Winston, 1964. (I: 3–8; R: 4–8)

———. *The Castle of Llyr*. New York: Holt, Rinehart and Winston, 1966. (I: 3–8; R: 4–8)

Andersen, Hans Christian. *The Nightingale*. Illustrated by Demi. New York: Harcourt Brace Jovanovich, 1985. (I: 2–6; R: 3–6)

Anglund, Joan Walsh. *Nibble, Nibble, Mousekin—A Tale of Hansel and Gretel*. New York: Harcourt, Brace and World, 1962. (I: 1–5; R: 2–4)

Atwater, Richard, and Florence Atwater. *Mr. Popper's Penguins*. Newbery Award. Illustrated by Robert Lawson. Boston: Little, Brown, 1958. (I: 2–5; R: 3–5)

Bailey, Carolyn Sherwin. *Miss Hickory*. Newbery Award. New York: Viking, 1946. (I: 2–5; R: 2–4)

Barrie, J. M. *Peter Pan*. Illustrated by Michael Hague. New York: Henry Holt, 1987. (I: 4–8; R: 4–8)

Bjork, Christina, and Lena Anderson. *Elliot's Extraordinary Cookbook*. Stockholm: Raben and Sjogren Books (distributed by Farrar, Strauss and Giroux), 1990. (I: 2–5; R: 2–5)

———. *Linnea in Monet's Garden*. Stockholm: Raben and Sjogren Books (distributed by Farrar, Straus and Giroux), 1985. (I: 2–5; R: 2–5)

Brittain, Bill. *The Wish Giver*. New York: Harper and Row, 1983. (I: 4–8; R: 4–6)

Burnett, Frances Hodgson. *The Secret Garden*. Illustrated by Tasha Tudor. New York: Dell, 1962 (1911). (I: 5–7; R: 5–7)

Burton, Virginia Lee. *Mike Mulligan and His Steam Shovel*. Boston: Houghton Mifflin, 1967 (1939). (I: K–3; R: 2–3)

Carle, Eric. *The Grouchy Ladybug*. New York: Crowell, 1977. (I: K–2; R: 1–2)

———. *A House for Hermit Crab*. Saxonville, Mass.: Picture Book Studio, 1987. (I: K–3; R: 2–3)

———. *Seven Stories by Hans Christian Andersen*. Illustrated and retold by Eric Carle. New York: Franklin Watts, 1978. (I: 2–5; R: 3–5)

———. *The Very Hungry Caterpillar*. New York: Philomel Books, 1987 (1969). (I: K–2; R: 1–2)

Carroll, Lewis. *Through the Looking Glass*. Illustrated by John Tenniel. New York: St. Martin's, 1977. (I: 2–8; R: 4–8)

Cazet, Denys. *Never Spit on Your Shoes*. New York: Orchard Books, 1990. (I: 1–2; R: 2–3)

Charney, Steve. *Daddy's Whiskers*. New York: Crown, 1989. (I: K–3; R: 2–3)

Clark, Margery. *The Poppyseed Cakes*. Illustrated by Maud and Miska Petersham. Garden City, N.Y.: Doubleday, 1924. (I: 1–3; R: 2–3)

Clements, Andrew. *Big Al*. Illustrated by Yoshi. Saxonville, Mass.: Picture Book Studio, 1988. (I: K–3; R: 2–3)

Climo, Shirley. *The Egyptian Cinderella*. Illustrated by Ruth Heller. New York: Crowell, 1989. (I: 2–5; R: 3–5)

Collodi, Carlo. *The Adventures of Pinocchio*. Translated by Nicholas J. Perrella. Berkeley: University of California Press, 1986. (I: 1–6; R: 3–6)

Dahl, Roald. *Charlie and the Chocolate Factory*. New York: Knopf, 1973. (I: K–5; R: 3–5)

———. *Danny, the Champion of the World*. Illustrated by Jill Bennett. New York: Knopf, 1975. (I: 2–6; R: 3–6)

———. *The Wonderful Story of Henry Sugar, and Six More*. New York: Knopf, 1977. (I: 2–8; R: 4–8)

Ehrlich, Amy. *Cinderella by Charles Perrault*. Illustrated by Susan Jeffers. New York: Dial Books for Young Readers, 1985. (I: 1–5; R: 2–5)

Field, Rachel. *Hitty, Her First Hundred Years*. Newbery Award. New York: Macmillan, 1929. (I: 3–5; R: 3–5)

Fish, Helen Dean. *When the Root Children Wake Up*. La Jolla, Calif.: Green Tiger Press, 1991 (1906). (I: 1–4; R: 2–4)

Fritz, Jean. *Can't You Make Them Behave, King George?* New York: Howard-McCann, 1977. (I: 5–8; R: 5–8)

Gág, Wanda. *Millions of Cats*. Newbery Award. New York: Coward-McCann, 1977 (1928). (I: K–2; R: 1–2)

———. *Three Gay Tales from Grimm*. Eau Claire, Wis.: E. M. Hale, 1943. (I: 1–5; R: 2–3)

Garfield, Leon. *The Wedding Ghost*. Illustrated by Charles Keeping. Toronto: Oxford University Press, 1988. (I: 7–12; R: 7–12)

Goble, Paul. *Buffalo Woman*. Scarsdale, N.Y.: Bradbury Press, 1984. (I: 3–5; R: 3–5)

———. *The Gift of the Sacred Dog*. Scarsdale, N.Y.: Bradbury Press, 1980. (I: 3–5; R: 3–5)

Grifalconi, Ann. *The Village of Round and Square Houses*. Boston: Little, Brown, 1986. (I: 2–4; R: 3–4)

Grimm, J., and W. Grimm. *Hansel and Gretel*. Illustrated by Adrienne Adams. Translated by Charles Scribner, Jr. New York: Scribner's, 1975. (I: K–6; R: 3–6)

Grimm, J., and W. Grimm. *Hansel and Gretel*. Illustrated by Lisbeth Zwerger. Translated by Elizabeth D. Crawford. New York: Morrow, 1979. (I: K–6; R: 3–6)

Hidaka, Masako. *Girl from the Snow Country*. Brooklyn, N.Y.: Kane/Miller, 1986. (I: K–3; R: 2–3)

Higgonet-Schnopper, Janet. *Tales from Atop a Russian Stove*. Chicago: Albert Whitman, 1973. (I: 3–7; R: 3–7)

Huck, Charlotte. *Princess Furball*. Illustrated by Anita Lobel. New York: Greenwillow Books, 1989. (I: 1–5; R: 3–5)

Jacques, Brian. *Redwall*. New York: Philomel Books, 1986. (I: 4–8; R: 5–8)

Kennedy, Jimmy. *The Teddy Bears' Picnic*. La Jolla, Calif.: Green Tiger Press, 1983. (I: K–3; R: 2–3)

Lawson, Robert. *Ben and Me*. New York: Little, Brown, 1953. (I: 4–7; R: 4–7)

———. *Mr. Revere and I*. New York: Little, Brown, 1953. (I: 4–7; R: 4–7)

———. *Rabbit Hill*. Newbery Award. New York: Viking Press, 1972 (1944). (I: K–5; R: 2–5)

Leaf, Munro. *Wee Gillis*. Illustrated by Robert Lawson. New York: Viking, 1938. (I: 1–4; R: 2–4)

Lear, Edward. *The Jumblies*. Illustrated by Ted Rand. New York: Putnam's, 1989. (I: 2–8; R: 4–8)

LeGuin, Ursula K. *The Farthest Shore*. New York: Atheneum, 1972. (I: 5–8; R: 5–8)

———. *The Tombs of Atuan*. New York: Atheneum, 1971. (I: 5–8; R: 5–8)

———. *A Wizard of Earthsea*. New York: Parnassus, 1968. (I: 5–8; R: 5–8)

L'Engle. Madeleine. *A Swiftly Tilting Planet*. New York: Farrar, Straus and Giroux, 1977. (I: 3–8; R: 4–8)

———. *A Wind in the Door*. New York: Farrar, Straus and Giroux, 1973. (I: 3–8; R: 4–8)

———. *A Wrinkle in Time*. New York: Farrar, Straus and Giroux, 1962. (I: 3–8; R: 4–8)

Lewis, C. S. *The Lion, the Witch and the Wardrobe*. New York: Collier, 1970 (1950). (I: 4–6; R: 4–6)

Lindgren, Astrid. *Pippi Longstocking*. New York: Viking, 1950. (I: 3–5; R: 3–5)

Louie, Ai-Ling. *Yeh-Shen—A Cinderella Story from China*. Illustrated by Ed Young. New York: Philomel Books, 1982. (I: 2–5; R: 3–5)

MacDonald, George. *At the Back of the North Wind*. Elgin, Ill.: David C. Cook, 1979 (1870). (I: 2–6; R: 5+)

———. *The Princess and the Goblin*. Baltimore, Md.: Penguin, 1975 (1872). (I: 2–6; R: 5+)

MacDonald, Golden. *The Little Island*. Illustrated by Leonard Weisgard. Caldecott Award. Garden City, N.Y.: Doubleday, 1946. (I: 1–4; R: 2–3)

Malotki, Ekkehart. *The Mouse Couple—A Hopi Folktale*. Illustrated by Michael Lacapa. Flagstaff, Ariz.: Northland Press, 1988. (I: 3–5; R: 3–5)

McCloskey, Robert. *Make Way for Ducklings*. Caldecott Award. New York: Viking, 1969 (1941). (I: K–2; R: 2–adult)

Milne, A. A. *Winnie the Pooh*. New York: Dutton, 1926. (I: 1–3; R: 3–5)

Mori, Tuyosi. *Socrates and the Three Little Pigs*. Illustrated by Mitsumasa Anno. New York: Philomel Books, 1986. (I: 3–8; R: 3–8)

Norton, Mary. *The Borrowers*. Illustrated by Beth and Joe Krush. New York: Harcourt Brace, 1953. (I: 1–5; R: 2–5)

O'Brien, Robert C. *Mrs. Frisby and the Rats of NIMH*. New York: Antheneum, 1971. (I: 5–8; R: 5–8)

———. *Z for Zachariah*. New York: Macmillan, 1974. (I: 6–8; R: 6–8)

Palmer, Robin. *Demons, Monsters & Abodes of the Dead*. New York: Scholastic, 1975. (I: 4–8; R: 4–8)

Parr, Letitia. *A Man and His Hat*. Clay animation by Paul Terrett. New York: Philomel Books, 1989. (I: 1–4; R: 2–4)

Perrault, Charles. *Cinderella and Other Tales from Perrault*. Illustrated by Michael Hague. (New York: Holt, 1989. (I: 1–5; R: 3–5)

Pinkwater, Daniel. *Bear's Picture*. New York: Dutton, 1972. (I: K–2; R: 1–2)

Potter, Beatrix. *The Tale of Peter Rabbit*. New York: Warne, 1902. (I: K–3; R: 2–3)

————. *The Tale of Squirrel Nutkin*. New York: Warne, 1903. (I: K–3; R: 2–3)

Ringgold, Faith. *Tar Beach*. New York: Crown, 1991. (I: 2–4; R: 3–4)

San Souci, Robert D. *Sukey and the Mermaid*. Illustrated by Brian Pinckey. New York: Four Winds, 1992. (I: 2–5; R: 3–5)

Scieszka, Jon. *The True Story of the Three Little Pigs*. New York: Viking Kestrel, 1989. (I: 1–5; R: 2–5)

Selden, George. *The Cricket in Times Square*. New York: Dell, 1960. (I: 5–7; R: 5+)

Seuss, Dr. *And to Think That I Saw It on Mulberry Street*. New York: Vanguard, 1964 (1934). (I: K–3; R: 2–3)

————. *The Cat in the Hat*. Boston: Houghton Mifflin, 1957. (I: K–3; R: 2–3)

Snyder, Dianne. *The Boy of the Three-Year Nap*. Boston: Houghton Mifflin, 1988. (I: 2–5; R: 3–5)

Steiner, Jorg. *Rabbit Island*. Translated by Ann Conrad Lammers. New York: Harcourt Brace Jovanovich, 1978. (I: 3–8; R: 4–8)

Steptoe, John. *The Story of Jumping Mouse*. Caldecott Award. New York: Lothrop, Lee and Shepard Books, 1984. (I: 3–4; R: 3–4)

Watts, Bernadette. *Snow White and Rose Red*. Retold and illustrated by Bernadette Watts. Faellanden, Switzerland: North-South Books, 1988. (I: 1–5; R: 2–5)

White, Anne Terry. *The Golden Treasury of Myths and Legends*. Illustrated by Alice and Martin Provensen. New York: Golden Press, 1959. (I: K–6; R: 4–6)

White, E. B. *Charlotte's Web*. New York: Harper and Row, 1952. (I: 2–5; R: 4–5)

Williams, Margery. *The Velveteen Rabbit*. New York: Holt, Rinehart and Winston, 1983 (1922). (I: 2–4; R: 3–4)

Young, Ed. *Lon Po Po: A Red Riding Hood Story from China*. New York: Philomel Books, 1989. (I: 1–5; R: 3–5)

Information Books

Adoff, Arnold. *Birds*. New York: Lippincott, 1982. (I: 2–5; R: 3–5)

Aliki. *A Medieval Feast*. New York: Crowell, 1983. (I: 2–8; R: 3–5)

Anno, Masaichiro, and Mitsumasa Anno. *Anno's Mysterious Multiplying Jar*. New York: Philomel Books, 1979. (I: 3–10+; R: 3–10+)

Anno, Mitsumasa. *Anno's Medieval World*. Translated by Ursula Synge. New York: Philomel Books, 1979. (I: 2–8; R: 3–8)

Baylor, Byrd. *Everybody Needs a Rock*. Illustrated by Peter Parnall. New York: Atheneum, 1974. (I: 1–5; R: 2–5)

Behn, Harry. *Trees*. Illustrated by James Endicott. New York: Henry Holt, 1992. (I: 2–5; R: 2–5)

Bjork, Christina, and Lena Anderson. *Elliot's Extraordinary Cookbook*. Stockholm: Raben and Sjogren Books (distributed by Farrar, Straus and Giroux), 1990. (I: 2–5; R: 2–5)

———. *Linnea in Monet's Garden*. Stockholm: Raben and Sjogren Books (distributed by Farrar, Straus and Giroux), 1985. (I: 2–5; R: 2–5)

———. *Linnea's Almanac*. Stockholm: Raben and Sjogren Books (distributed by Farrar, Straus and Giroux), 1982. (I: 2–5; R: 2–5)

———. *Linnea's Windowsill Garden*. Stockholm: Raben and Sjogren Books (distributed by Farrar, Straus and Giroux), 1988. (I: 2–5; R: 2–5)

Bonners, Susan. *Panda*. New York: Dell, 1978. (I: K–3; R: 1–3)

Carle, Eric. *The Grouchy Ladybug*. New York: Crowell, 1977. (I: K–2; R: 1–2)

———. *A House for Hermit Crab*. Saxonville, Mass.: Picture Book Studio, 1987. (I: K–3; R: 2–3)

———. *Today Is Monday*. New York: Philomel Books, 1993. (I: K–2; R: 1–2)

———. *The Very Hungry Caterpillar*. New York: Philomel Books, 1987 (1969). (I: K–2; R: 1–2)

Cherry, Lynne. *A River Ran Wild: An Environmental History*. San Diego: Harcourt Brace Jovanovich, 1992. (I: 2–5; R: 3–5)

Chicago—A Picture Book to Remember Her By. Designed by David Gibbon. Produced by Ted Smart. New York: Crescent Books, 1979. (All ages)

Cohen, Barbara. *Gooseberries to Oranges*. Illustrated by Beverly Brodsky. New York: Lothrop, Lee and Shepard Books, 1982. (I: 2–6; R: 3–6)

Collier, James Lincoln, and Christopher Collier. *My Brother Sam Is Dead*. New York: Four Winds, 1974. (I: 5–8; R: 5–8)

Cooney, Barbara. *Island Boy*. New York: Viking Kestrel, 1988. (I: 1–4; R: 2–4)

deAngeli, Marguerite. *The Door in the Wall*. Newbery Award. New York: Scholastic, 1949. (I: 5–8; R: 4–6)

———. *Yonie Wondernose*. Caldecott Award. New York: Doubleday, 1938. (I: 3–5; R: 3–5)

dePaola, Tomie. *The Kids' Cat Book*. New York: Holiday House, 1979. (I: 1–4; R: 3–4)

Dewey, Jennifer. *Can You Find Me? A Book About Animal Camouflage*. New York: Scholastic, 1989. (I: 1–3; R: 2–3)

Dionetti, Michelle. *Coal Mine Peaches*. New York: Orchard Books, 1991. (I: 2–5; R: 3–4)

Fish, Helen Dean. *When the Root Children Wake Up*. La Jolla, Calif.: Green Tiger Press, 1991 (1906). (I: 1–4; R: 2–4)

Freedman, Russell. *Lincoln—A Photobiography*. Newbery Award. New York: Clarion Books, 1987. (I: 5–8; R: 5–8)

Fritz, Jean. *Can't You Make Them Behave, King George?* New York: Howard-McCann, 1977. (I: 5–8; R: 5–8)

Goble, Paul. *Buffalo Woman*. Scarsdale, N.Y.: Bradbury Press, 1984. (I: 3–5; R: 3–5)

———. *The Gift of the Sacred Dog*. Scarsdale, N.Y.: Bradbury Press, 1980. (I: 3–5; R: 3–5)

Gray, Elizabeth Janet. *Adam of the Road*. Illustrated by Robert Lawson. New York: Viking, 1942. (I: 5–8; R: 5–8)

Greene, Bette. *Summer of My German Soldier*. New York: Bantam Books, 1988 (1973). (I: 5–8; R: 5–8)

Heller, Ruth. *Animals Born Alive and Well*. New York: Grosset and Dunlap, 1982. (I: 2–8; R: 3–8)

———. *Chickens Aren't the Only Ones*. New York: Grosset and Dunlap, 1982. (I: 2–8; R: 3–8)

———. *Kites Sail High—A Book About Verbs*. New York: Grosset and Dunlap, 1988. (I: 2–8; R: 3–8)

———. *Plants That Never Ever Bloom*. New York: Grosset and Dunlap, 1984. (I: 2–8; R: 3–8)

———. *The Reason for a Flower*. New York: Grosset and Dunlap, 1986. (I: 2–8; R: 3–8)

Hendershot, Judith. *In Coal Country*. New York: Knopf, 1987. (I: 2–5; R: 3–5)

Knight, Margy Burne. *Talking Walls*. Gardiner, Me.: Tilbury House, 1992. (I: 3–8; R: 4–6)

Lasker, Joe. *A Tournament of Knights*. New York: Harper and Row, 1986. (I: 3–5; R: 3–5)

Lasky, Kathryn. *Sugaring Time*. Photographs by Christopher G. Knight. New York: Macmillan, 1983. (I: 3–5; R: 3–5)

Lawson, Robert. *Ben and Me*. New York: Little, Brown, 1953. (I: 4–7; R: 4–7)

———. *Mr. Revere and I*. New York: Little, Brown, 1953. (I: 4–7; R: 4–7)

Lewis, Claudia. *Long Ago in Oregon*. New York: Dell, 1987. (I: 3–4; R: 3–4)

Levinson, Nancy Smiler. *I Lift My Lamp—Emma Lazarus and the Statue of Liberty*. New York: Lodestar Books, 1986. (I: 5–8; R: 5–8)

Longfellow, Henry Wadsworth. *Paul Revere's Ride*. Illustrated by Ted Rand. New York: Dutton Children's Books, 1990. (I: 2–adult; R: 4–adult)

Lowry, Lois. *Number the Stars*. Newbery Award. Boston: Houghton Mifflin, 1990. (I: 4–6; R: 4–6)

MacDonald, Golden. *The Little Island*. Illustrated by Leonard Weisgard. Caldecott Award. Garden City, N.Y.: Doubleday, 1946. (I: 1–4; R: 2–3)

MacDonald, Suse. *Numblers*. New York: Dial Books for Young Readers, 1988. (I: K–2; R: 1–2)

MacLachlan, Patricia. *Sarah, Plain and Tall*. Newbery Award. New York: Harper and Row Junior Books, 1985. (I: 3–5; R: 3–5)

Maruki, Toshi. *Hiroshima No Pika*. New York: Lothrop, Lee and Shepard Books, 1980. (I: 5–8; R: 5–8)

May, Julian. *The Big Island*. Chicago: Follett, 1968. (I: 2–5; R: 3–5)

McGovern, Ann. *The Runaway Slave—The Story of Harriet Tubman*. New York: Scholastic, 1965. (I: 2–5; R: 2–5)

Mori, Tuyosi. *Socrates and the Three Little Pigs*. Illustrated by Mitsumasa Anno. New York: Philomel Books, 1986. (I: 3–8; R: 3–8)

Morris, Neil, and Ting Morris. *Tales of the American West*. New York: Derrydale Books, 1988. (I: 3–5; R: 3–5)

Murray, Elizabeth. *Monet's Passion: Ideas, Inspiration and Insights from the Painter's Garden*. San Francisco: Pomegranate Artbooks, 1989. (All ages)

Nozaki, Akihiro. *Anno's Hat Tricks*. Illustrated by Mitsumasa Anno. New York: Philomel Books, 1985. (I: 3–8; R: 3–8)

Palmer, Robin. *Demons, Monsters & Abodes of the Dead*. New York: Scholastic, 1975. (I: 4–8; R: 4–8)

Provensen, Alice, and Martin Provenson. *Leonardo da Vinci*. Paper engineering by John Strejan. New York: Viking, 1984. (I: 2–8; R: 4–8)

Ringgold, Faith. *Tar Beach*. New York: Crown, 1991. (I: 2–4; R: 3–4)

Rius, Maria. *Life Underground*. New York: Woodbury, 1987. (I: 2–5; R: 2–5)

———. *The Middle Ages*. New York: Barron's, 1988. (I: 2–5; R: 2–5)

Rylant, Cynthia. *When I Was Young in the Mountains*. Illustrated by Diane Goode. Caldecott Award. New York: Dutton, 1982. (I: 2–4; R: 2–4)

Schwartz, David M. *How Much Is a Million?* Illustrated by Steven Kellogg. New York: Scholastic, 1985. (I: K–5; R: 2–5)

Skelsey, Alice, and Gloria Huckaby. *Growing Up Green*. New York: Workman, 1973. (I: 2–5; R: 3–5)

Skolnick, Peter L. *Jump Rope*. Illustrated by Marty Norman. Photography by Jerry Darvin. New York: Workman, 1974. (I: 1–5; R: 1–5)

Smothers, Ethel Footman. *Down in the Piney Woods*. New York: Knopf, 1992. (I: 5–8; R: 5–8)

Steiner, Jorg. *Rabbit Island*. Illustrated by Jorg Muller. Translated by Ann Conrad Lammers. New York: Harcourt Brace Jovanovich, 1978. (I: 3–8; R: 4–8)

Thornhill, Jan. *The Wildlife 1.2.3.* New York: Simon and Schuster, 1989. (I: K–2; R: 1–2)

Turkle, Brinton. *Obadiah the Bold*. New York: Viking, 1969. (I: 1–3; R: 2–3)

White, Anne Terry. *The Golden Treasury of Myths and Legends*. Illustrated by Alice and Martin Provensen. New York: Golden Press, 1959. (I: K–6; R: 4–6)

Yarbrough, Camille. *Cornrows*. New York: Coward-McCann, 1979. (I: 1–5; R: 2–5)

Yoshi. *Who's Hiding Here?* Natick, Mass.: Picture Book Studio, 1987. (I: K–3; R: 2–3)

Index

Credits

Photo Credits